Shojo Beat

La Corda d'Oro

10
Story & Art by Yuki Kure

La Corda d'Oro

CONTENTS
Volume 10

Characters

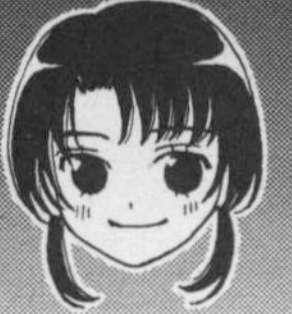

Kahoko Hino
(General Education School, 2nd year)

The heroine. She knows nothing about music, but she finds herself participating in the school music competition equipped with a magic violin.

Len Tsukimori
(Music School, 2nd year)

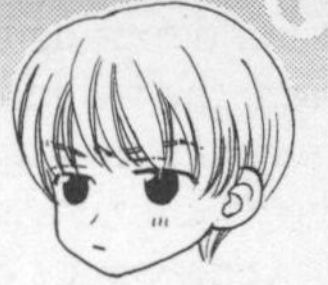

A violin major and a cold perfectionist from a musical family of unquestionable talent.

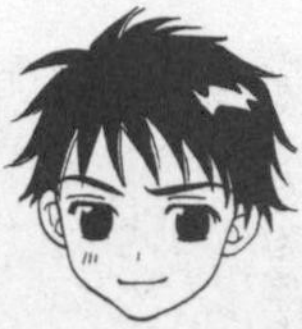

Ryotaro Tsuchiura
(General Education School, 2nd year)

A member of the soccer team who seems to be looking after Kahoko. A talented pianist.

Keiichi Shimizu
(Music school, 1st year)

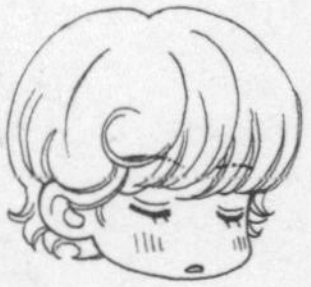

A cello major who walks to the beat of his own drum and is often lost in the world of music. He is also often asleep.

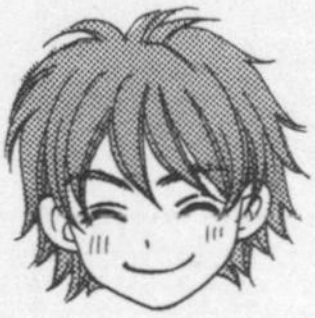

Kazuki Hihara
(Music school, 3rd year)

An energetic and friendly trumpet major and a fan of anything fun.

Azuma Yunoki
(Music school, 3rd year)

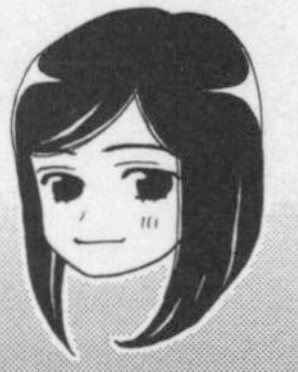

A flute major and the son of a graceful and kind traditional flower arrangement master. He has a dedicated fan club called the "Yunoki Guard."

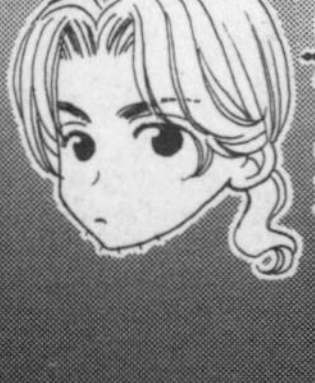

Hiroto Kanazawa
(Music teacher)

The contest coordinator, whose lazy demeanor suggests he is avoiding any hassle.

Story

Our story is set at Seiso Academy, which is split into the General Education School and the Music School. Kahoko, a Gen Ed student, encounters a music fairy named Lili who gives her a magic violin that anyone can play. Suddenly Kahoko finds herself in the school's music competition, with good-looking, quirky Music School students as her fellow contestants! Kahoko comes to accept her daunting task and discovers a love of music. But during the Third Selection, the violin loses its power and disappears. Although Kahoko is discouraged at first, she decides to continue playing with a normal violin. The Final Selection approaches and the final stage unfolds, leading to the end of each contestant's emotional journey...

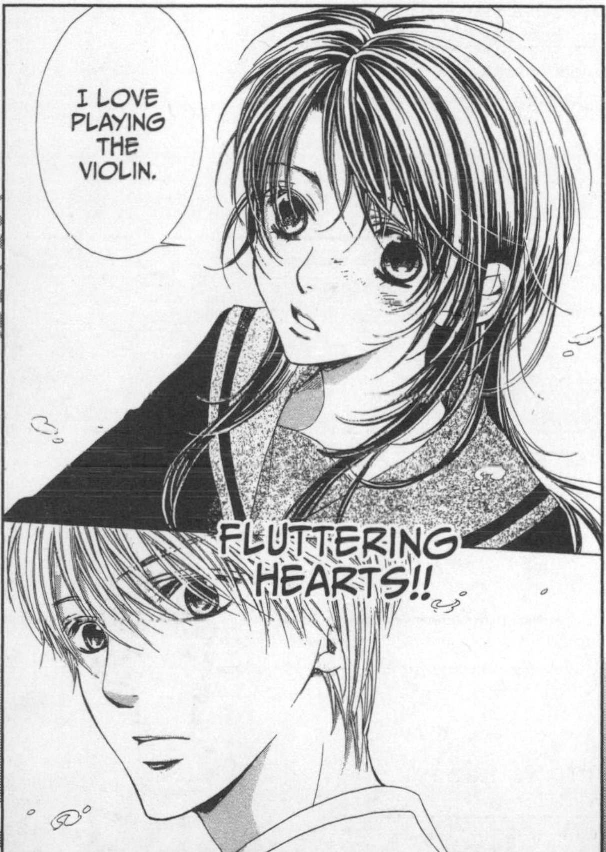
I LOVE PLAYING THE VIOLIN.
FLUTTERING HEARTS!!

Previously...

Everyone at school notices that Kahoko isn't playing as well as she used to. Ryotaro, Kazuki and Len all talk to her about it, and through them Kahoko realizes how important music has become to her.

The music fairy Lili, who got Kahoko caught up in this affair. ↓

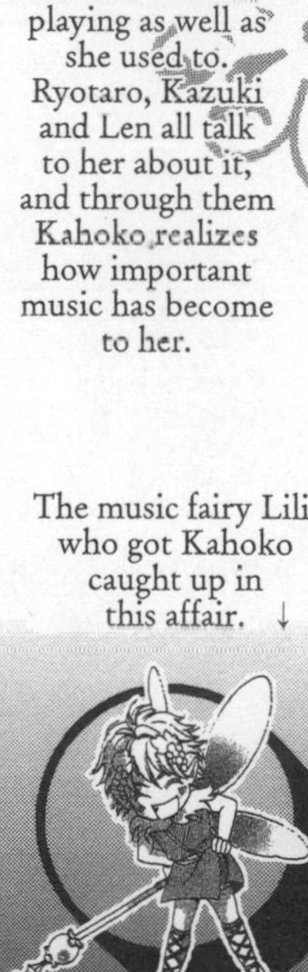

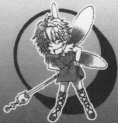

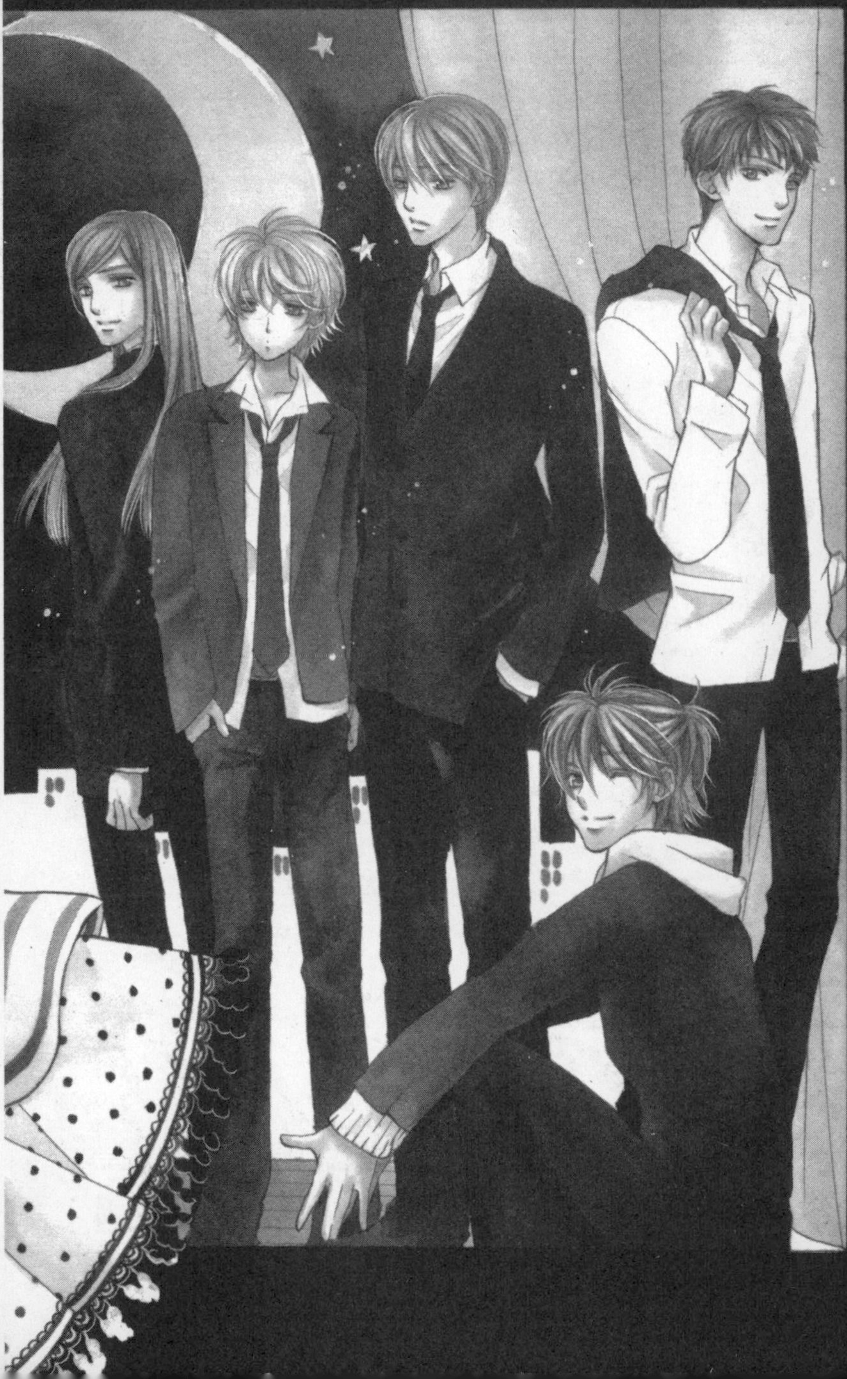

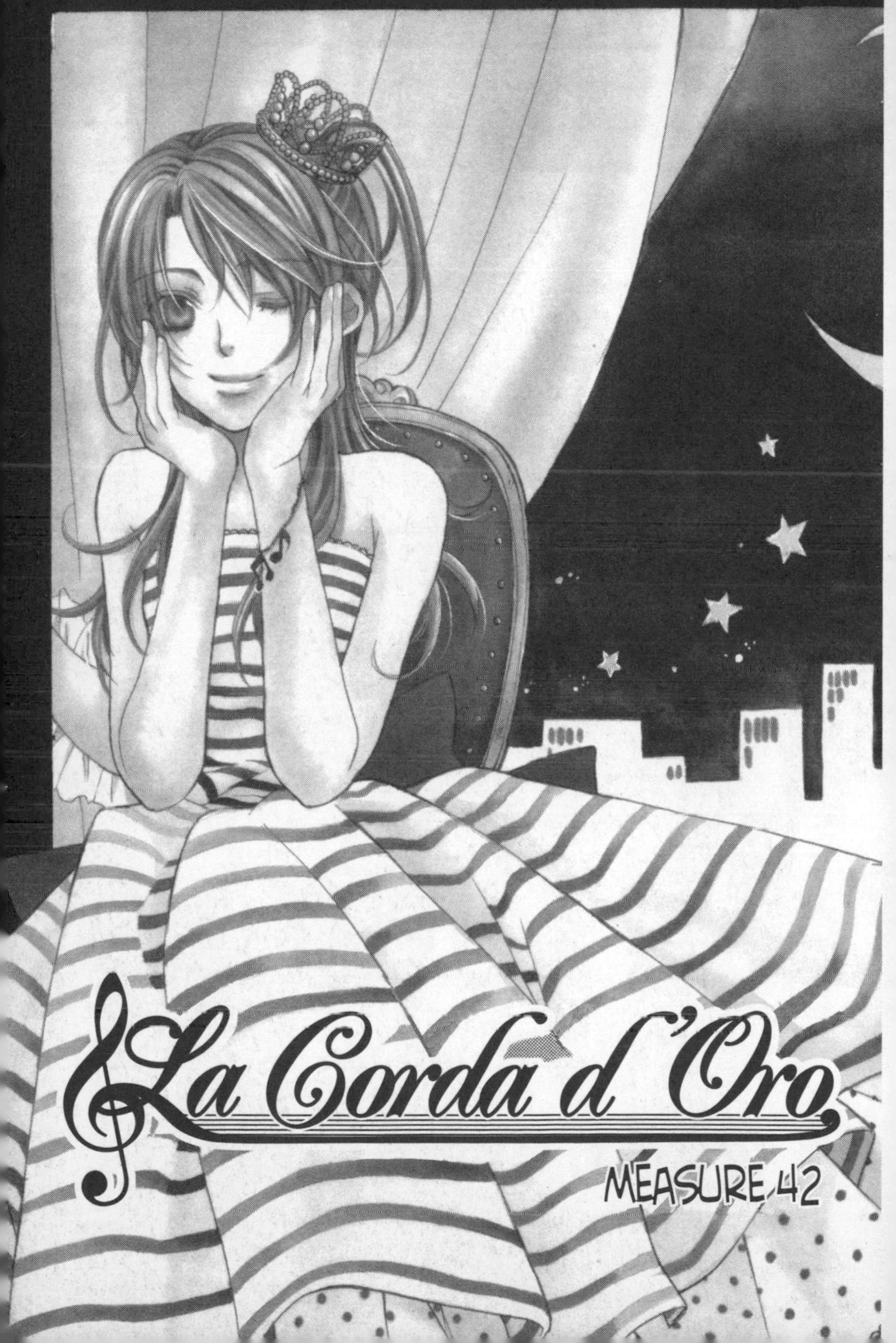
La Corda d'Oro
MEASURE 42

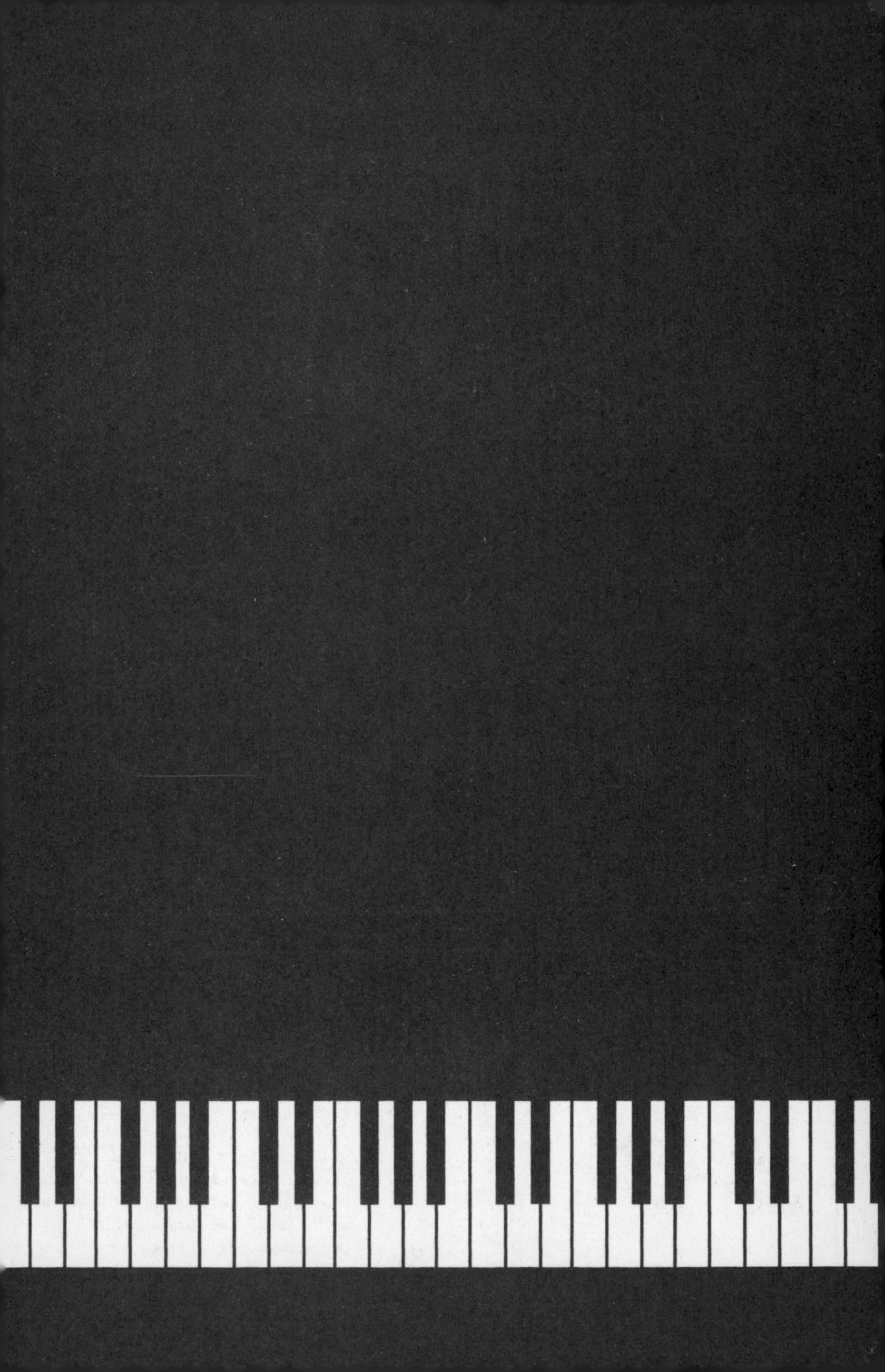

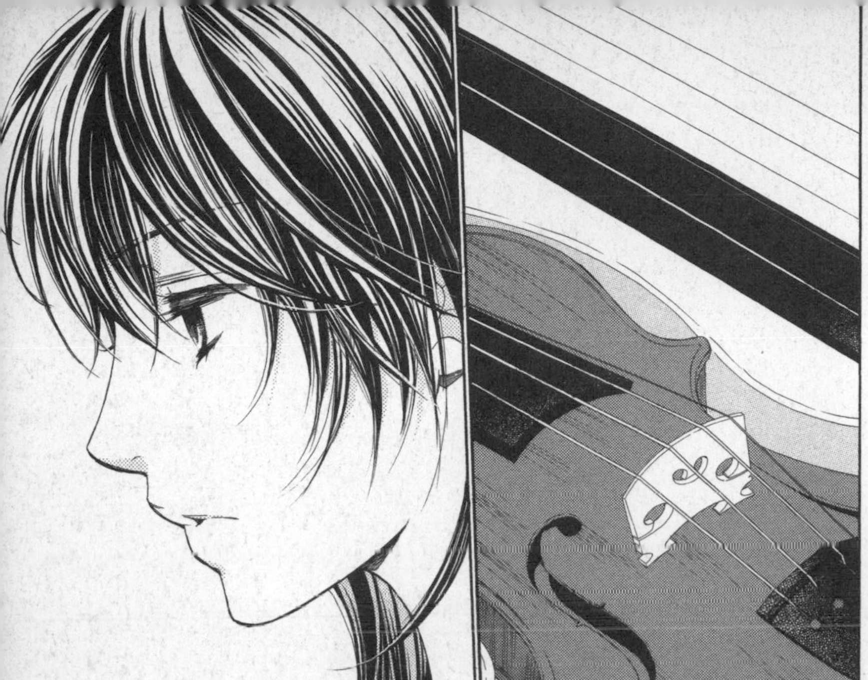

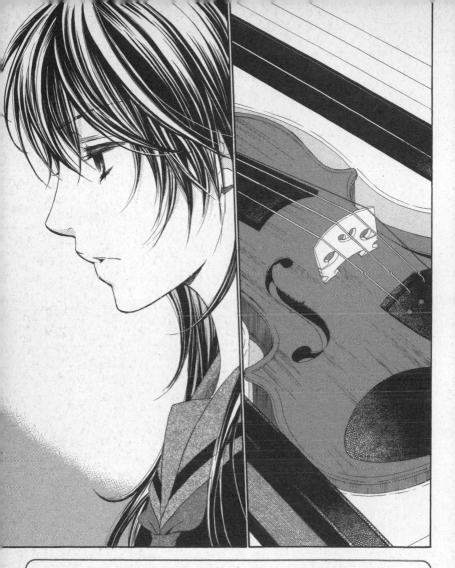

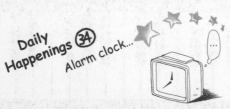

Daily Happenings ㉞

Alarm clock...

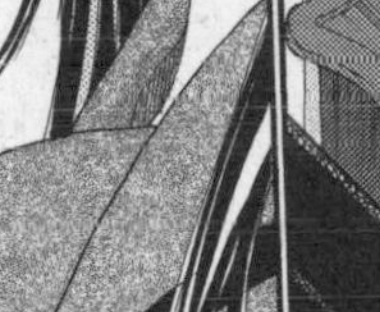

I am REEAAALLLLY bad at getting up. I don't know what it is. The other day on TV I saw an ad for an alarm clock that's "guaranteed to get you up." Really? I'm suspicious... but maybe just a little curious.

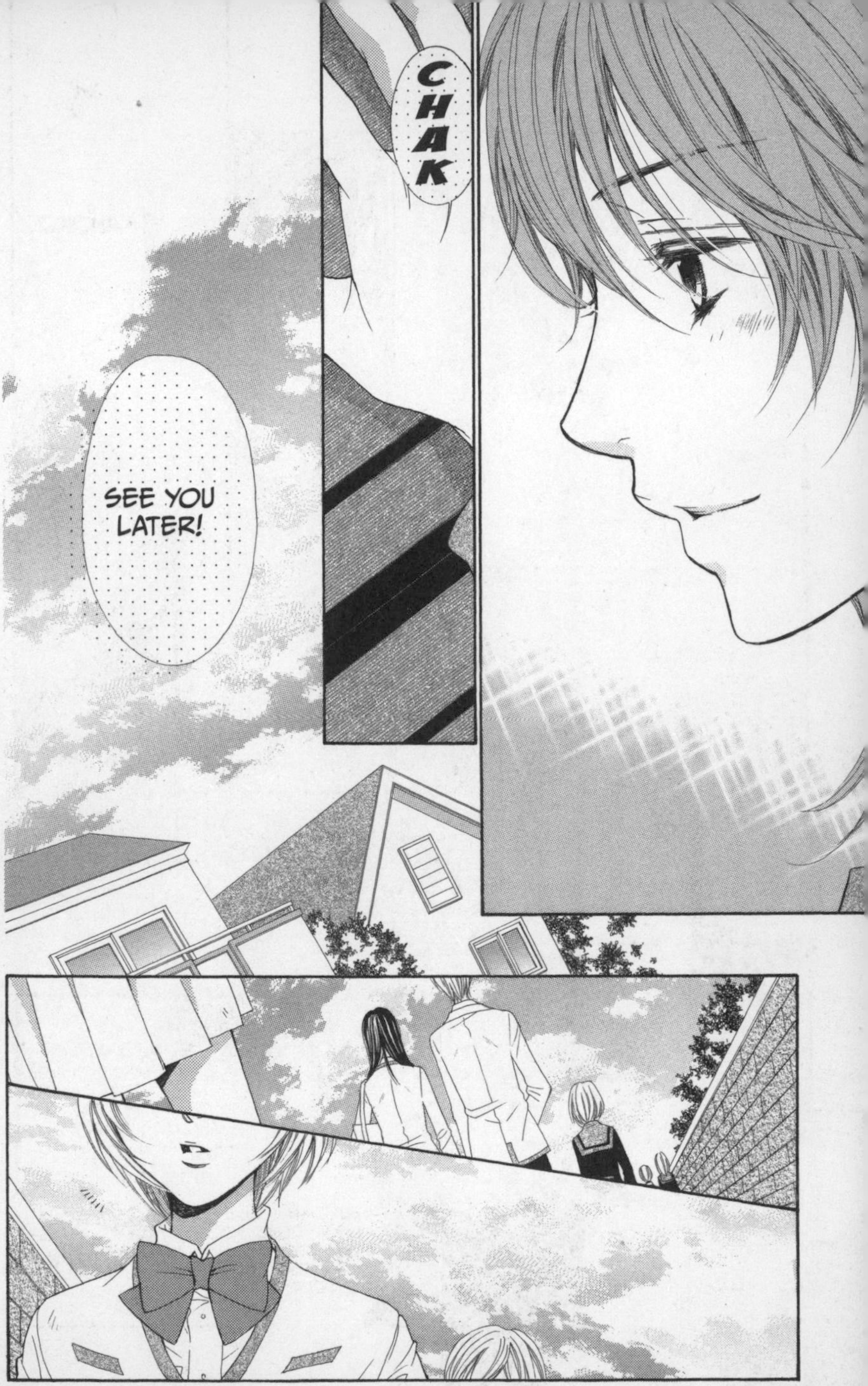
CHAK
SEE YOU LATER!

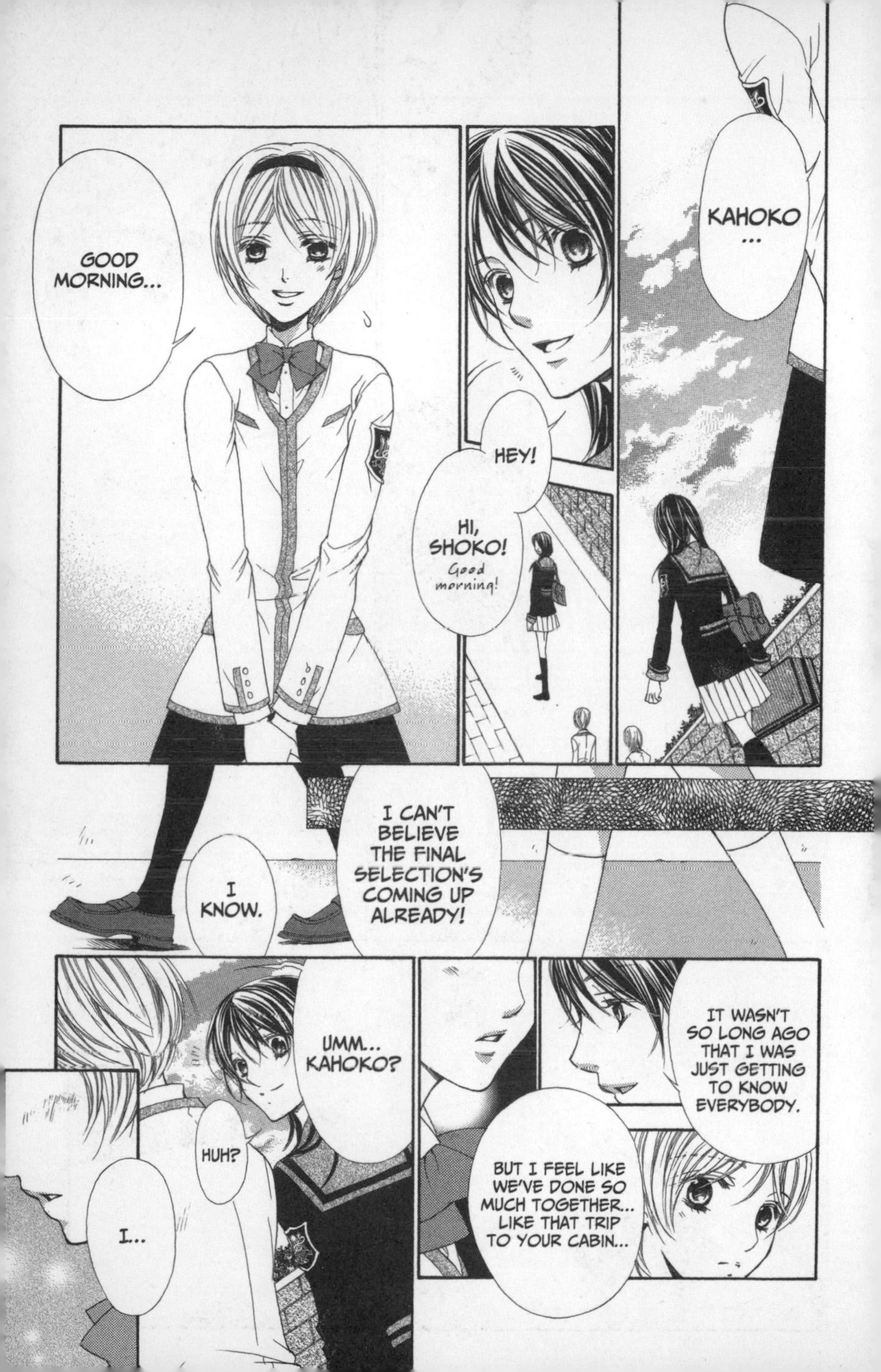
KAHOKO ...
HEY!
HI, SHOKO! Good morning!
GOOD MORNING...
I CAN'T BELIEVE THE FINAL SELECTION'S COMING UP ALREADY!
I KNOW.
IT WASN'T SO LONG AGO THAT I WAS JUST GETTING TO KNOW EVERYBODY.
BUT I FEEL LIKE WE'VE DONE SO MUCH TOGETHER... LIKE THAT TRIP TO YOUR CABIN...
UMM... KAHOKO?
HUH?
I...

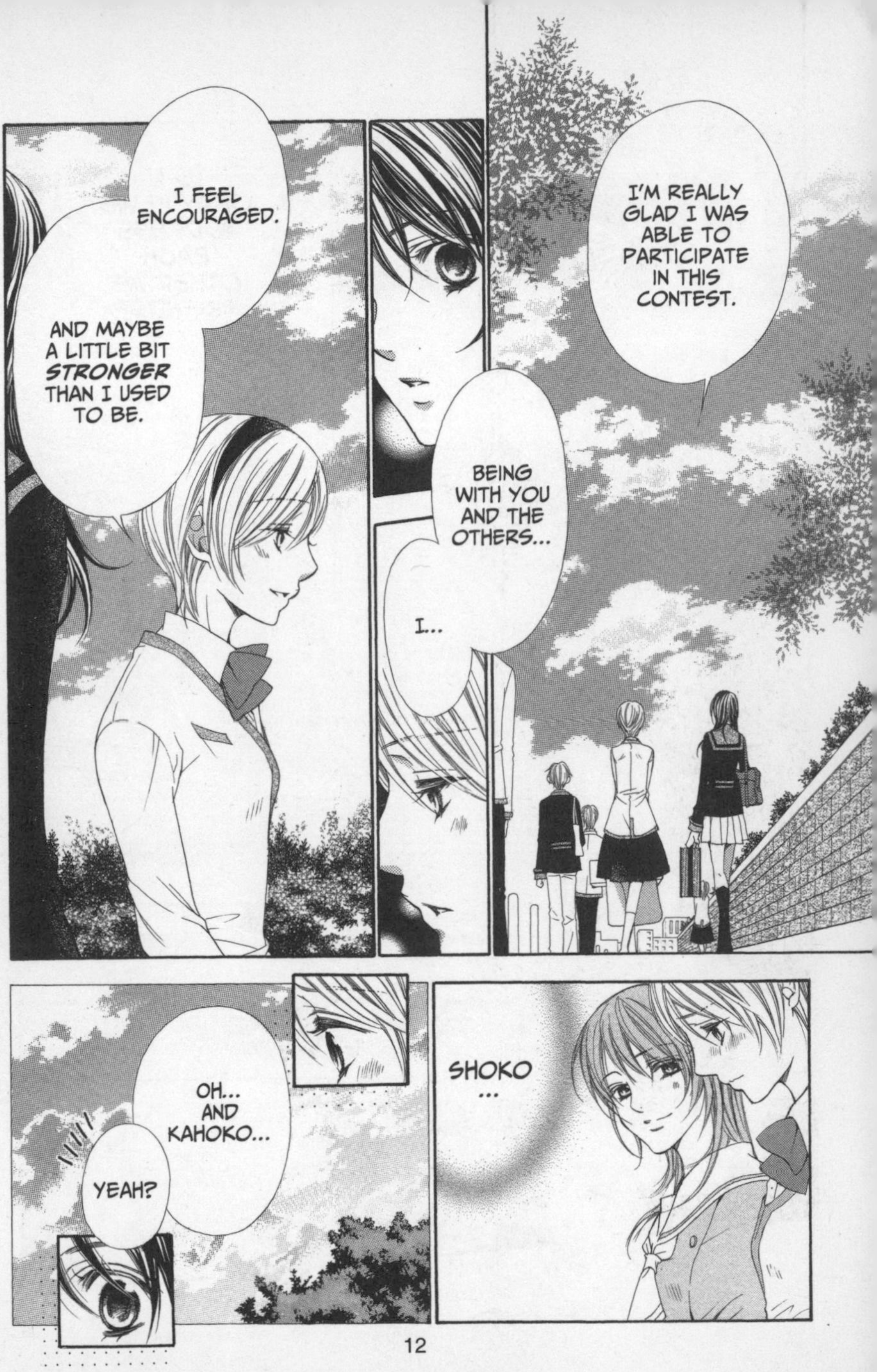
I'M REALLY GLAD I WAS ABLE TO PARTICIPATE IN THIS CONTEST.
BEING WITH YOU AND THE OTHERS...
I...
I FEEL ENCOURAGED.
AND MAYBE A LITTLE BIT *STRONGER* THAN I USED TO BE.
SHOKO ...
OH... AND KAHOKO...
YEAH?

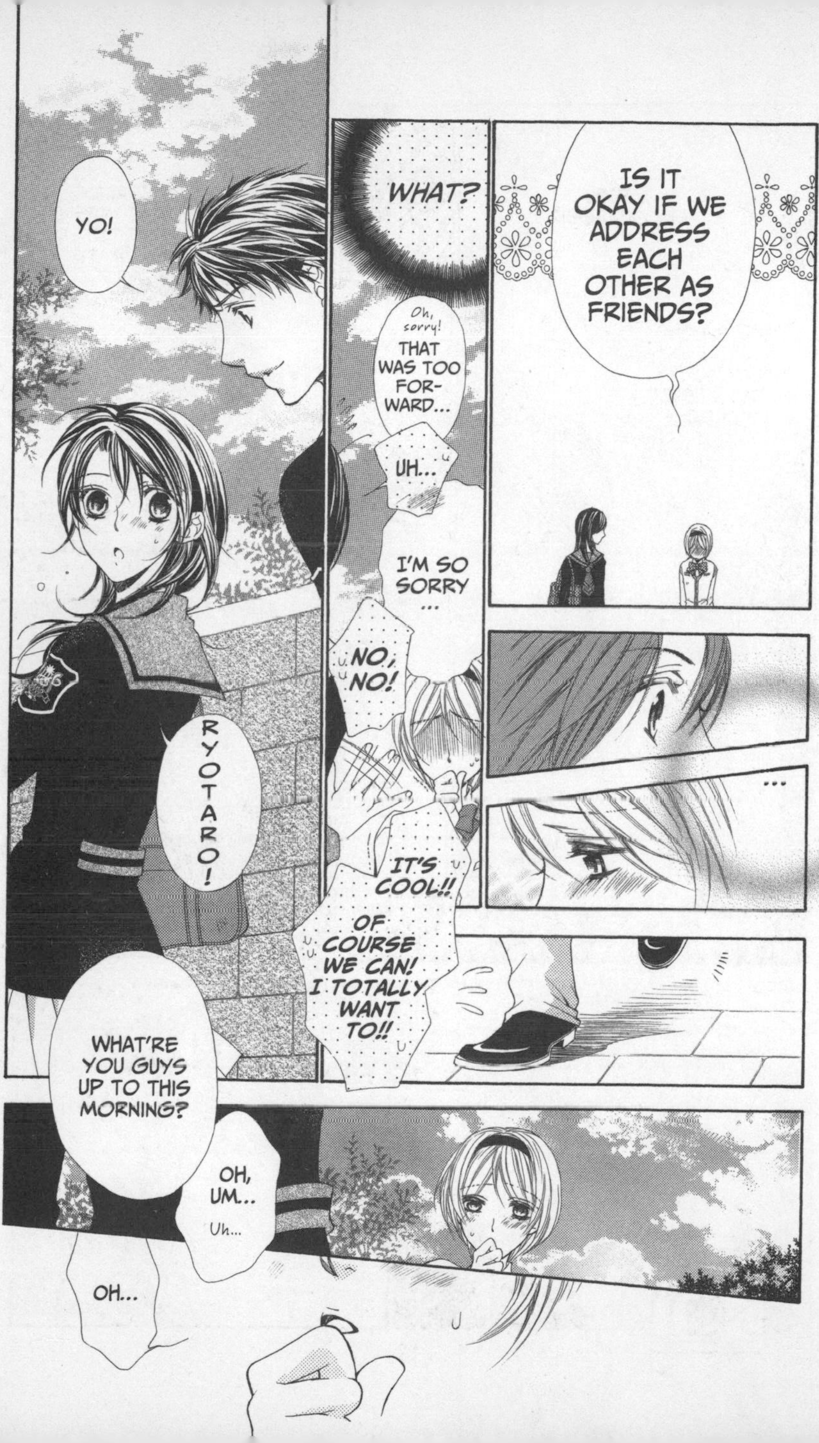
IS IT OKAY IF WE ADDRESS EACH OTHER AS FRIENDS?
...
WHAT?
Oh, sorry!
THAT WAS TOO FOR-WARD...
UH...
I'M SO SORRY...
NO, NO!
IT'S COOL!!
OF COURSE WE CAN! I TOTALLY WANT TO!!
YO!
RYOTARO!
WHAT'RE YOU GUYS UP TO THIS MORNING?
OH, UM...
Uh...
OH...

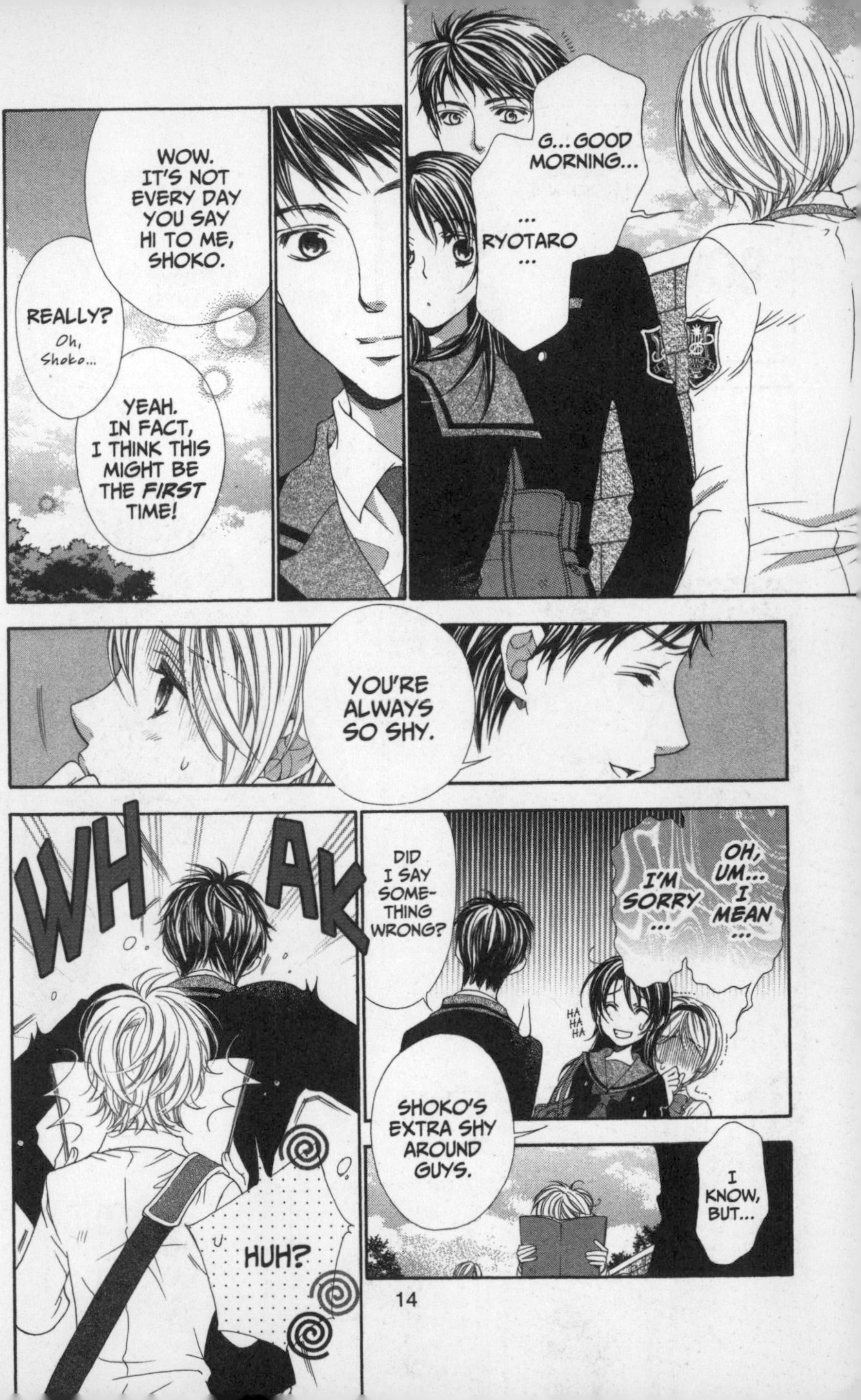
G...GOOD MORNING...
...RYOTARO...
WOW. IT'S NOT EVERY DAY YOU SAY HI TO ME, SHOKO.
REALLY?
Oh, Shoko...
YEAH. IN FACT, I THINK THIS MIGHT BE THE *FIRST* TIME!
YOU'RE ALWAYS SO SHY.
OH, UM... I MEAN...
I'M SORRY...
DID I SAY SOMETHING WRONG?
HA HA HA
SHOKO'S EXTRA SHY AROUND GUYS.
I KNOW, BUT...
WHAK
HUH?

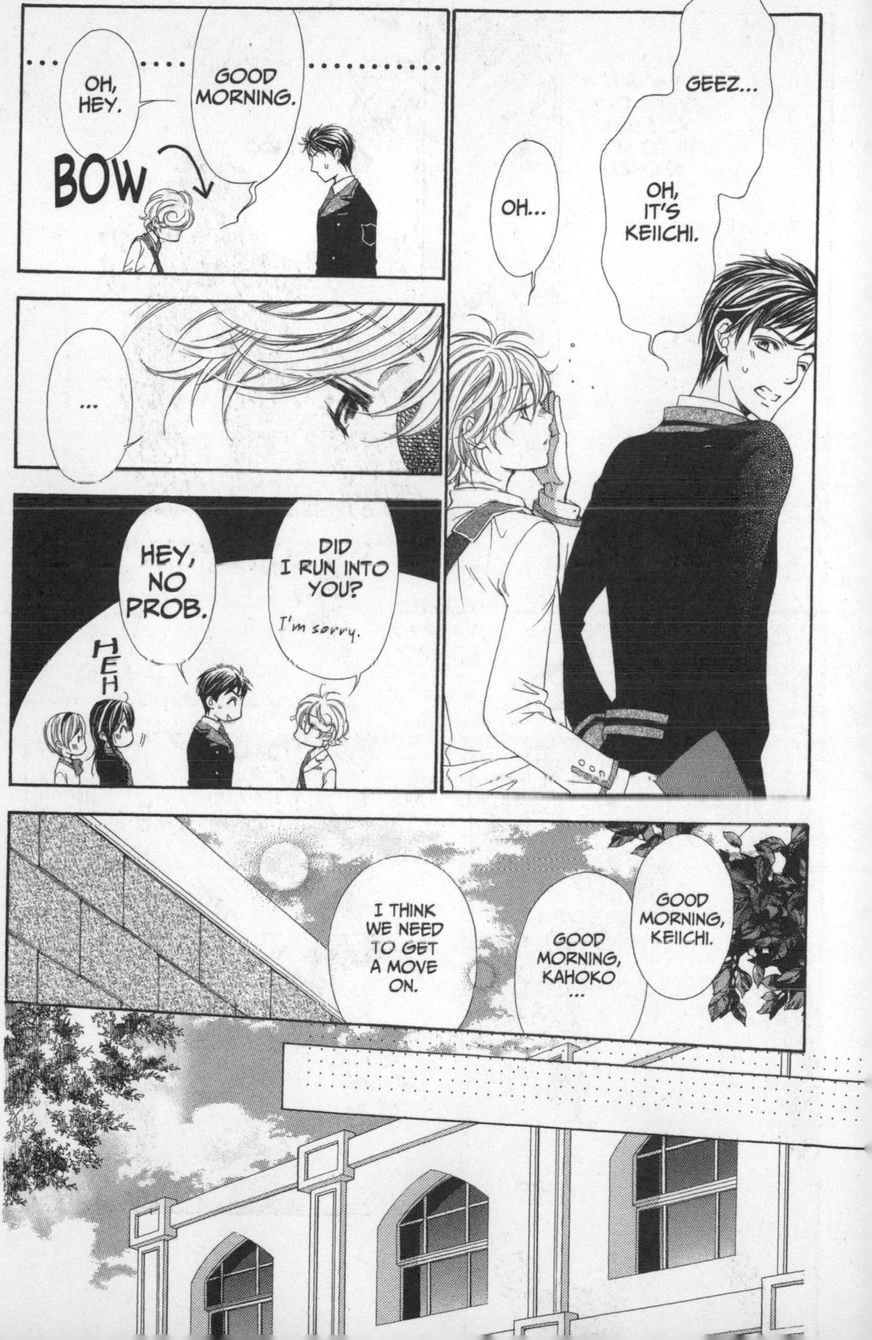
GEEZ... OH, IT'S KEIICHI.
OH...
GOOD MORNING.
OH, HEY.
BOW
...
DID I RUN INTO YOU?
I'm sorry.
HEY, NO PROB.
HEH
GOOD MORNING, KEIICHI.
GOOD MORNING, KAHOKO...
I THINK WE NEED TO GET A MOVE ON.

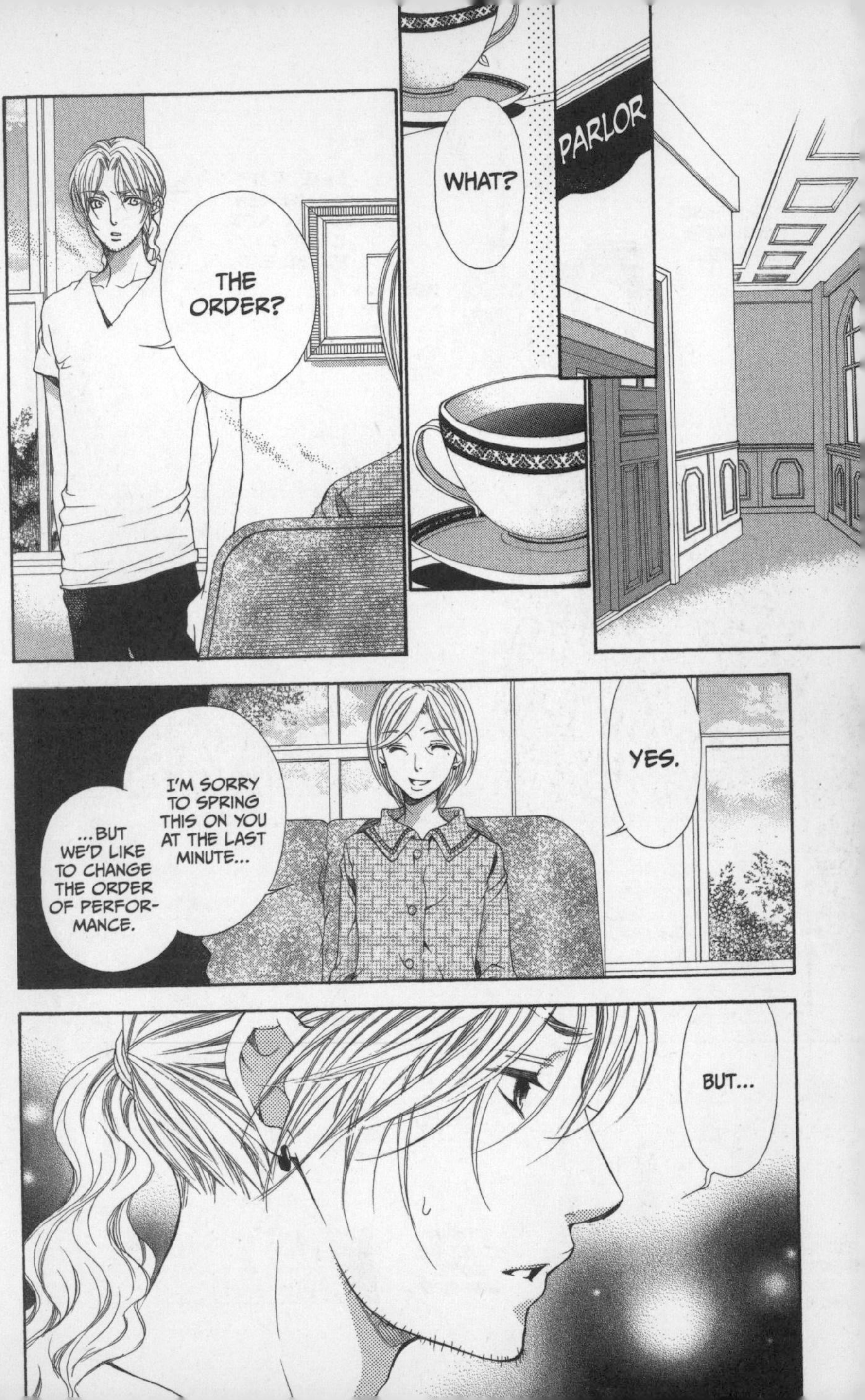
PARLOR
WHAT?
THE ORDER?
YES.
I'M SORRY TO SPRING THIS ON YOU AT THE LAST MINUTE...
...BUT WE'D LIKE TO CHANGE THE ORDER OF PERFORMANCE.
BUT...

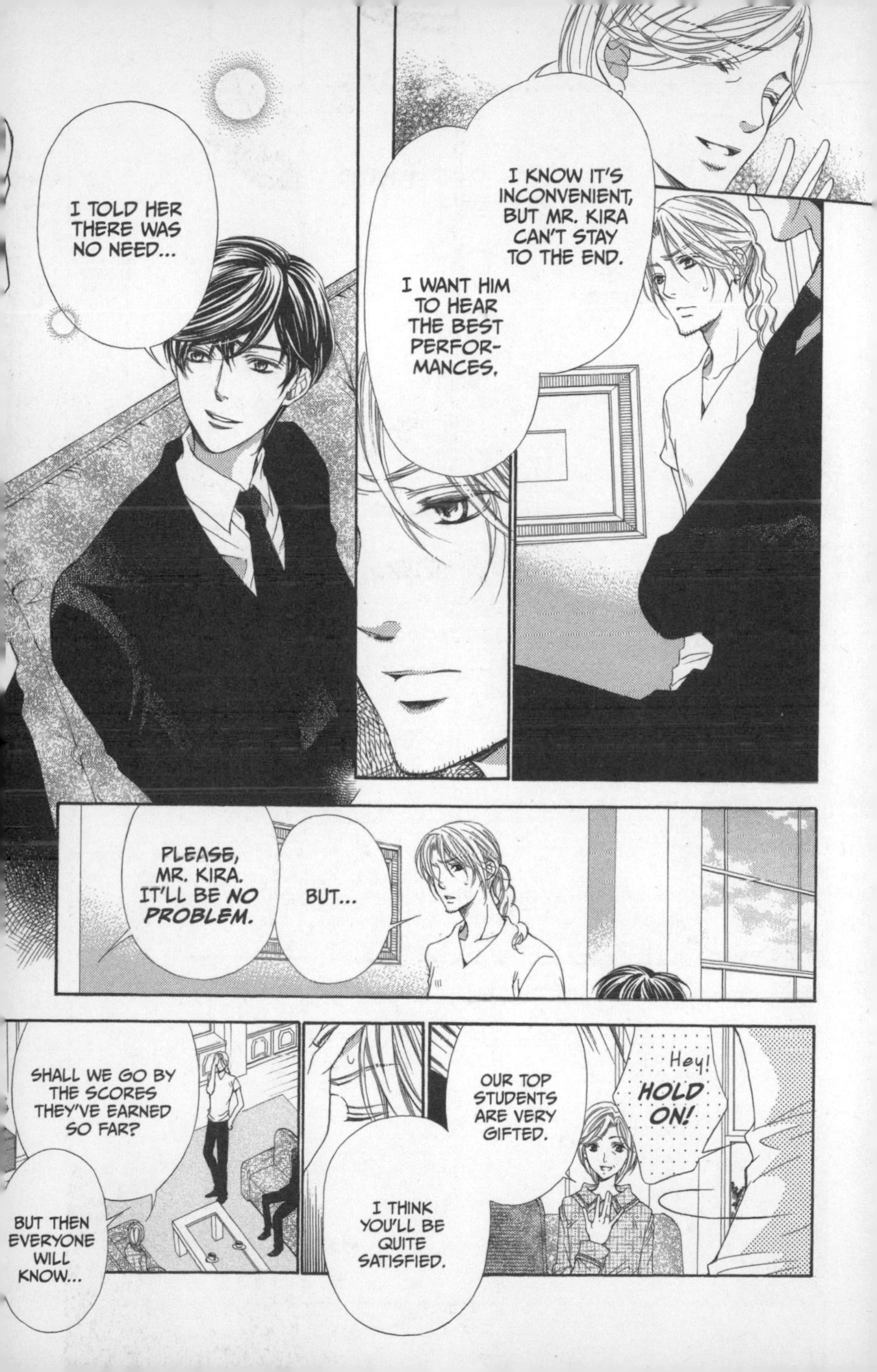
I KNOW IT'S INCONVENIENT, BUT MR. KIRA CAN'T STAY TO THE END.
I WANT HIM TO HEAR THE BEST PERFOR-MANCES.
I TOLD HER THERE WAS NO NEED...
BUT...
PLEASE, MR. KIRA. IT'LL BE *NO PROBLEM.*
Hey! **HOLD ON!**
OUR TOP STUDENTS ARE VERY GIFTED.
I THINK YOU'LL BE QUITE SATISFIED.
SHALL WE GO BY THE SCORES THEY'VE EARNED SO FAR?
BUT THEN EVERYONE WILL KNOW...

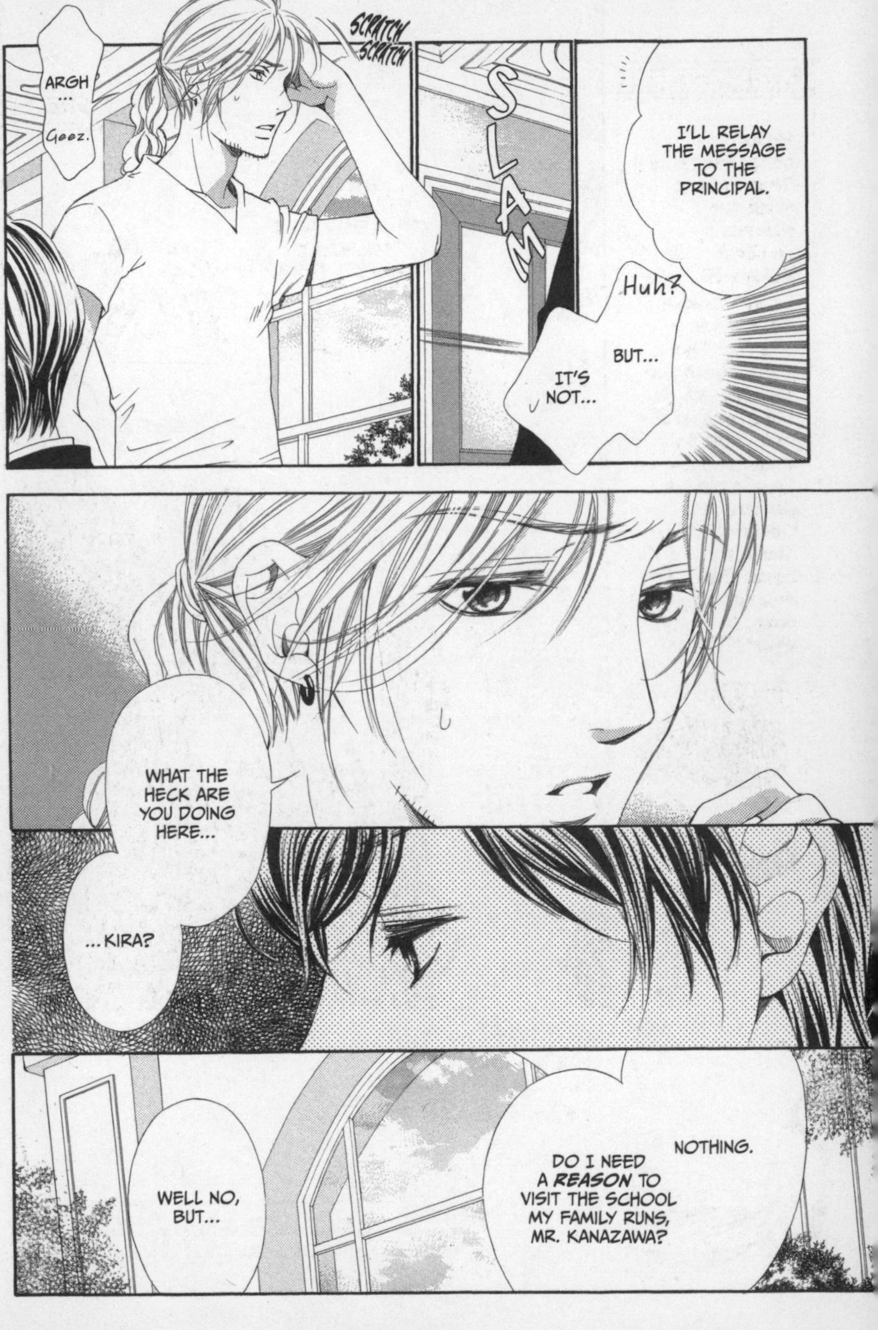
I'LL RELAY THE MESSAGE TO THE PRINCIPAL.
Huh?
BUT... IT'S NOT...
SLAM
SCRATCH SCRATCH
ARGH ... Geez.
WHAT THE HECK ARE YOU DOING HERE...
...KIRA?
NOTHING.
DO I NEED A *REASON* TO VISIT THE SCHOOL MY FAMILY RUNS, MR. KANAZAWA?
WELL NO, BUT...

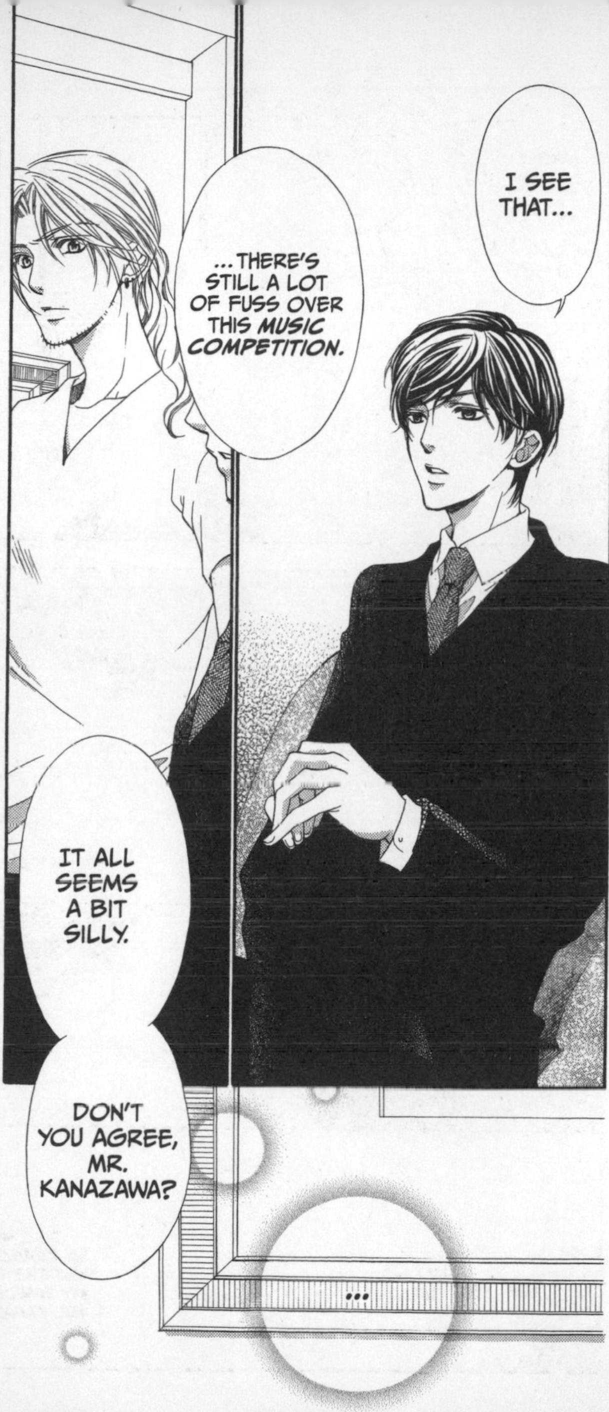
I SEE THAT...
...THERE'S STILL A LOT OF FUSS OVER THIS *MUSIC COMPETITION.*
IT ALL SEEMS A BIT SILLY.
DON'T YOU AGREE, MR. KANAZAWA?
...

Hello!
Long time no see!
Thank you so much for purchasing *La Corda d'Oro* Volume 10.
I can't believe we've made it this far. Thank you so much for your loyalty.
I'm so grateful to be able to draw so much.
This volume is all about the Final Selection.
There's also a bonus story. I hope you enjoy it.
Wow...
Volume 10...

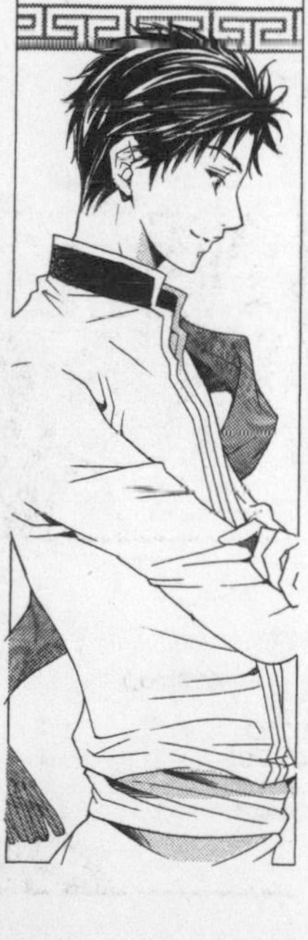

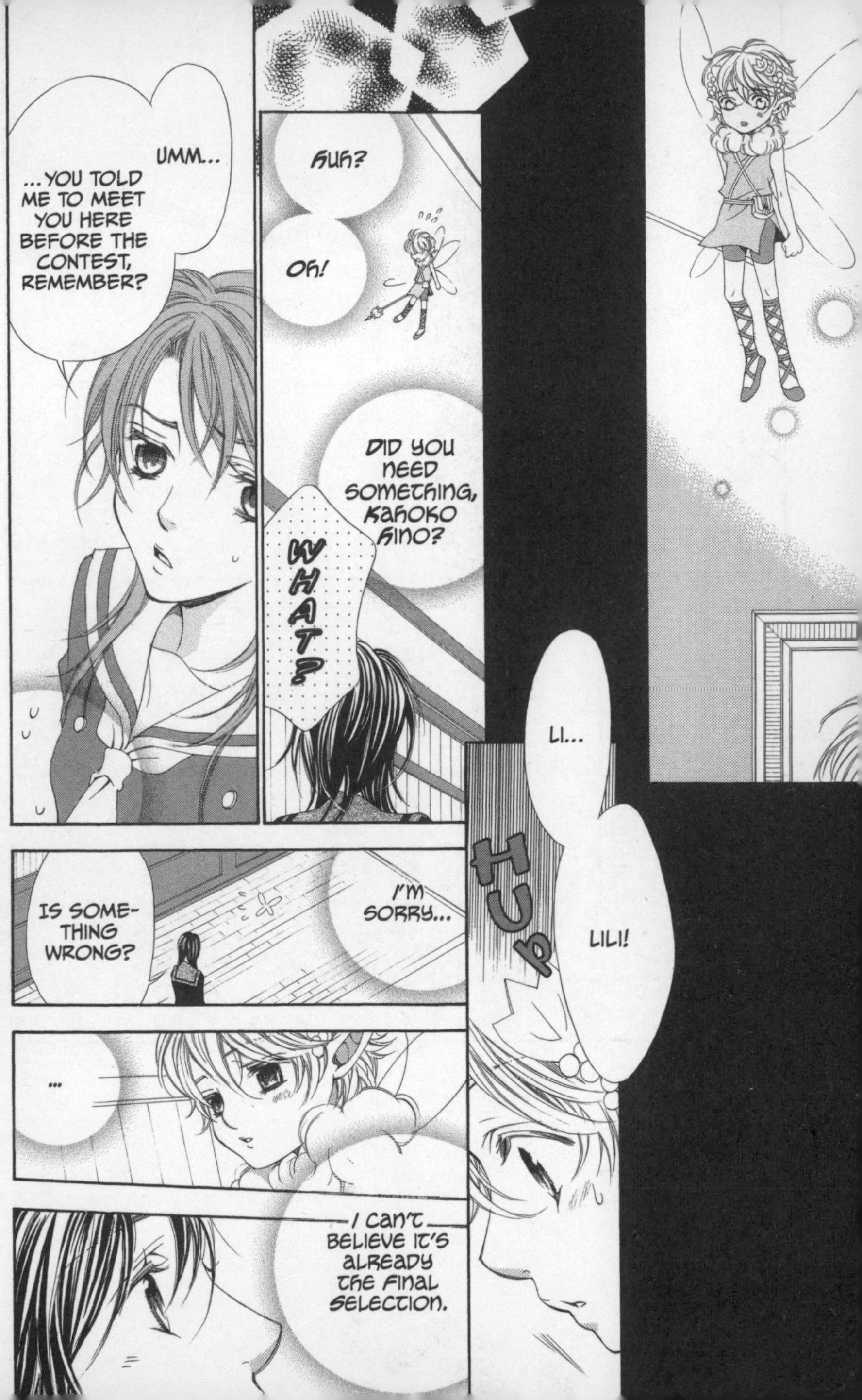
LI...
LILI!
HUP
HUH?
OH!
DID YOU NEED SOMETHING, KAHOKO HINO?
WHAT?
UMM...
...YOU TOLD ME TO MEET YOU HERE BEFORE THE CONTEST, REMEMBER?
I'M SORRY...
IS SOME-THING WRONG?
...
I CAN'T BELIEVE IT'S ALREADY THE FINAL SELECTION.

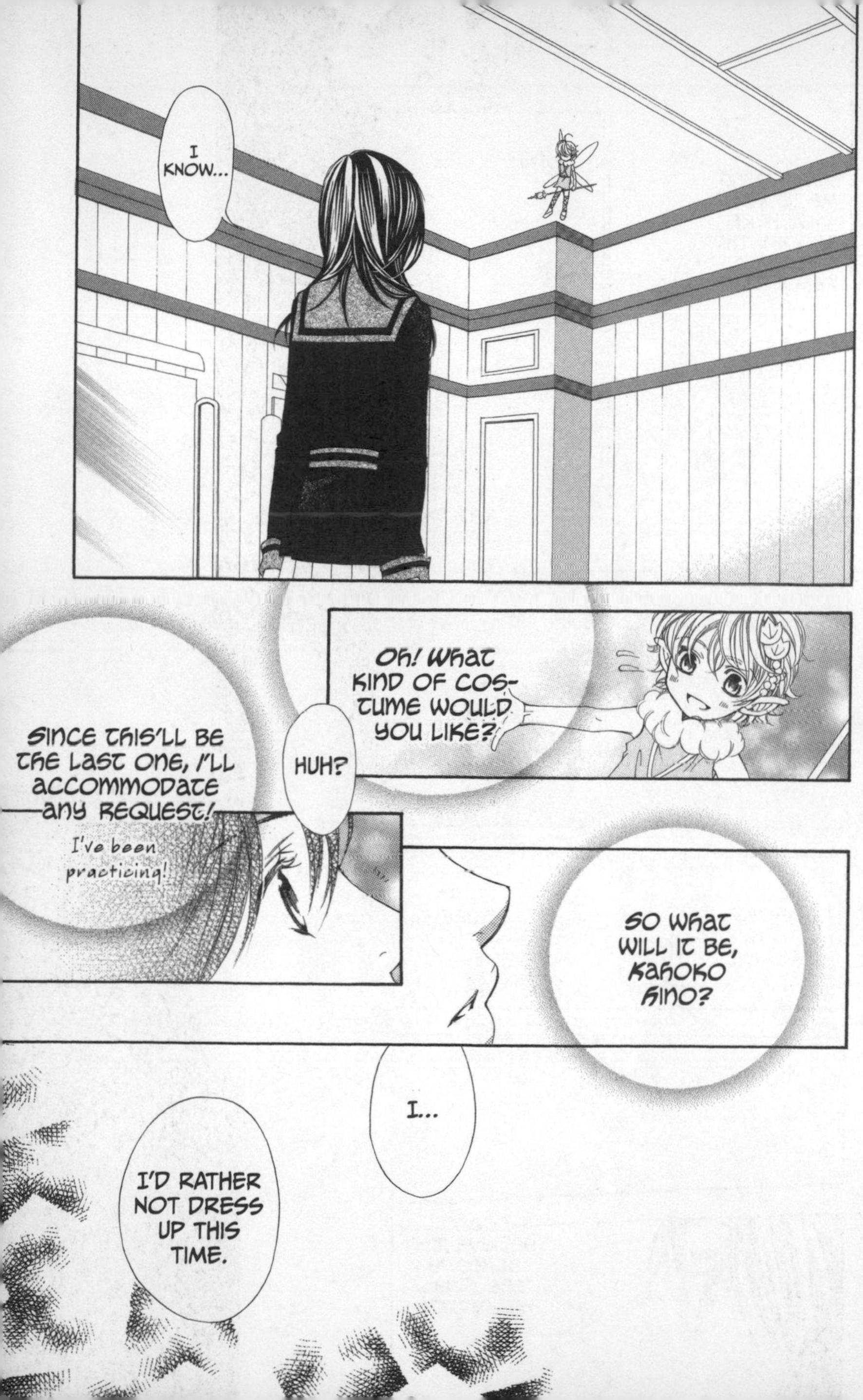
I KNOW...
OH! WHAT KIND OF COSTUME WOULD YOU LIKE?
HUH?
SINCE THIS'LL BE THE LAST ONE, I'LL ACCOMMODATE —ANY REQUEST!
I've been practicing!
SO WHAT WILL IT BE, KAHOKO HINO?
I...
I'D RATHER NOT DRESS UP THIS TIME.

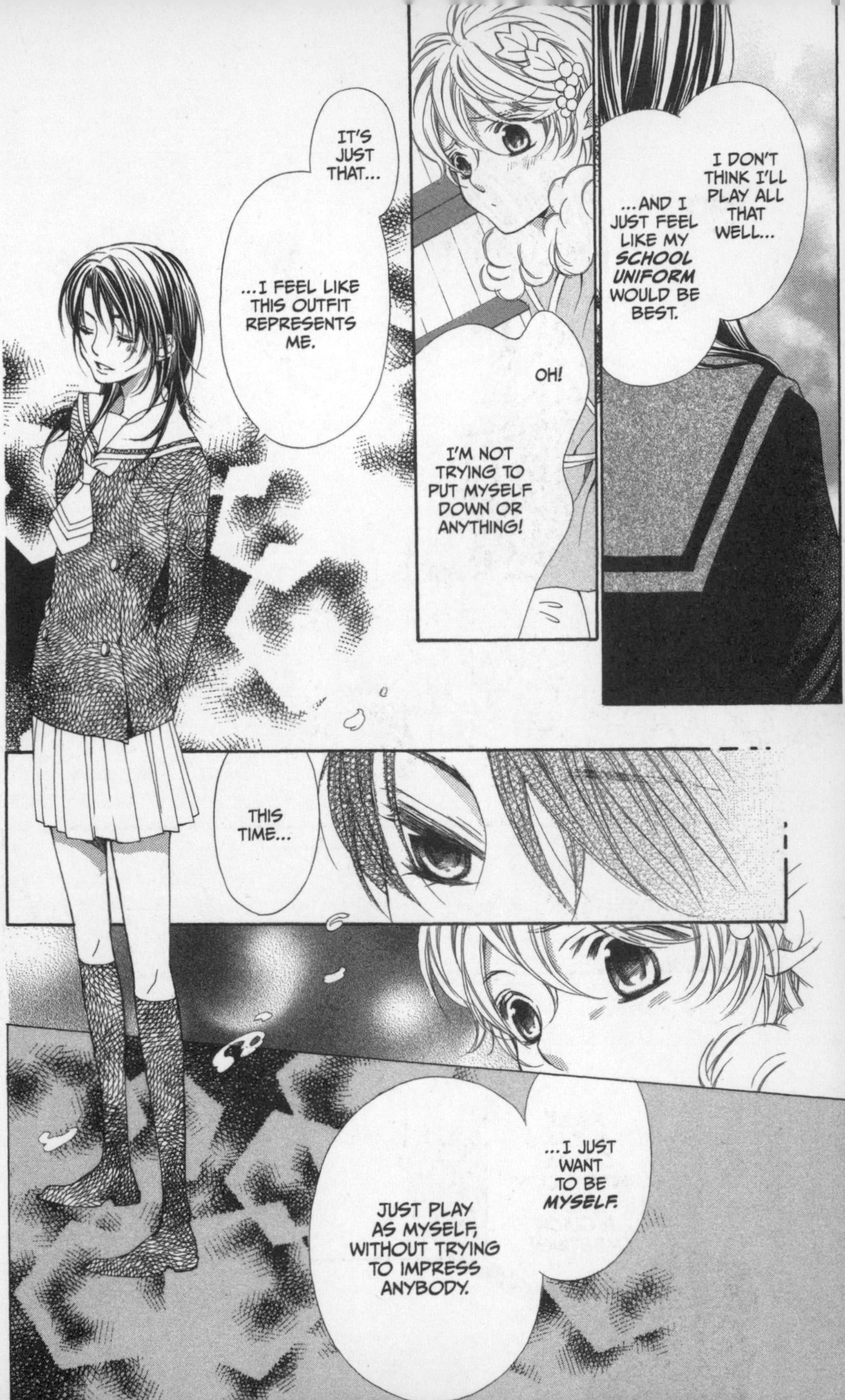

I DON'T THINK I'LL PLAY ALL THAT WELL...
...AND I JUST FEEL LIKE MY *SCHOOL UNIFORM* WOULD BE BEST.
OH!
I'M NOT TRYING TO PUT MYSELF DOWN OR ANYTHING!
IT'S JUST THAT...
...I FEEL LIKE THIS OUTFIT REPRESENTS ME.
THIS TIME...
...I JUST WANT TO BE *MYSELF*.
JUST PLAY AS MYSELF, WITHOUT TRYING TO IMPRESS ANYBODY.

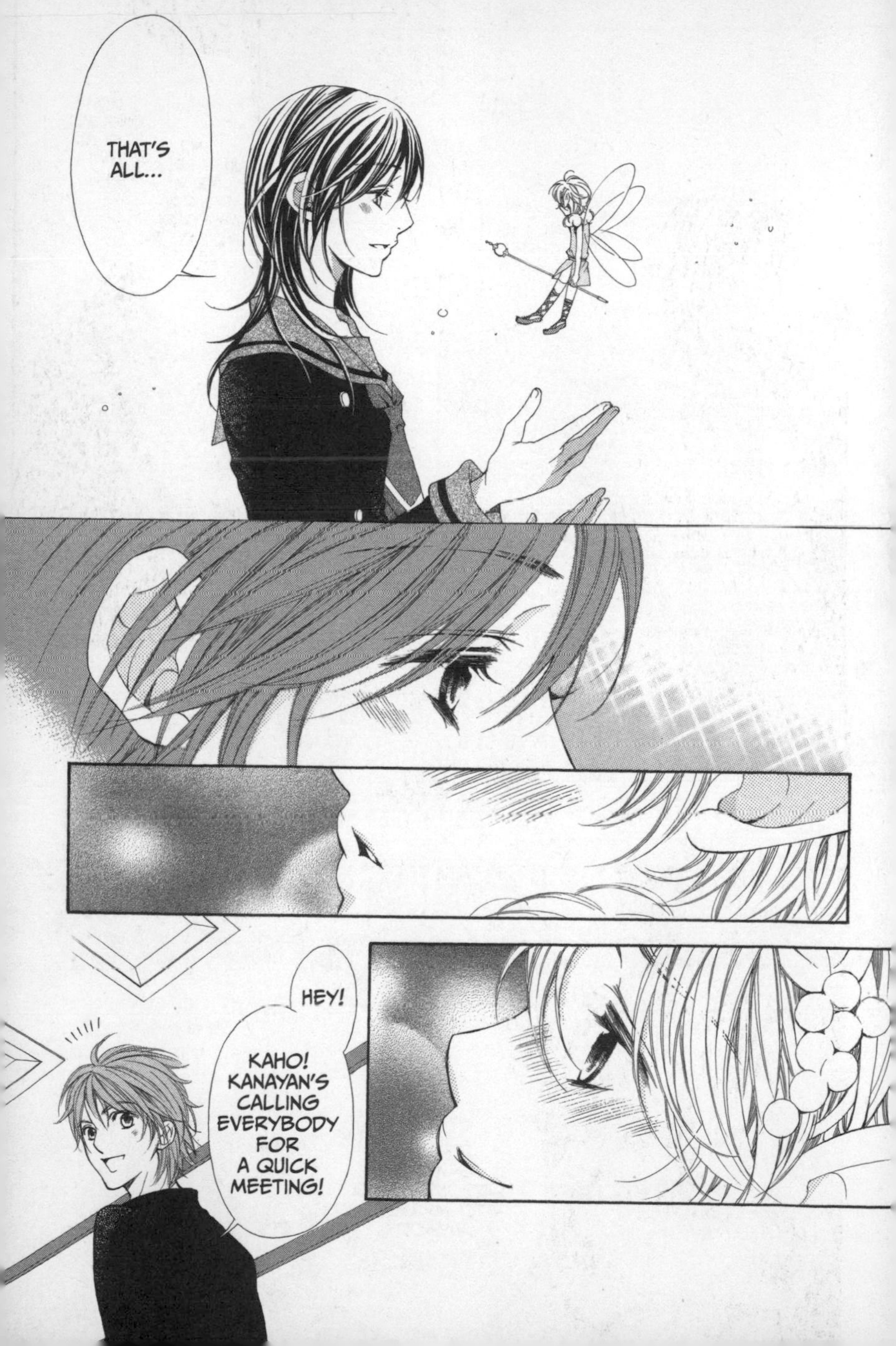
THAT'S ALL...
HEY!
KAHO! KANAYAN'S CALLING EVERYBODY FOR A QUICK MEETING!

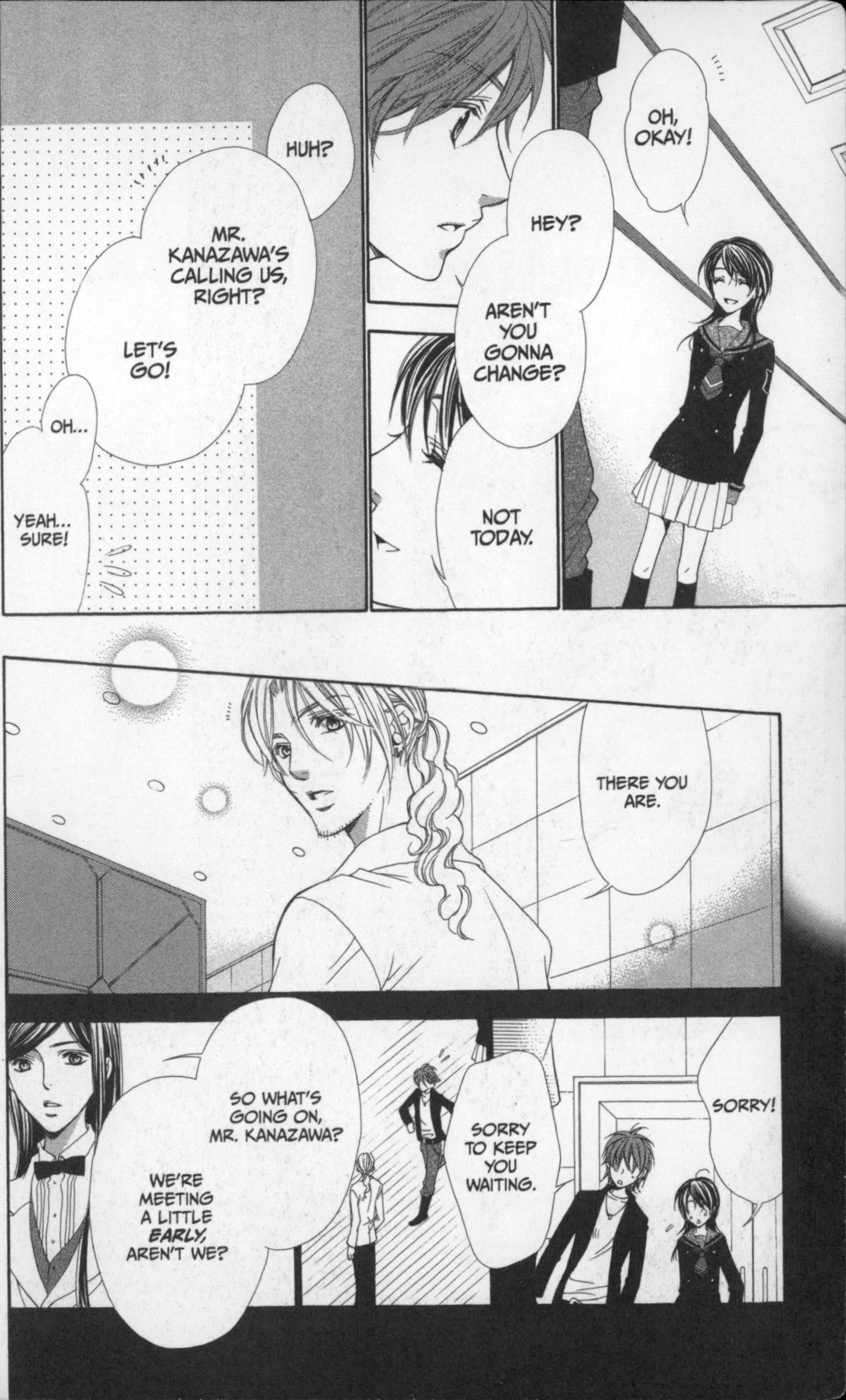
OH, OKAY!
HEY?
AREN'T YOU GONNA CHANGE?
NOT TODAY.
HUH?
MR. KANAZAWA'S CALLING US, RIGHT?
LET'S GO!
OH...
YEAH... SURE!
THERE YOU ARE.
SORRY!
SORRY TO KEEP YOU WAITING.
SO WHAT'S GOING ON, MR. KANAZAWA?
WE'RE MEETING A LITTLE *EARLY*, AREN'T WE?

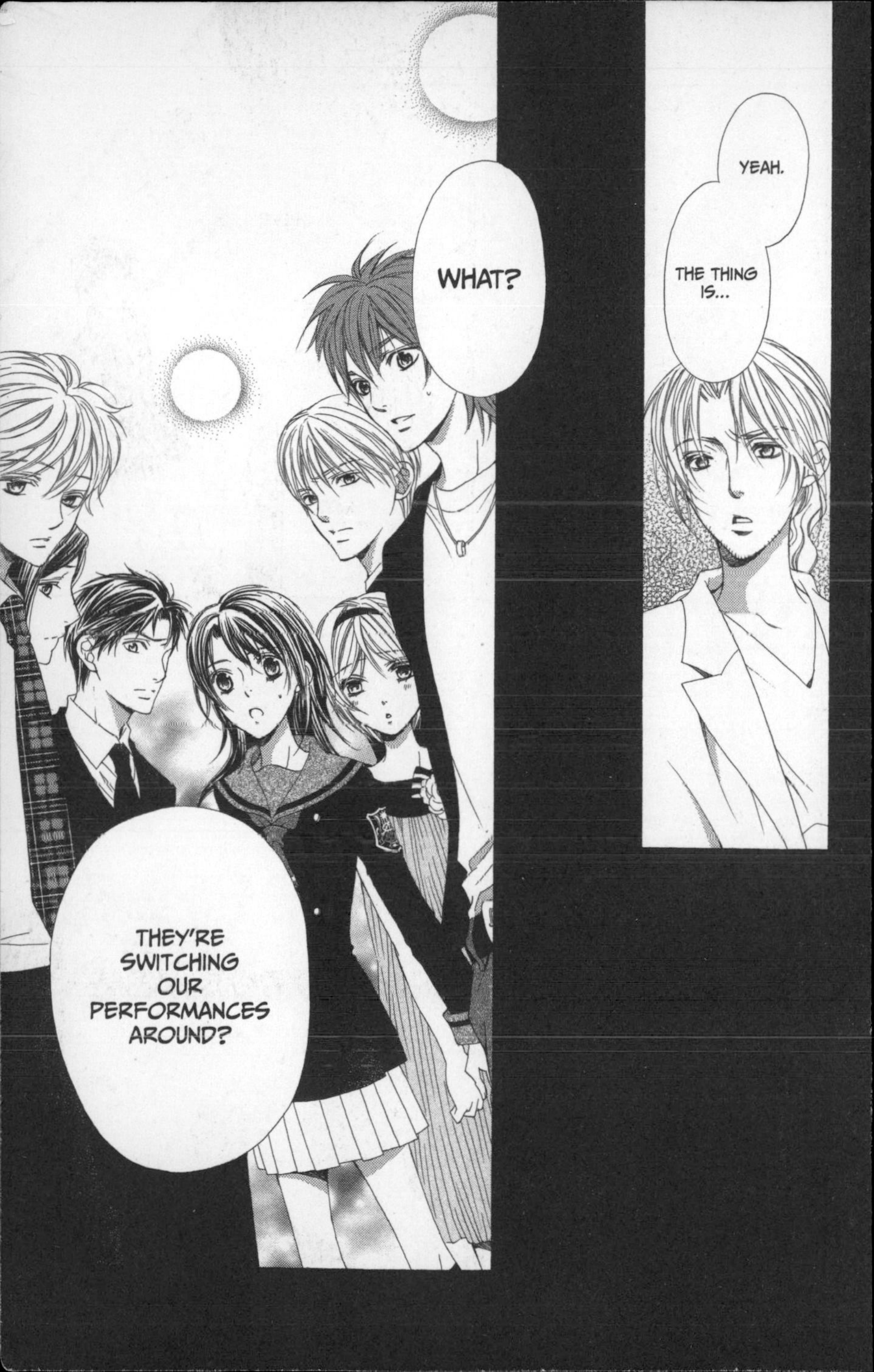
YEAH.
THE THING IS...
WHAT?
THEY'RE SWITCHING OUR PERFORMANCES AROUND?

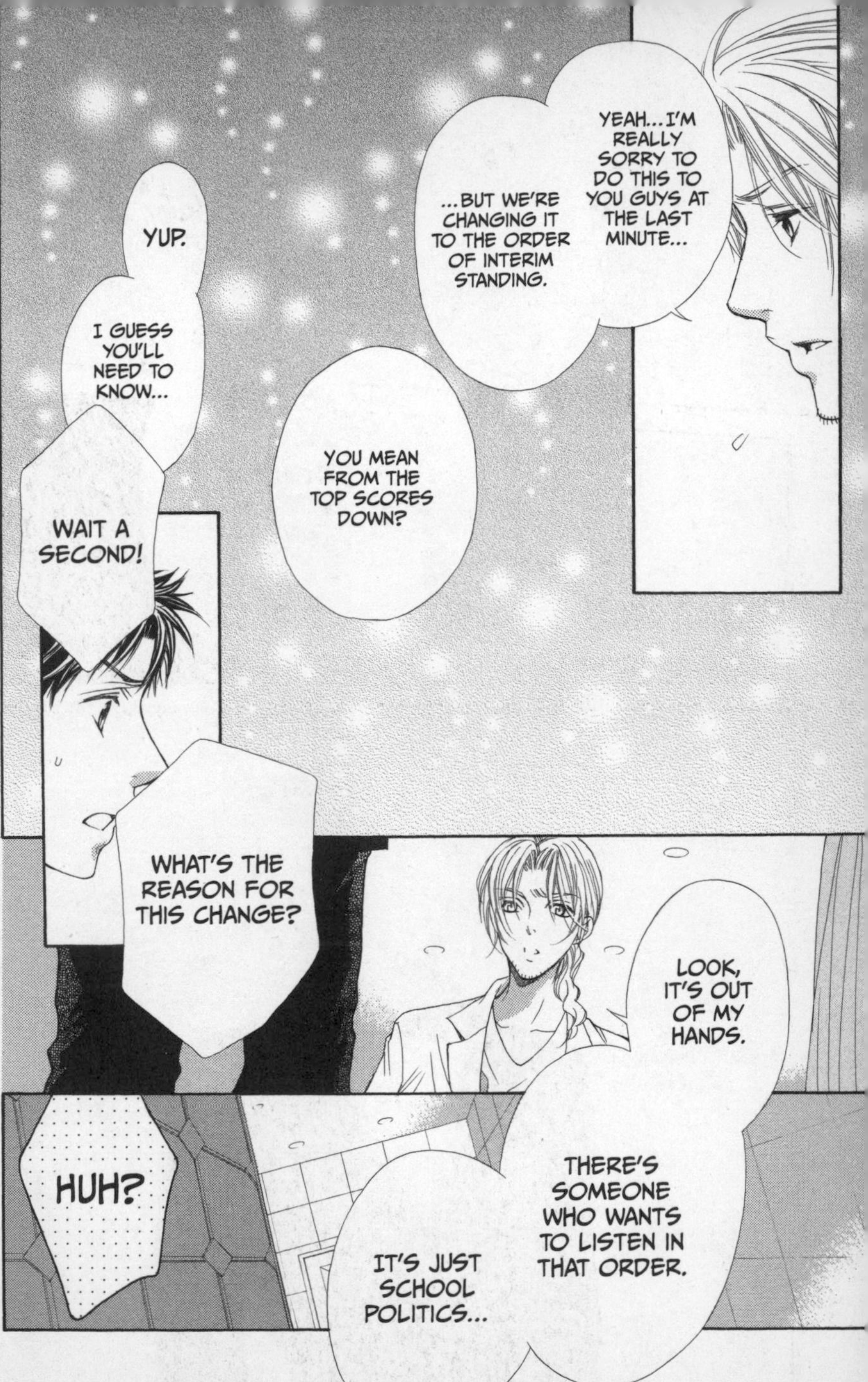
YEAH...I'M REALLY SORRY TO DO THIS TO YOU GUYS AT THE LAST MINUTE...
...BUT WE'RE CHANGING IT TO THE ORDER OF INTERIM STANDING.
YOU MEAN FROM THE TOP SCORES DOWN?
YUP.
I GUESS YOU'LL NEED TO KNOW...
WAIT A SECOND!
WHAT'S THE REASON FOR THIS CHANGE?
LOOK, IT'S OUT OF MY HANDS.
THERE'S SOMEONE WHO WANTS TO LISTEN IN THAT ORDER.
IT'S JUST SCHOOL POLITICS...
HUH?

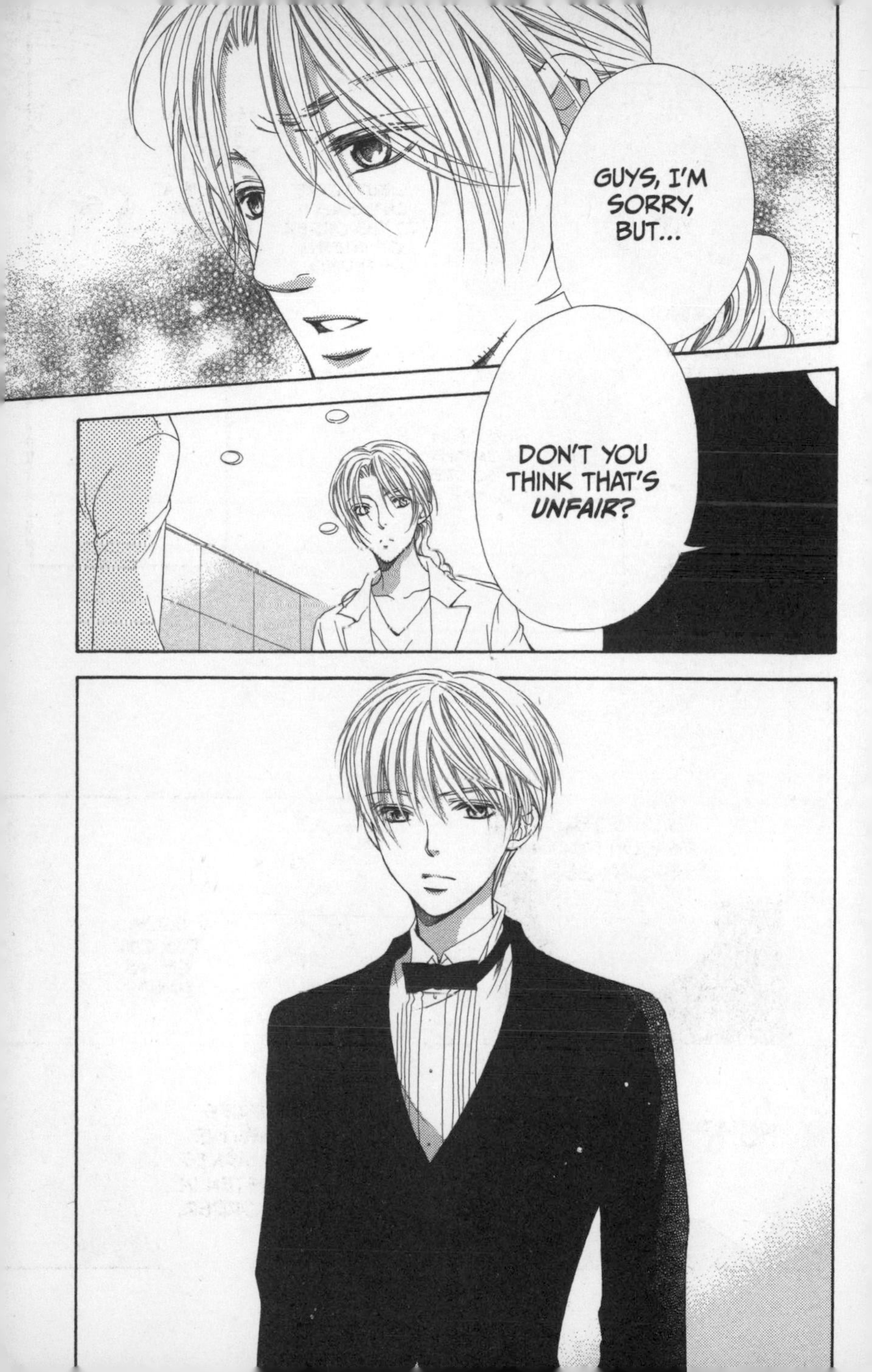
GUYS, I'M SORRY, BUT...
DON'T YOU THINK THAT'S *UNFAIR?*

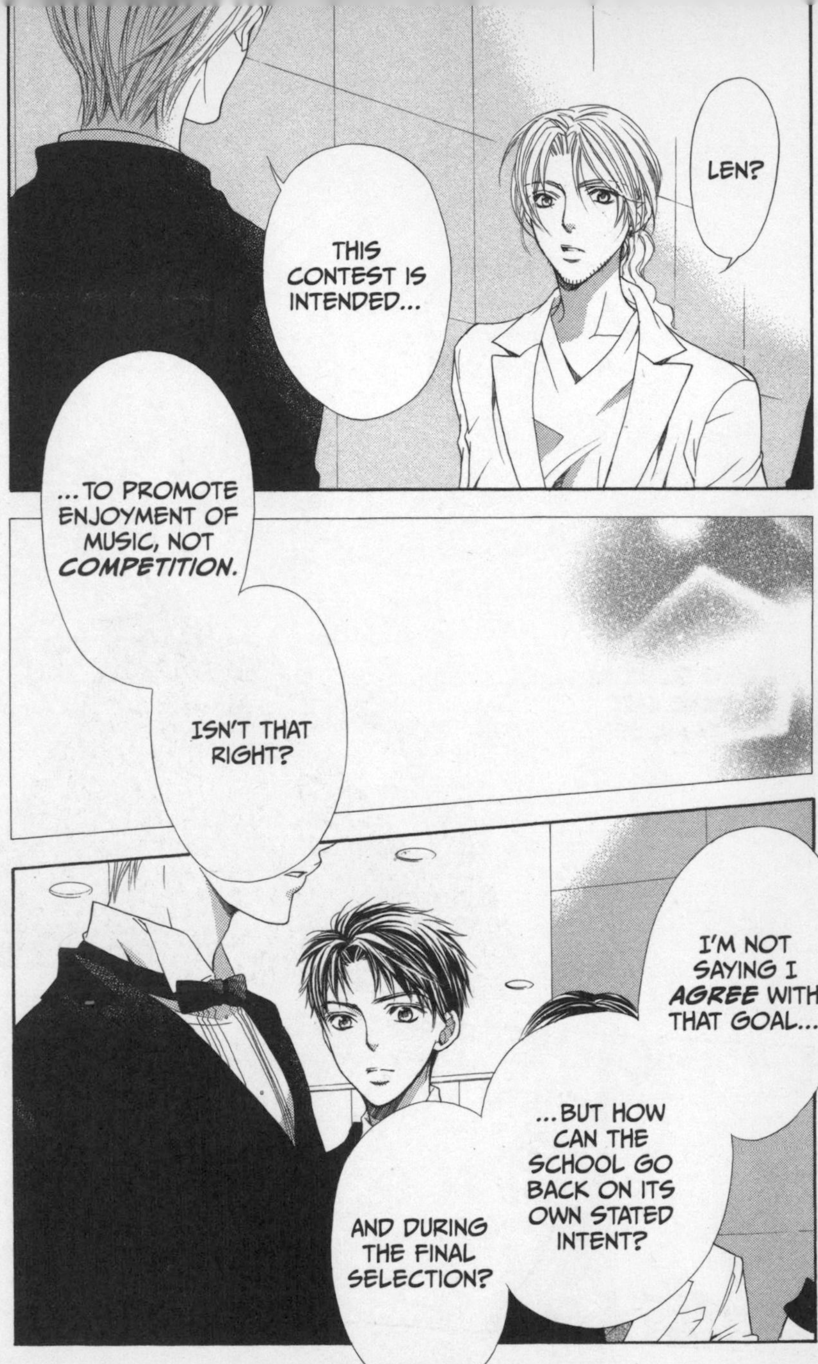
LEN?
THIS CONTEST IS INTENDED...
...TO PROMOTE ENJOYMENT OF MUSIC, NOT *COMPETITION*.
ISN'T THAT RIGHT?
I'M NOT SAYING I *AGREE* WITH THAT GOAL...
...BUT HOW CAN THE SCHOOL GO BACK ON ITS OWN STATED INTENT?
AND DURING THE FINAL SELECTION?

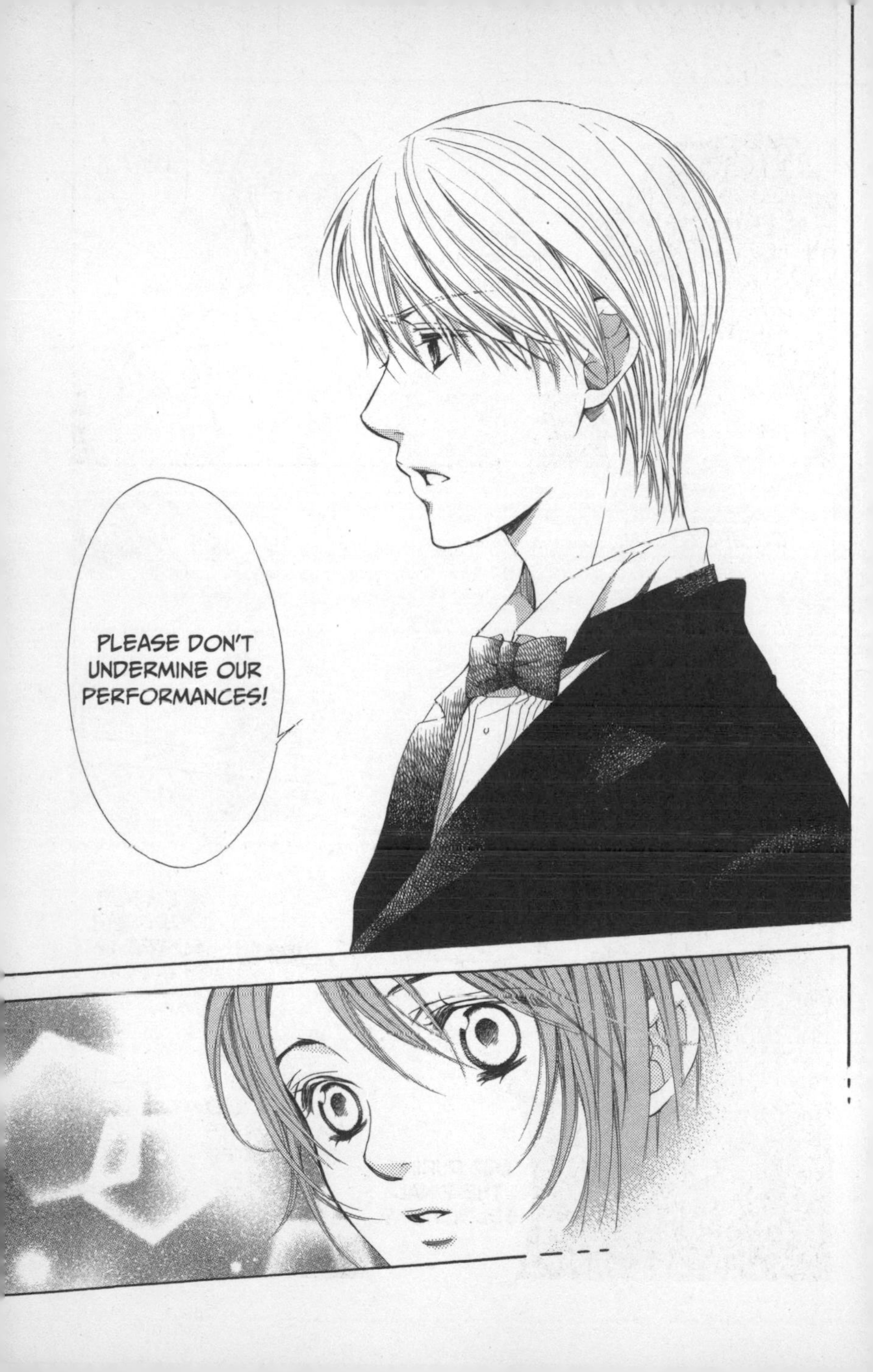
PLEASE DON'T UNDERMINE OUR PERFORMANCES!

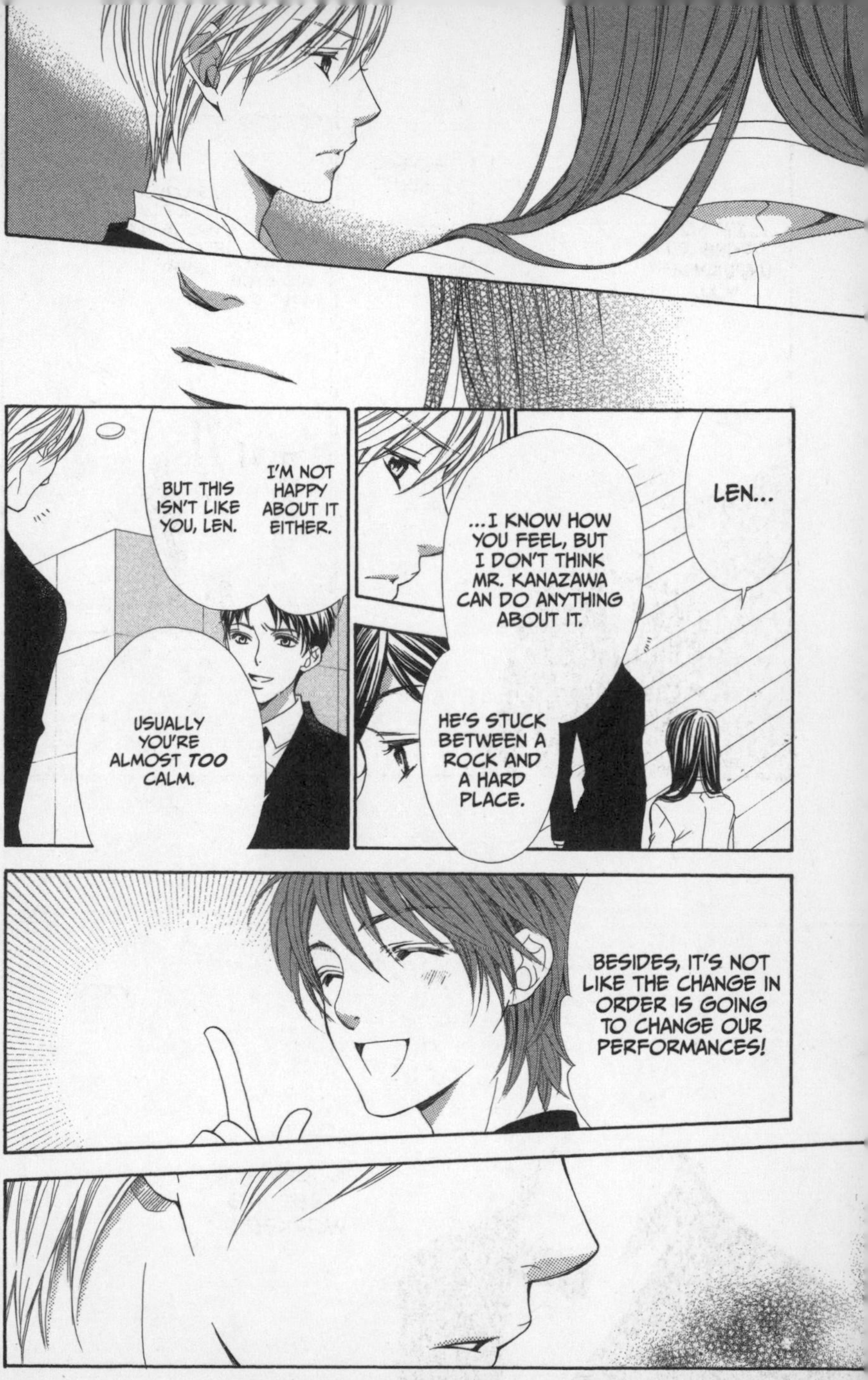
LEN...
...I KNOW HOW YOU FEEL, BUT I DON'T THINK MR. KANAZAWA CAN DO ANYTHING ABOUT IT.
HE'S STUCK BETWEEN A ROCK AND A HARD PLACE.
I'M NOT HAPPY ABOUT IT EITHER.
BUT THIS ISN'T LIKE YOU, LEN.
USUALLY YOU'RE ALMOST *TOO* CALM.
BESIDES, IT'S NOT LIKE THE CHANGE IN ORDER IS GOING TO CHANGE OUR PERFORMANCES!

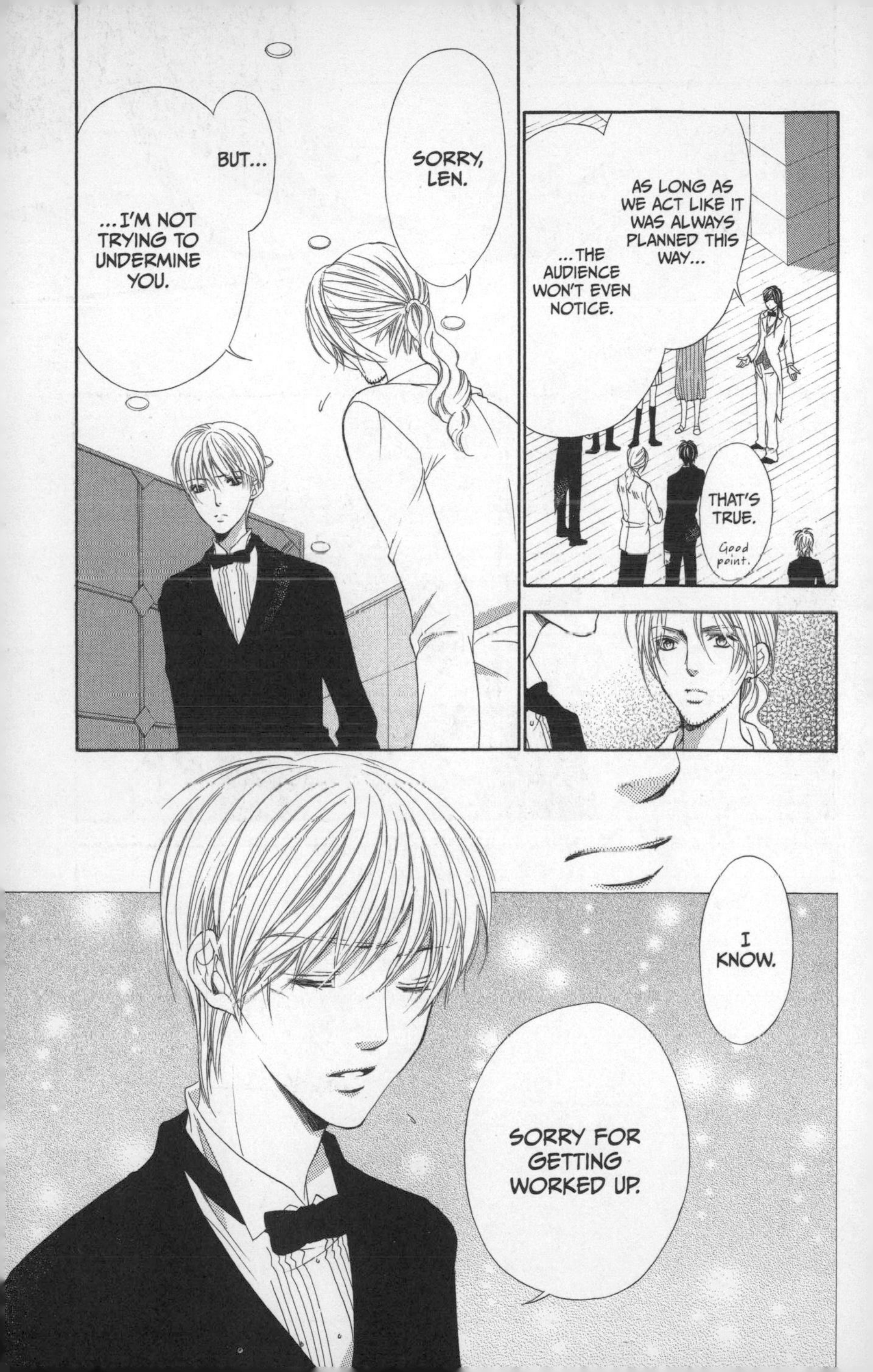
AS LONG AS WE ACT LIKE IT WAS ALWAYS PLANNED THIS WAY...
...THE AUDIENCE WON'T EVEN NOTICE.
THAT'S TRUE.
Good point.
SORRY, LEN.
BUT...
...I'M NOT TRYING TO UNDERMINE YOU.
I KNOW.
SORRY FOR GETTING WORKED UP.

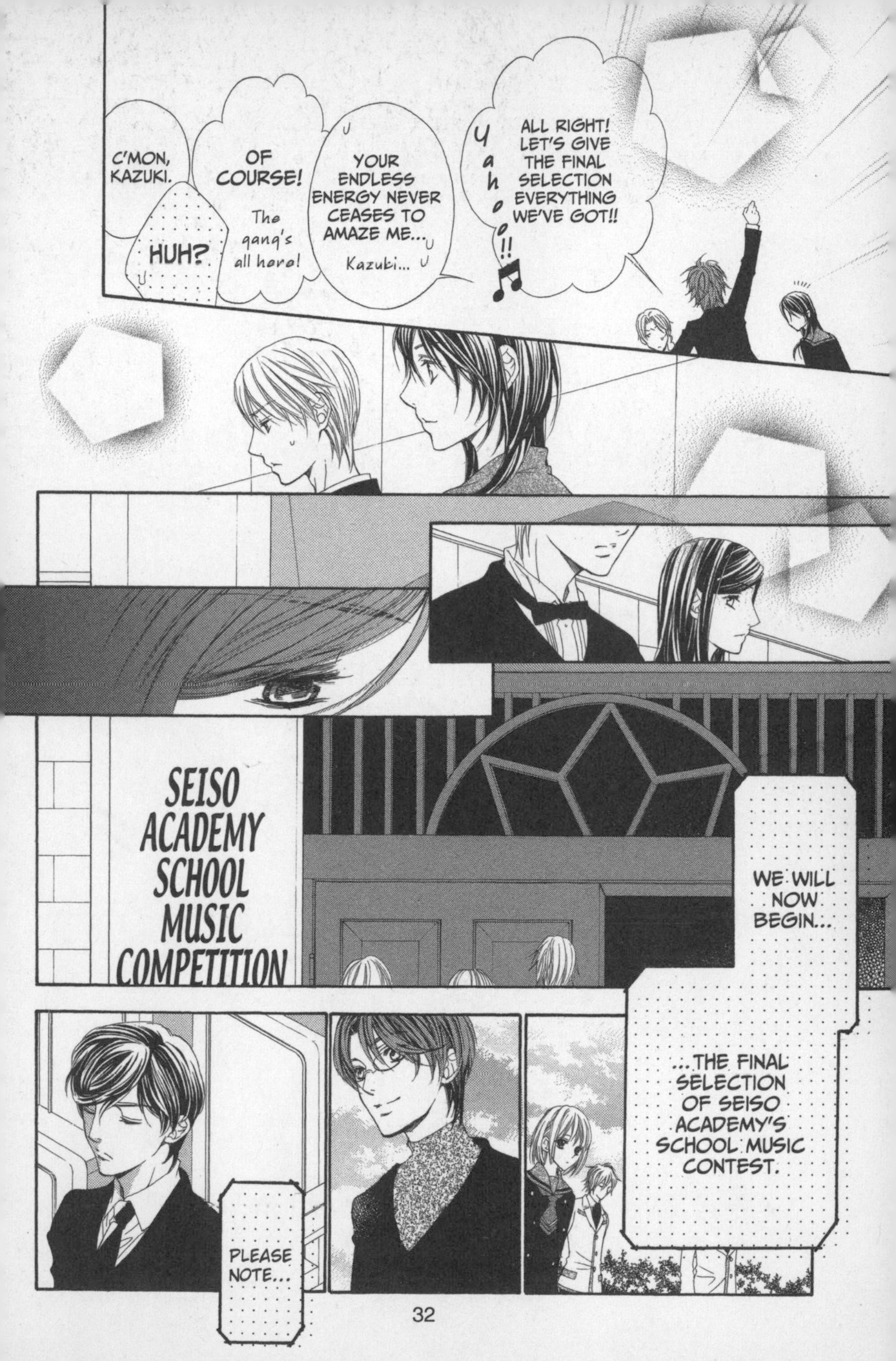
ALL RIGHT! LET'S GIVE THE FINAL SELECTION EVERYTHING WE'VE GOT!!
Yahoo!!
YOUR ENDLESS ENERGY NEVER CEASES TO AMAZE ME...
Kazuki...
OF COURSE!
The gang's all here!
C'MON, KAZUKI.
HUH?
WE WILL NOW BEGIN...
SEISO ACADEMY SCHOOL MUSIC COMPETITION
...THE FINAL SELECTION OF SEISO ACADEMY'S SCHOOL MUSIC CONTEST.
PLEASE NOTE...

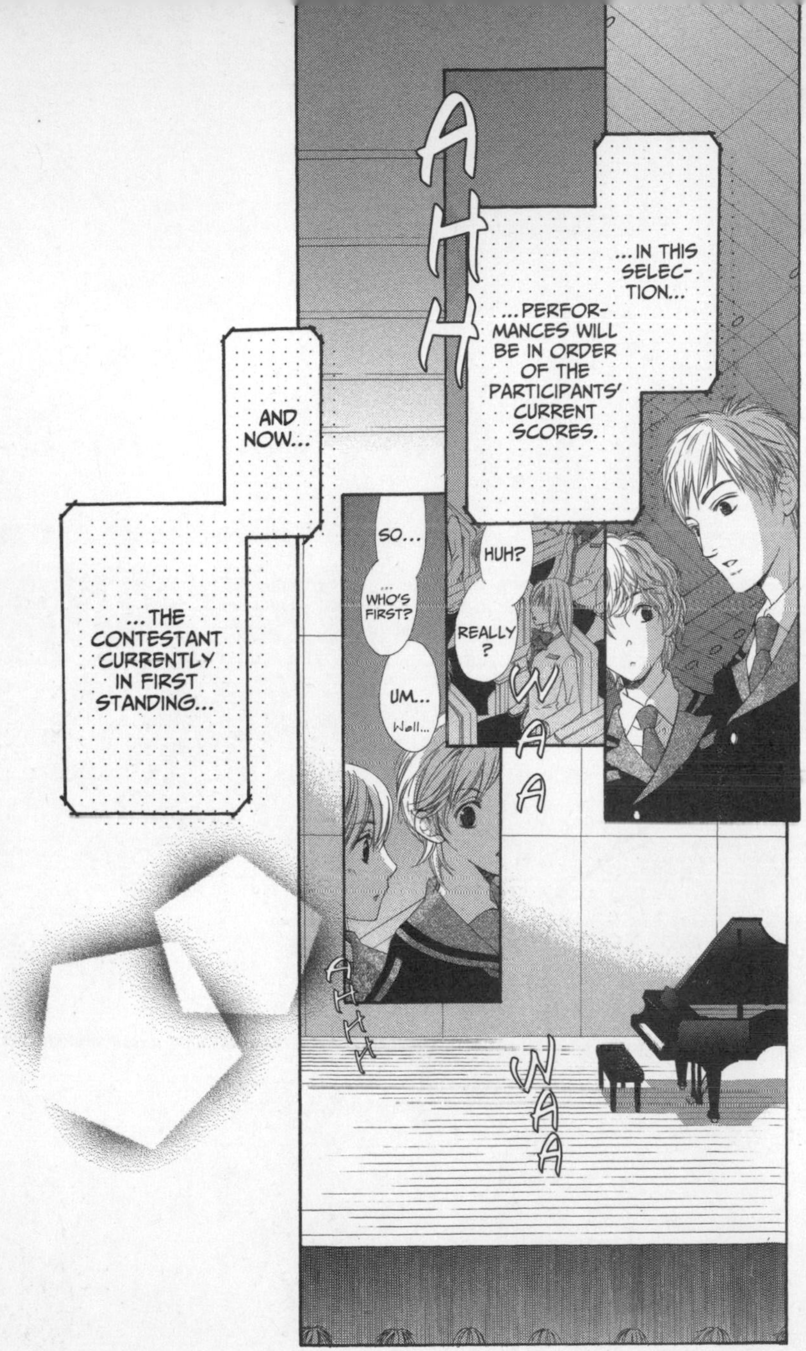
...IN THIS SELECTION...
...PERFORMANCES WILL BE IN ORDER OF THE PARTICIPANTS' CURRENT SCORES.
AHH
HUH?
REALLY?
WAA
SO...
...WHO'S FIRST?
UM...
Well...
AND NOW...
...THE CONTESTANT CURRENTLY IN FIRST STANDING...
AHH
WAA

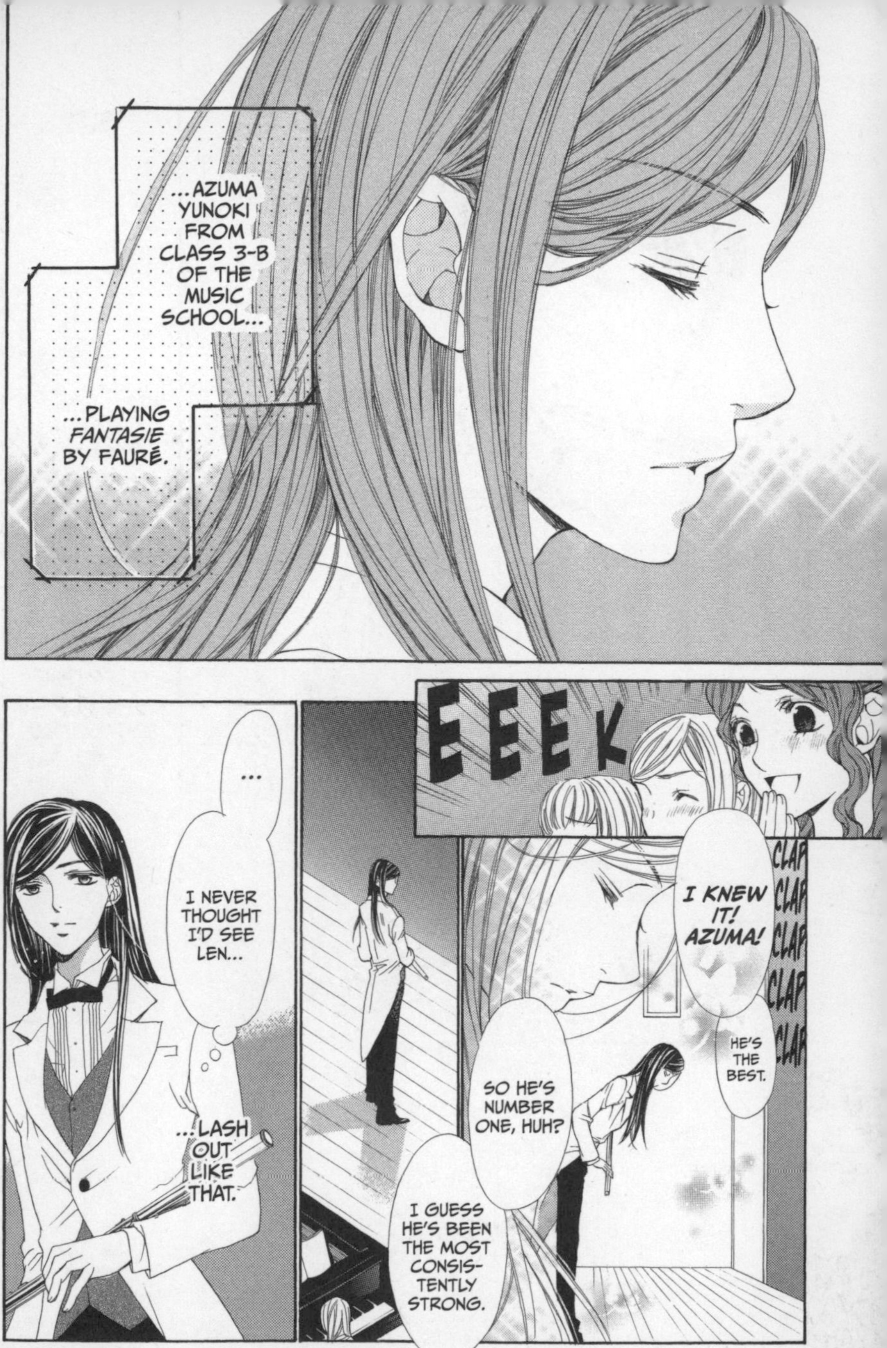
...AZUMA YUNOKI FROM CLASS 3-B OF THE MUSIC SCHOOL...
...PLAYING *FANTASIE* BY FAURÉ.
EEEK
CLAP CLAP CLAP CLAP CLAP
I KNEW IT! AZUMA!
HE'S THE BEST.
SO HE'S NUMBER ONE, HUH?
I GUESS HE'S BEEN THE MOST CONSIS-TENTLY STRONG.
...
I NEVER THOUGHT I'D SEE LEN...
...LASH OUT LIKE THAT.

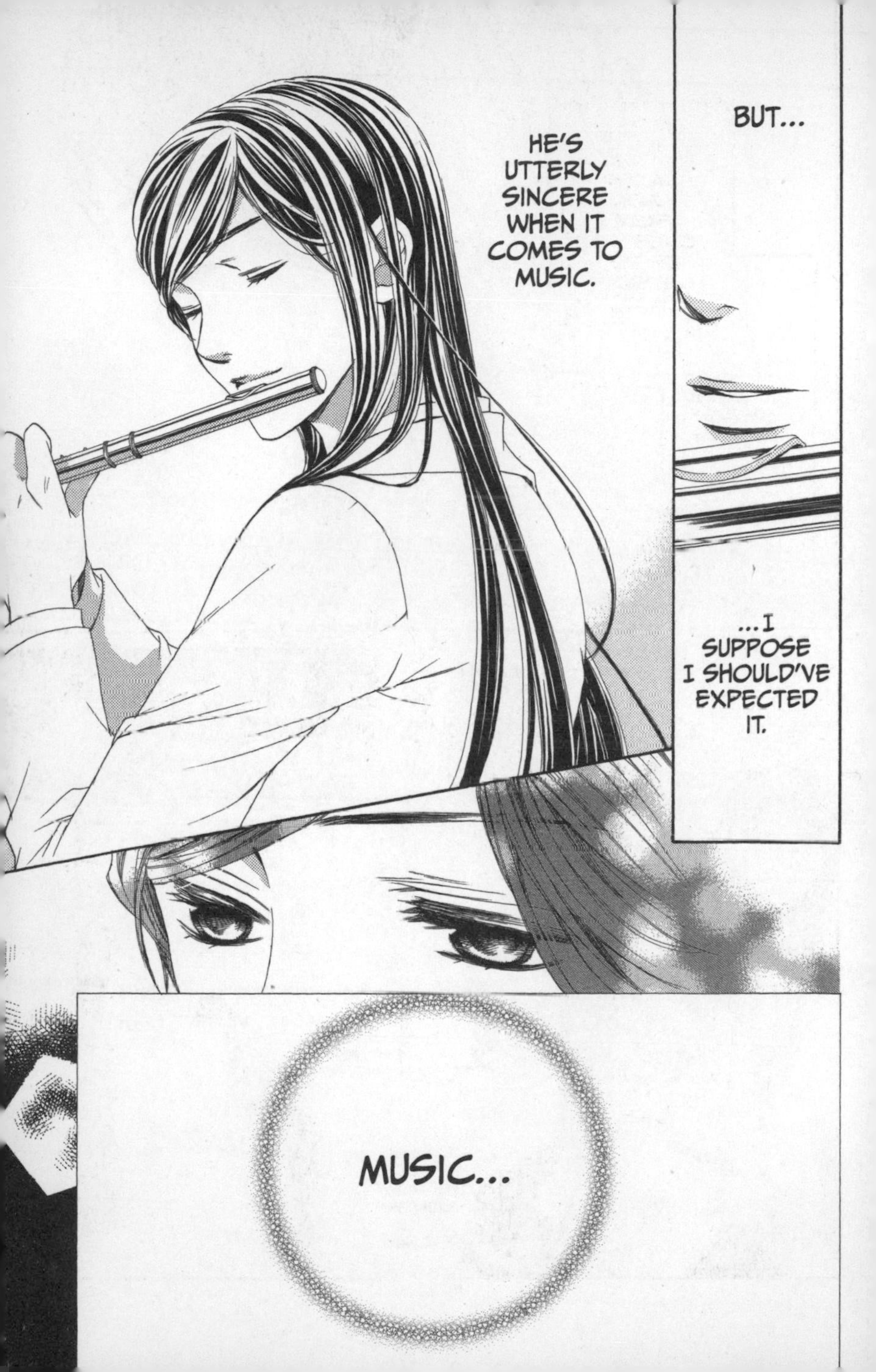
BUT...
...I SUPPOSE I SHOULD'VE EXPECTED IT.
HE'S UTTERLY SINCERE WHEN IT COMES TO MUSIC.
MUSIC...

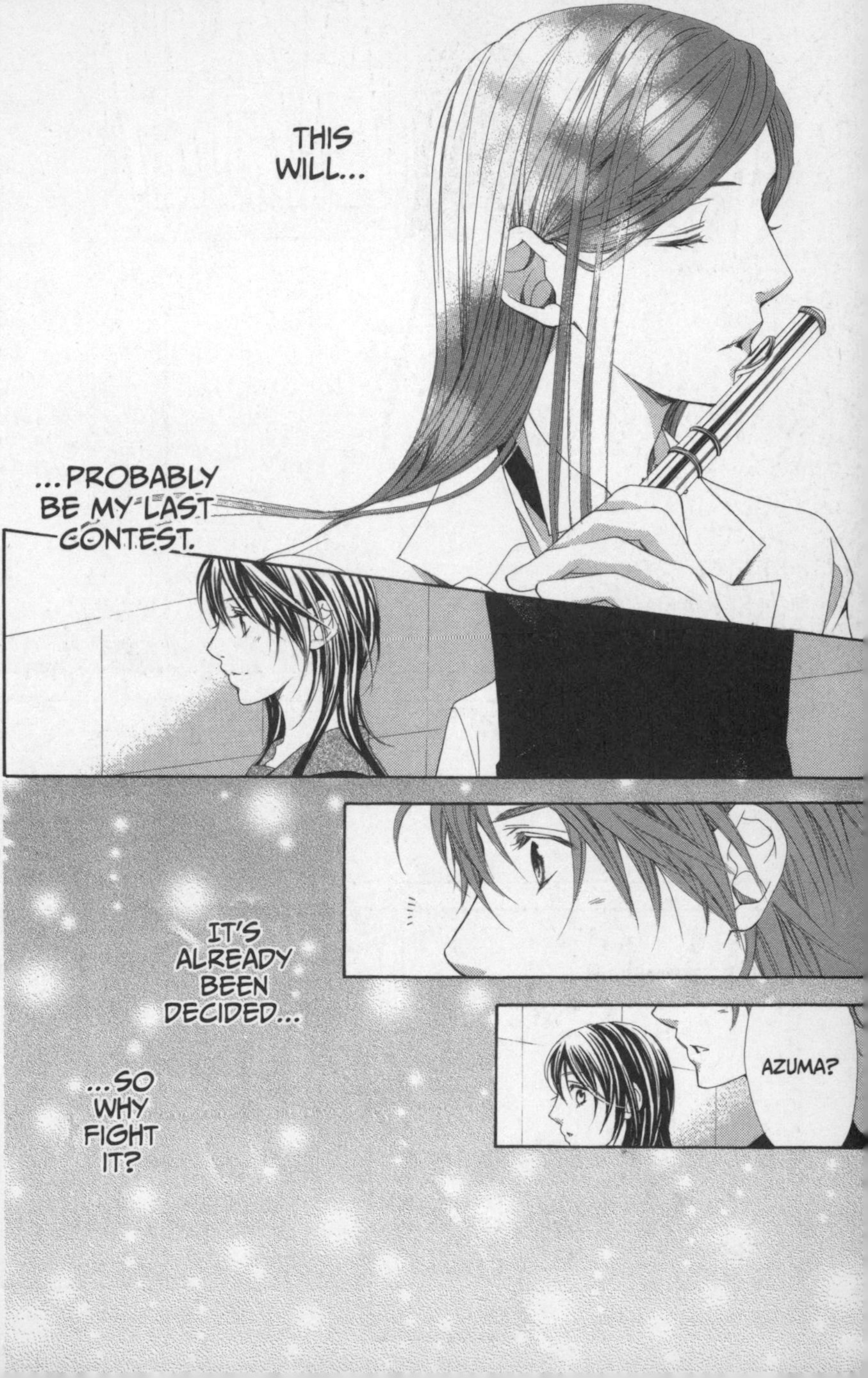
THIS WILL...
...PROBABLY BE MY LAST CONTEST.
IT'S ALREADY BEEN DECIDED...
...SO WHY FIGHT IT?
AZUMA?

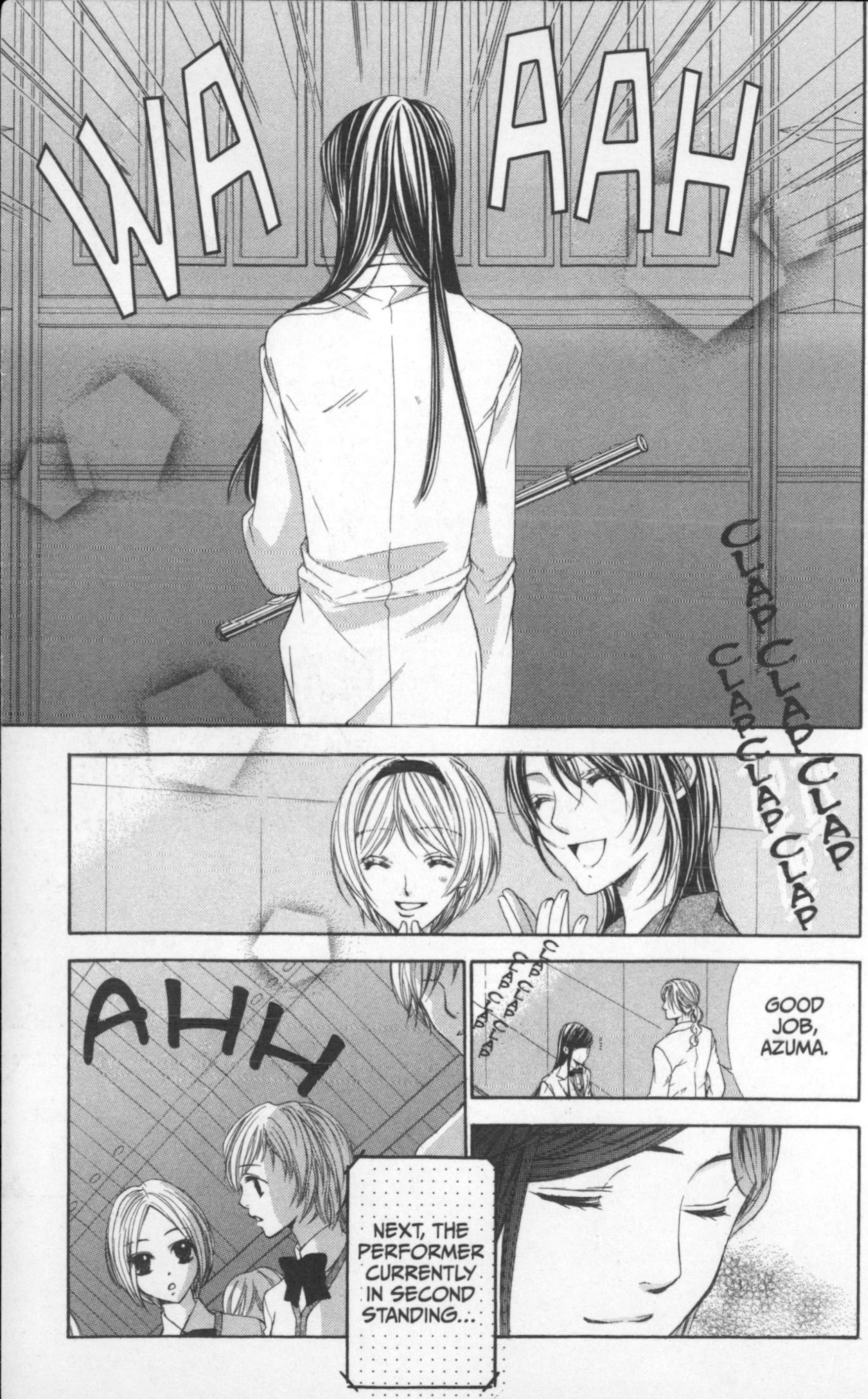
WA AAH
CLAP CLAP CLAP
CLAP CLAP CLAP
CLAP CLAP CLAP CLAP
GOOD JOB, AZUMA.
AHH
NEXT, THE PERFORMER CURRENTLY IN SECOND STANDING...

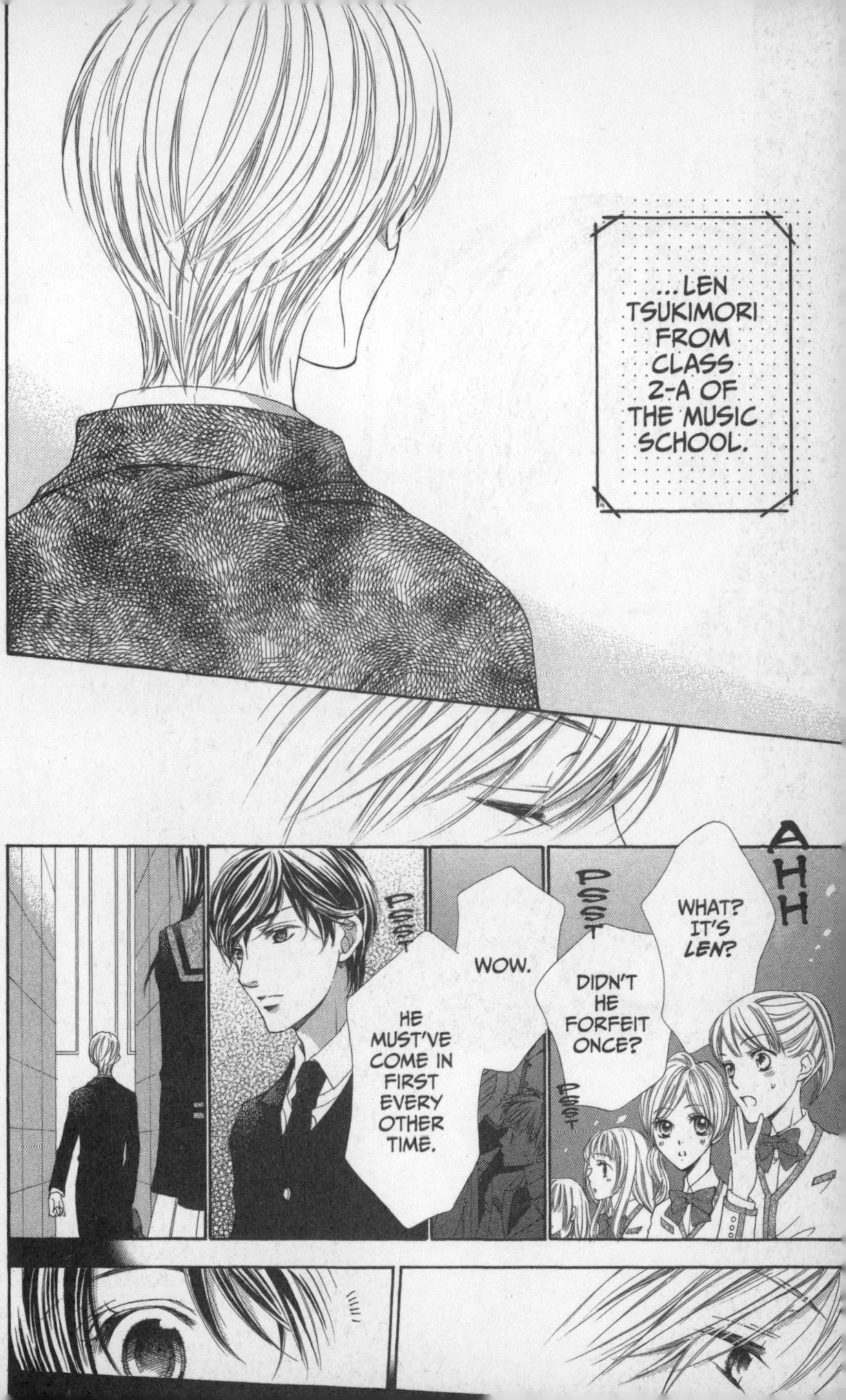
...LEN TSUKIMORI FROM CLASS 2-A OF THE MUSIC SCHOOL.
AHH
WHAT? IT'S LEN?
PSST
DIDN'T HE FORFEIT ONCE?
PSST
WOW.
HE MUST'VE COME IN FIRST EVERY OTHER TIME.
PSST

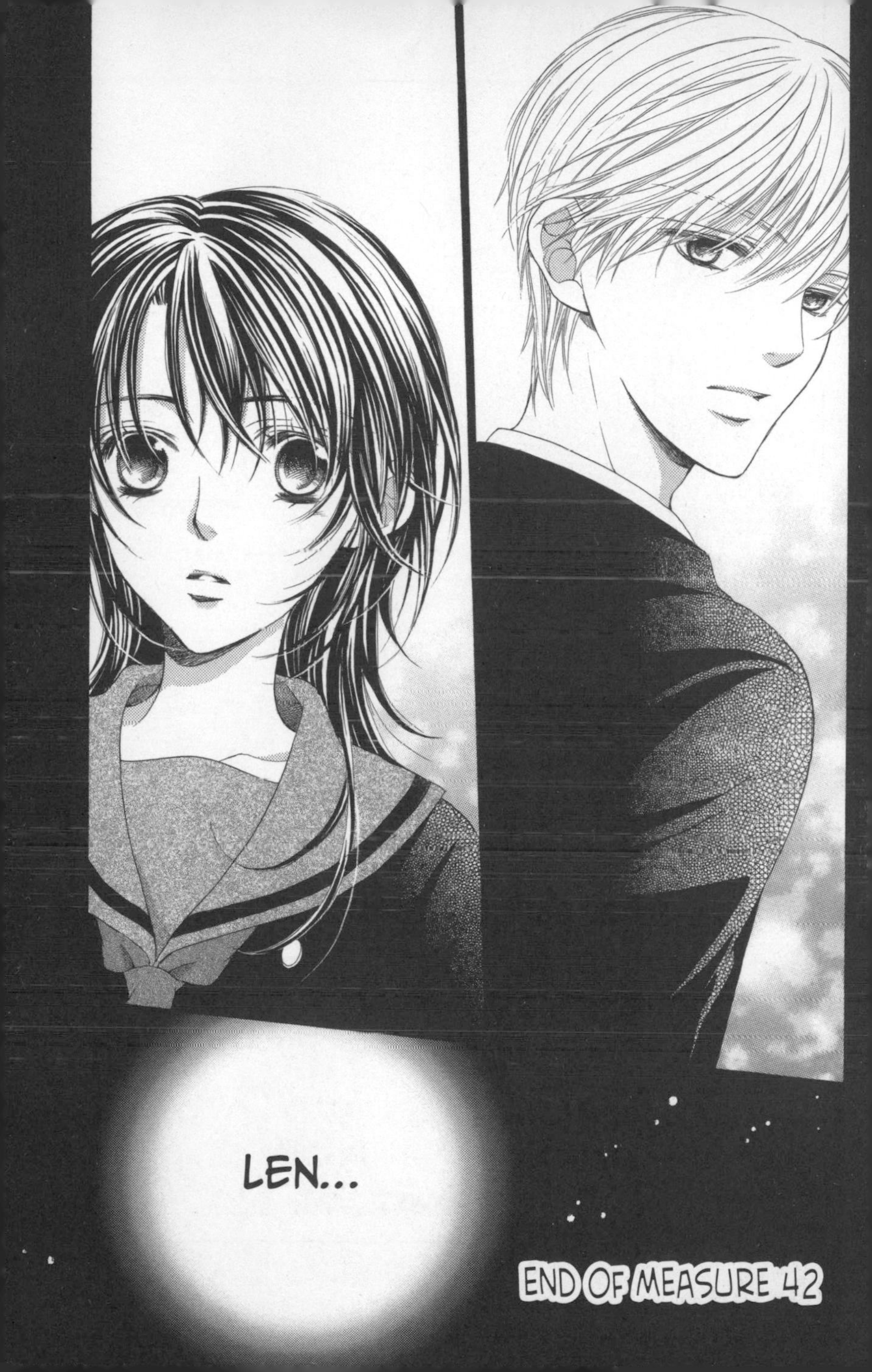
LEN...
END OF MEASURE 42

...

LEN TSUKIMORI.

I PLAY THE VIOLIN, LIKE YOU.

Daily Happenings 35 Babies...

My cousin had a baby... and everyone in the family is totally smitten. This is the only baby around, so it makes it worse. Carrying that little weight... ♥

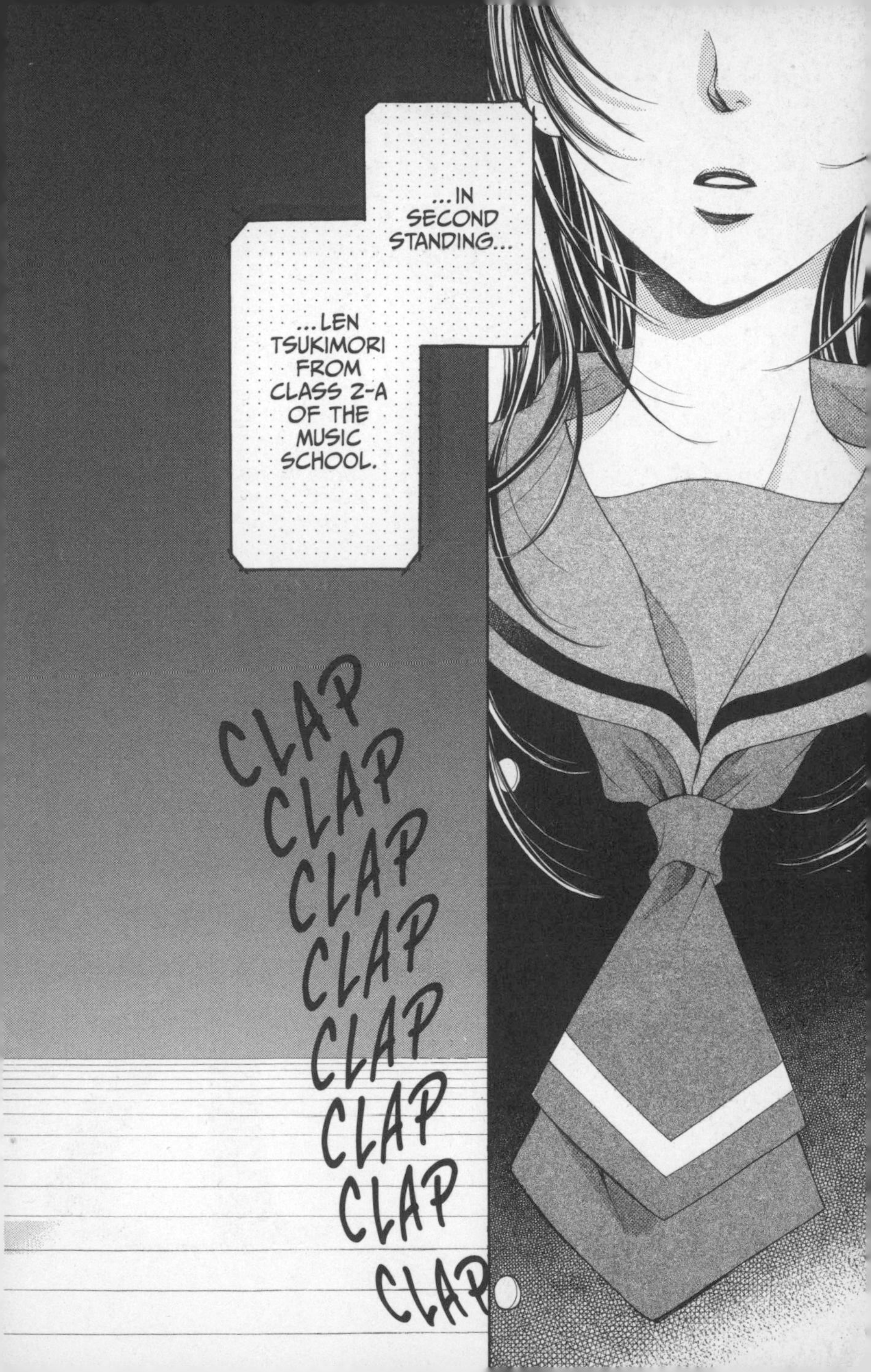
...IN SECOND STANDING...
...LEN TSUKIMORI FROM CLASS 2-A OF THE MUSIC SCHOOL.
CLAP CLAP CLAP CLAP CLAP CLAP CLAP CLAP

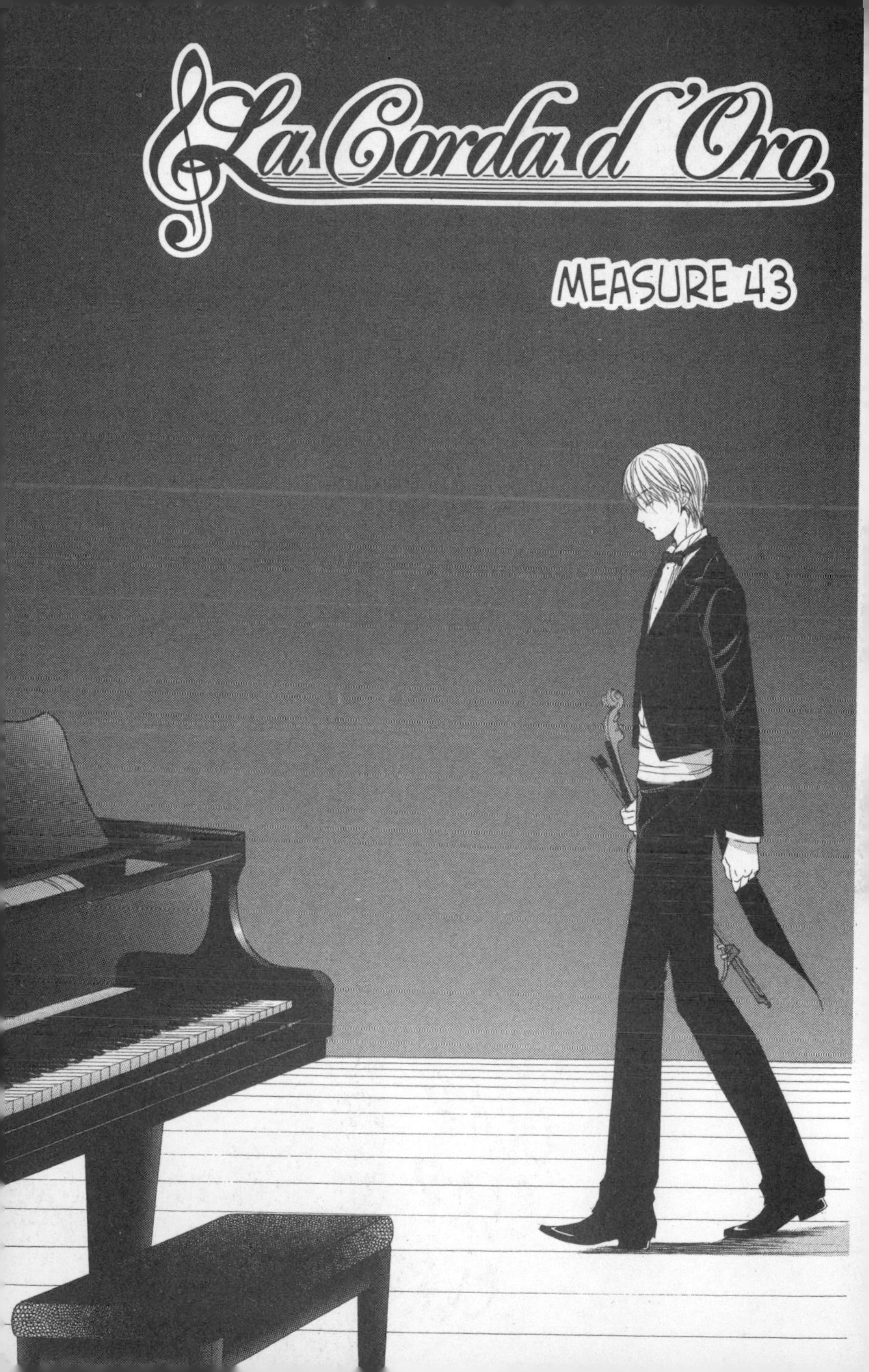
La Corda d'Oro
MEASURE 43

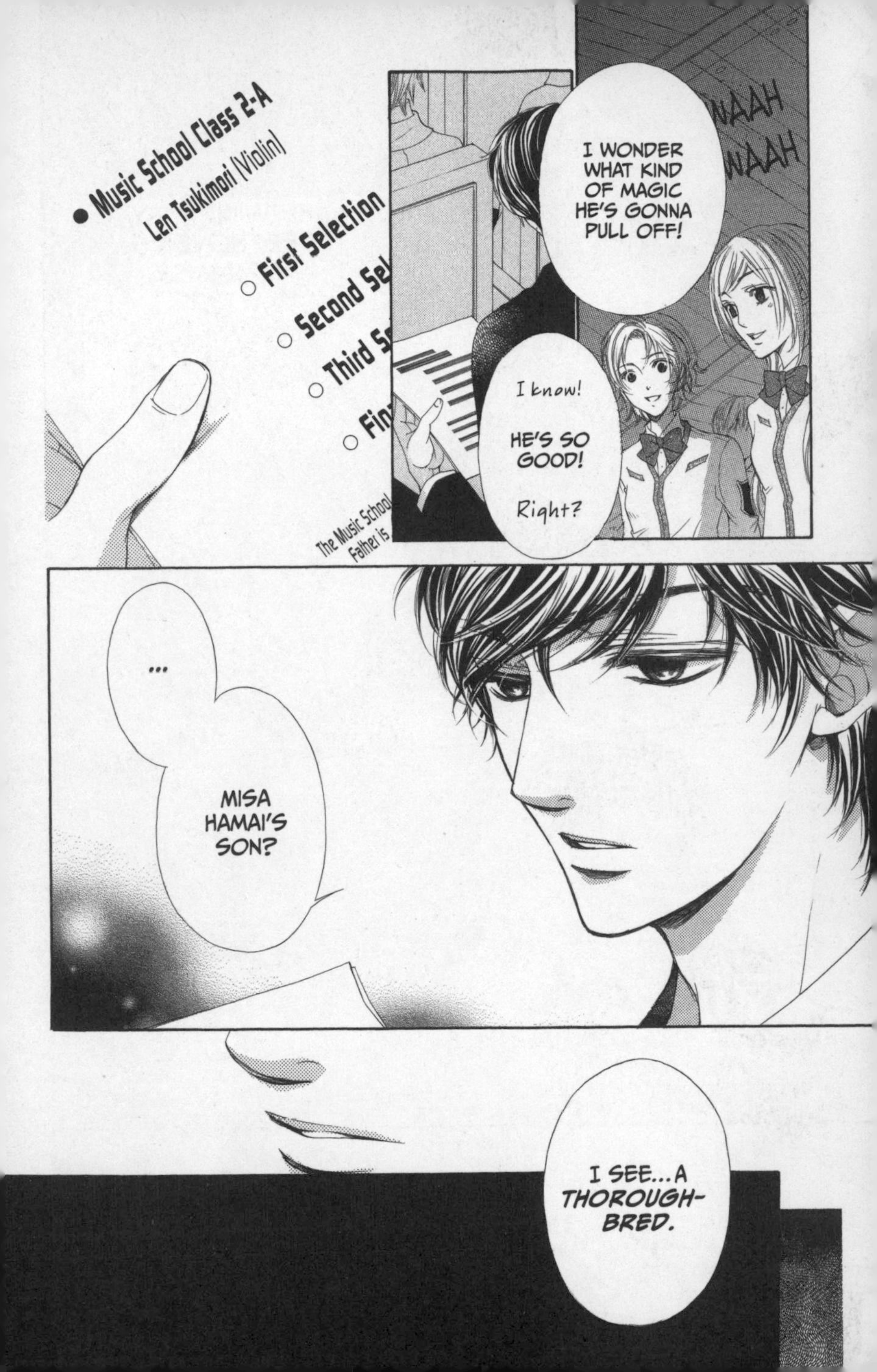
WAAH
I WONDER WHAT KIND OF MAGIC HE'S GONNA PULL OFF!
I know!
HE'S SO GOOD!
Right?
● Music School Class 2-A
Len Tsukimori (Violin)
○ First Selection
○ Second Se
○ Third S
○ Fin
The Music School
Father is
...
MISA HAMAI'S SON?
I SEE...A THOROUGH-BRED.

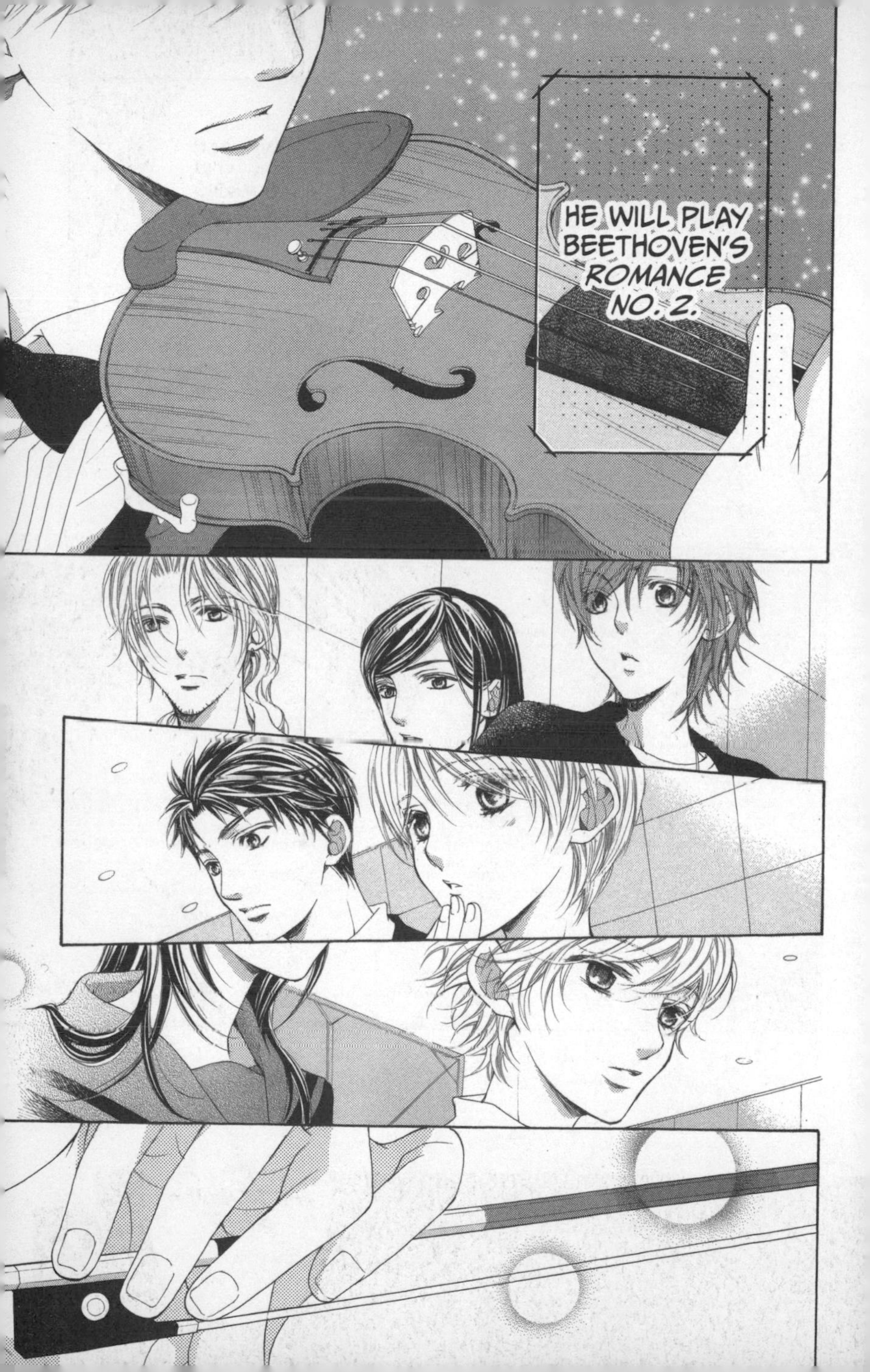
HE WILL PLAY BEETHOVEN'S ROMANCE NO. 2.

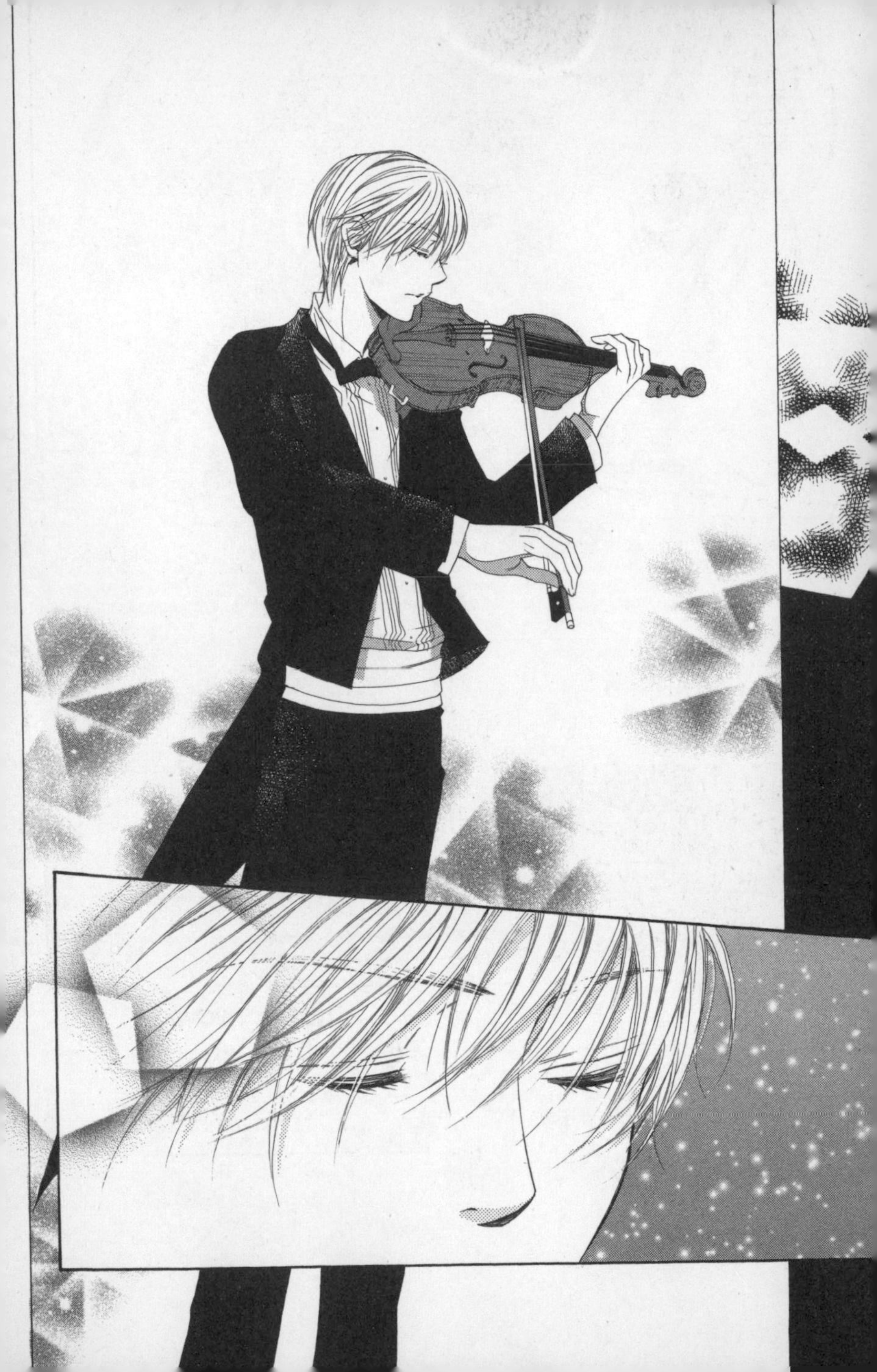

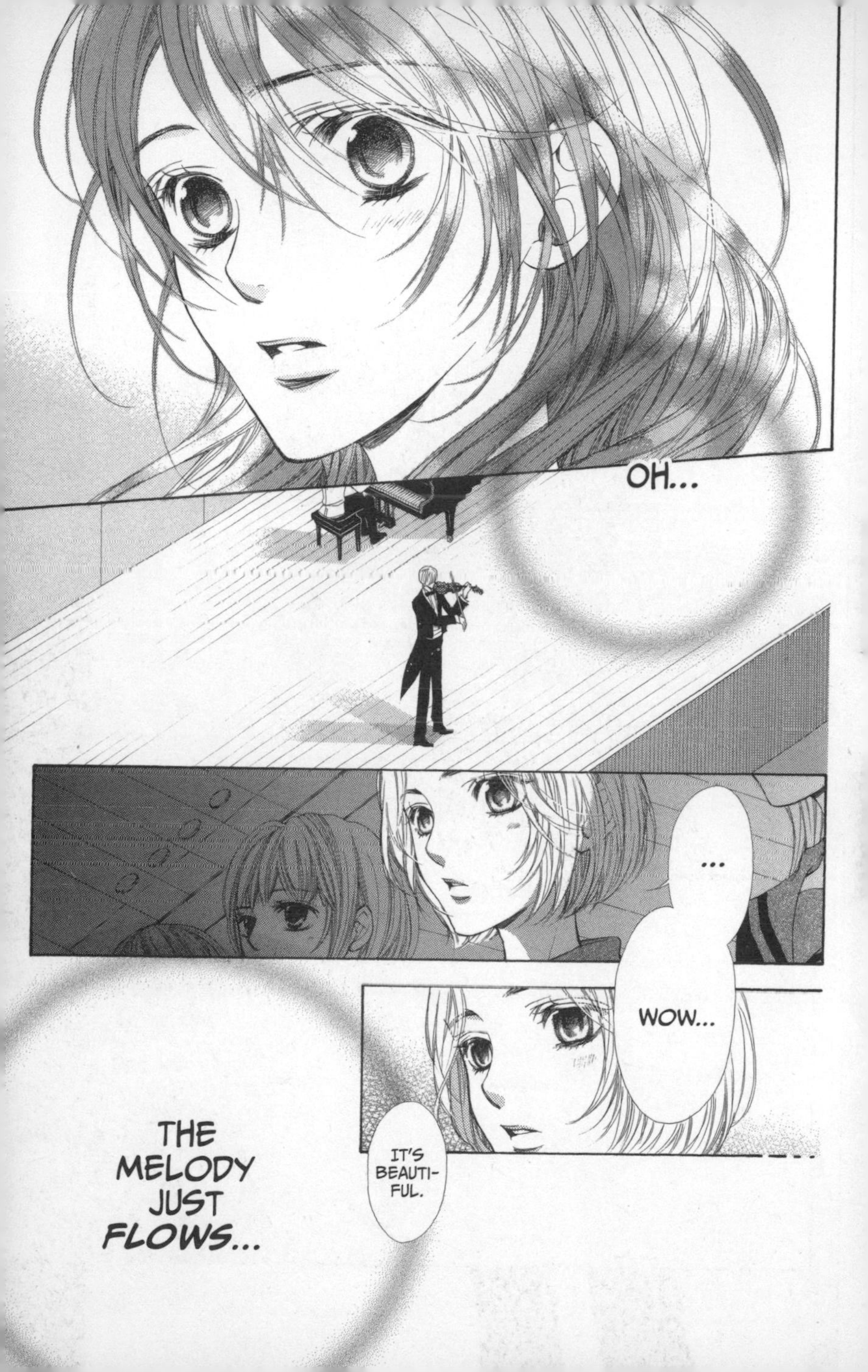
OH...
...
WOW...
IT'S BEAUTI-FUL.
THE MELODY JUST FLOWS...

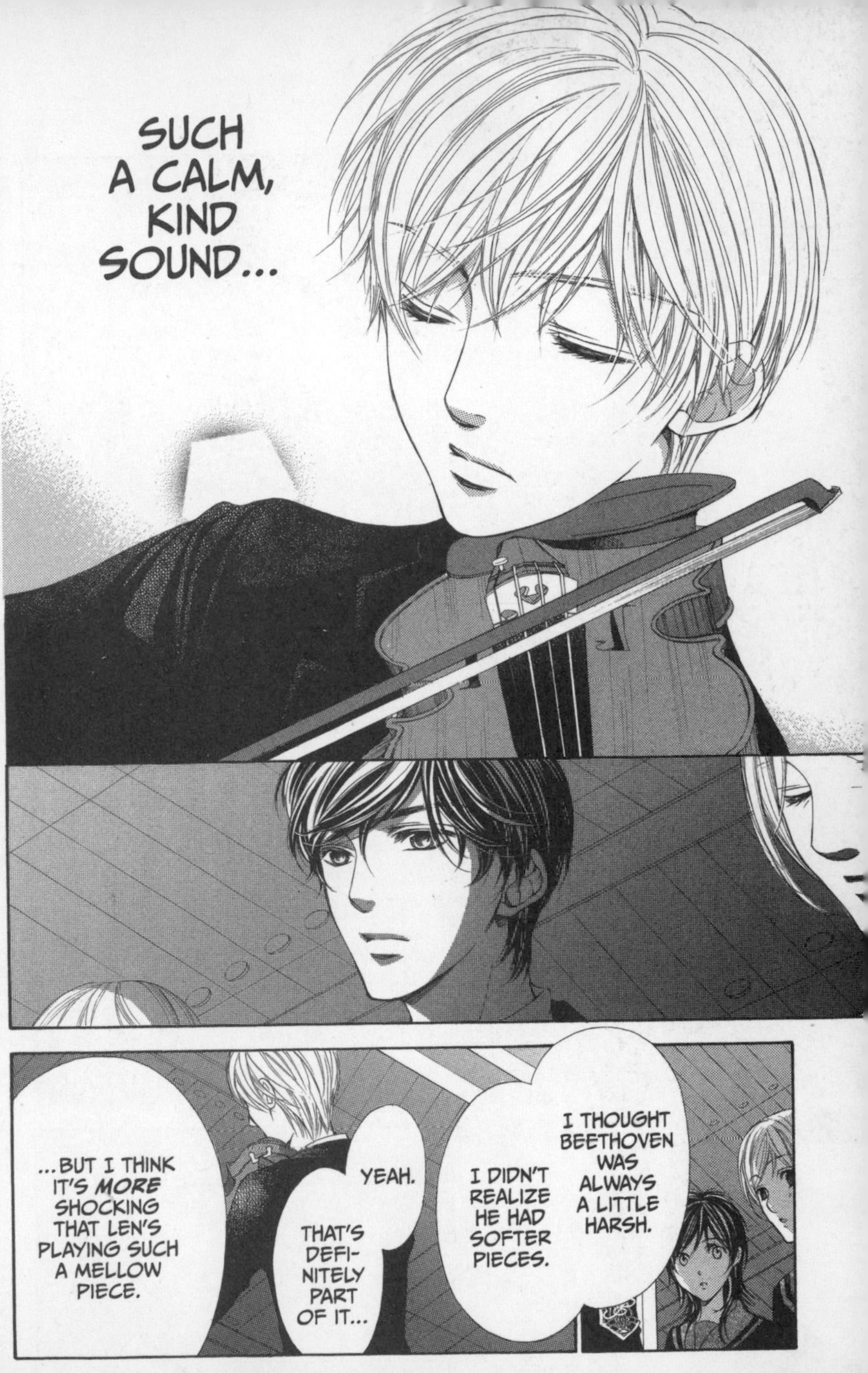
SUCH A CALM, KIND SOUND...
I THOUGHT BEETHOVEN WAS ALWAYS A LITTLE HARSH.
I DIDN'T REALIZE HE HAD SOFTER PIECES.
YEAH.
THAT'S DEFI-NITELY PART OF IT...
...BUT I THINK IT'S *MORE* SHOCKING THAT LEN'S PLAYING SUCH A MELLOW PIECE.

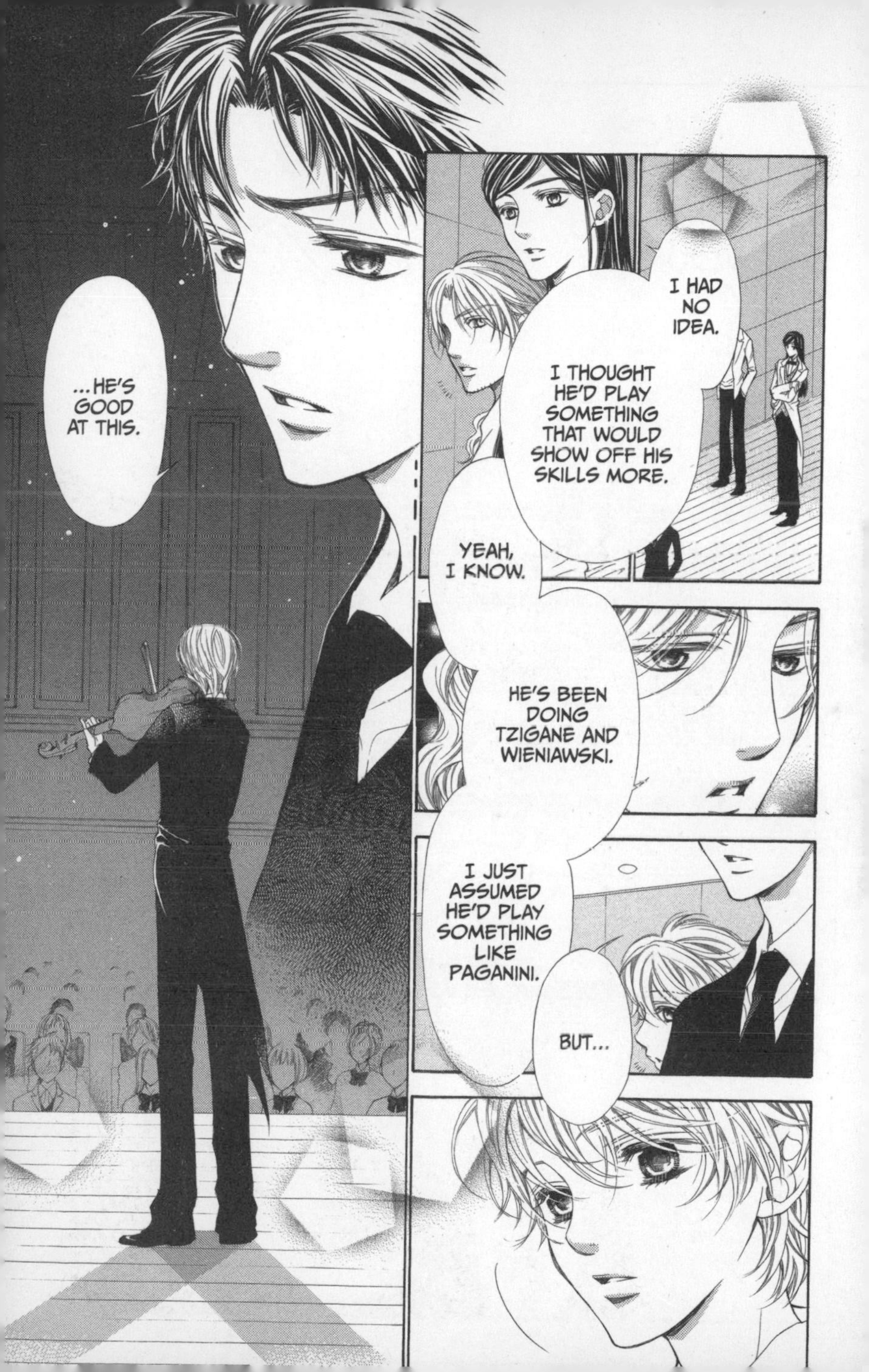
...HE'S GOOD AT THIS.
I HAD NO IDEA.
I THOUGHT HE'D PLAY SOMETHING THAT WOULD SHOW OFF HIS SKILLS MORE.
YEAH, I KNOW.
HE'S BEEN DOING TZIGANE AND WIENIAWSKI.
I JUST ASSUMED HE'D PLAY SOMETHING LIKE PAGANINI.
BUT...

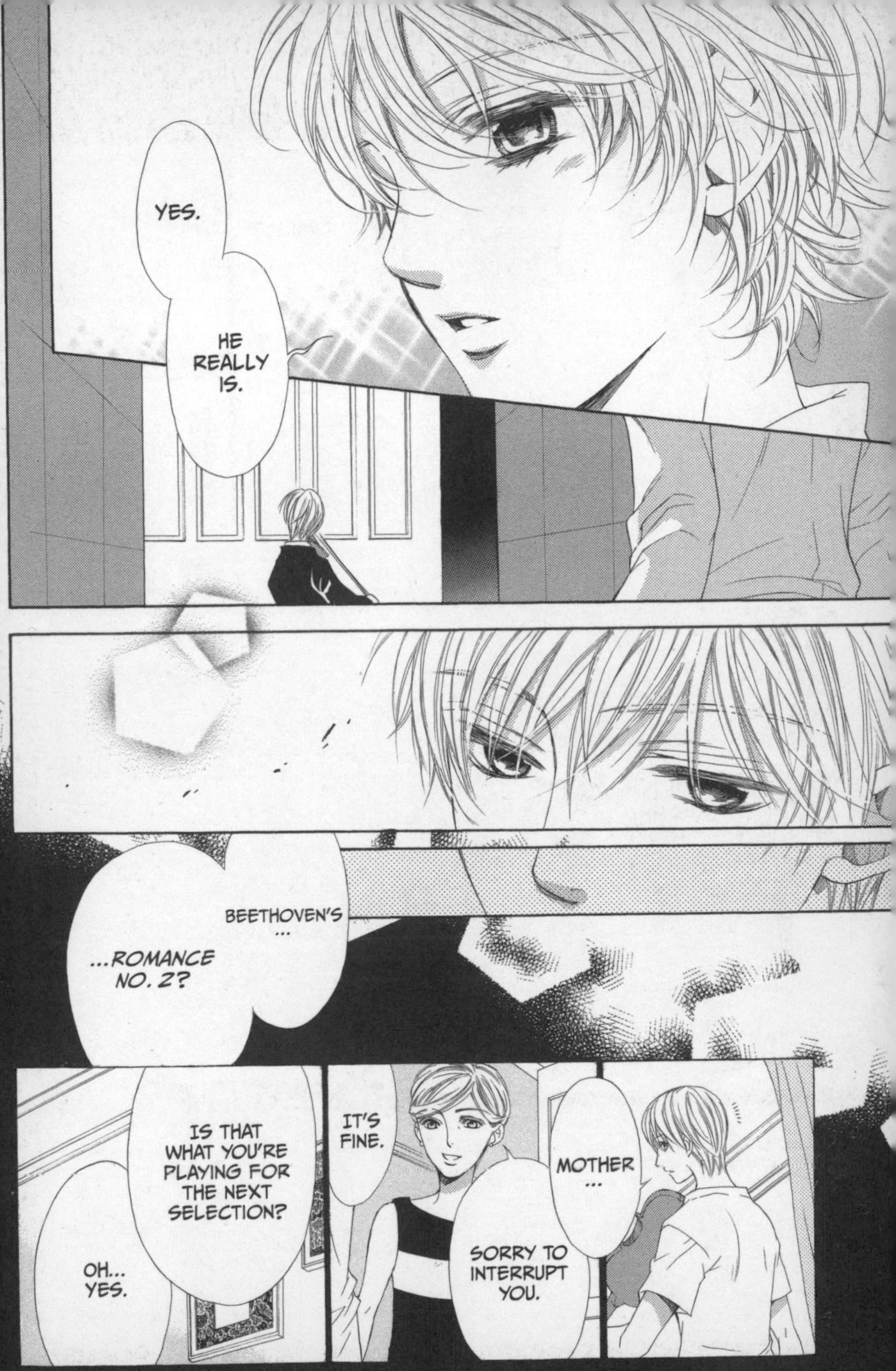
YES.
HE REALLY IS.
BEETHOVEN'S...
...ROMANCE NO. 2?
MOTHER...
SORRY TO INTERRUPT YOU.
IT'S FINE.
IS THAT WHAT YOU'RE PLAYING FOR THE NEXT SELECTION?
OH... YES.

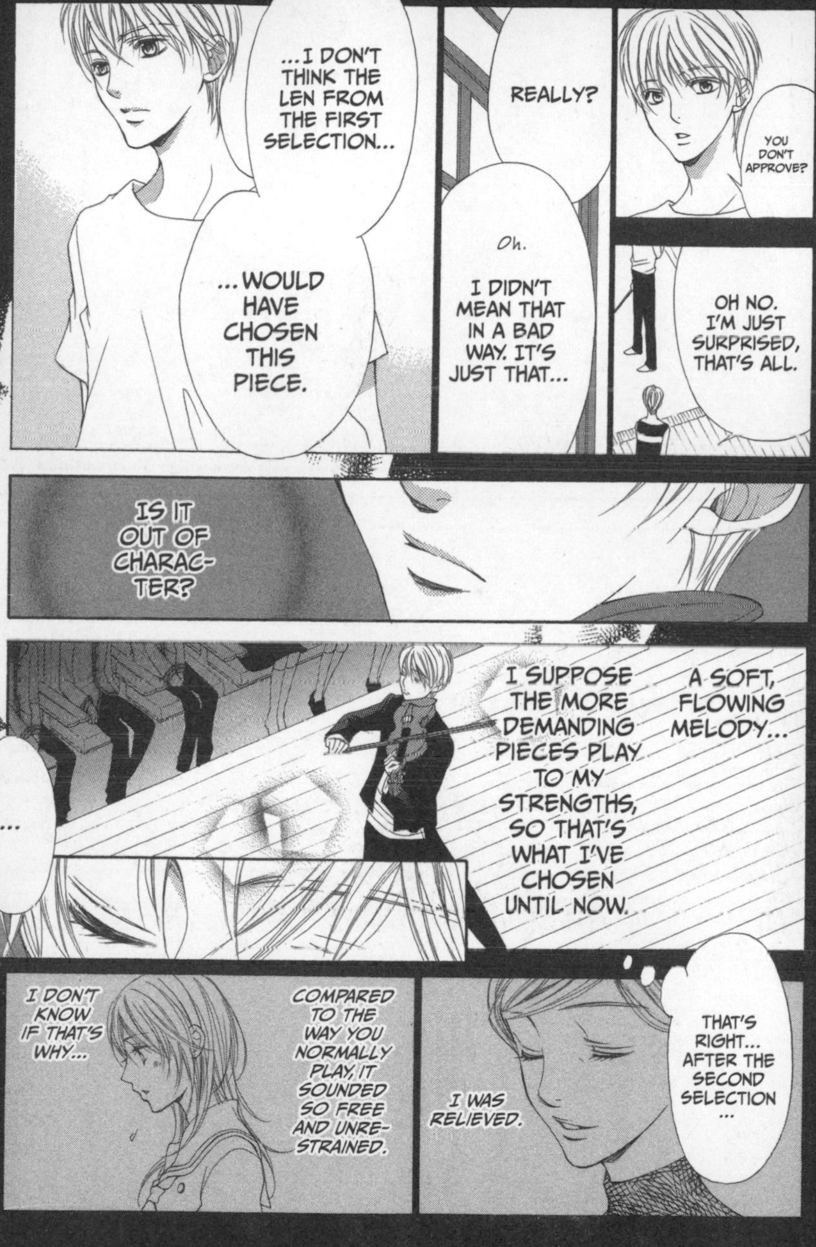
YOU DON'T APPROVE?
OH NO. I'M JUST SURPRISED, THAT'S ALL.
REALLY?
Oh.
I DIDN'T MEAN THAT IN A BAD WAY. IT'S JUST THAT...
...I DON'T THINK THE LEN FROM THE FIRST SELECTION...
...WOULD HAVE CHOSEN THIS PIECE.
IS IT OUT OF CHARAC-TER?
A SOFT, FLOWING MELODY...
I SUPPOSE THE MORE DEMANDING PIECES PLAY TO MY STRENGTHS, SO THAT'S WHAT I'VE CHOSEN UNTIL NOW.
...
THAT'S RIGHT... AFTER THE SECOND SELECTION ...
I WAS RELIEVED.
COMPARED TO THE WAY YOU NORMALLY PLAY, IT SOUNDED SO FREE AND UNRE-STRAINED.
I DON'T KNOW IF THAT'S WHY...

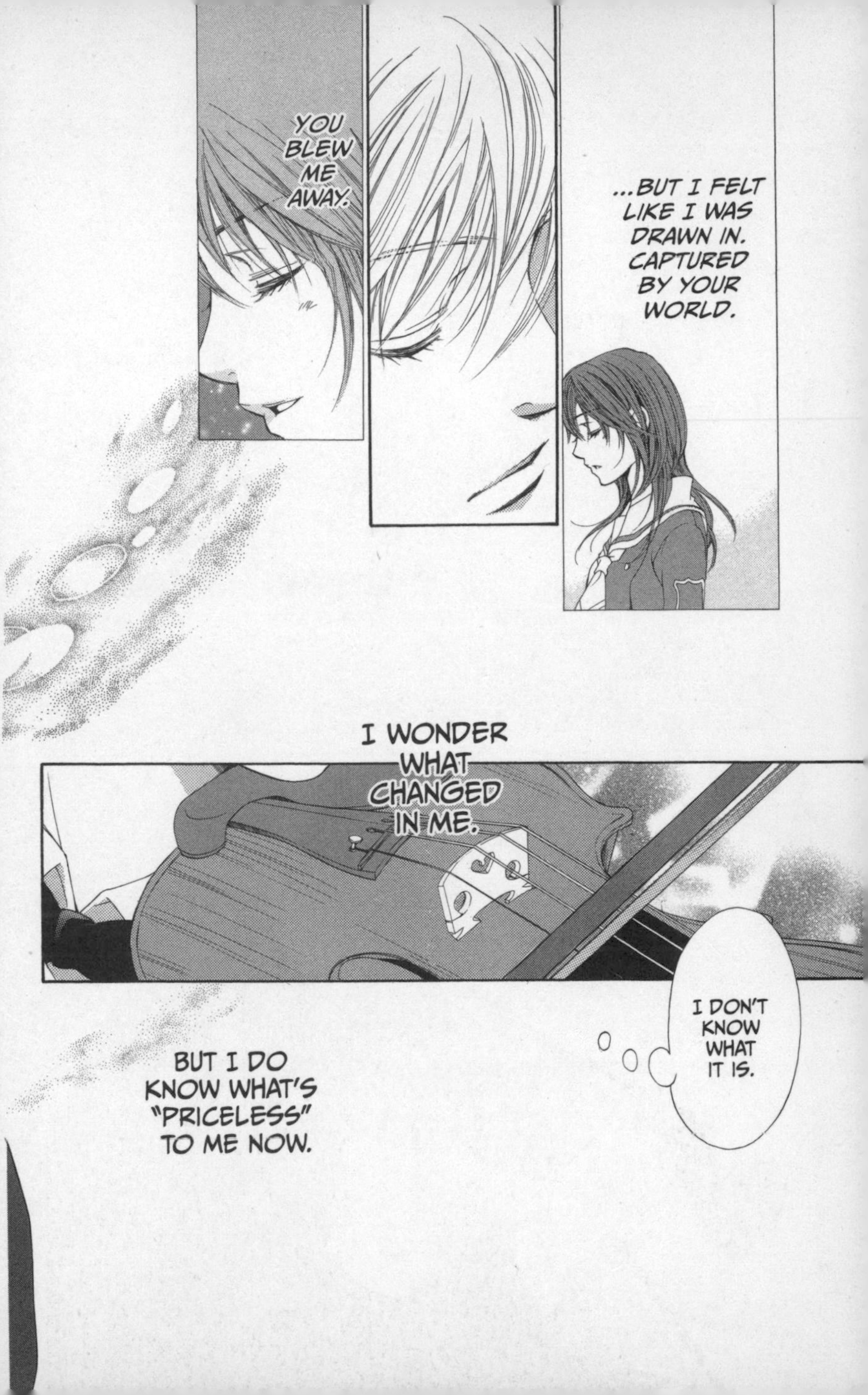
...BUT I FELT LIKE I WAS DRAWN IN. CAPTURED BY YOUR WORLD.
YOU BLEW ME AWAY.
I WONDER WHAT CHANGED IN ME.
I DON'T KNOW WHAT IT IS.
BUT I DO KNOW WHAT'S "PRICELESS" TO ME NOW.

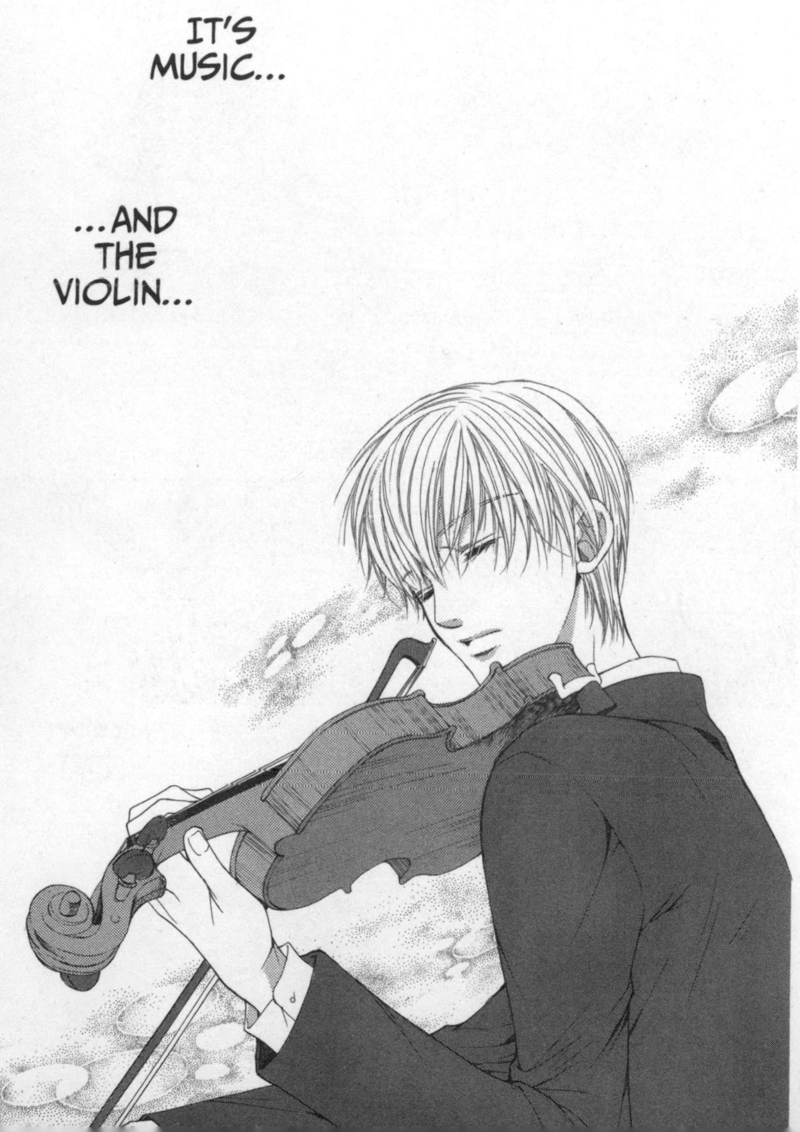
IT'S MUSIC...
...AND THE VIOLIN...

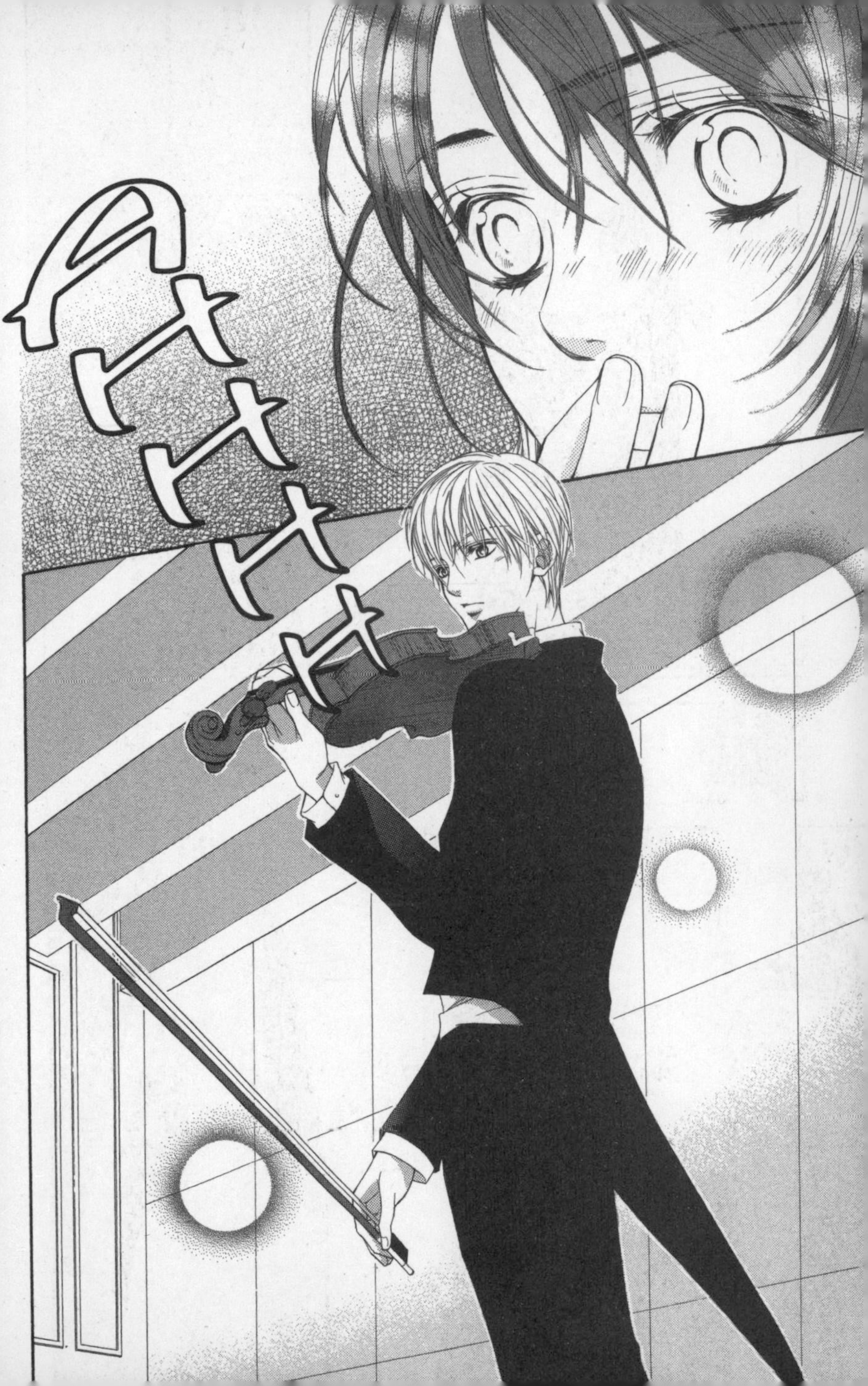

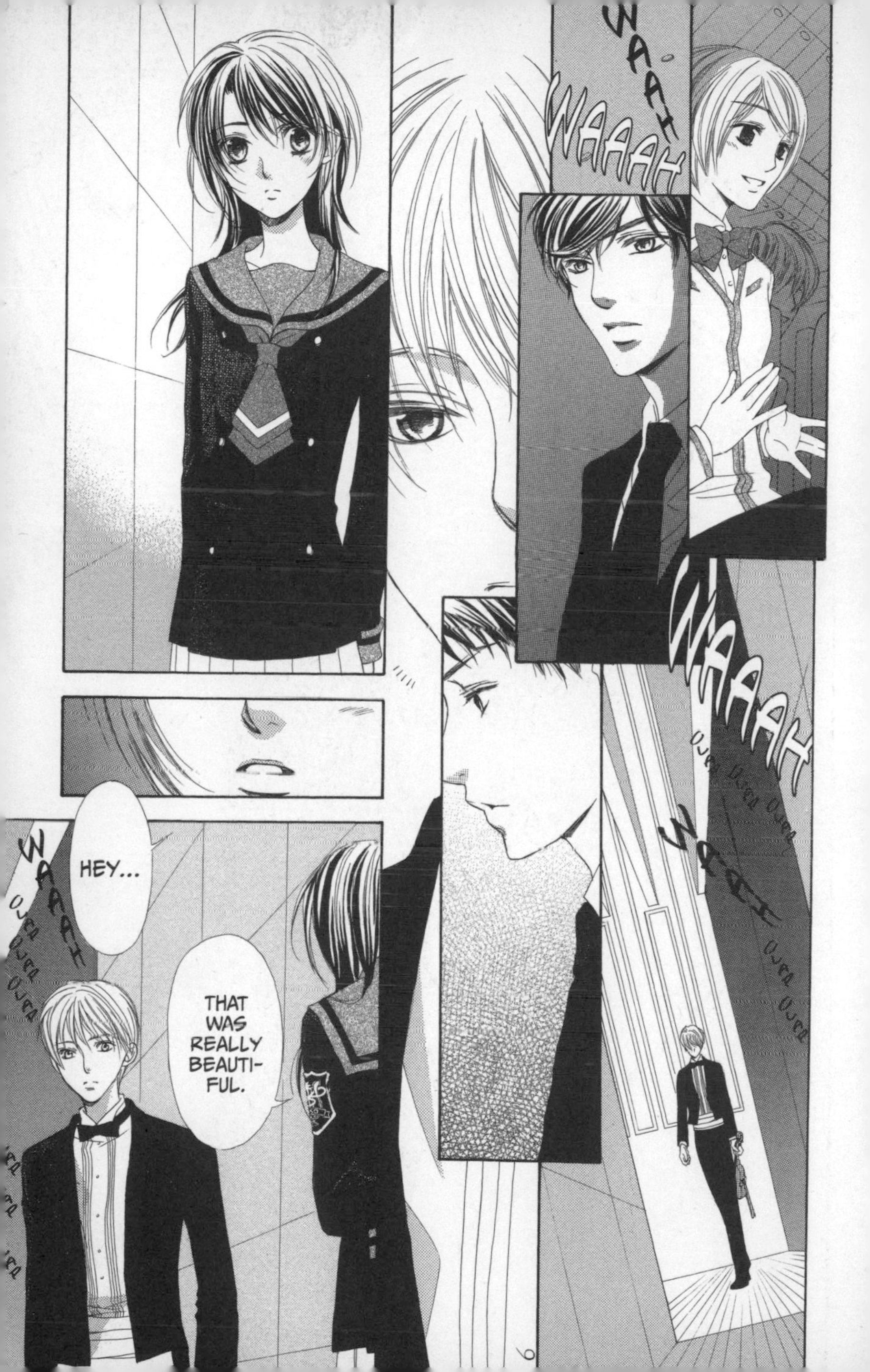
WAAAH
WAAAH
WAAAH
HEY...
THAT WAS REALLY BEAUTI-FUL.
WAAAH

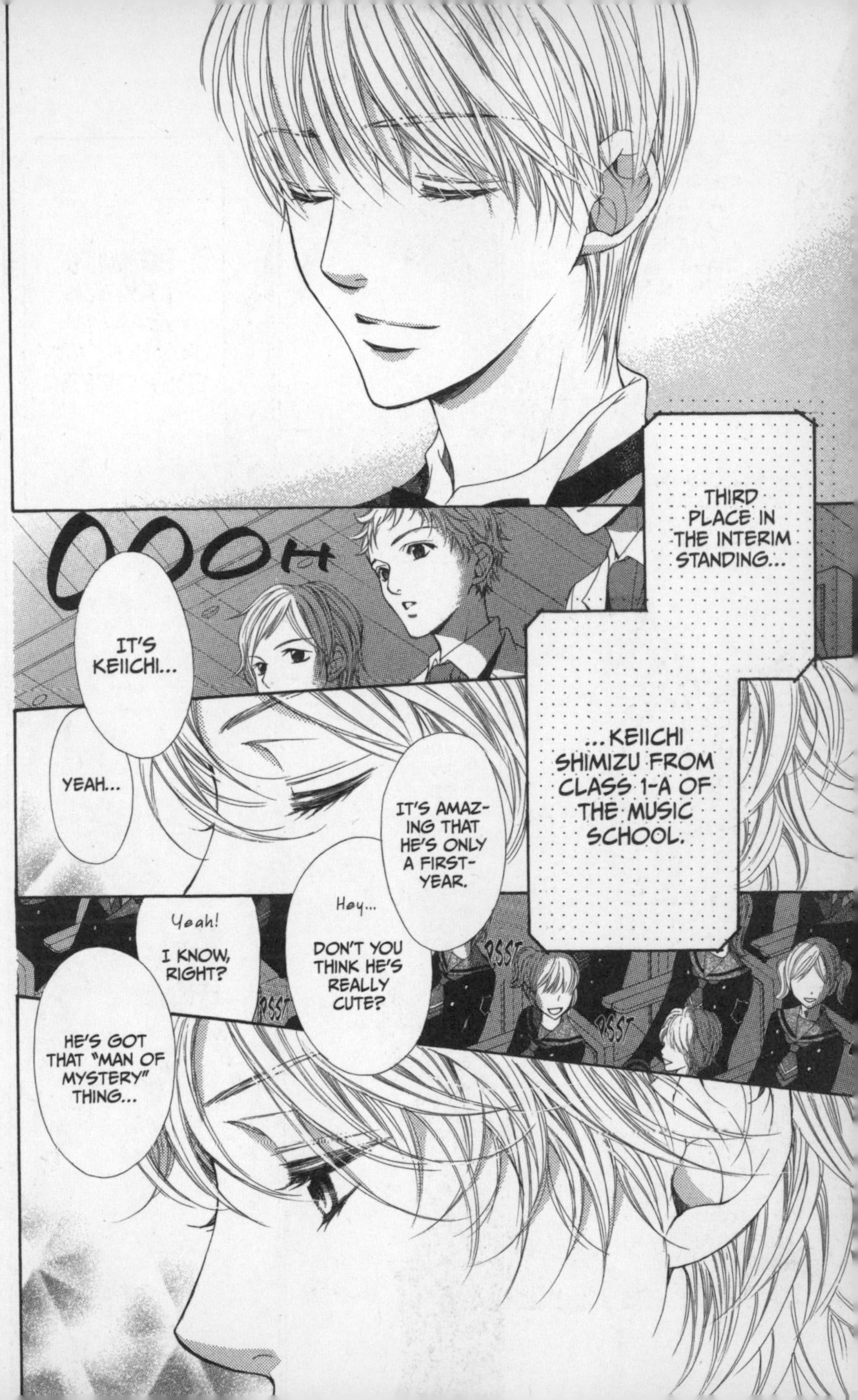
THIRD PLACE IN THE INTERIM STANDING...
OOOH
IT'S KEIICHI...
...KEIICHI SHIMIZU FROM CLASS 1-A OF THE MUSIC SCHOOL.
YEAH...
IT'S AMAZ-ING THAT HE'S ONLY A FIRST-YEAR.
PSST
PSST
Hey... DON'T YOU THINK HE'S REALLY CUTE?
PSST
Yeah! I KNOW, RIGHT?
HE'S GOT THAT "MAN OF MYSTERY" THING...

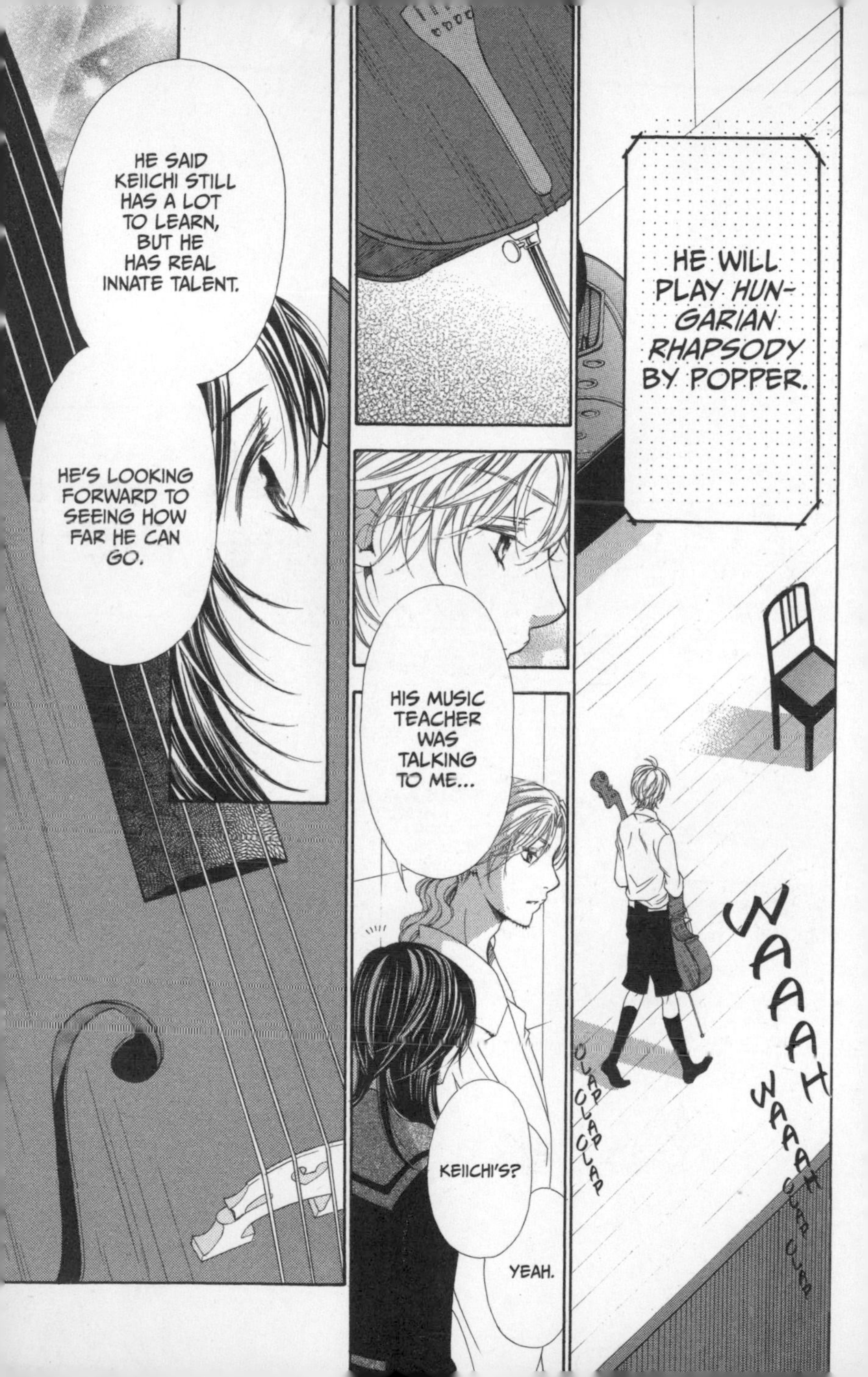
HE WILL PLAY HUNGARIAN RHAPSODY BY POPPER.
WAAAAH
WAAAAH
CLAP CLAP CLAP
CLAP CLAP CLAP
HIS MUSIC TEACHER WAS TALKING TO ME...
KEIICHI'S?
YEAH.
HE SAID KEIICHI STILL HAS A LOT TO LEARN, BUT HE HAS REAL INNATE TALENT.
HE'S LOOKING FORWARD TO SEEING HOW FAR HE CAN GO.

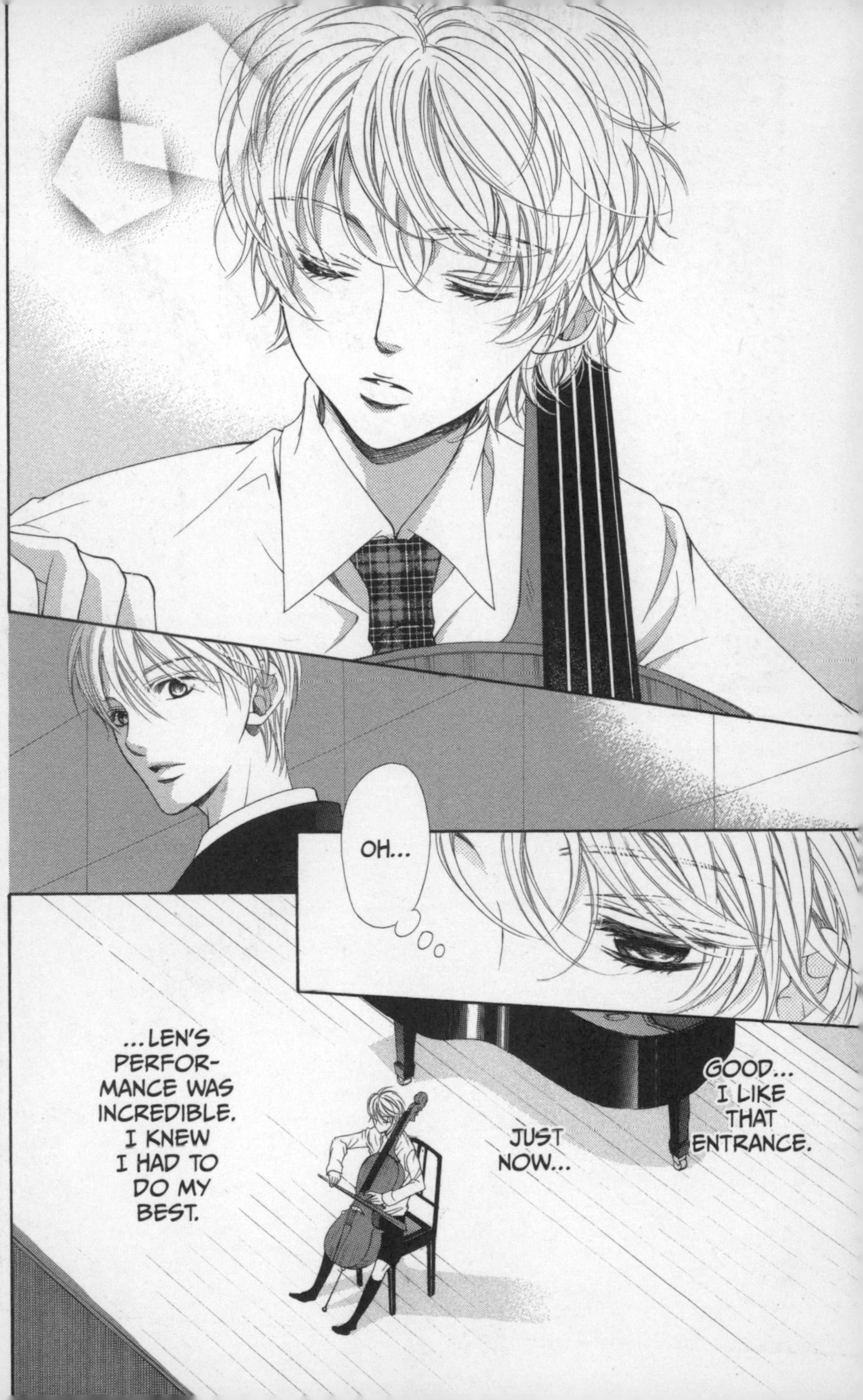
OH...
GOOD... I LIKE THAT ENTRANCE.
JUST NOW...
...LEN'S PERFOR-MANCE WAS INCREDIBLE. I KNEW I HAD TO DO MY BEST.

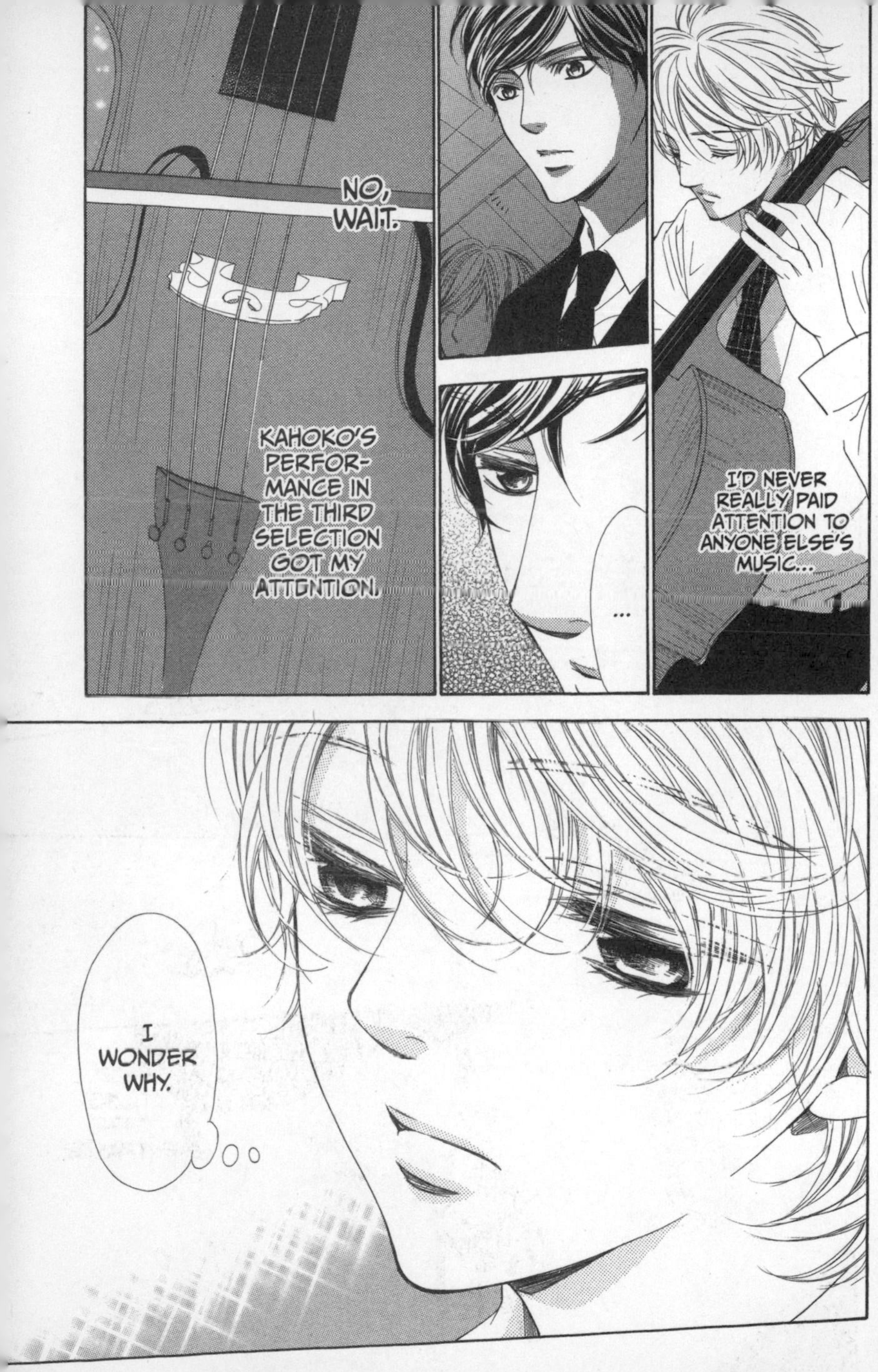
I'D NEVER REALLY PAID ATTENTION TO ANYONE ELSE'S MUSIC...
...
NO, WAIT.
KAHOKO'S PERFORMANCE IN THE THIRD SELECTION GOT MY ATTENTION.
I WONDER WHY.

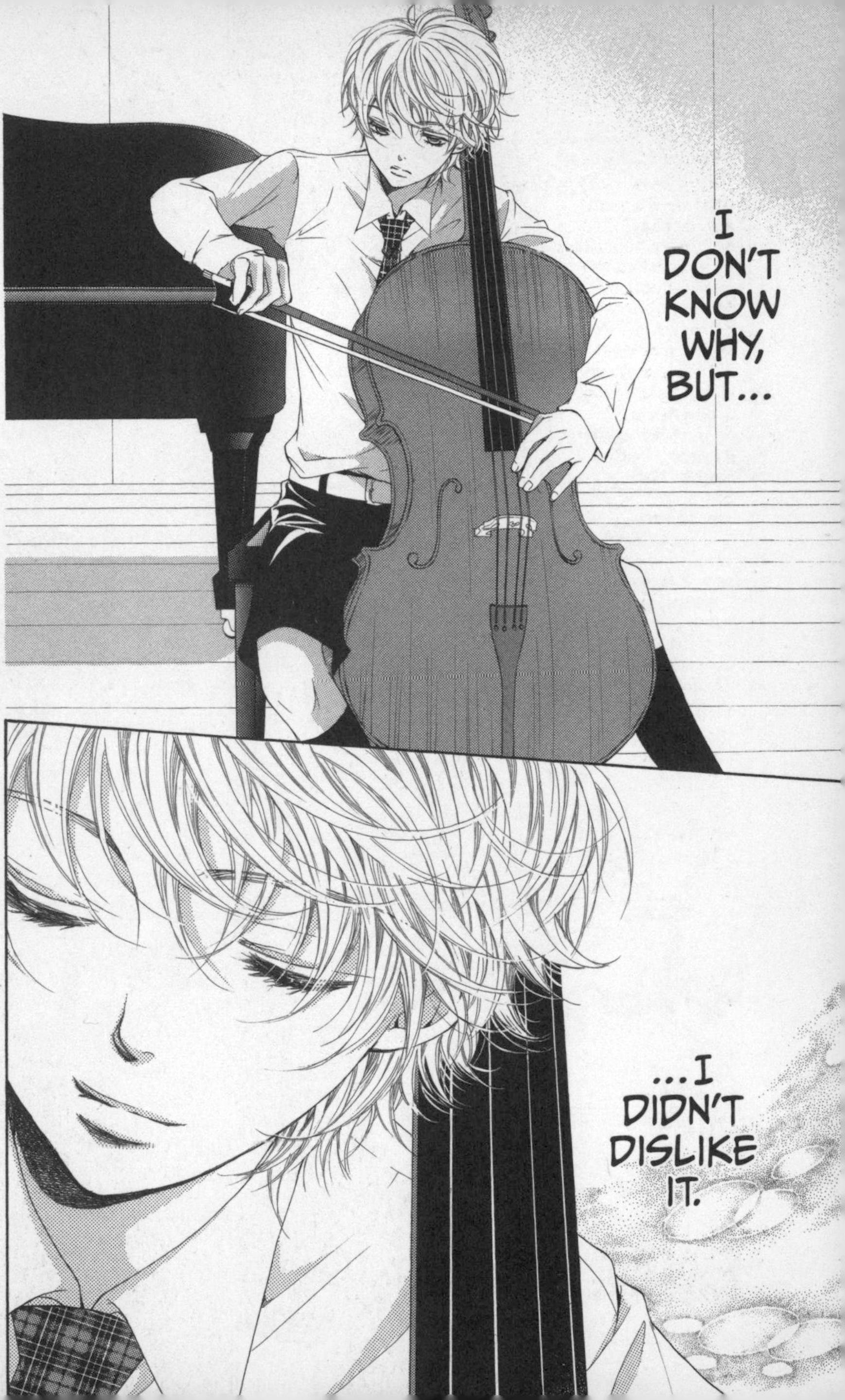
I DON'T KNOW WHY, BUT...
...I DIDN'T DISLIKE IT.

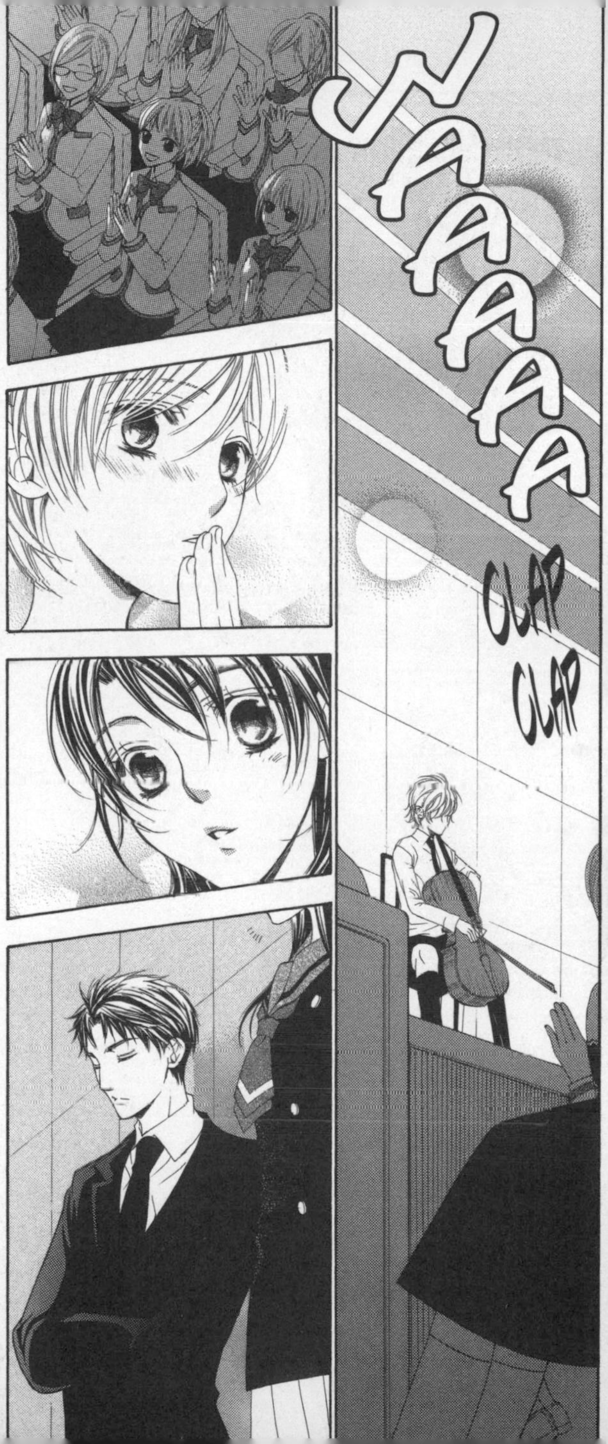
JAAAAA
CLAP
CLAP

I don't know whether I should say "already" or "finally," but we've reached the Final Selection! It's been a long journey. I'm sorry that the contest outfits are always so boring...although apparently a lot of you liked seeing Ryotaro's hair combed back. Speaking of costumes, I've added some little pinups to this set of notes. I wanted to give them a twist, so there's a Chinese theme. I know it's not the first time...

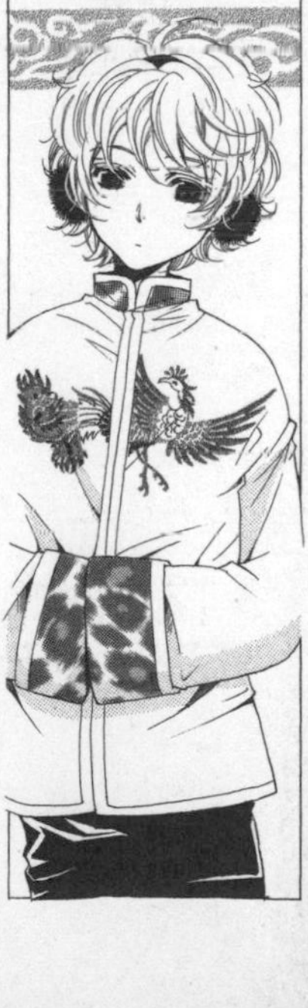

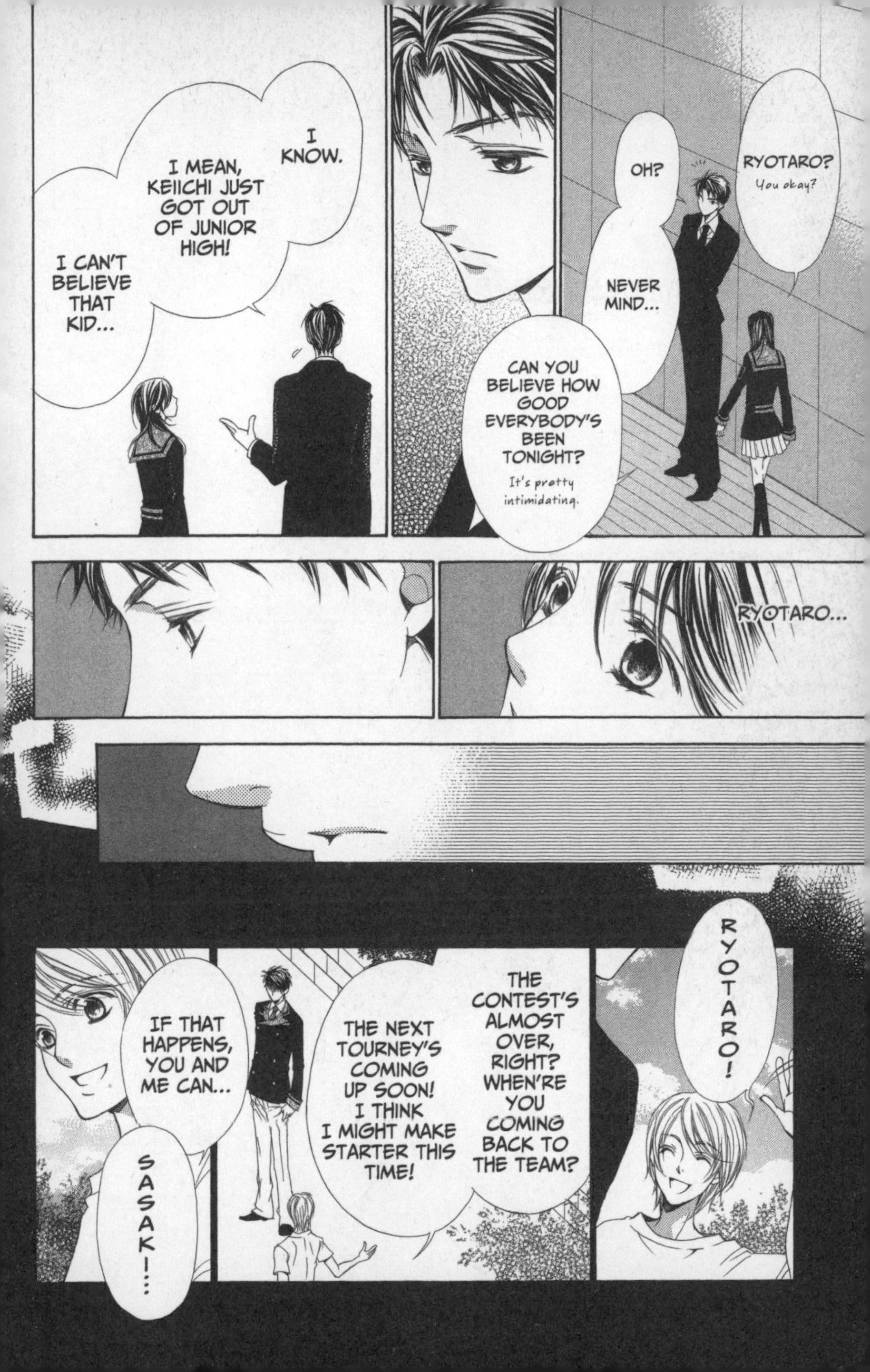
RYOTARO?
You okay?
OH?
NEVER MIND...
CAN YOU BELIEVE HOW GOOD EVERYBODY'S BEEN TONIGHT?
It's pretty intimidating.
I KNOW.
I MEAN, KEIICHI JUST GOT OUT OF JUNIOR HIGH!
I CAN'T BELIEVE THAT KID...
RYOTARO...
RYOTARO!
THE CONTEST'S ALMOST OVER, RIGHT? WHEN'RE YOU COMING BACK TO THE TEAM?
THE NEXT TOURNEY'S COMING UP SOON! I THINK I MIGHT MAKE STARTER THIS TIME!
IF THAT HAPPENS, YOU AND ME CAN...
SASAKI!...

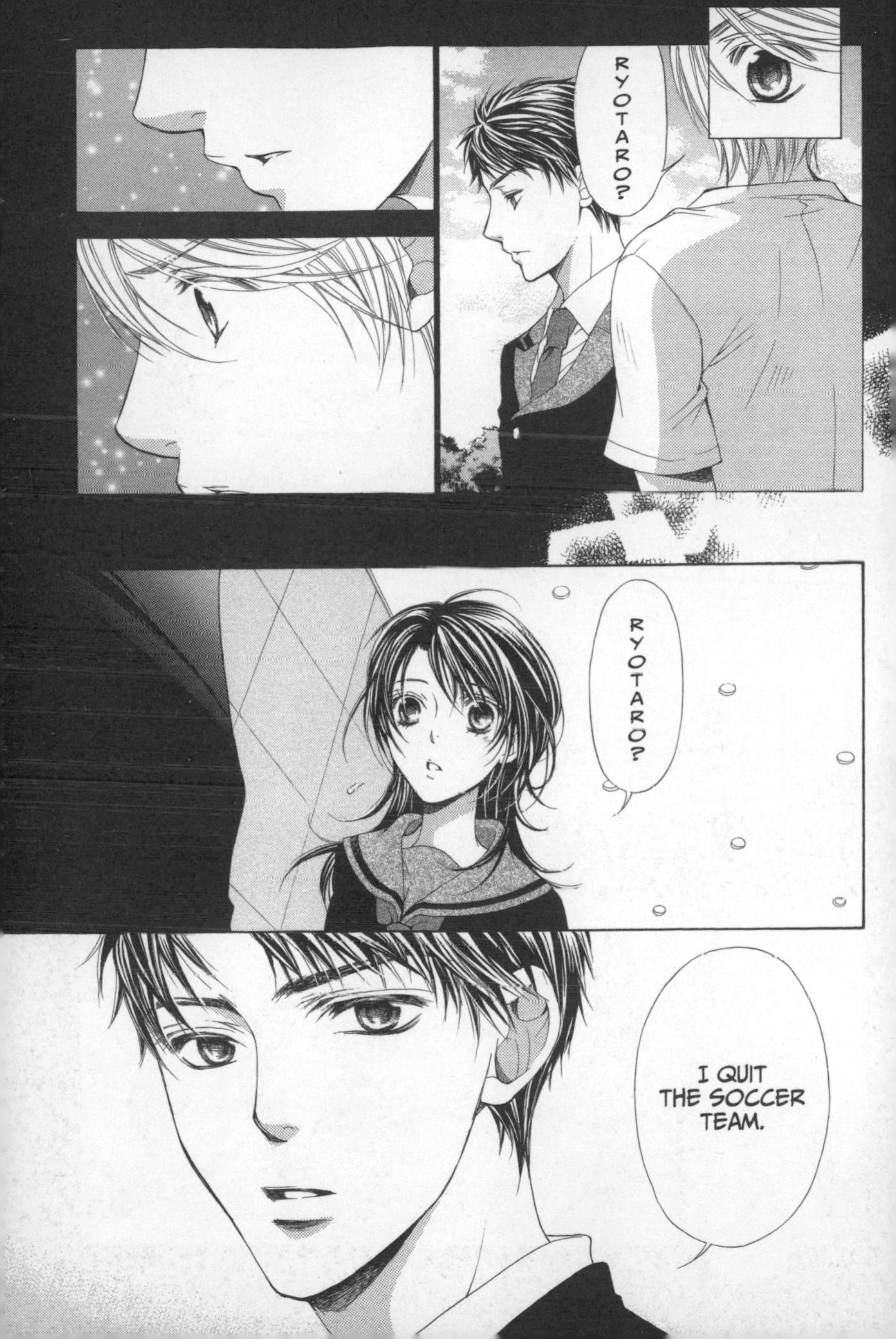
RYOTARO?
RYOTARO?
I QUIT THE SOCCER TEAM.

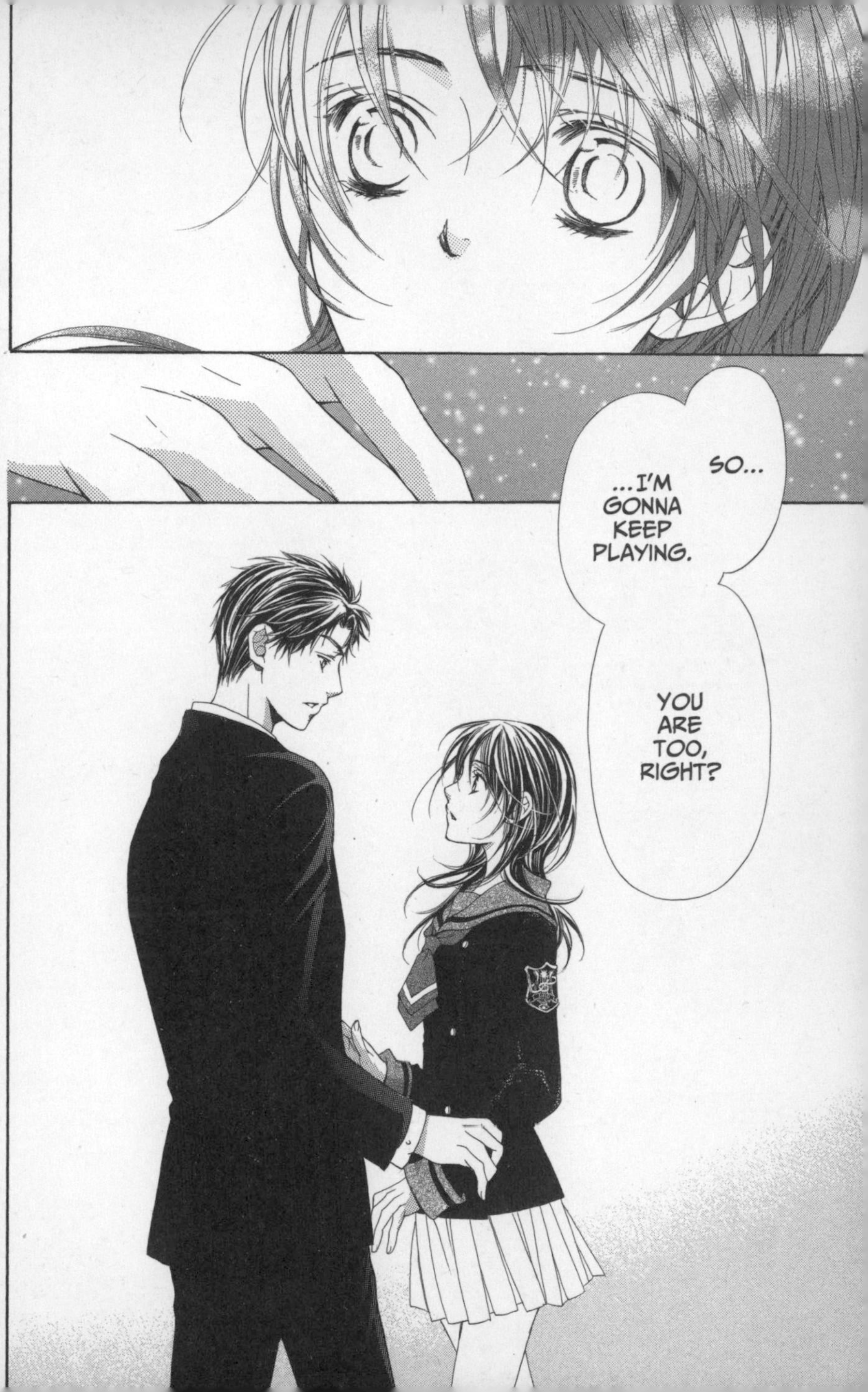
SO...
...I'M GONNA KEEP PLAYING.
YOU ARE TOO, RIGHT?

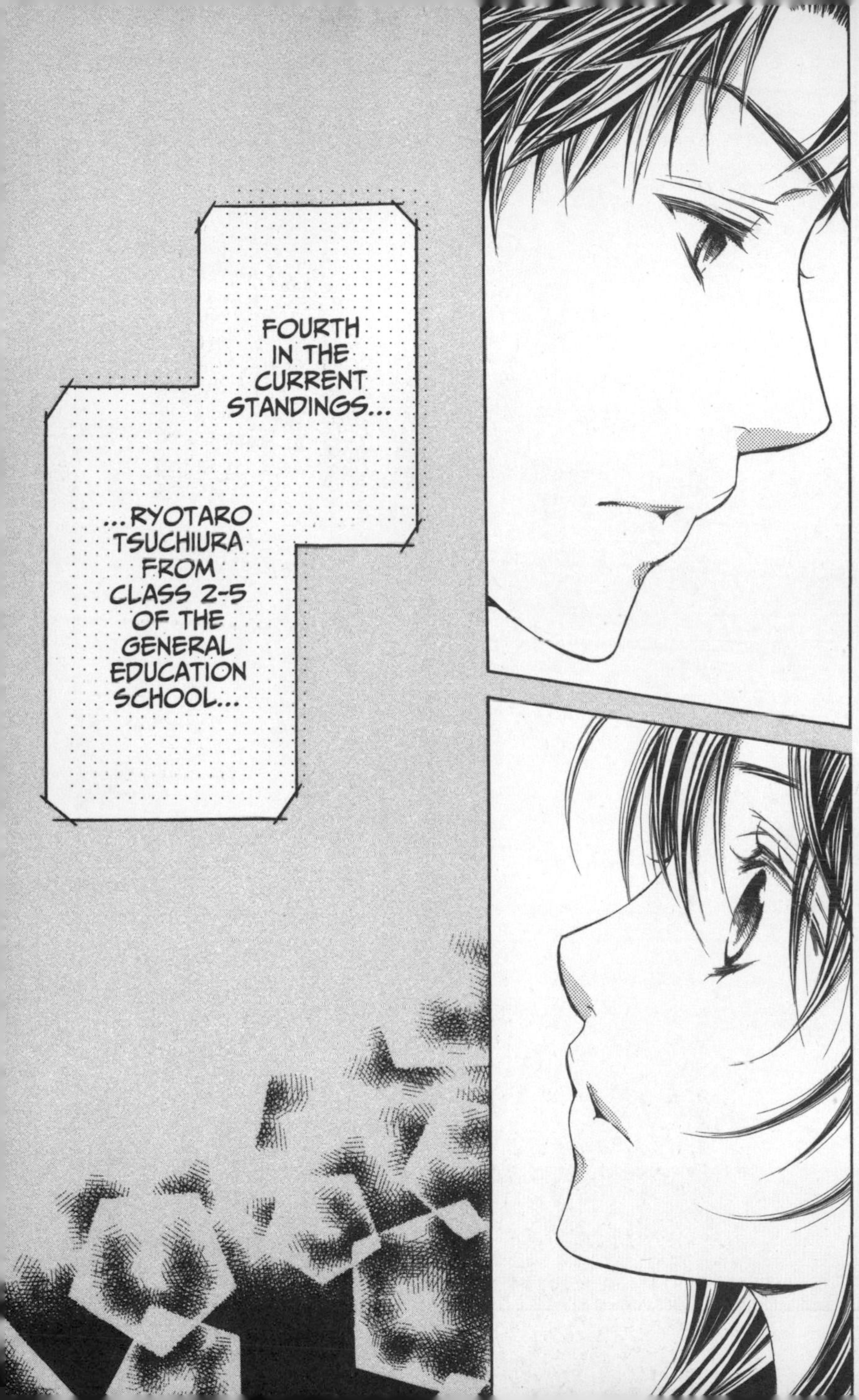
FOURTH IN THE CURRENT STANDINGS...
...RYOTARO TSUCHIURA FROM CLASS 2-5 OF THE GENERAL EDUCATION SCHOOL...

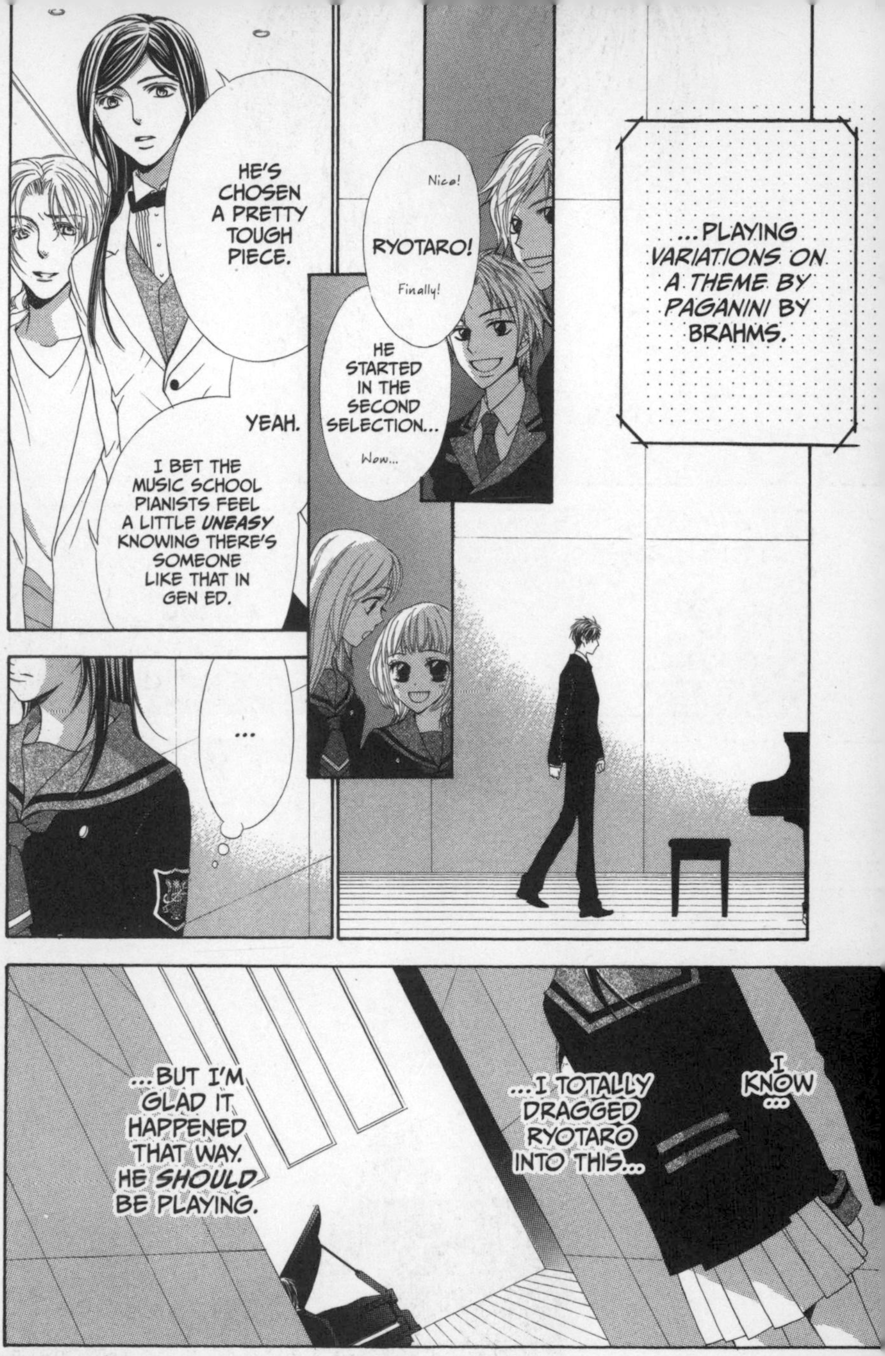
...PLAYING VARIATIONS ON A THEME BY PAGANINI BY BRAHMS.
Nico!
RYOTARO!
Finally!
HE STARTED IN THE SECOND SELECTION...
Wow...
HE'S CHOSEN A PRETTY TOUGH PIECE.
YEAH.
I BET THE MUSIC SCHOOL PIANISTS FEEL A LITTLE *UNEASY* KNOWING THERE'S SOMEONE LIKE THAT IN GEN ED.
...
I KNOW...
...I TOTALLY DRAGGED RYOTARO INTO THIS...
...BUT I'M GLAD IT HAPPENED THAT WAY. HE *SHOULD* BE PLAYING.

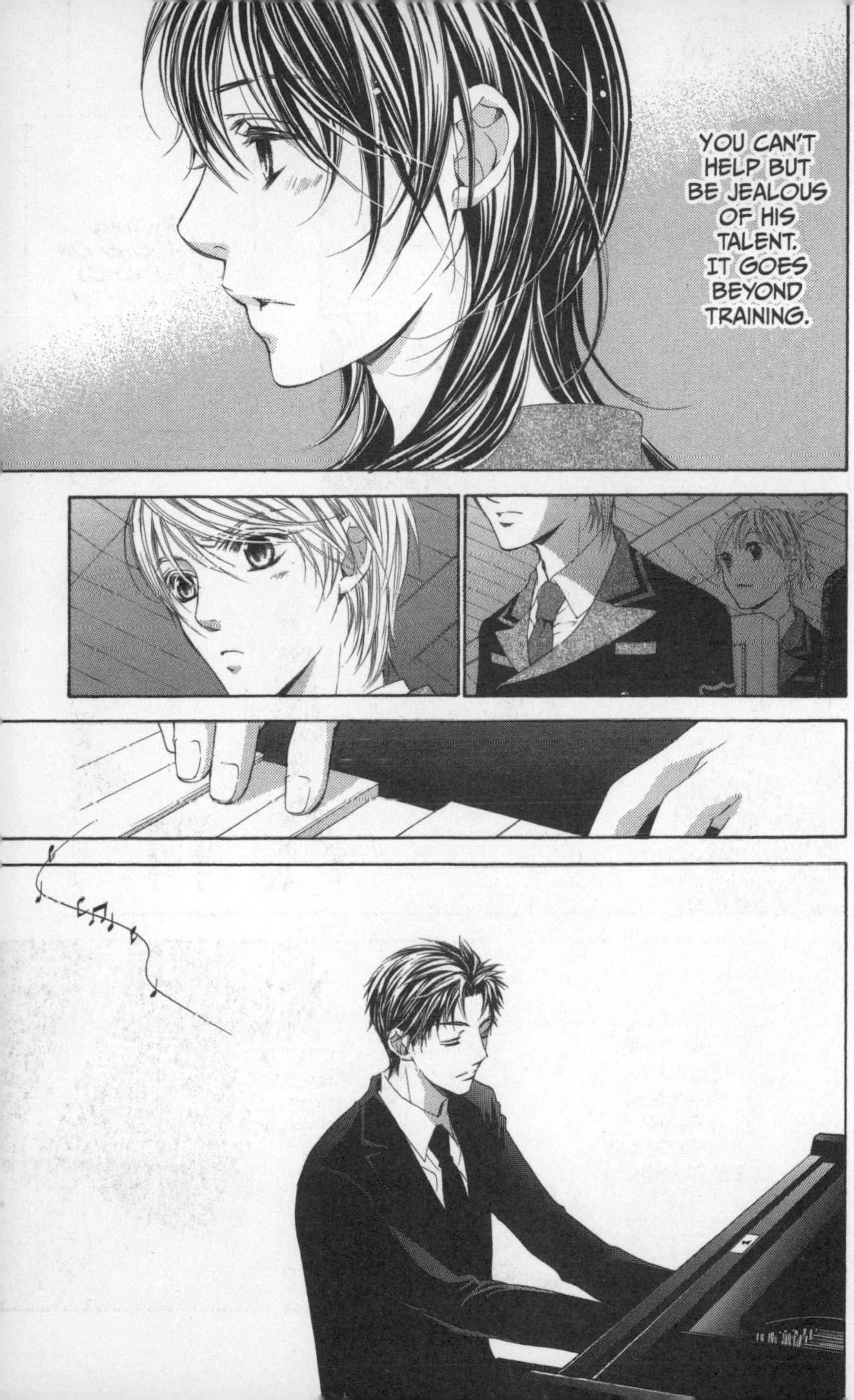
YOU CAN'T HELP BUT BE JEALOUS OF HIS TALENT. IT GOES BEYOND TRAINING.

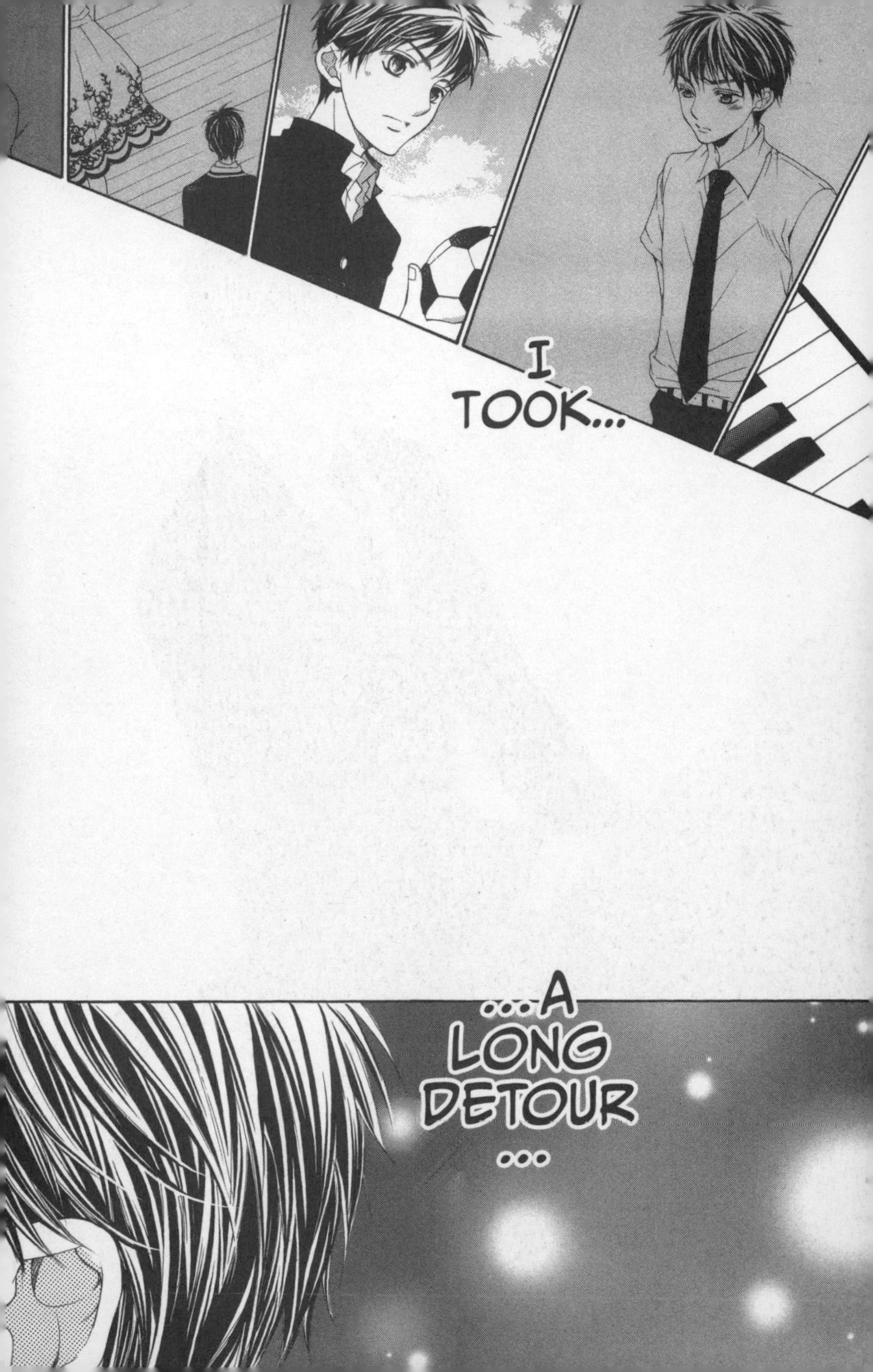
I TOOK...
...A LONG DETOUR
...

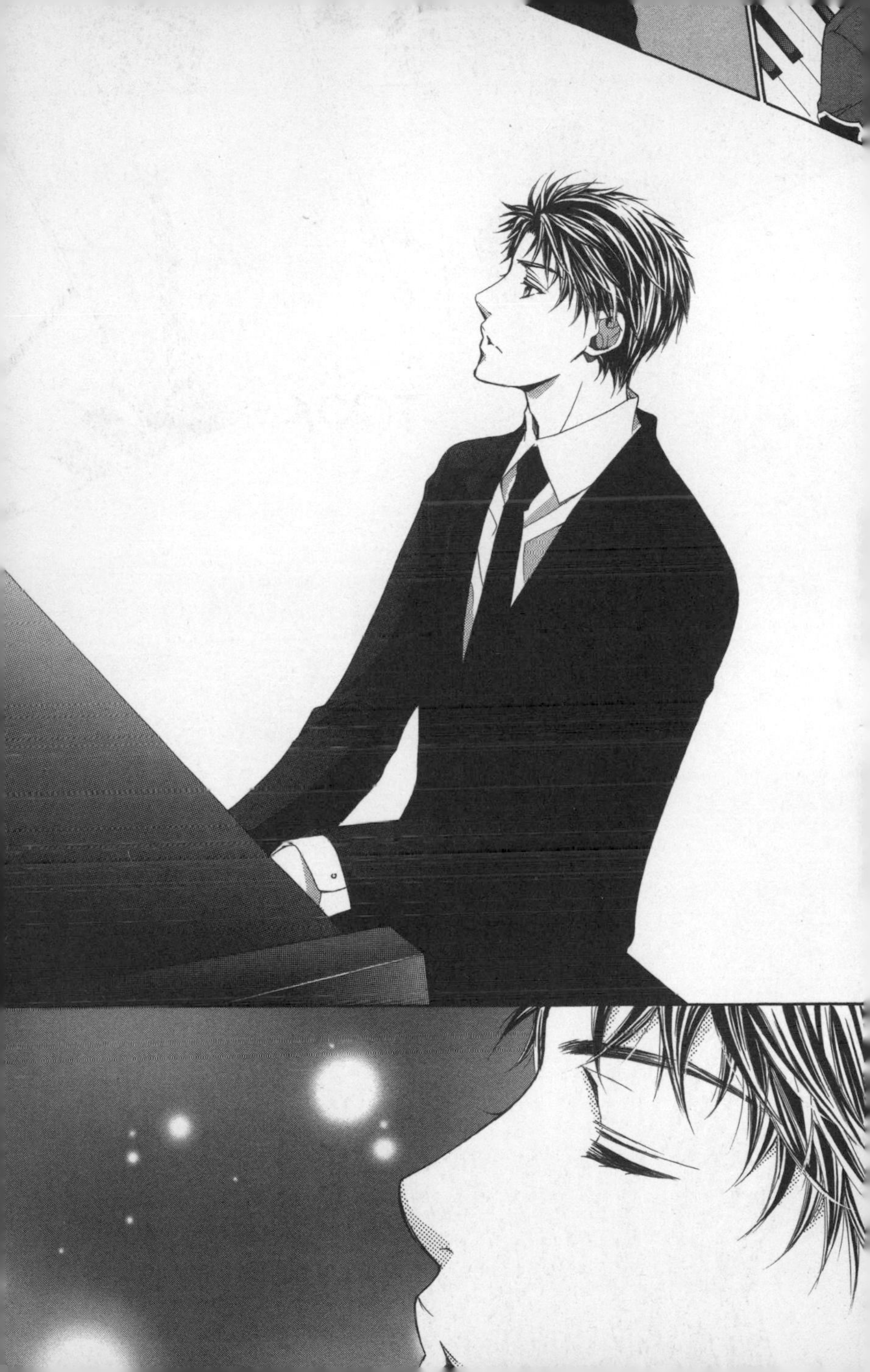

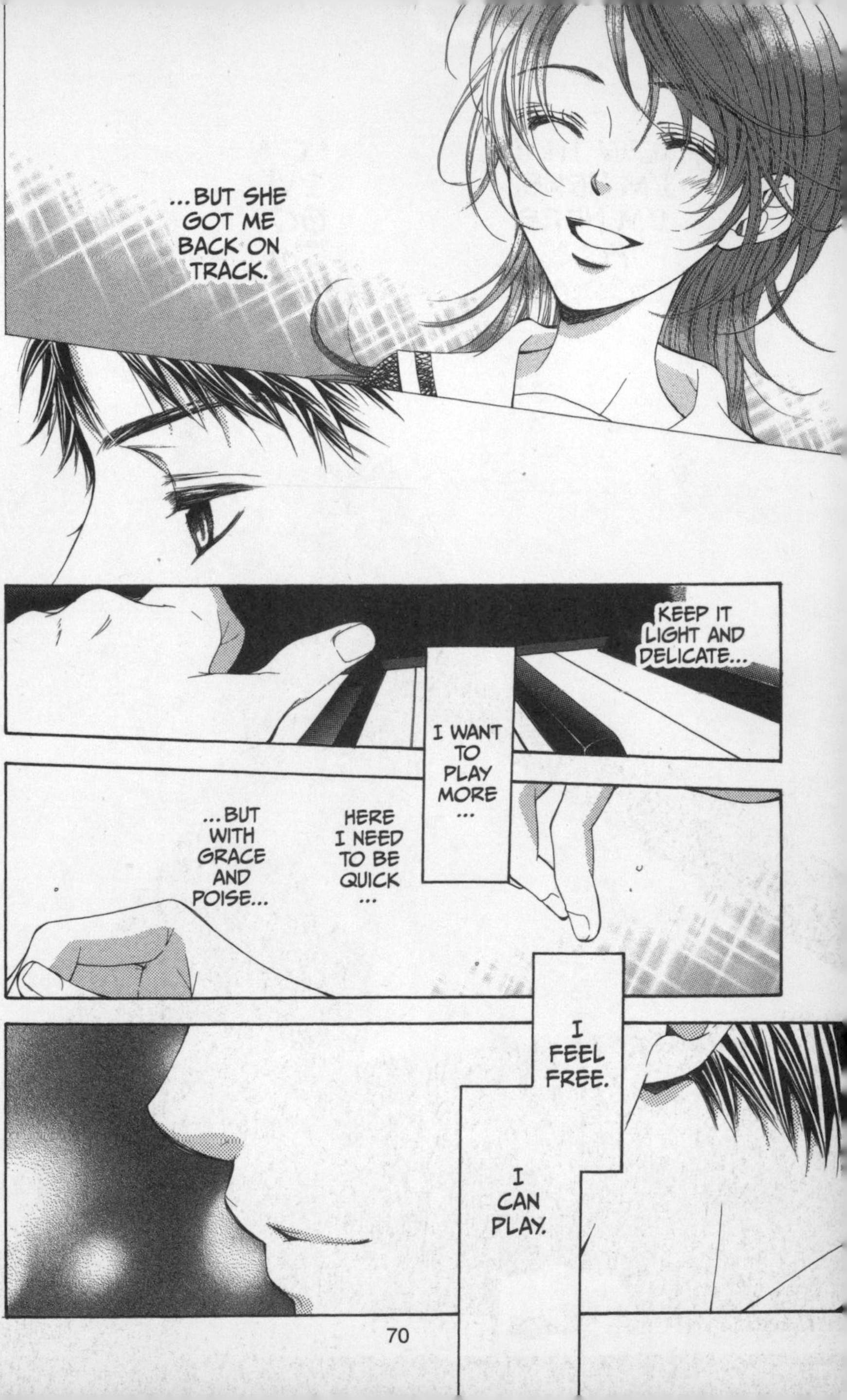

...BUT SHE GOT ME BACK ON TRACK.
KEEP IT LIGHT AND DELICATE...
I WANT TO PLAY MORE...
HERE I NEED TO BE QUICK...
...BUT WITH GRACE AND POISE...
I FEEL FREE.
I CAN PLAY.

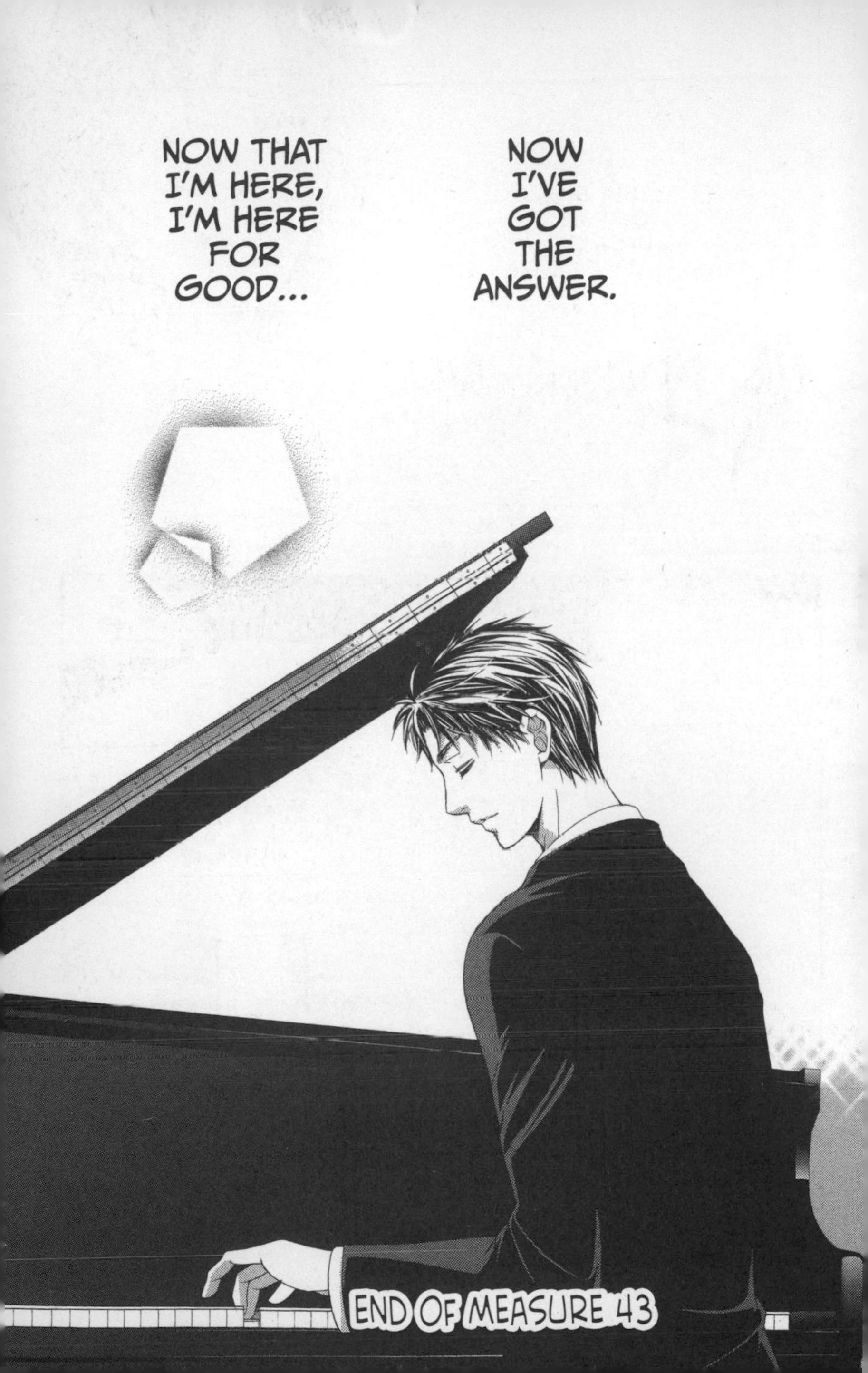
NOW I'VE GOT THE ANSWER.
NOW THAT I'M HERE, I'M HERE FOR GOOD...
END OF MEASURE 43

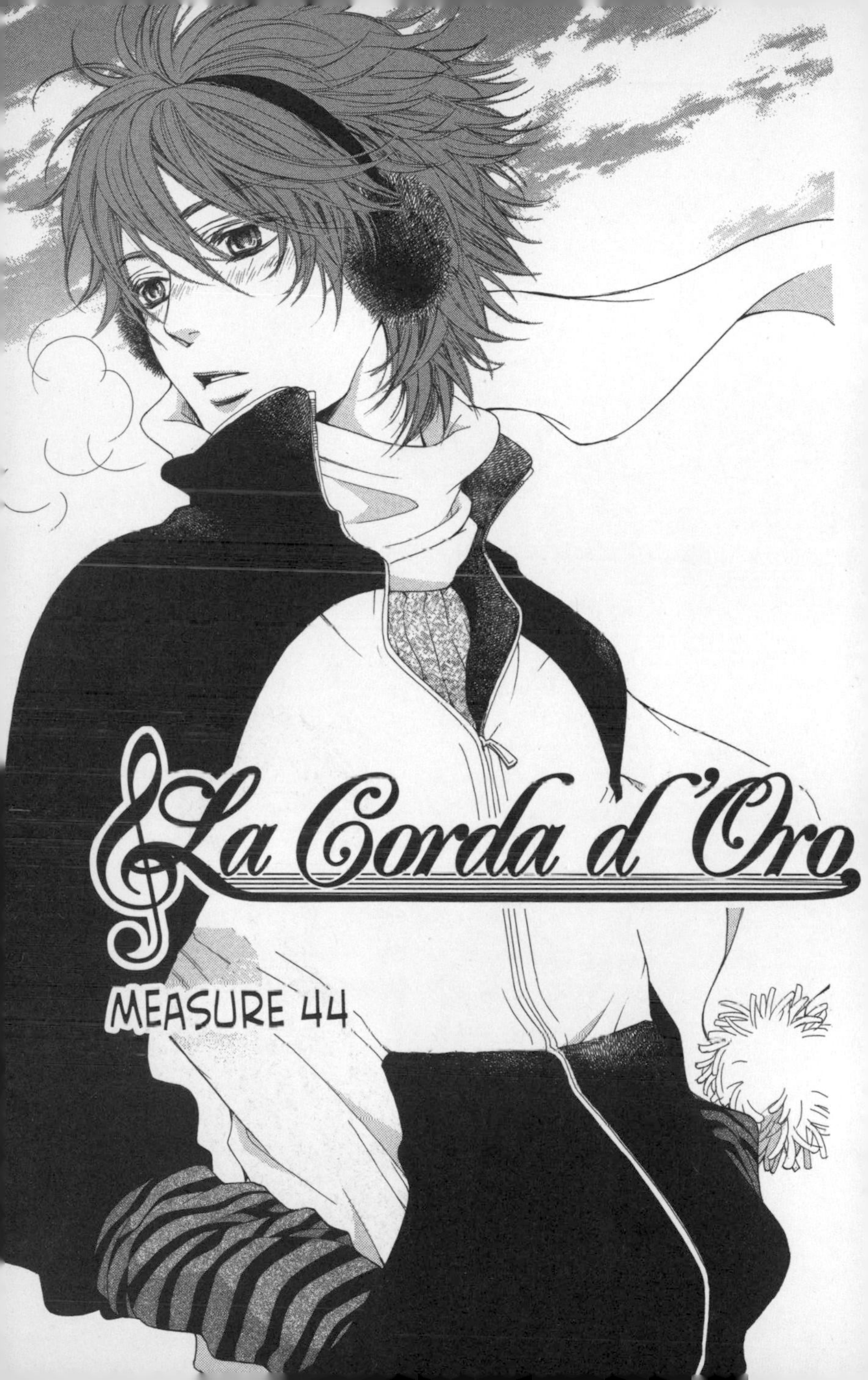
La Corda d'Oro
MEASURE 44

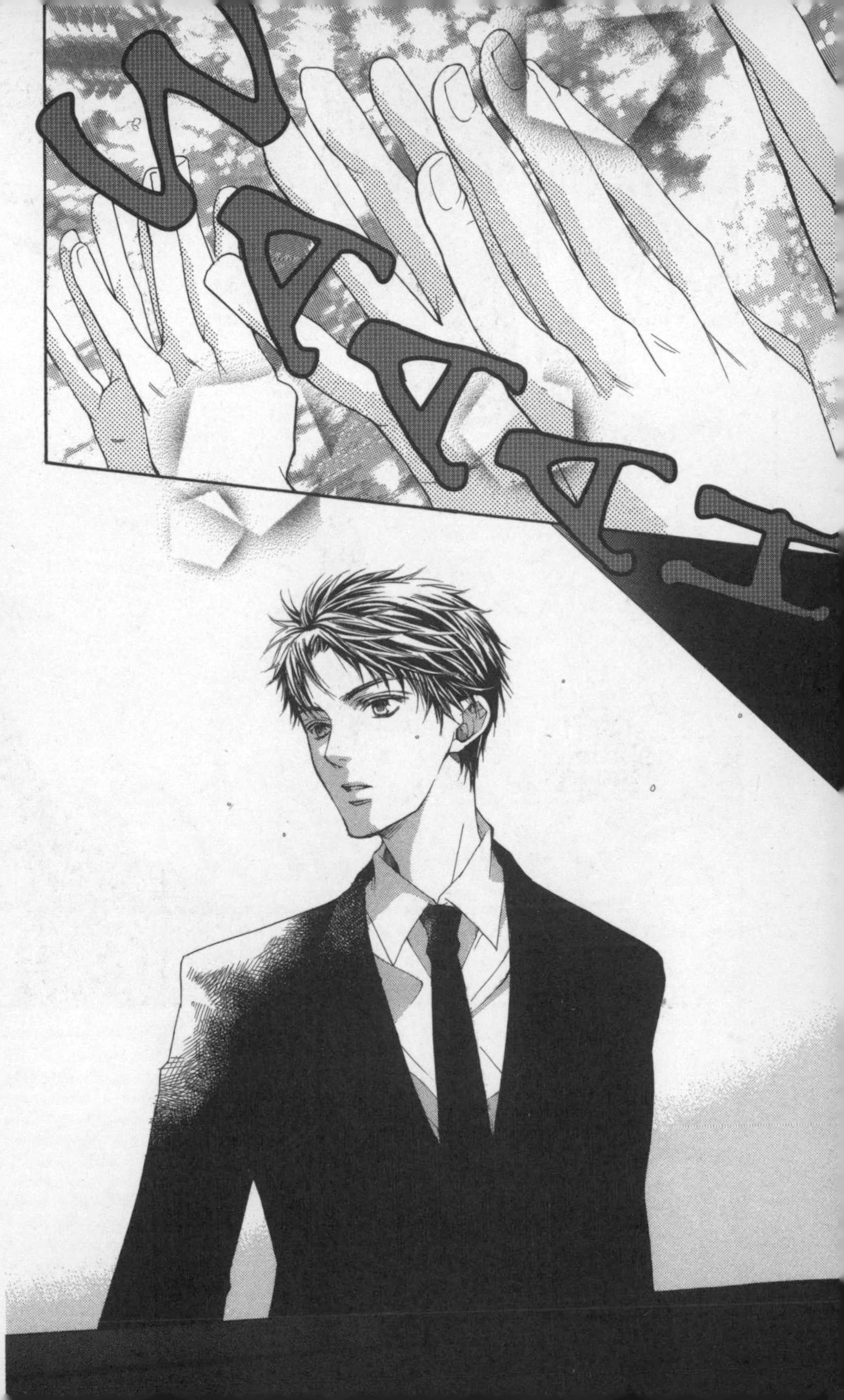
WAAAAH

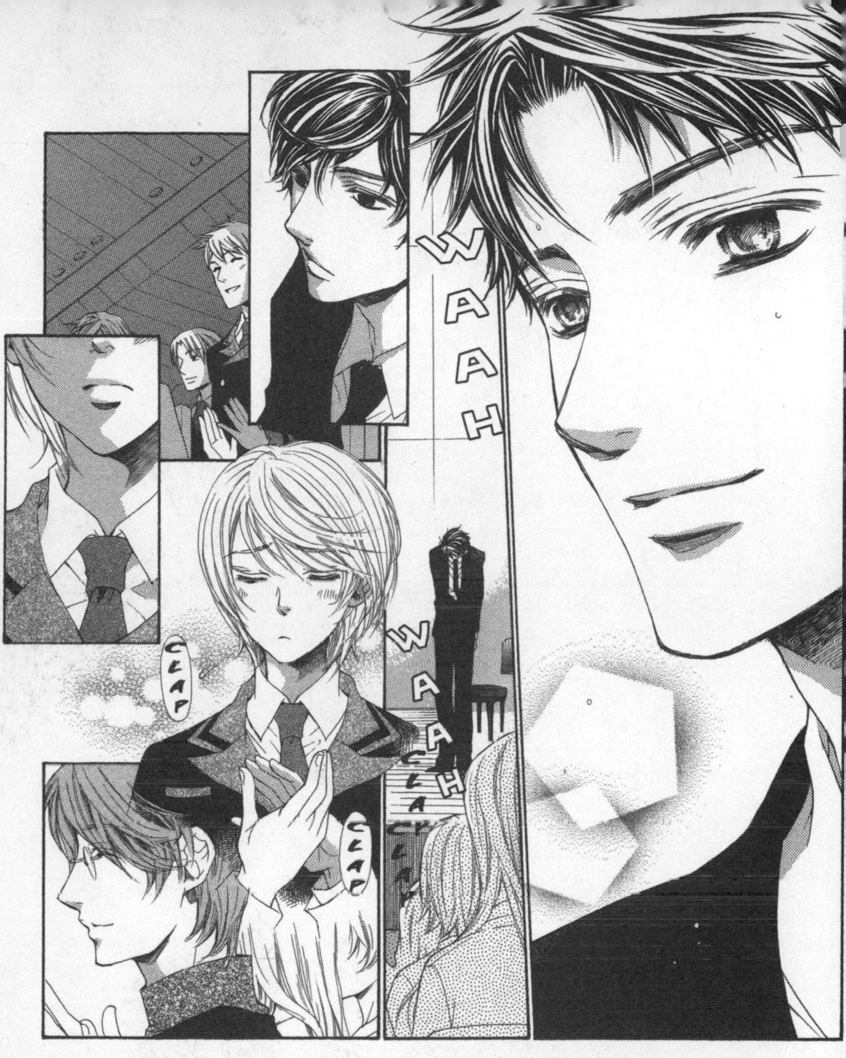
WAAH
WAAH
CLAP CLAP
CLAP
CLAP

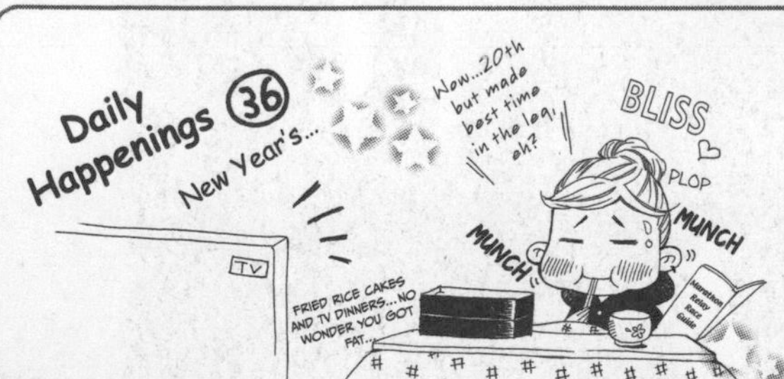
Daily Happenings 36
New Year's...
Wow...20th but made best time in the leg, eh?
BLISS
PLOP
MUNCH
MUNCH
TV
FRIED RICE CAKES AND TV DINNERS...NO WONDER YOU GOT FAT...

For New Year's, I just ate a bunch of rice cakes and watched the annual marathon relay race. I can't believe how much weight a person can gain in three days! Ha ha ha...I'm actually a huge fan of the marathon. I watch the business group, Hakone, and the prefectural race...I look forward to them so much! The varsity team was so good! ♡

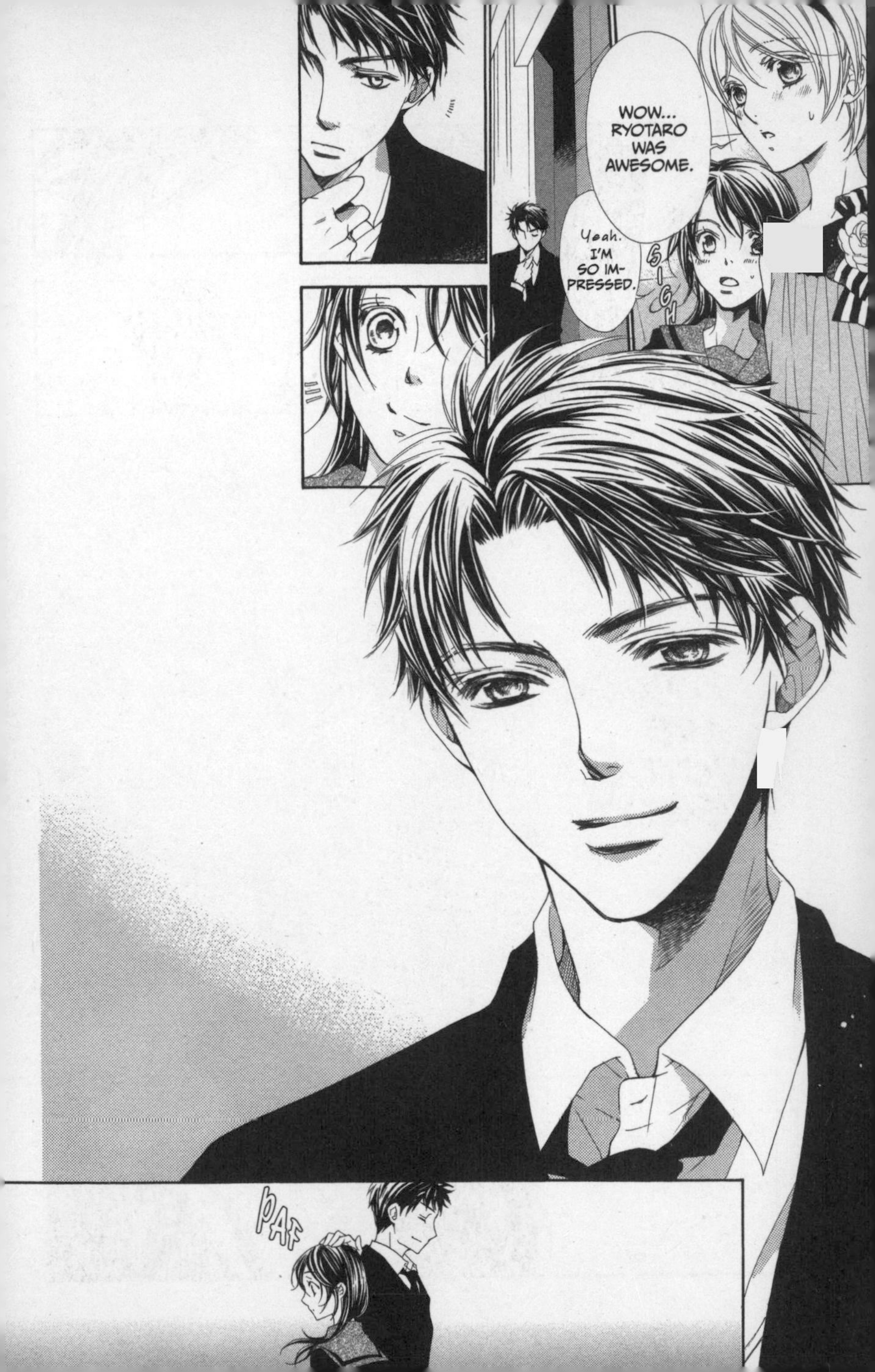
WOW... RYOTARO WAS AWESOME.
Yeah. I'M SO IM-PRESSED.
SIGH
PAF

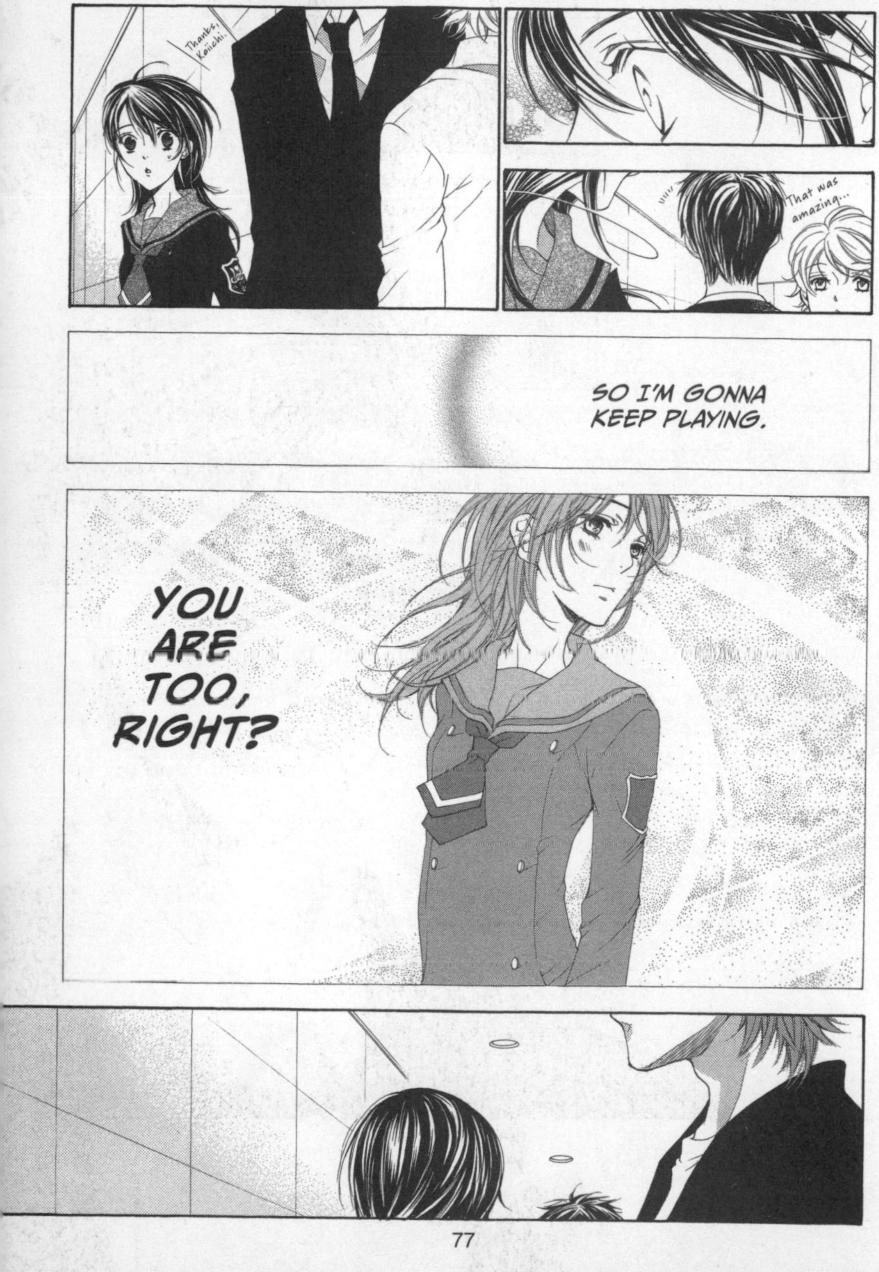
That was amazing...
Thanks, Keiichi.
SO I'M GONNA KEEP PLAYING.
YOU ARE TOO, RIGHT?

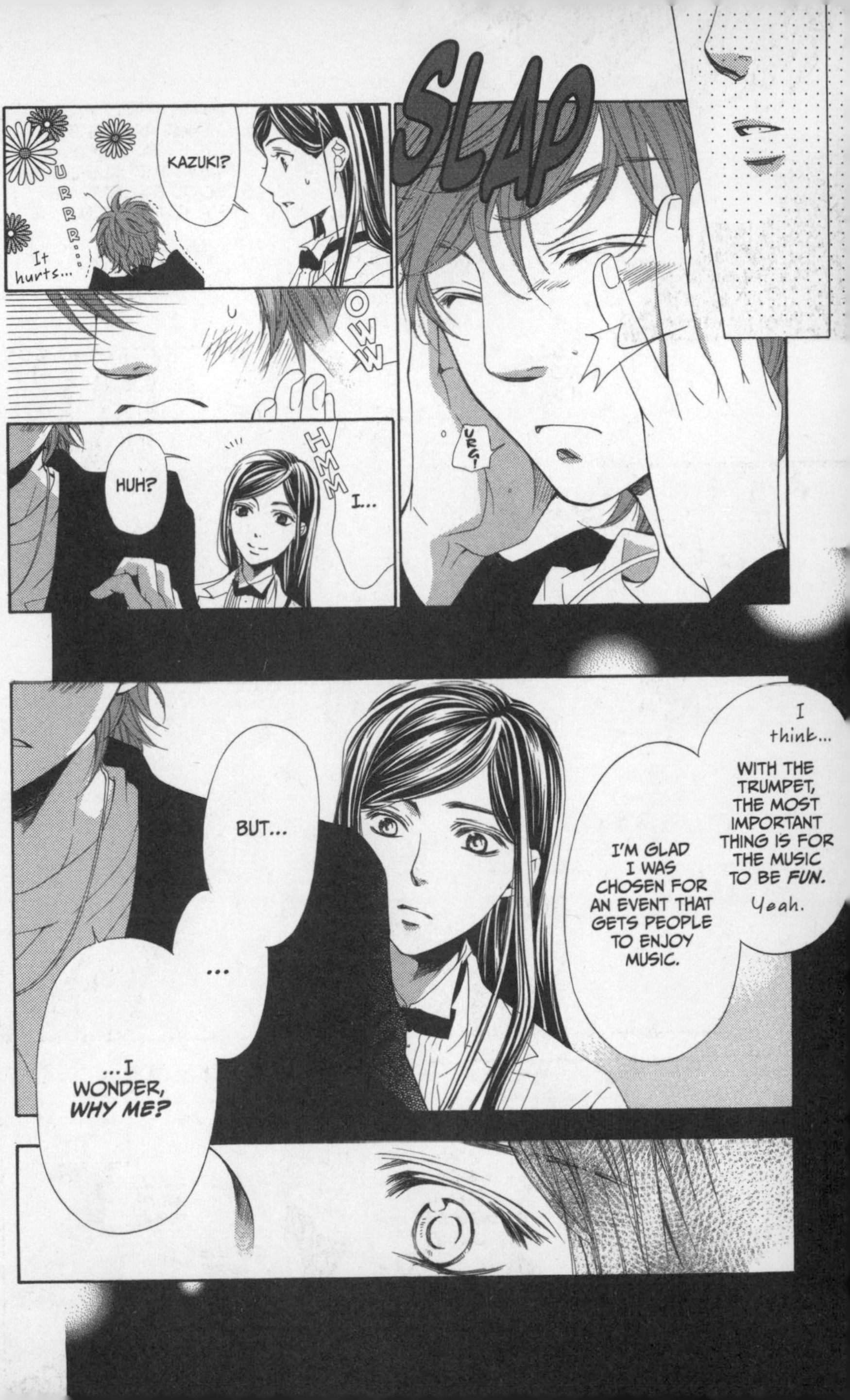
SLAP
URG!
KAZUKI?
URRR...
It hurts...
OWW
HMM I...
HUH?
I think...
WITH THE TRUMPET, THE MOST IMPORTANT THING IS FOR THE MUSIC TO BE FUN.
Yeah.
I'M GLAD I WAS CHOSEN FOR AN EVENT THAT GETS PEOPLE TO ENJOY MUSIC.
BUT...
...
...I WONDER, WHY ME?

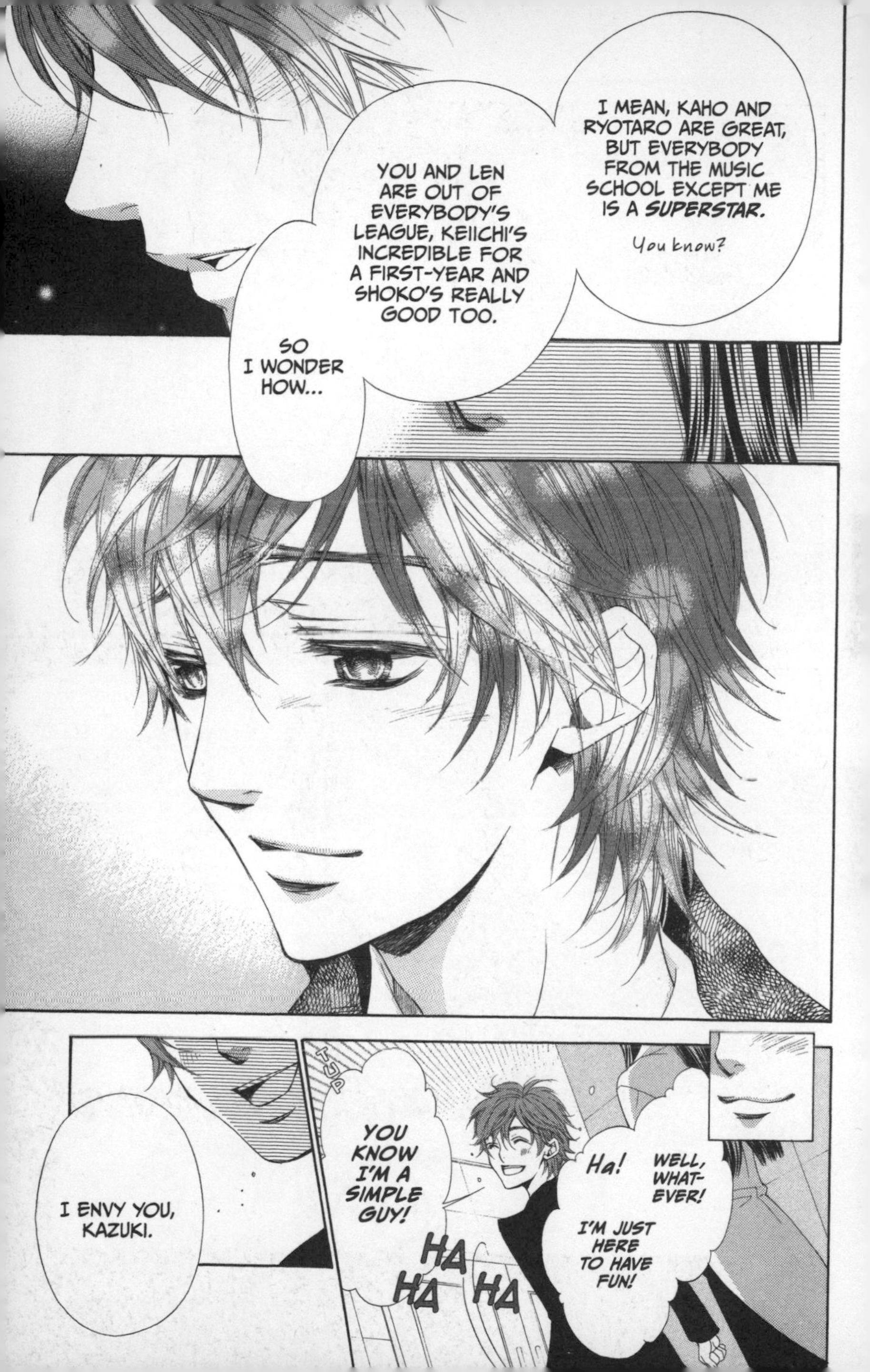
I MEAN, KAHO AND RYOTARO ARE GREAT, BUT EVERYBODY FROM THE MUSIC SCHOOL EXCEPT ME IS A *SUPERSTAR.*
You know?
YOU AND LEN ARE OUT OF EVERYBODY'S LEAGUE, KEIICHI'S INCREDIBLE FOR A FIRST-YEAR AND SHOKO'S REALLY GOOD TOO.
SO I WONDER HOW...
Ha! WELL, WHATEVER!
I'M JUST HERE TO HAVE FUN!
TUP
YOU KNOW I'M A SIMPLE GUY!
HA HA HA
I ENVY YOU, KAZUKI.

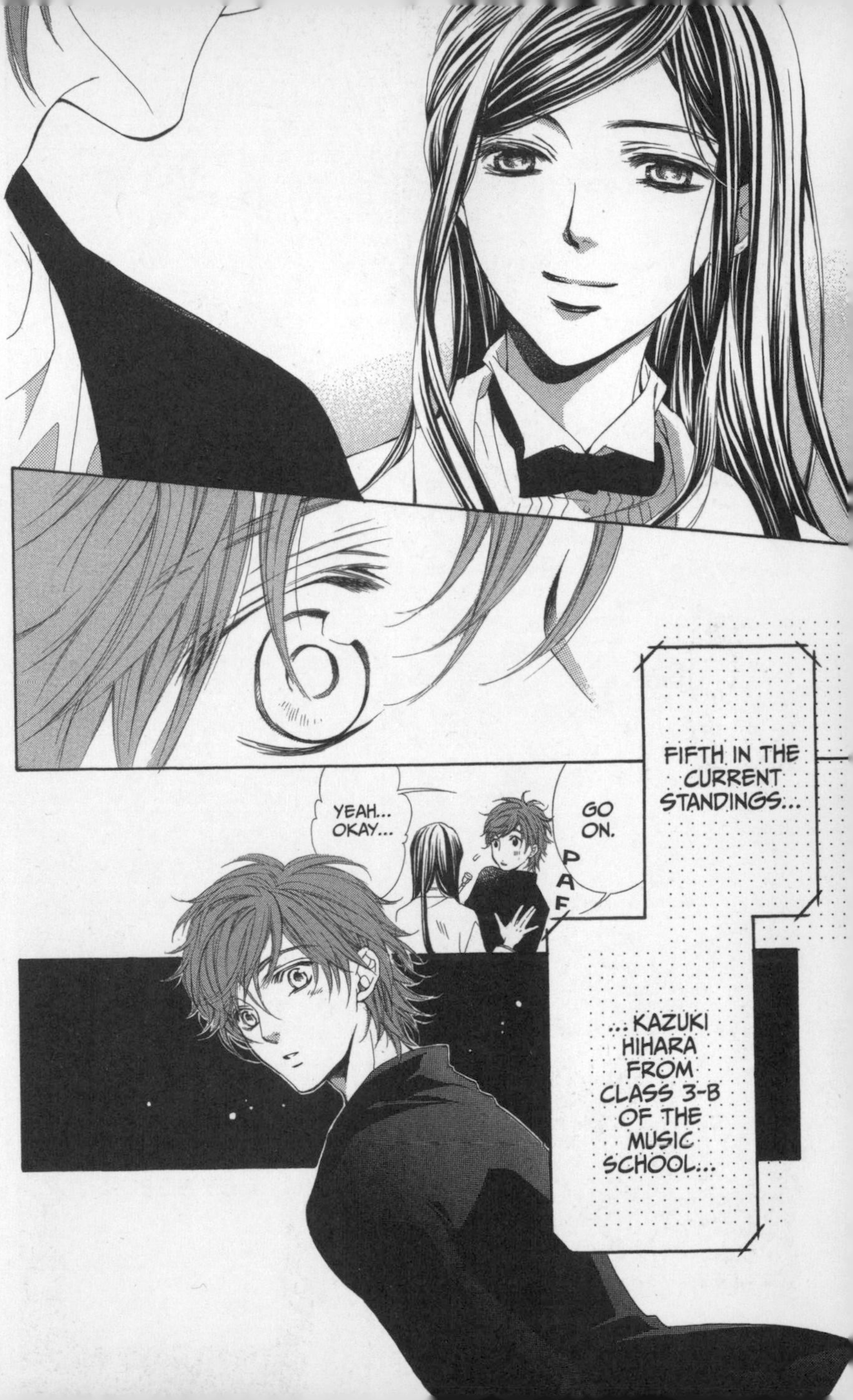
FIFTH IN THE CURRENT STANDINGS...
GO ON.
PAF
YEAH... OKAY...
...KAZUKI HIHARA FROM CLASS 3-B OF THE MUSIC SCHOOL...

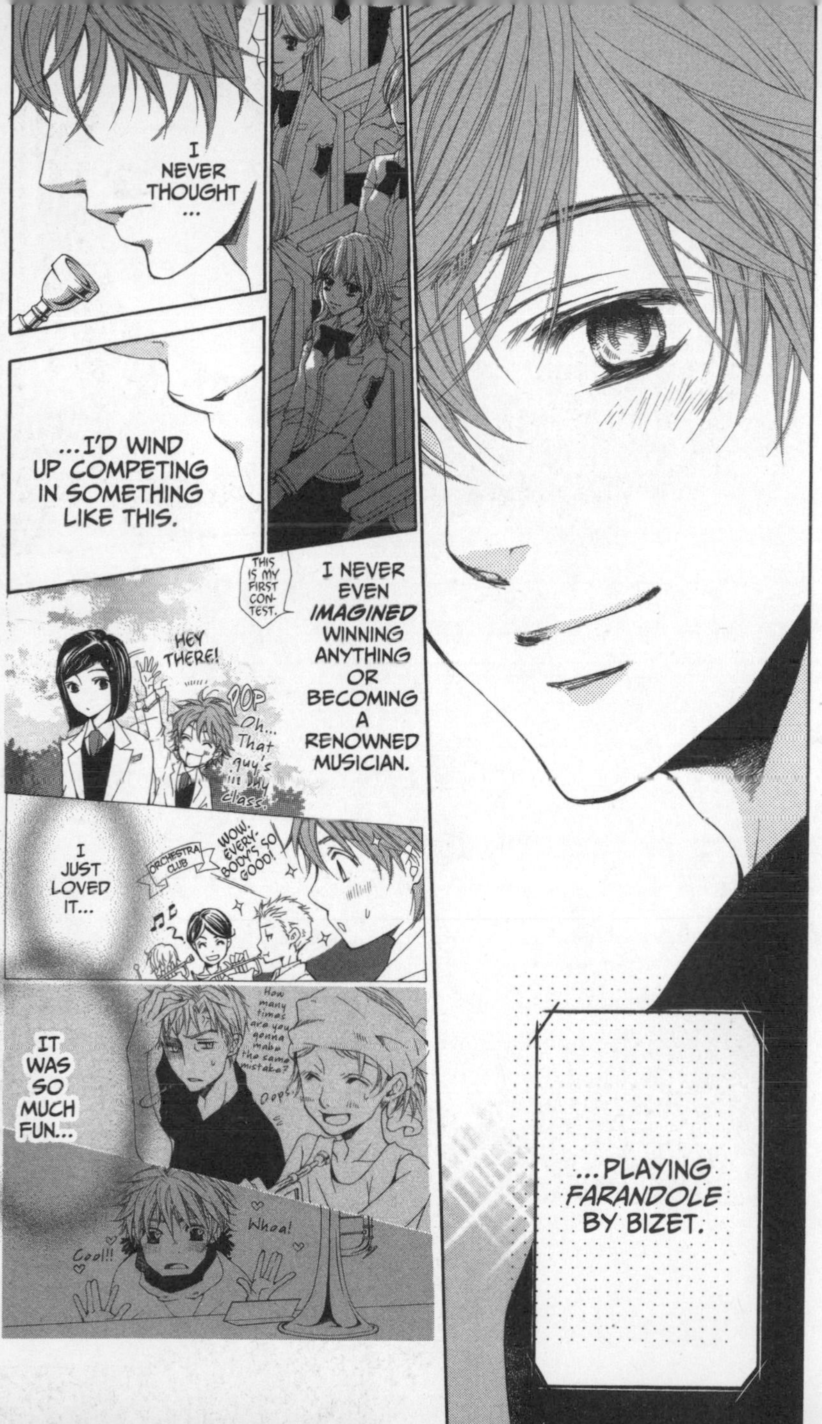
I NEVER THOUGHT...
...I'D WIND UP COMPETING IN SOMETHING LIKE THIS.
THIS IS MY FIRST CON-TEST.
I NEVER EVEN *IMAGINED* WINNING ANYTHING OR BECOMING A RENOWNED MUSICIAN.
HEY THERE!
POP
Oh... That guy's in my class.
WOW. EVERY-BODY'S SO GOOD!
ORCHESTRA CLUB
I JUST LOVED IT...
How many times are you gonna make the same mistake?
Oops!
IT WAS SO MUCH FUN...
Whoa!
Cool!!
...PLAYING *FARANDOLE* BY BIZET.

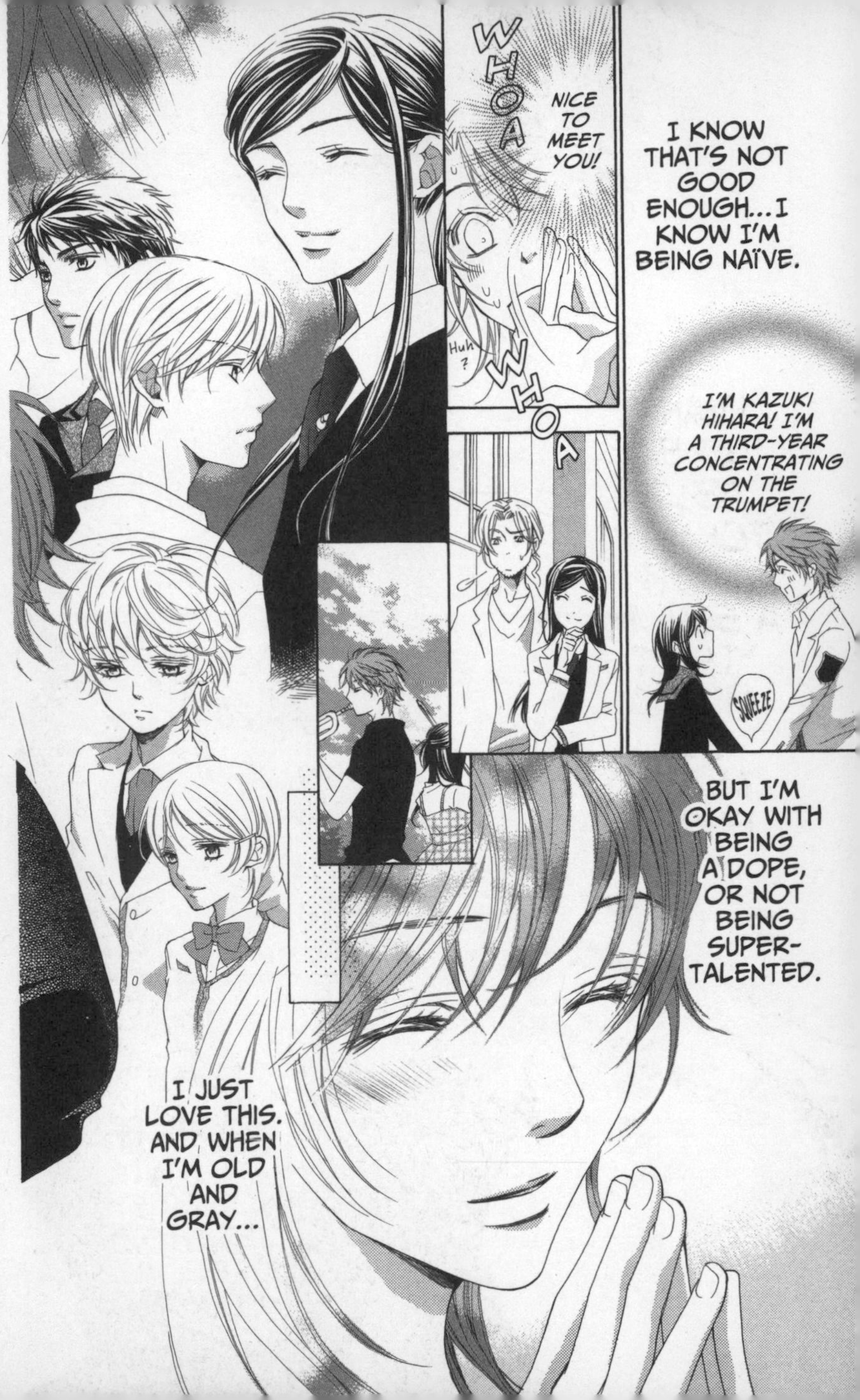

I KNOW THAT'S NOT GOOD ENOUGH...I KNOW I'M BEING NAÏVE.
WHOA
NICE TO MEET YOU!
Huh?
WHOA
I'M KAZUKI HIHARA! I'M A THIRD-YEAR CONCENTRATING ON THE TRUMPET!
SQUEEZE
BUT I'M OKAY WITH BEING A DOPE, OR NOT BEING SUPER-TALENTED.
I JUST LOVE THIS. AND WHEN I'M OLD AND GRAY...

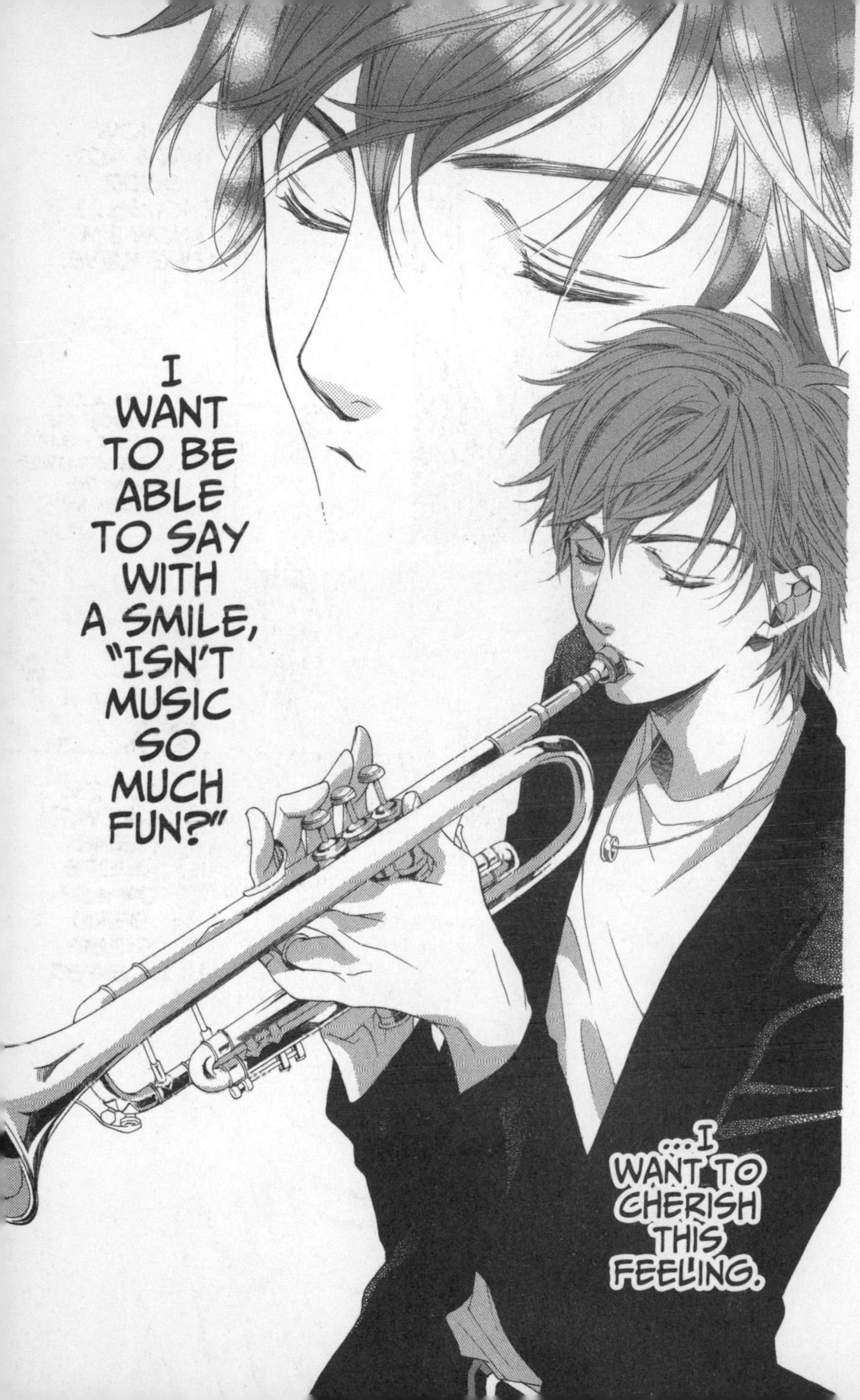
I WANT TO BE ABLE TO SAY WITH A SMILE, "ISN'T MUSIC SO MUCH FUN?"
...I WANT TO CHERISH THIS FEELING.

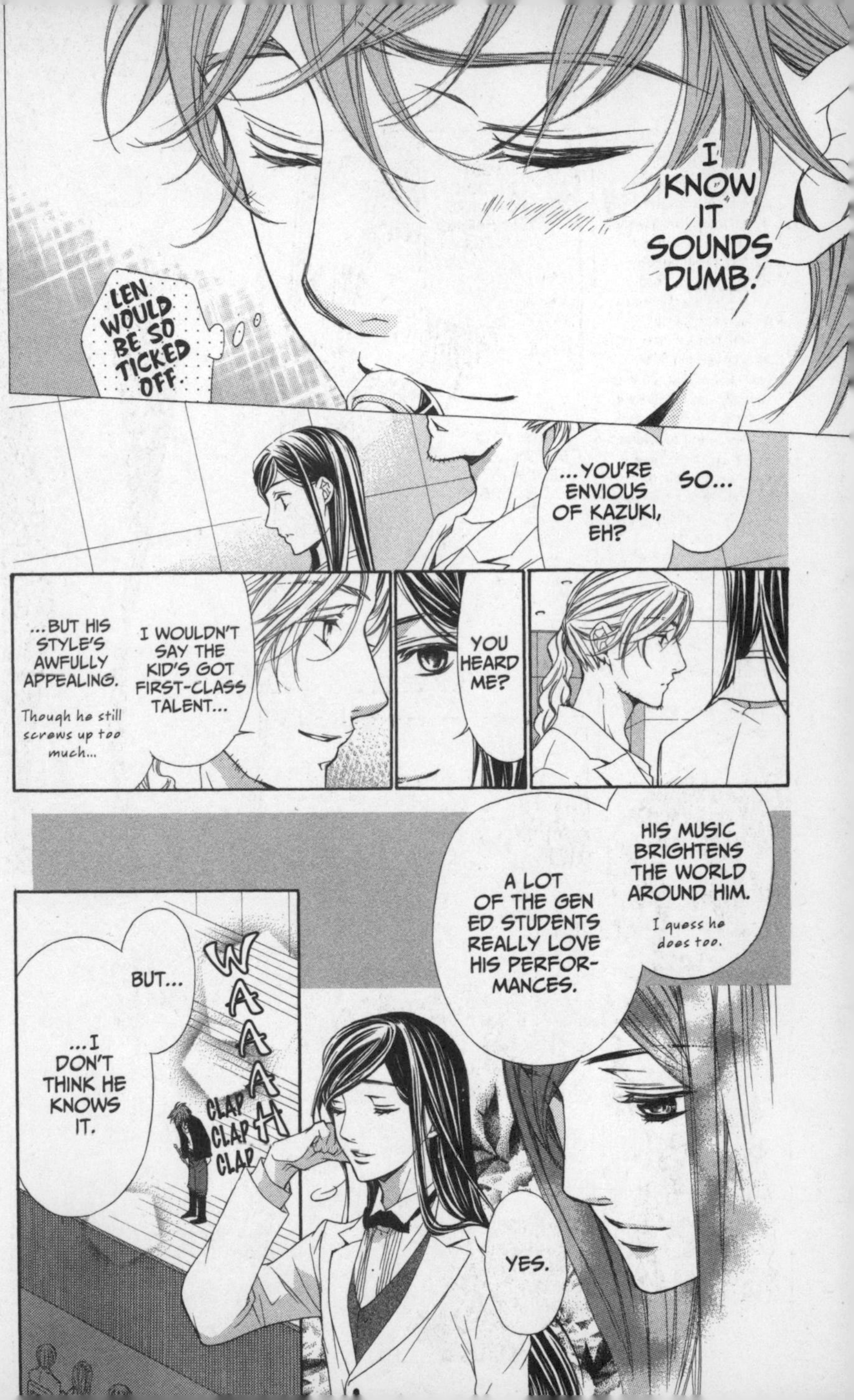
I KNOW IT SOUNDS DUMB.
LEN WOULD BE SO TICKED OFF
SO...
...YOU'RE ENVIOUS OF KAZUKI, EH?
YOU HEARD ME?
I WOULDN'T SAY THE KID'S GOT FIRST-CLASS TALENT...
...BUT HIS STYLE'S AWFULLY APPEALING.
Though he still screws up too much...
HIS MUSIC BRIGHTENS THE WORLD AROUND HIM.
I guess he does too.
A LOT OF THE GEN ED STUDENTS REALLY LOVE HIS PERFORMANCES.
WAAAAH
CLAP CLAP CLAP
BUT...
...I DON'T THINK HE KNOWS IT.
YES.

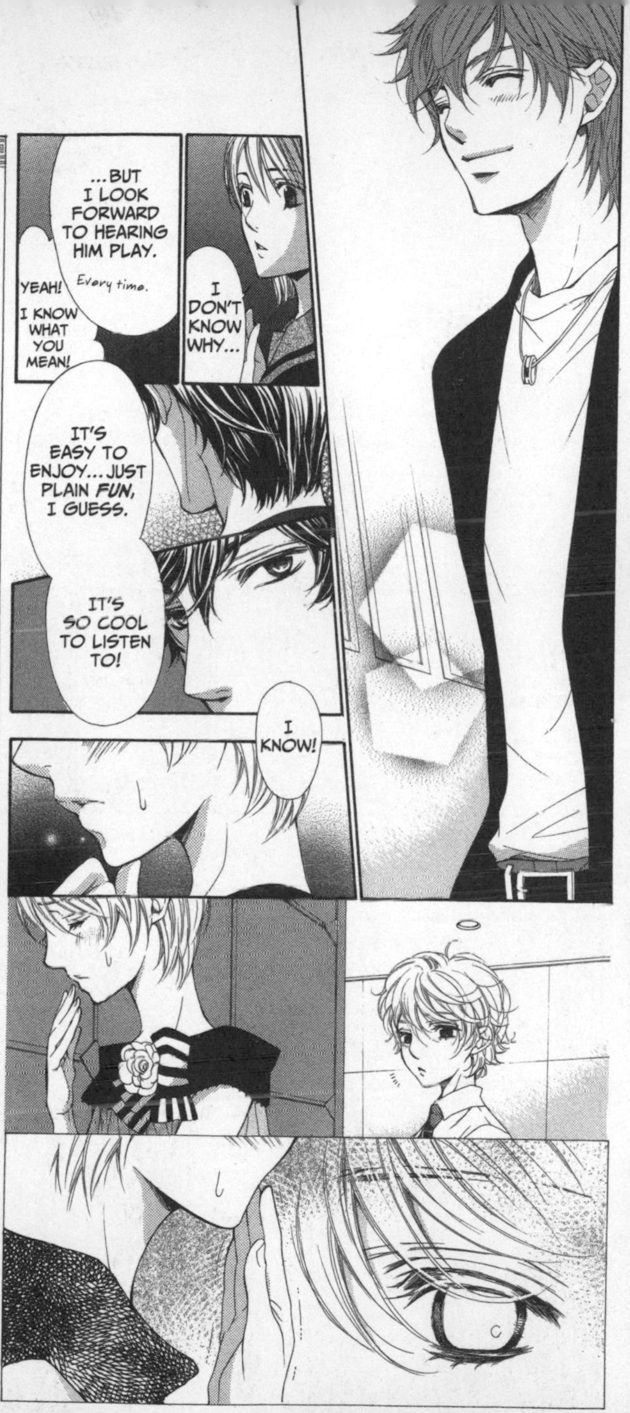
I DON'T KNOW WHY...
...BUT I LOOK FORWARD TO HEARING HIM PLAY.
Every time.
YEAH! I KNOW WHAT YOU MEAN!
IT'S EASY TO ENJOY... JUST PLAIN FUN, I GUESS.
IT'S SO COOL TO LISTEN TO!
I KNOW!

It's fun to dress the characters in different outfits once in a while. Originally I wanted to try a commando, RPG-type look, but I ended up with just a Chinese theme. It was really hard to brainstorm RPG versions of the characters. Brave Kazuki and Warrior Ryotaro were actually kind of bland. Maybe I could have Azuma and Keiichi as the stalwart heroes and Len as a playboy monk who's also a thief...umm...anyway, I kept changing my mind and finally I just gave up. Personally, I think Keiichi is the most fun to play dress-up with. ♡

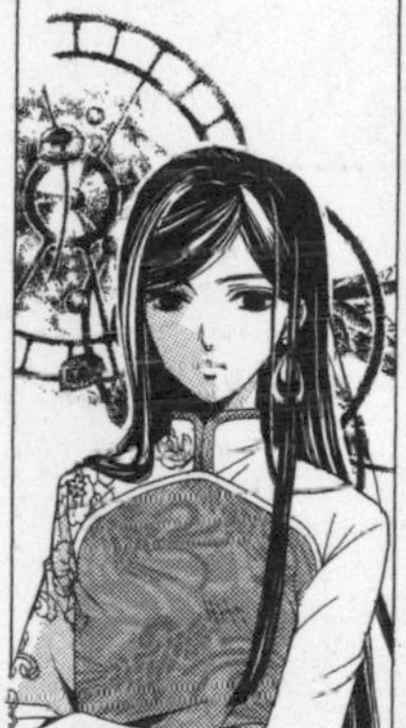

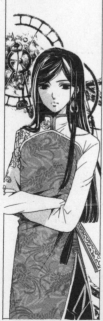

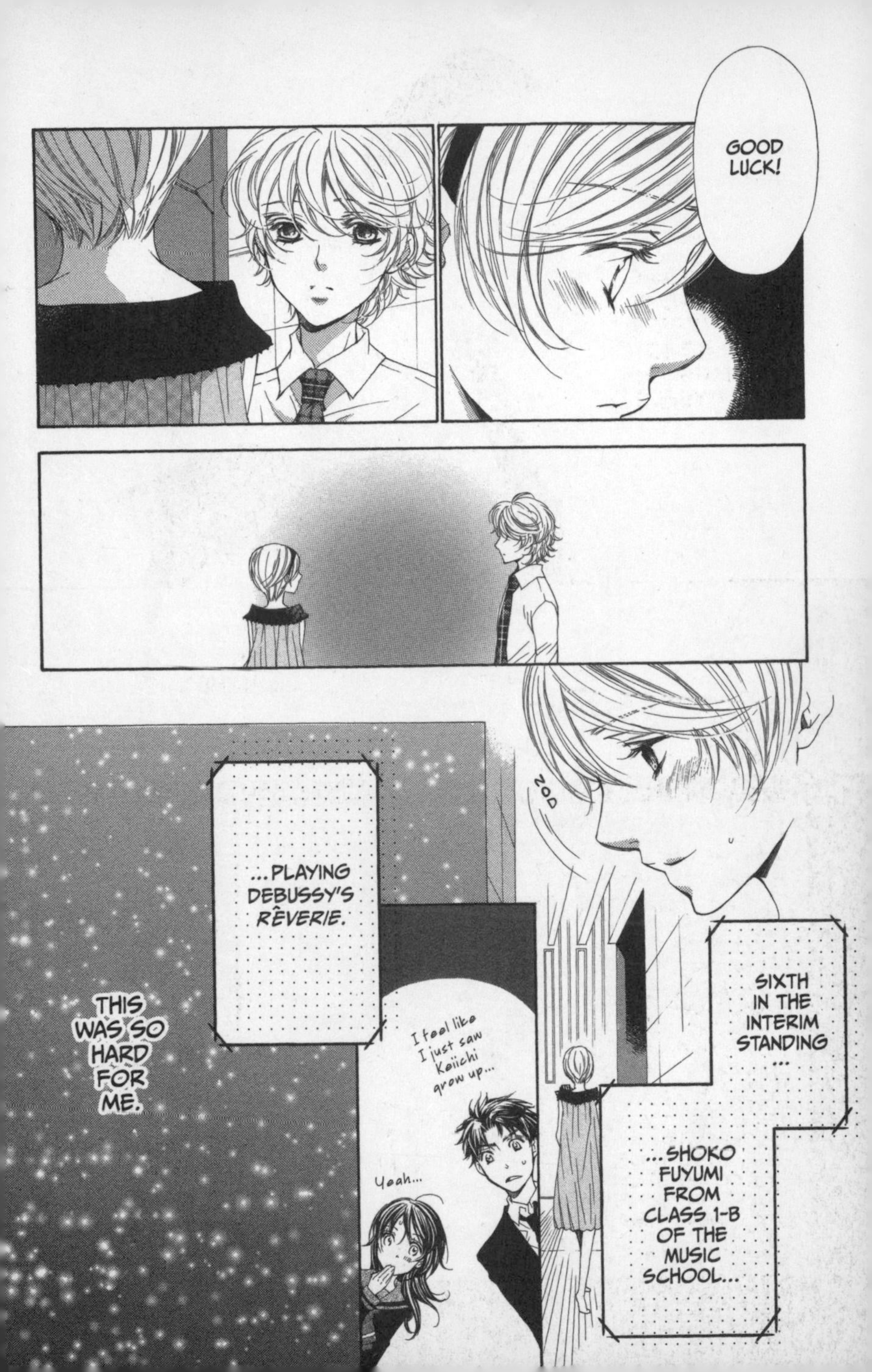
GOOD LUCK!
ZOD
SIXTH IN THE INTERIM STANDING...
...SHOKO FUYUMI FROM CLASS 1-B OF THE MUSIC SCHOOL...
...PLAYING DEBUSSY'S RÊVERIE.
I feel like I just saw Keiichi grow up...
Yeah...
THIS WAS SO HARD FOR ME.

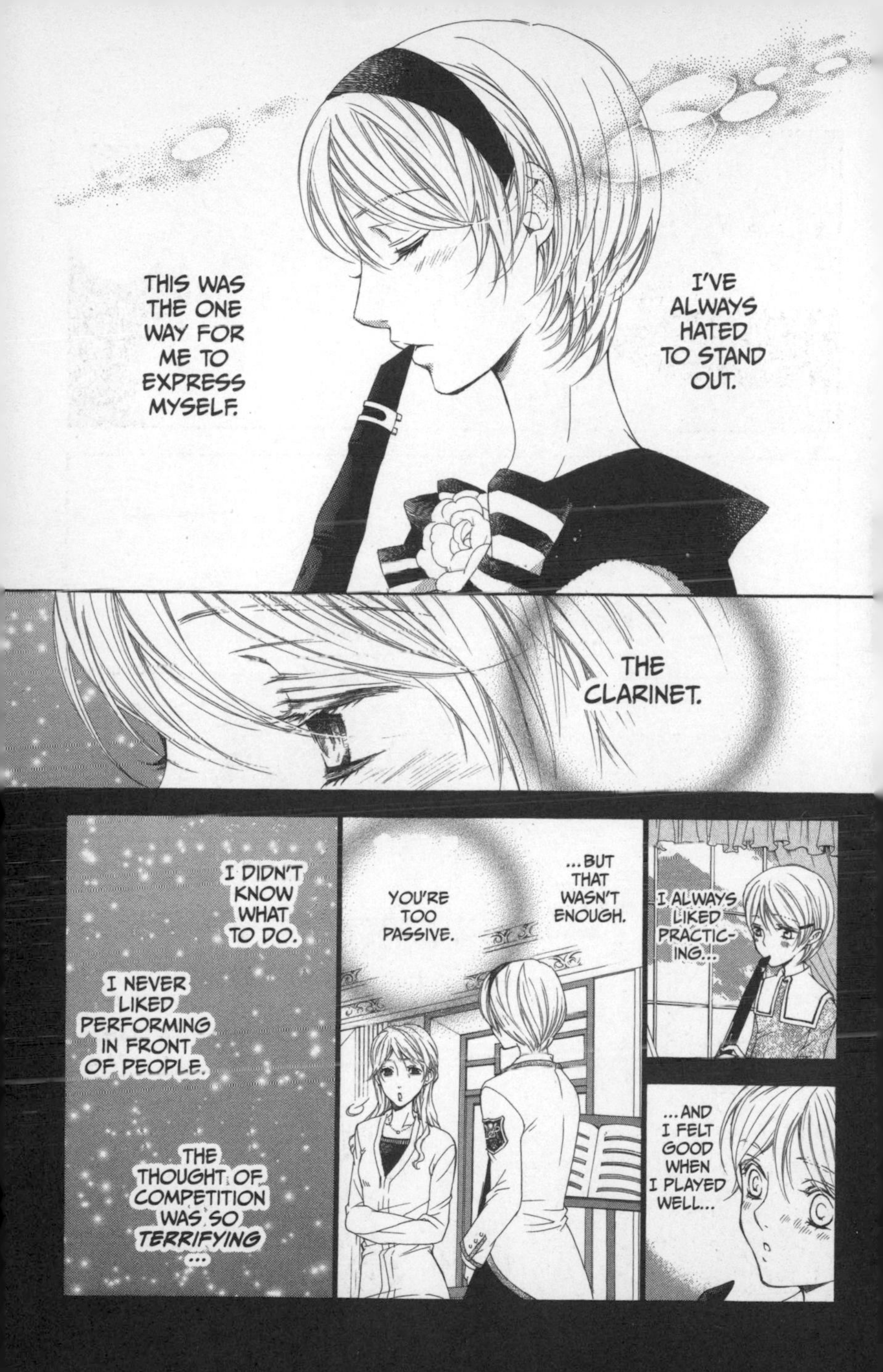
I'VE ALWAYS HATED TO STAND OUT.
THIS WAS THE ONE WAY FOR ME TO EXPRESS MYSELF.
THE CLARINET.
I ALWAYS LIKED PRACTICING...
...AND I FELT GOOD WHEN I PLAYED WELL...
...BUT THAT WASN'T ENOUGH.
YOU'RE TOO PASSIVE.
I DIDN'T KNOW WHAT TO DO.
I NEVER LIKED PERFORMING IN FRONT OF PEOPLE.
THE THOUGHT OF COMPETITION WAS SO *TERRIFYING*...

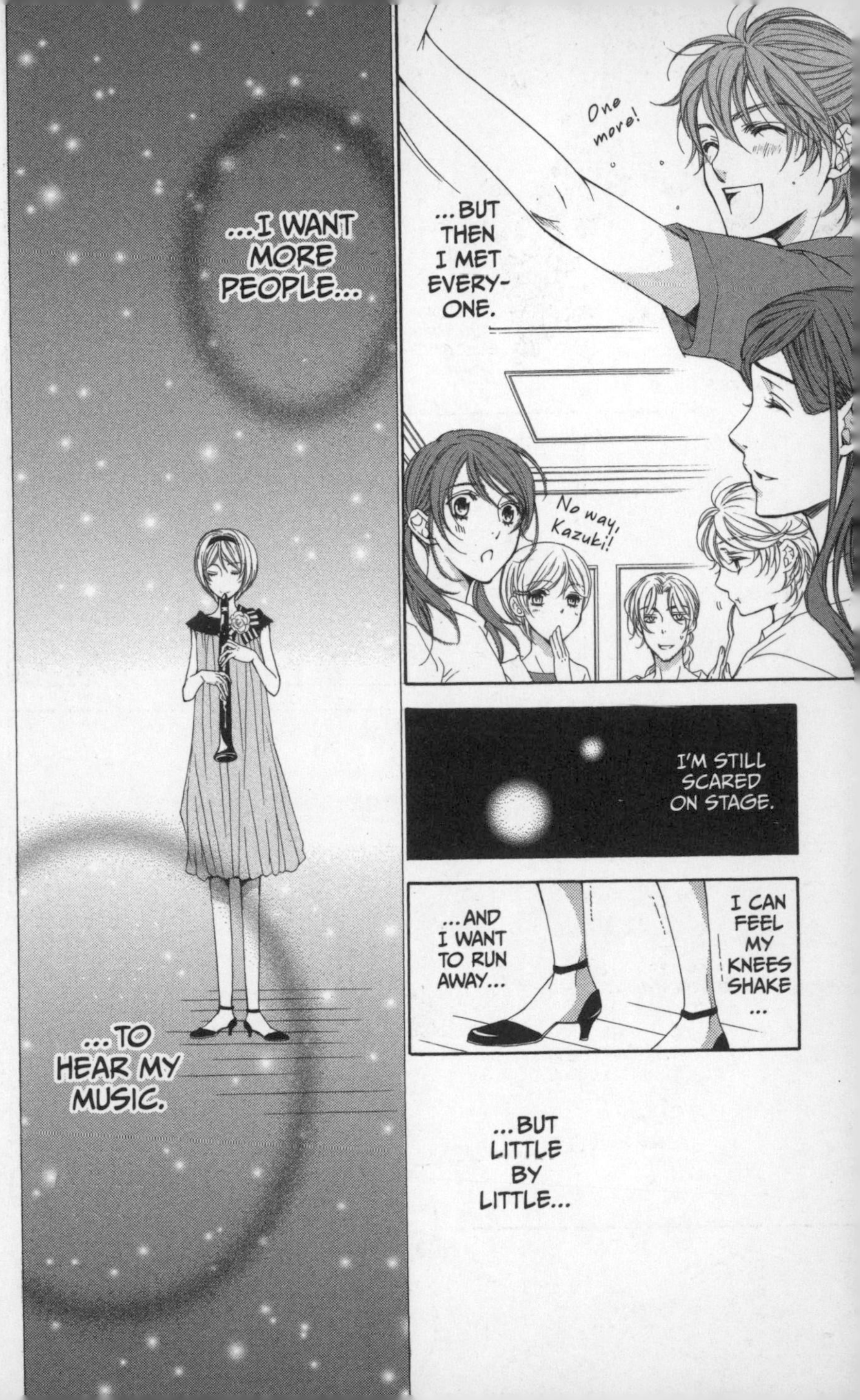
One more!
...BUT THEN I MET EVERY-ONE.
No way, Kazuki!
I'M STILL SCARED ON STAGE.
I CAN FEEL MY KNEES SHAKE ...
...AND I WANT TO RUN AWAY...
...BUT LITTLE BY LITTLE...
...I WANT MORE PEOPLE...
...TO HEAR MY MUSIC.

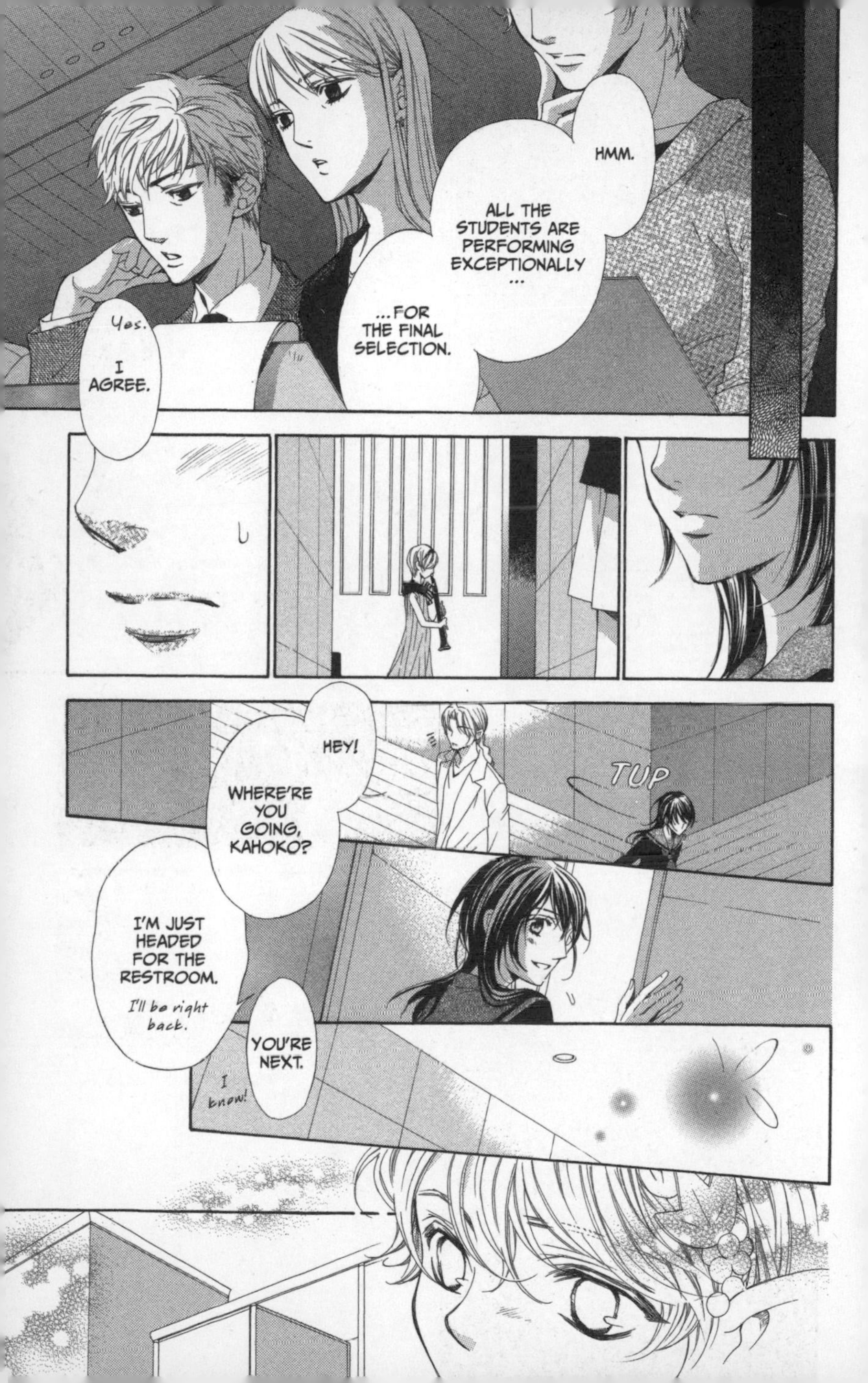
HMM.
ALL THE STUDENTS ARE PERFORMING EXCEPTIONALLY ...
...FOR THE FINAL SELECTION.
Yes.
I AGREE.
HEY!
WHERE'RE YOU GOING, KAHOKO?
TUP
I'M JUST HEADED FOR THE RESTROOM.
I'll be right back.
YOU'RE NEXT.
I know!

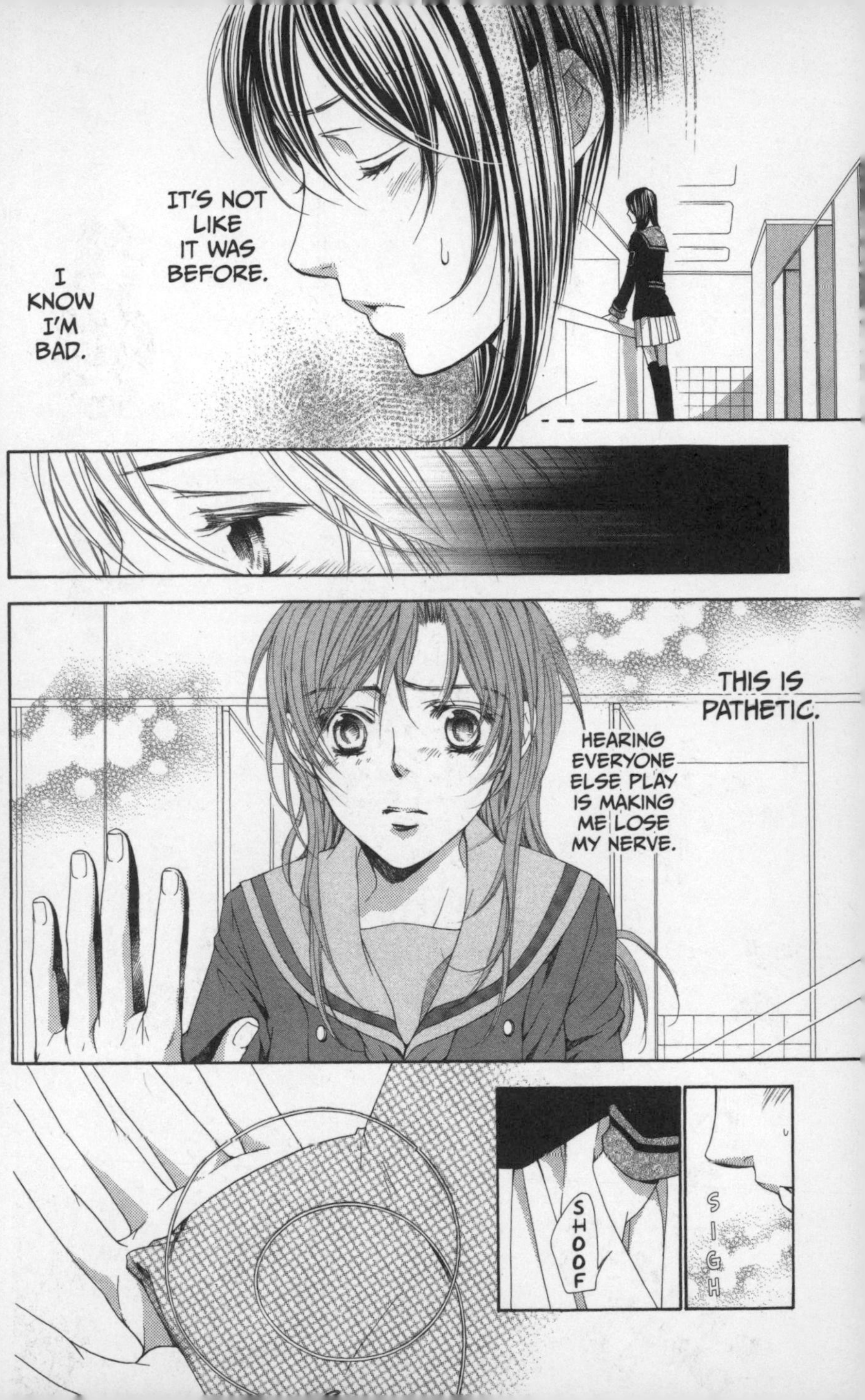

IT'S NOT LIKE IT WAS BEFORE.
I KNOW I'M BAD.
THIS IS PATHETIC.
HEARING EVERYONE ELSE PLAY IS MAKING ME LOSE MY NERVE.
SIGH
SHOOF

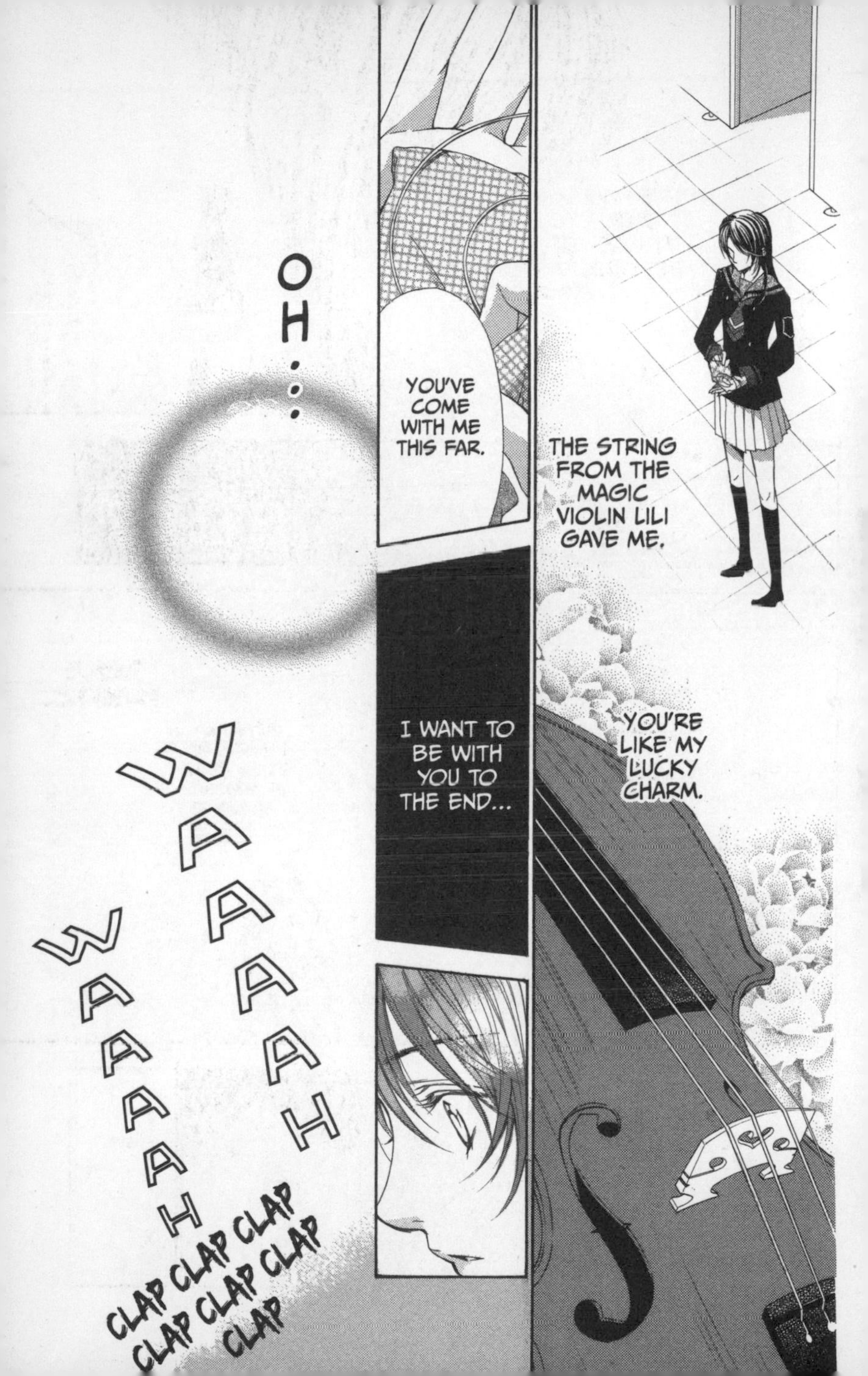
THE STRING FROM THE MAGIC VIOLIN LILI GAVE ME.
YOU'RE LIKE MY LUCKY CHARM.
YOU'VE COME WITH ME THIS FAR.
I WANT TO BE WITH YOU TO THE END...
OH...
WAAAAH
WAAAAH
CLAP CLAP CLAP CLAP CLAP CLAP CLAP

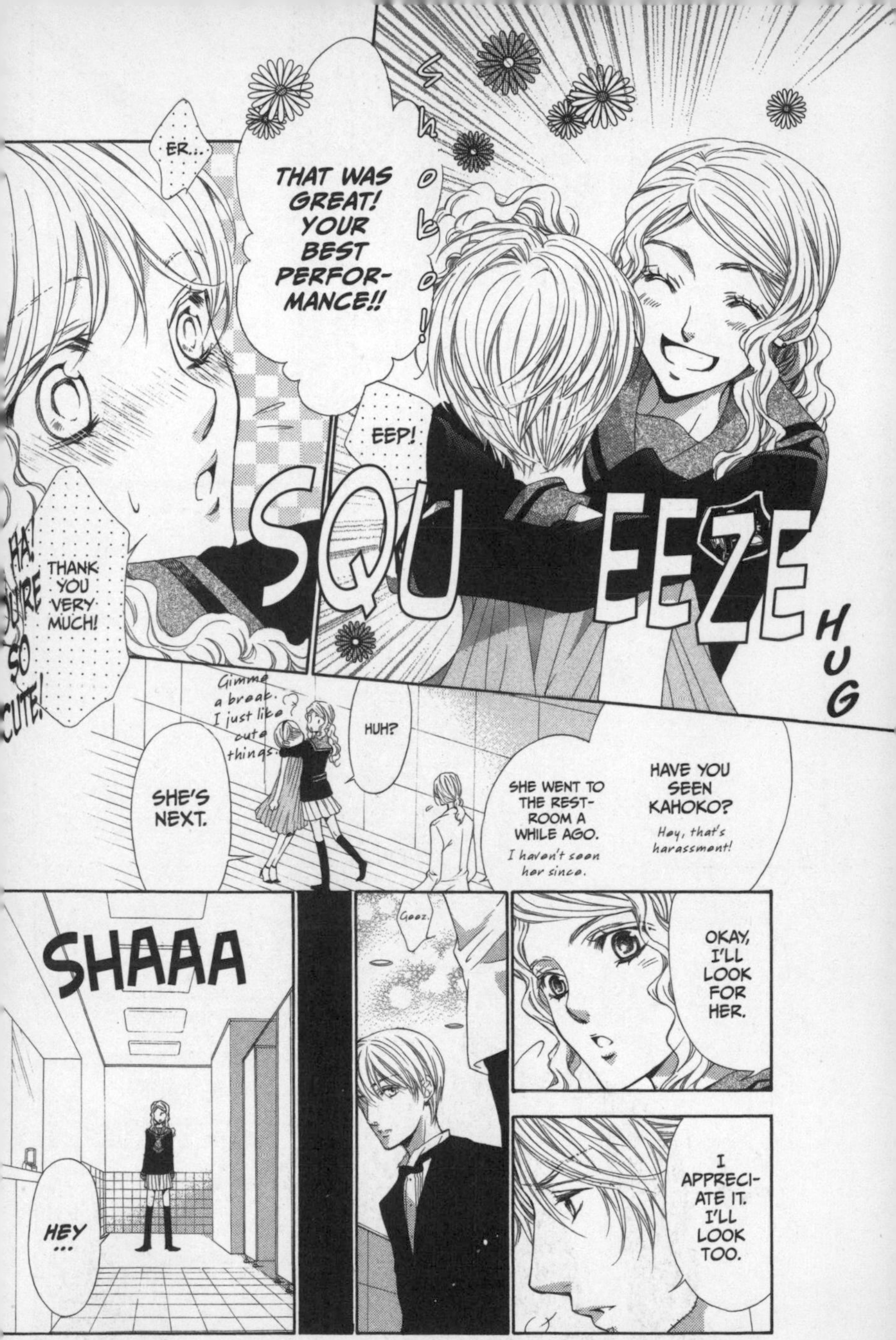
THAT WAS GREAT! YOUR BEST PERFORMANCE!!
EEP!
SQUEEZE
HUG
ER...
HA! OU'RE SO CUTE!
THANK YOU VERY MUCH!
HAVE YOU SEEN KAHOKO?
Hey, that's harassment!
SHE WENT TO THE REST-ROOM A WHILE AGO.
I haven't seen her since.
HUH?
Gimme a break. I just like cute things.
SHE'S NEXT.
OKAY, I'LL LOOK FOR HER.
I APPRECIATE IT. I'LL LOOK TOO.
Geez.
SHAAA
HEY ...

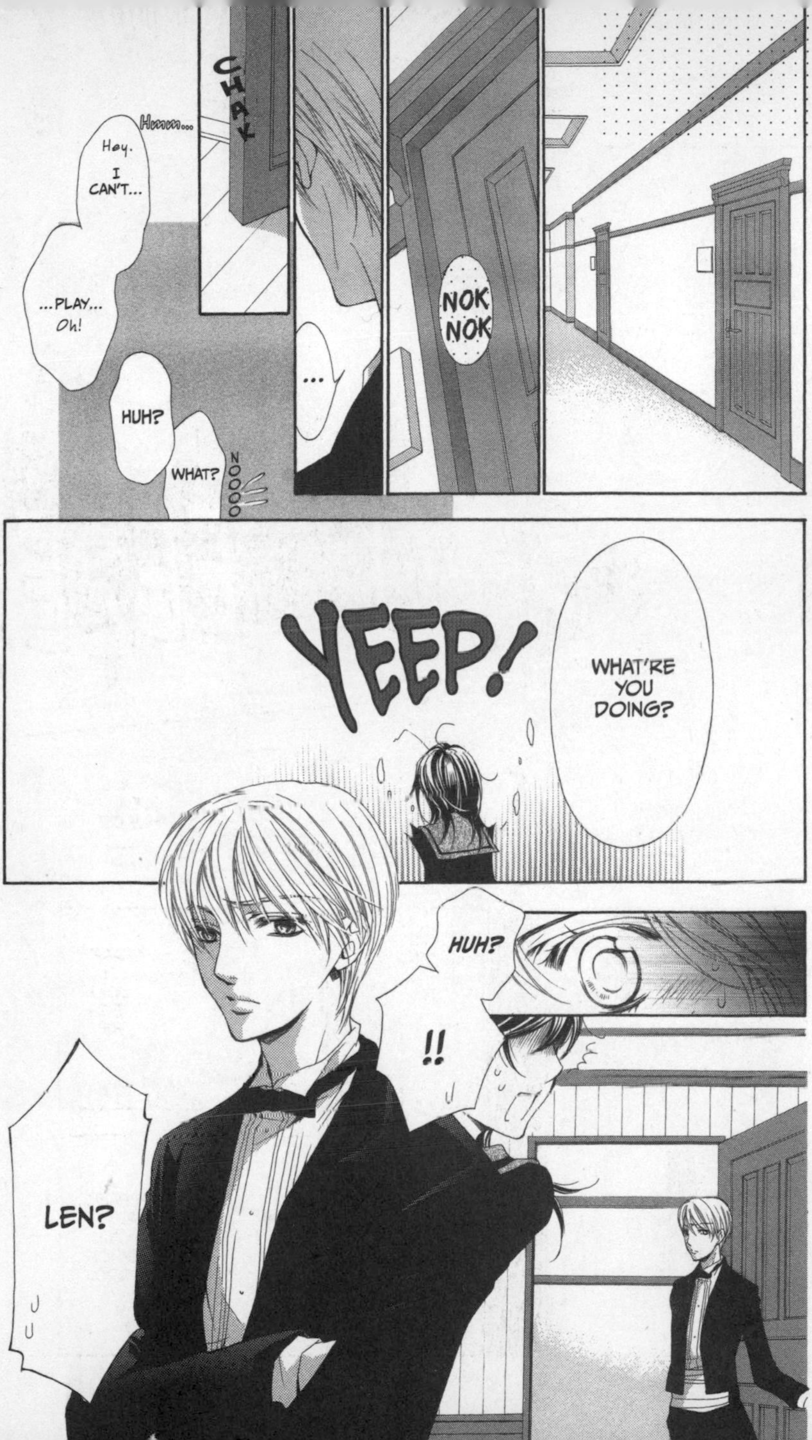
NOK NOK
...
CHAK
Hmm...
Hey.
I CAN'T...
...PLAY...
Oh!
HUH?
NOOOO
WHAT?
WHAT'RE YOU DOING?
YEEP!
HUH?
!!
LEN?

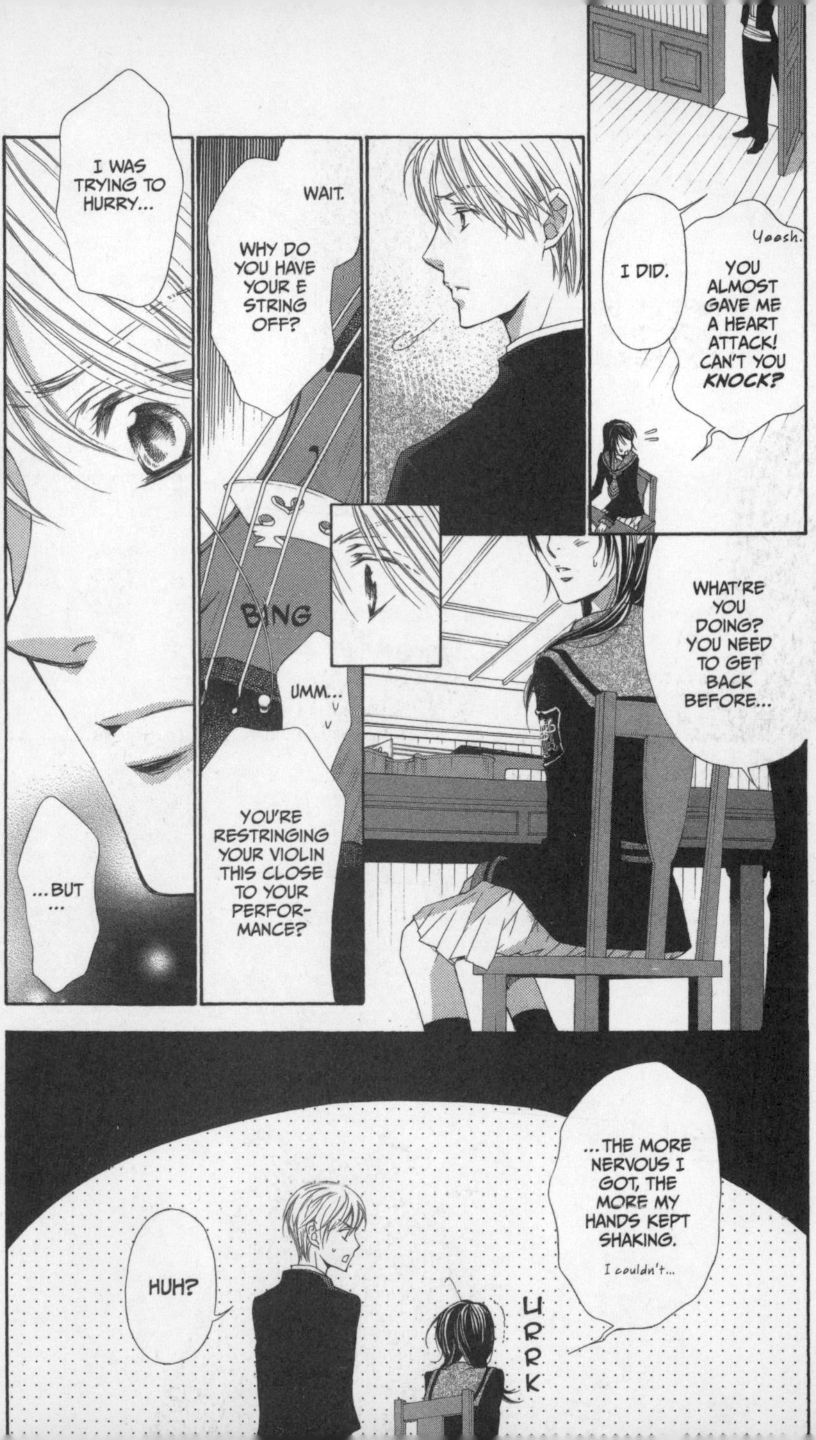
Yeesh.
YOU ALMOST GAVE ME A HEART ATTACK! CAN'T YOU *KNOCK?*
I DID.
WHAT'RE YOU DOING? YOU NEED TO GET BACK BEFORE...
WAIT.
WHY DO YOU HAVE YOUR E STRING OFF?
BING
UMM...
YOU'RE RESTRINGING YOUR VIOLIN THIS CLOSE TO YOUR PERFORMANCE?
I WAS TRYING TO HURRY...
...BUT ...
...THE MORE NERVOUS I GOT, THE MORE MY HANDS KEPT SHAKING.
I couldn't...
URRK
HUH?

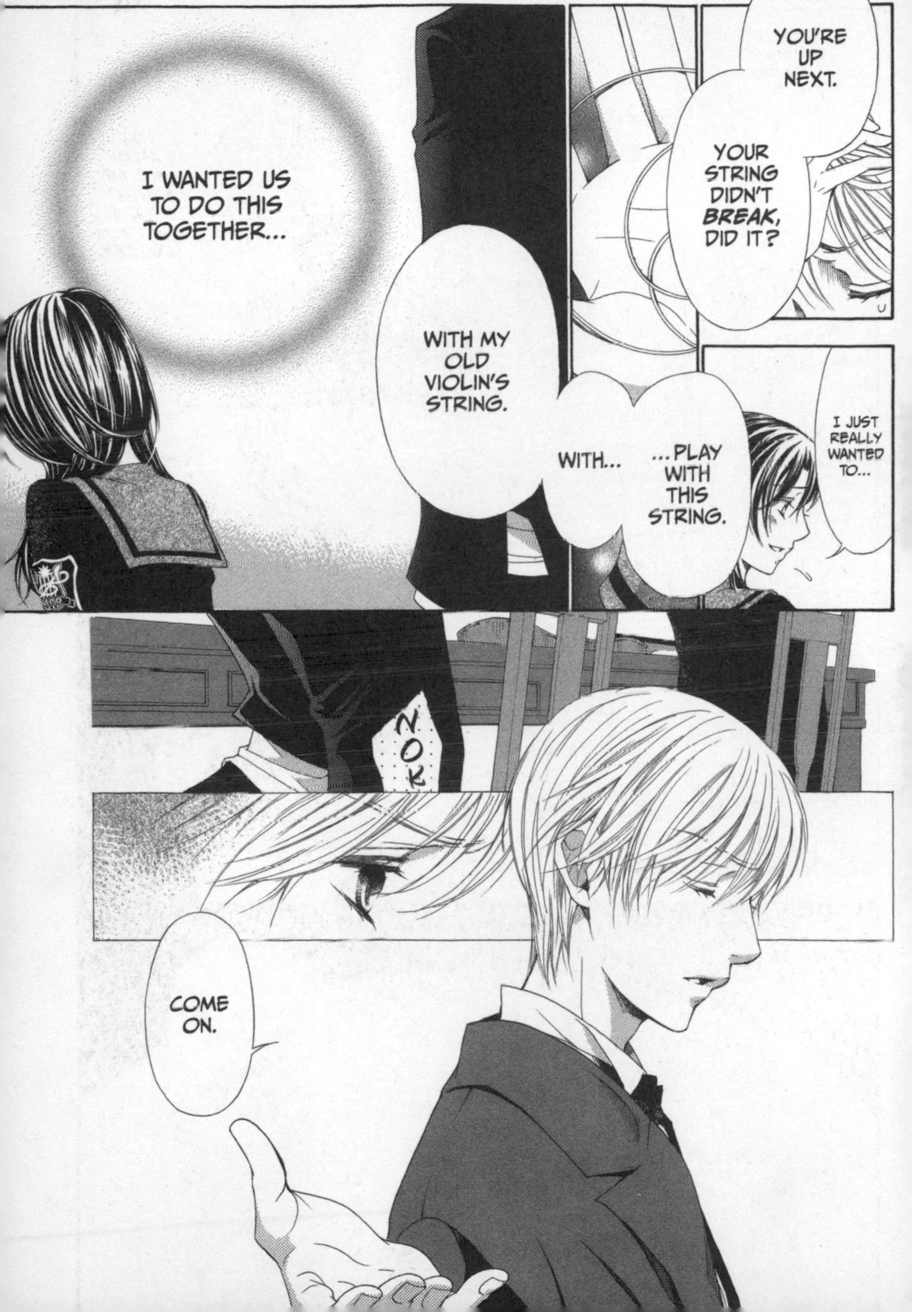
YOU'RE UP NEXT.
YOUR STRING DIDN'T *BREAK*, DID IT?
I JUST REALLY WANTED TO...
...PLAY WITH THIS STRING.
WITH...
WITH MY OLD VIOLIN'S STRING.
I WANTED US TO DO THIS TOGETHER...
NOK
COME ON.

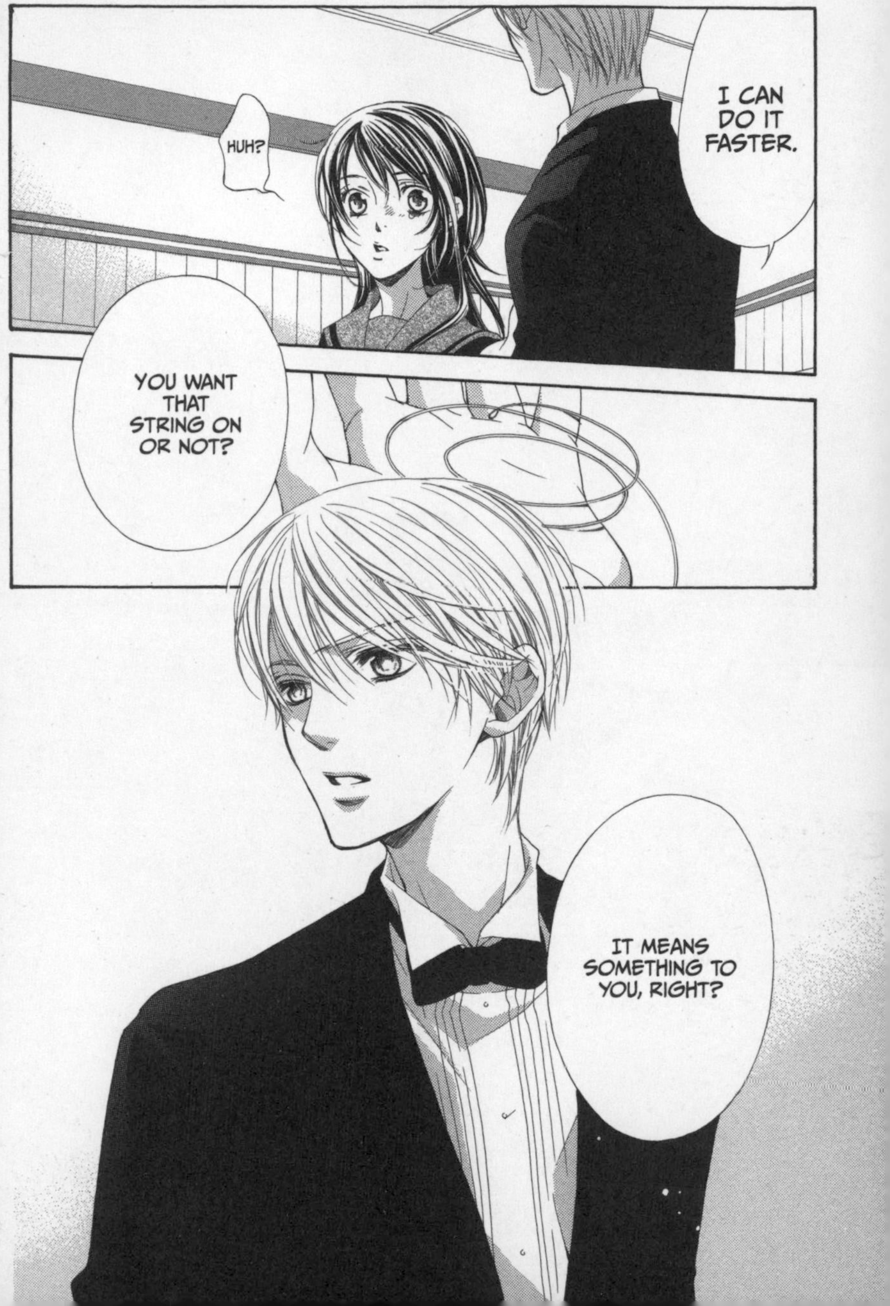
I CAN DO IT FASTER.
HUH?
YOU WANT THAT STRING ON OR NOT?
IT MEANS SOMETHING TO YOU, RIGHT?

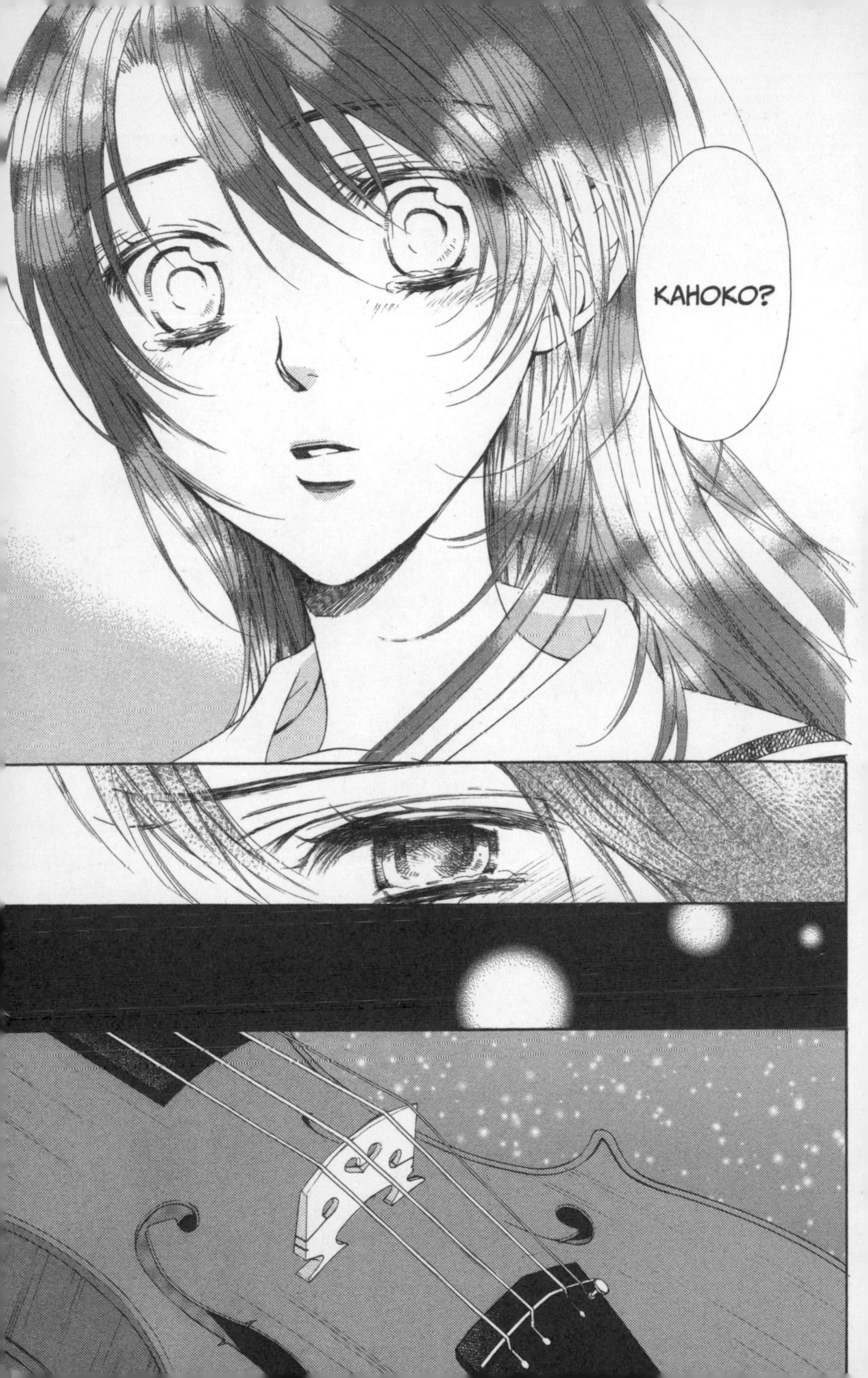
KAHOKO?

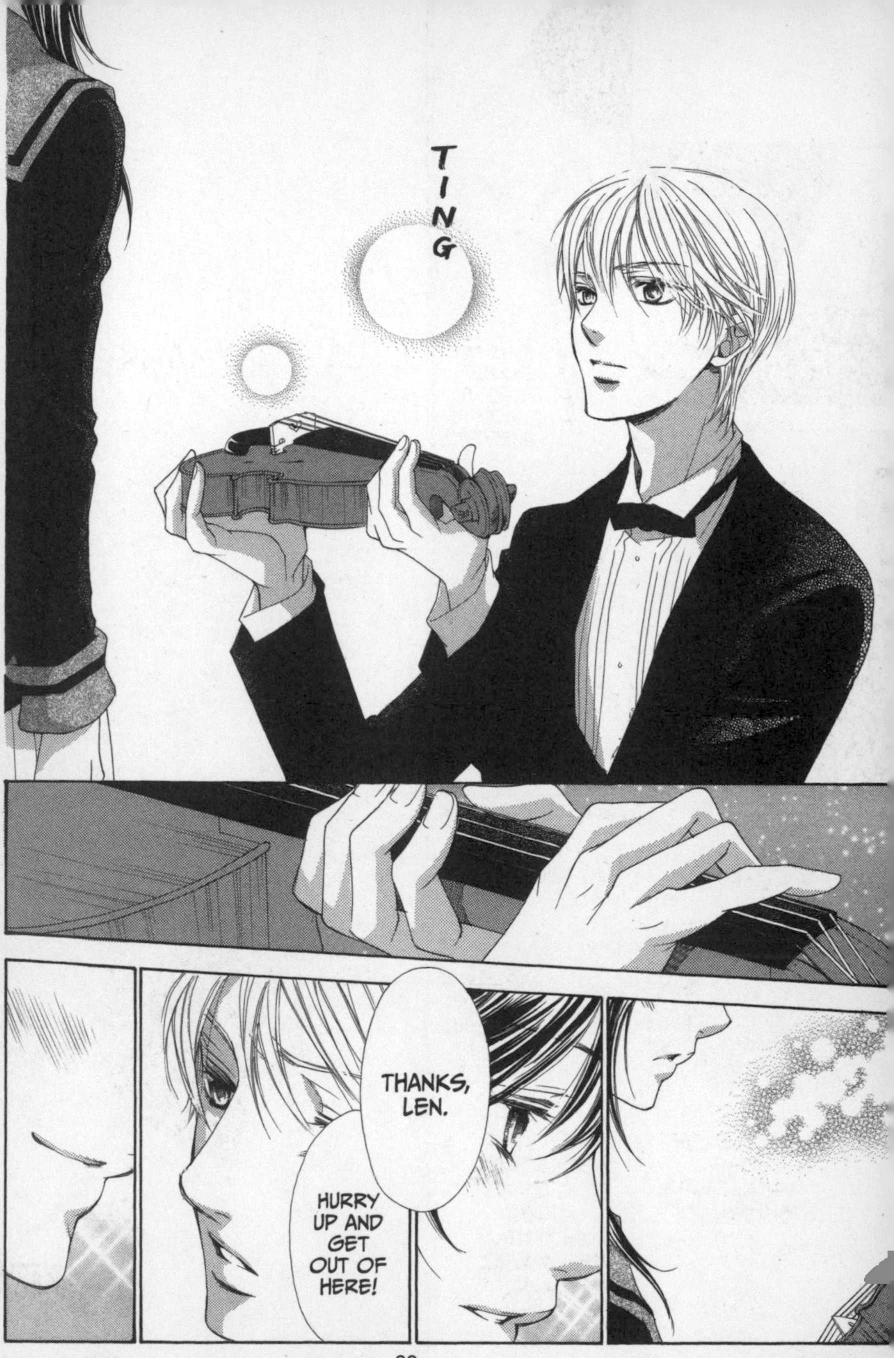
TING
THANKS, LEN.
HURRY UP AND GET OUT OF HERE!

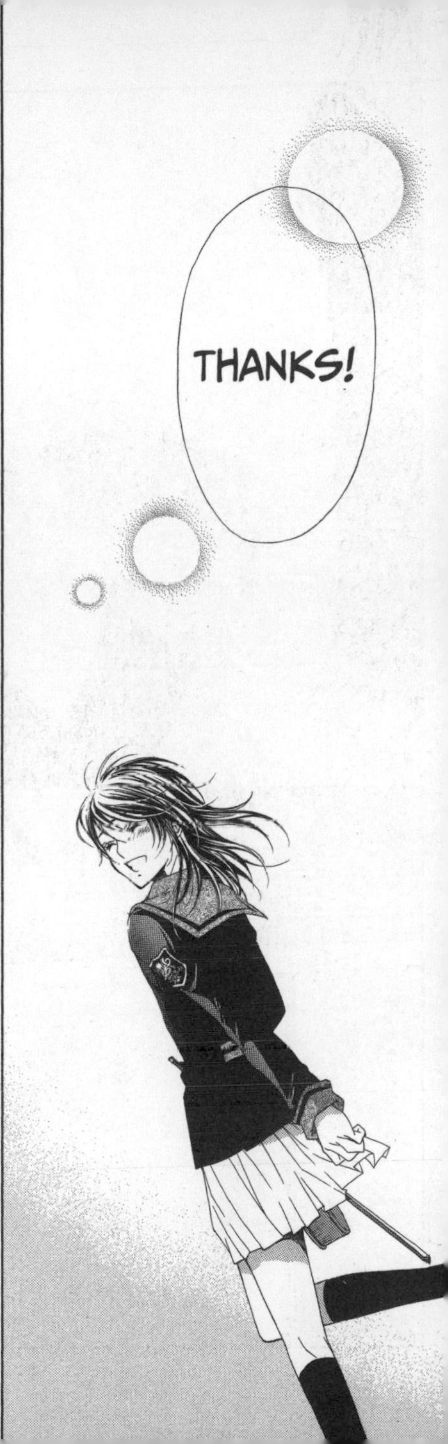
THANKS!

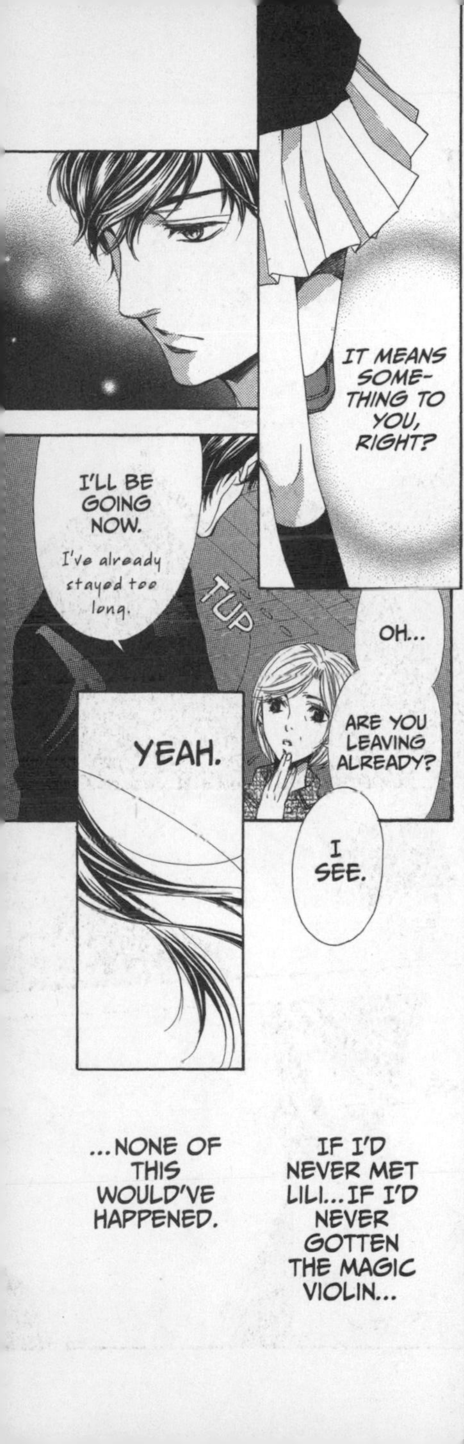
IT MEANS SOME-THING TO YOU, RIGHT?
I'LL BE GOING NOW.
I've already stayed too long.
TUP
OH...
ARE YOU LEAVING ALREADY?
YEAH.
I SEE.
IF I'D NEVER MET LILI...IF I'D NEVER GOTTEN THE MAGIC VIOLIN...
...NONE OF THIS WOULD'VE HAPPENED.

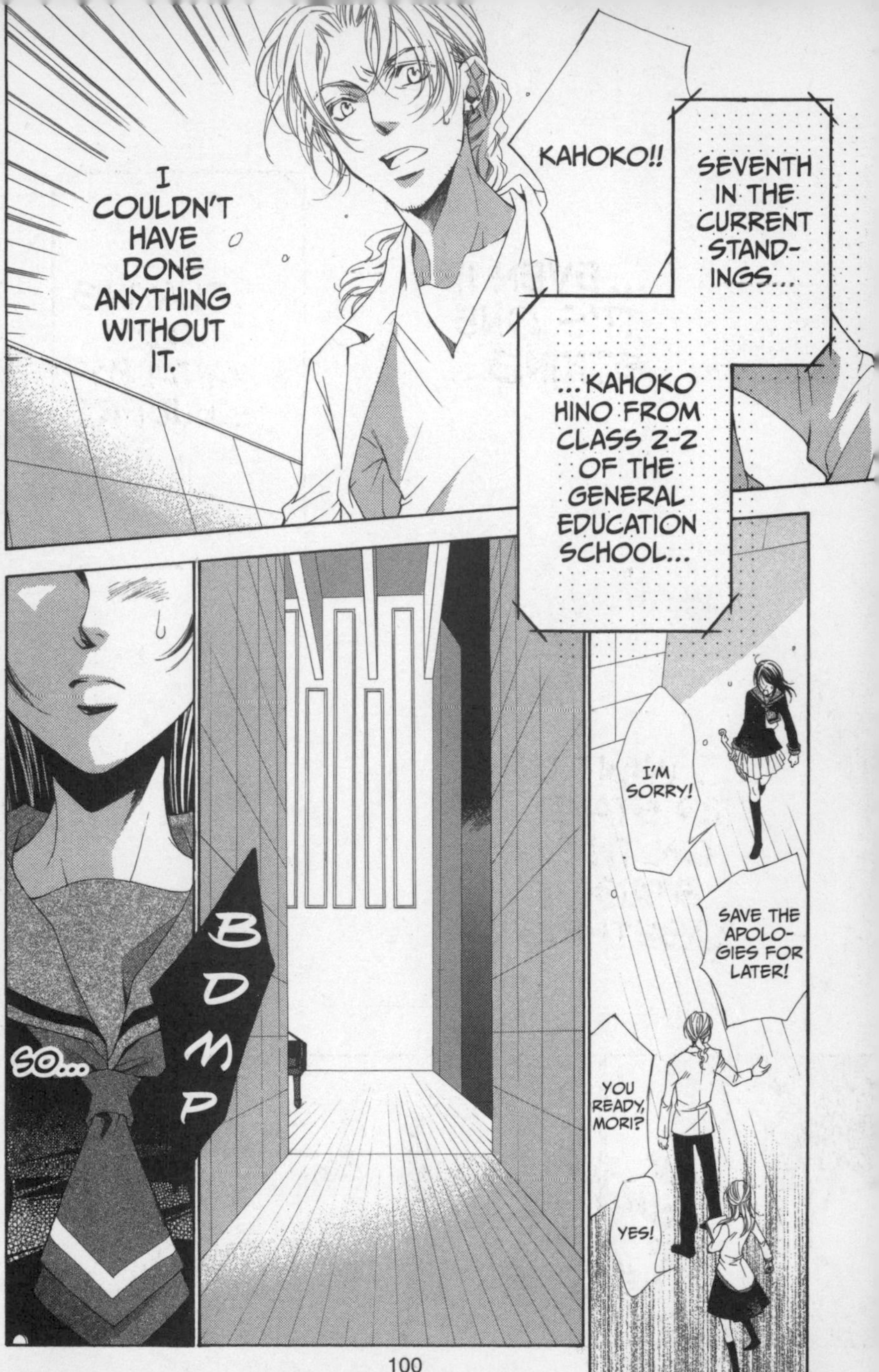
SEVENTH IN THE CURRENT STANDINGS...
...KAHOKO HINO FROM CLASS 2-2 OF THE GENERAL EDUCATION SCHOOL...
KAHOKO!!
I COULDN'T HAVE DONE ANYTHING WITHOUT IT.
I'M SORRY!
SAVE THE APOLOGIES FOR LATER!
YOU READY, MORI?
YES!
BDMP
SO...

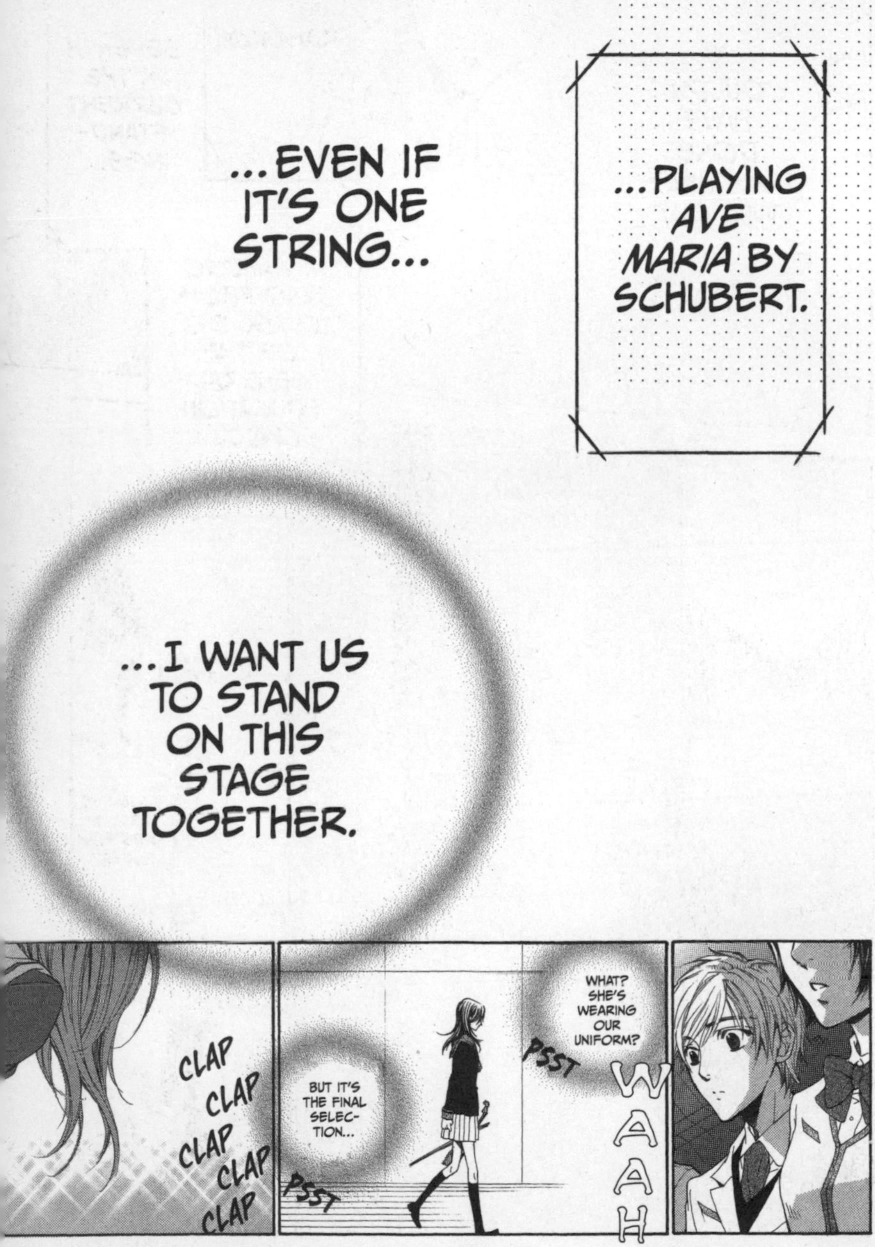
...PLAYING AVE MARIA BY SCHUBERT.
...EVEN IF IT'S ONE STRING...
...I WANT US TO STAND ON THIS STAGE TOGETHER.
WAAH
WHAT? SHE'S WEARING OUR UNIFORM?
PSST
BUT IT'S THE FINAL SELECTION...
PSST
CLAP CLAP CLAP CLAP CLAP

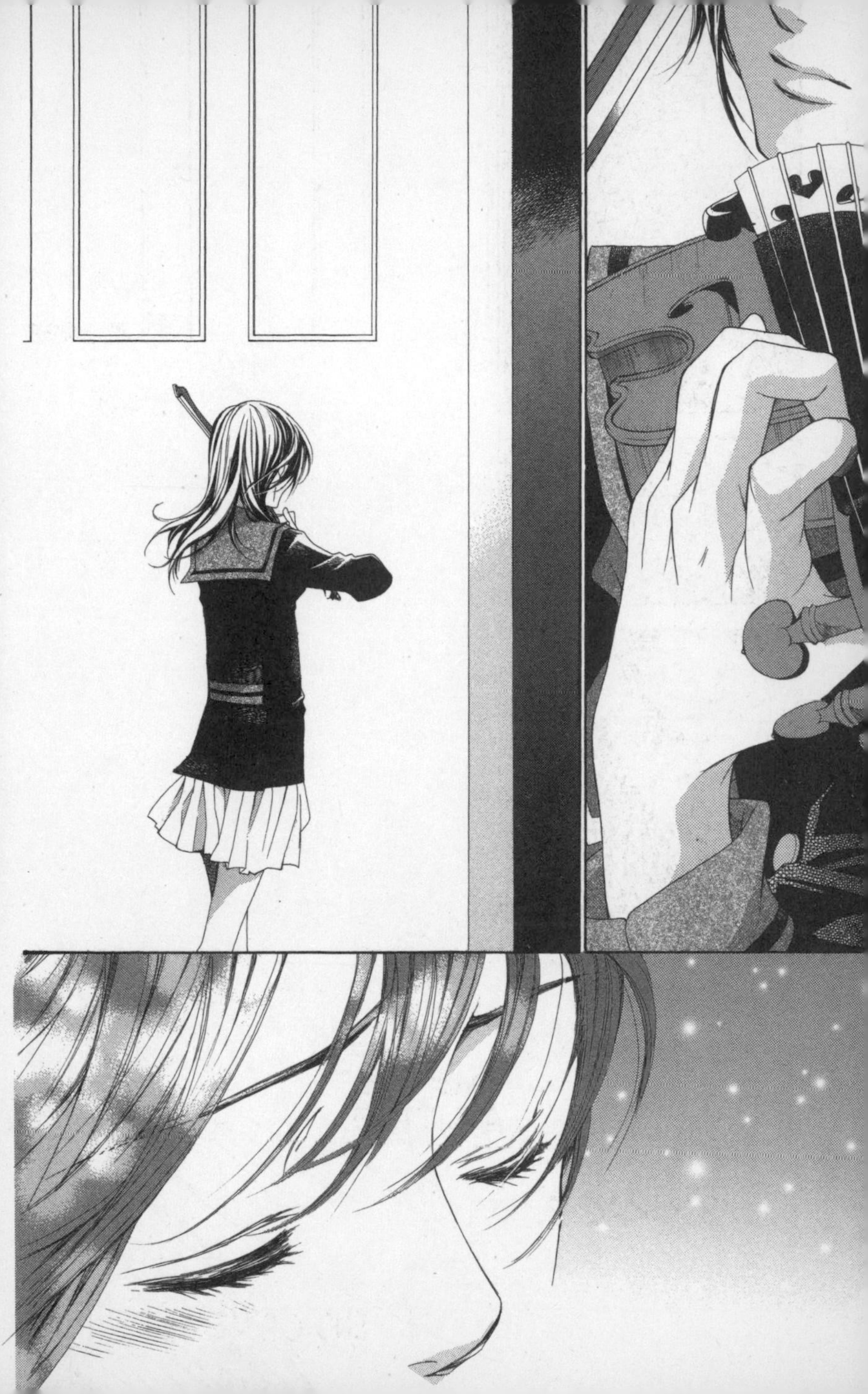

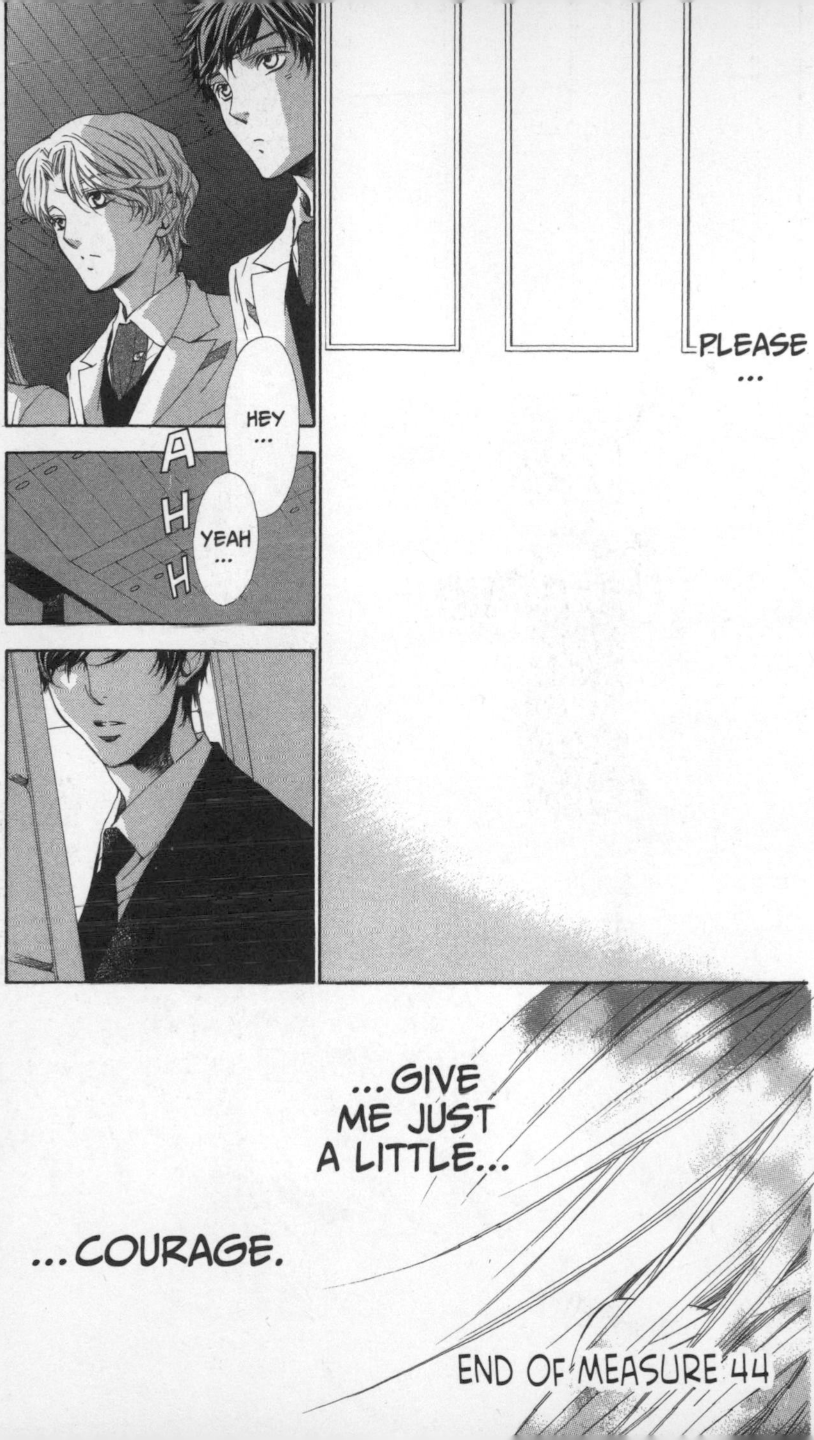
PLEASE ...
HEY ...
AHH
YEAH ...
...GIVE ME JUST A LITTLE...
...COURAGE.
END OF MEASURE 44

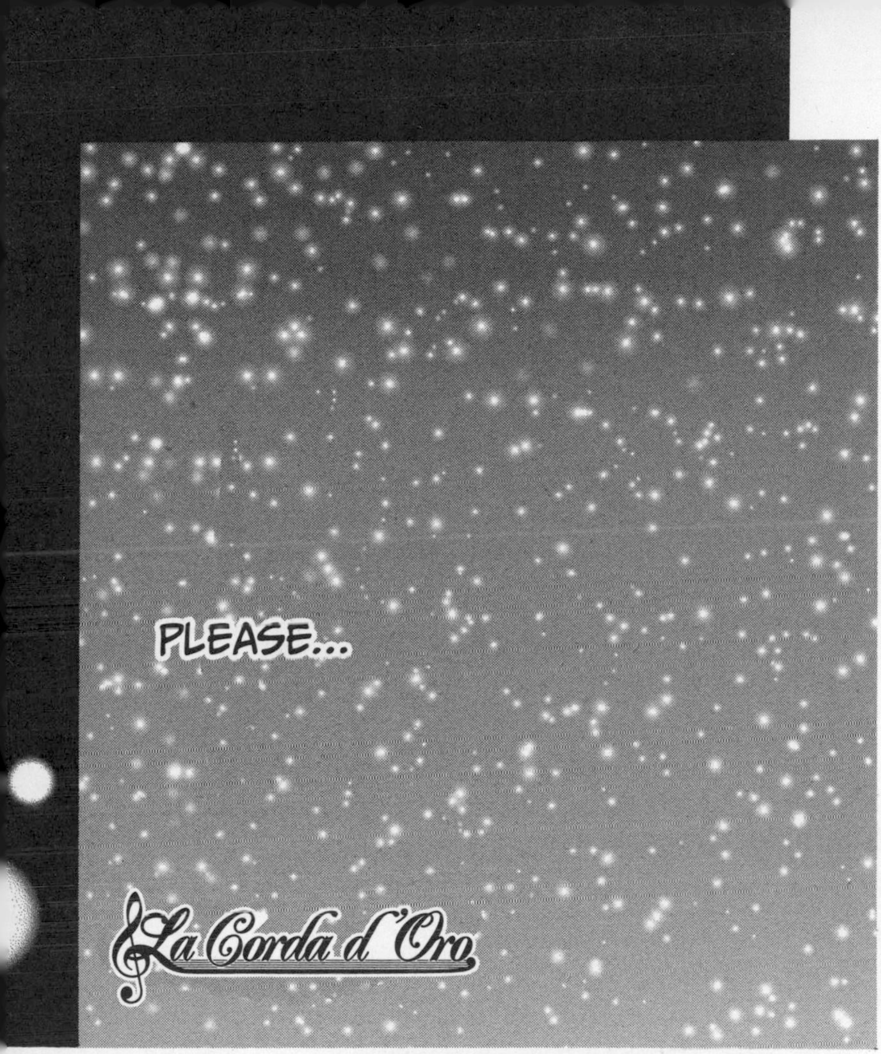

Daily Happenings (37)

This is connected to my story in (34) about the alarm clock...I always set my alarm early, determined to wake up at the crack of dawn. (In fact, I set two or three alarms, including my cell.) But of course I oversleep anyway. My little sister let me have it after suffering through my early alarms:

"You have too much faith in yourself!"

I'm sorry, I swear...

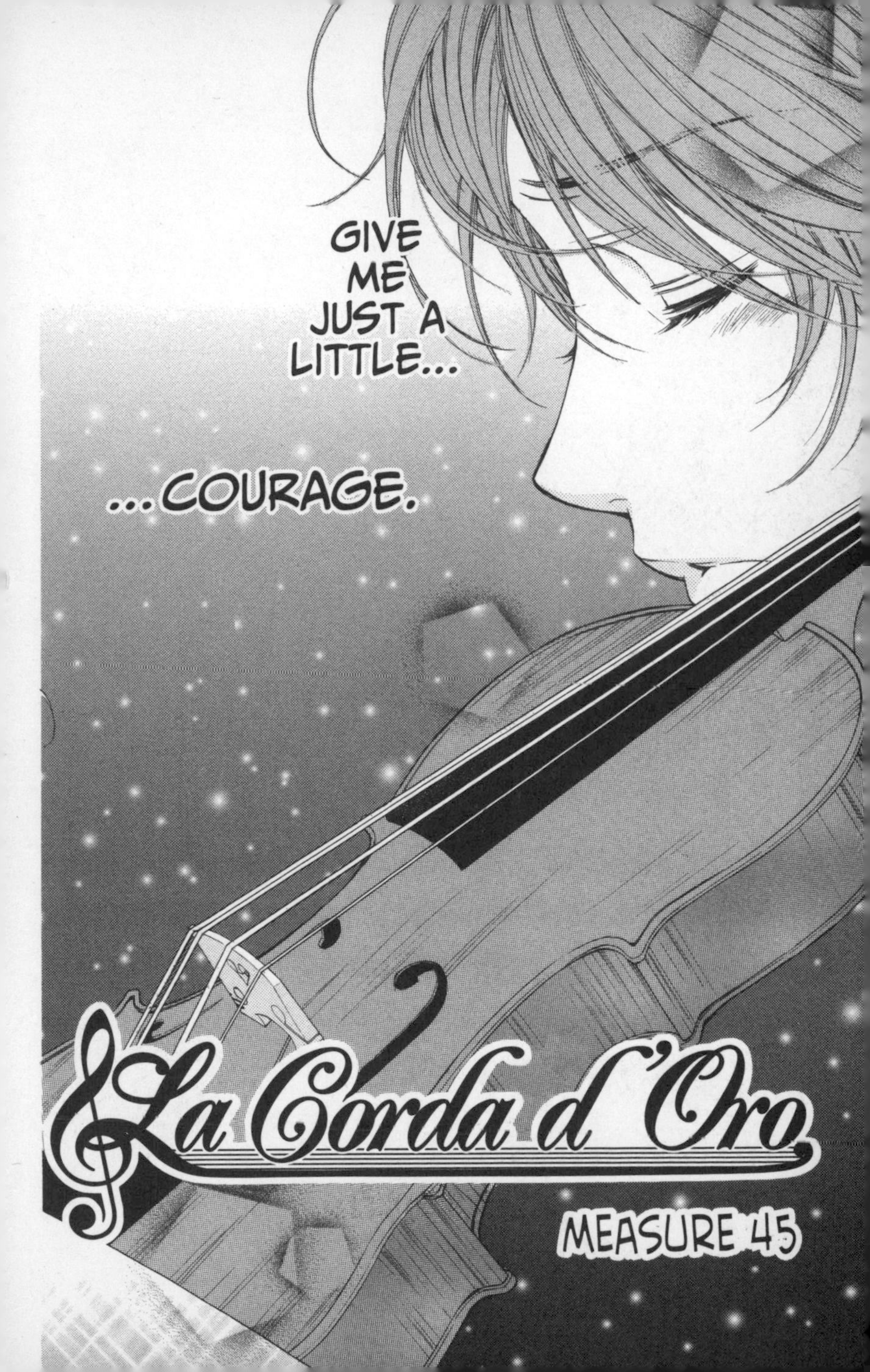
GIVE ME JUST A LITTLE...
...COURAGE.
La Corda d'Oro
MEASURE 45

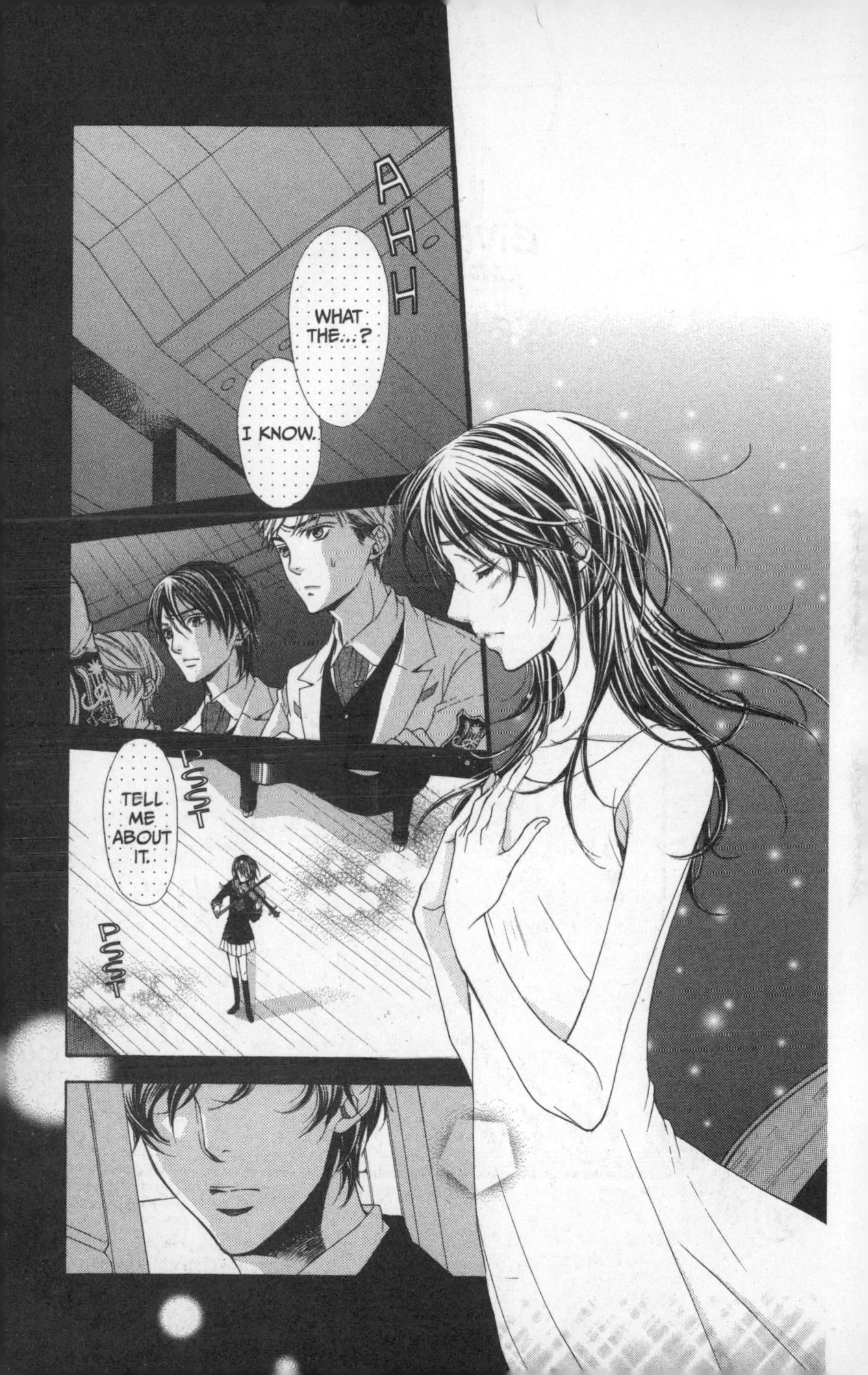
AHHH
WHAT THE...?
I KNOW.
PSST
TELL ME ABOUT IT.
PSST

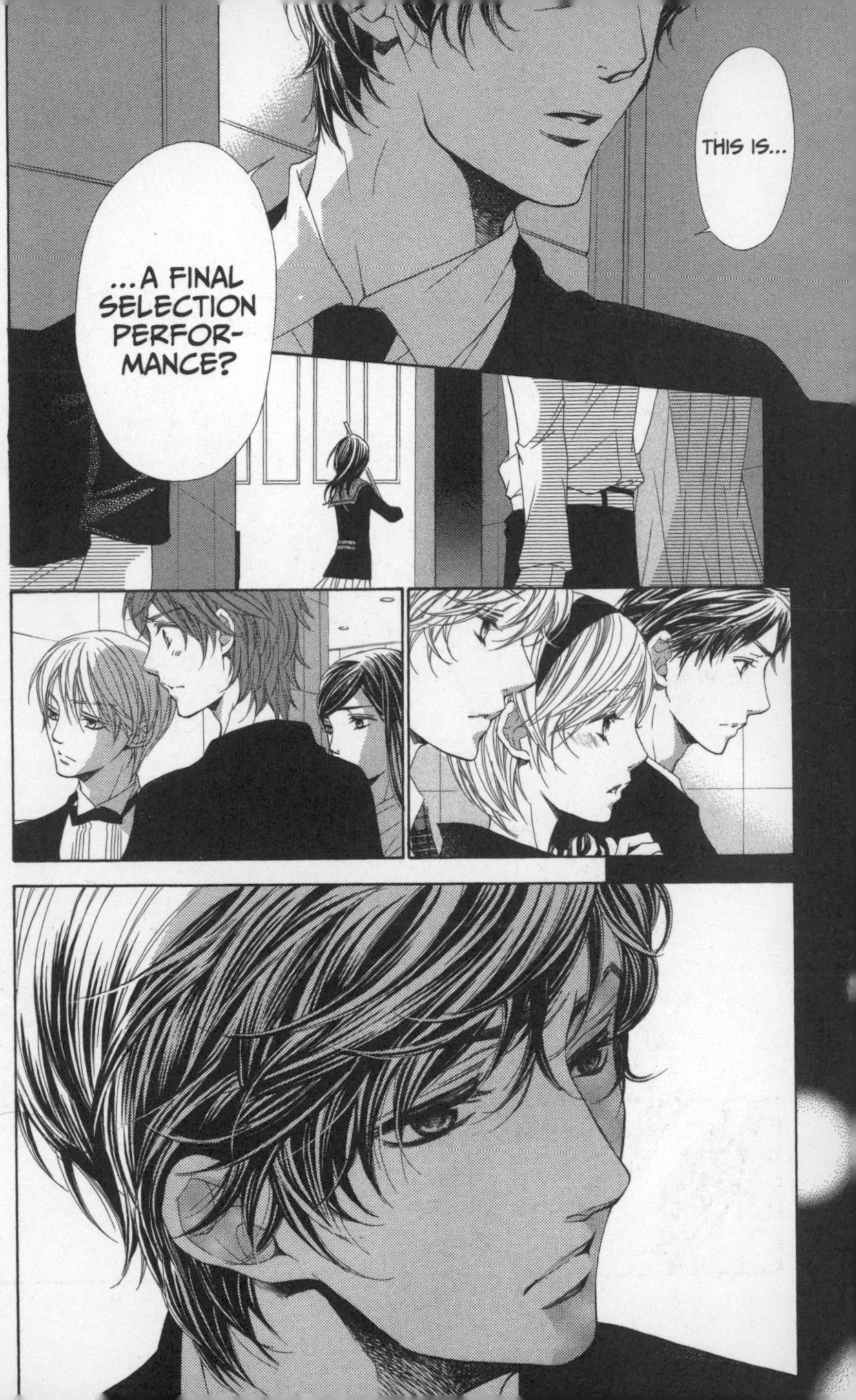
THIS IS...
...A FINAL SELECTION PERFORMANCE?

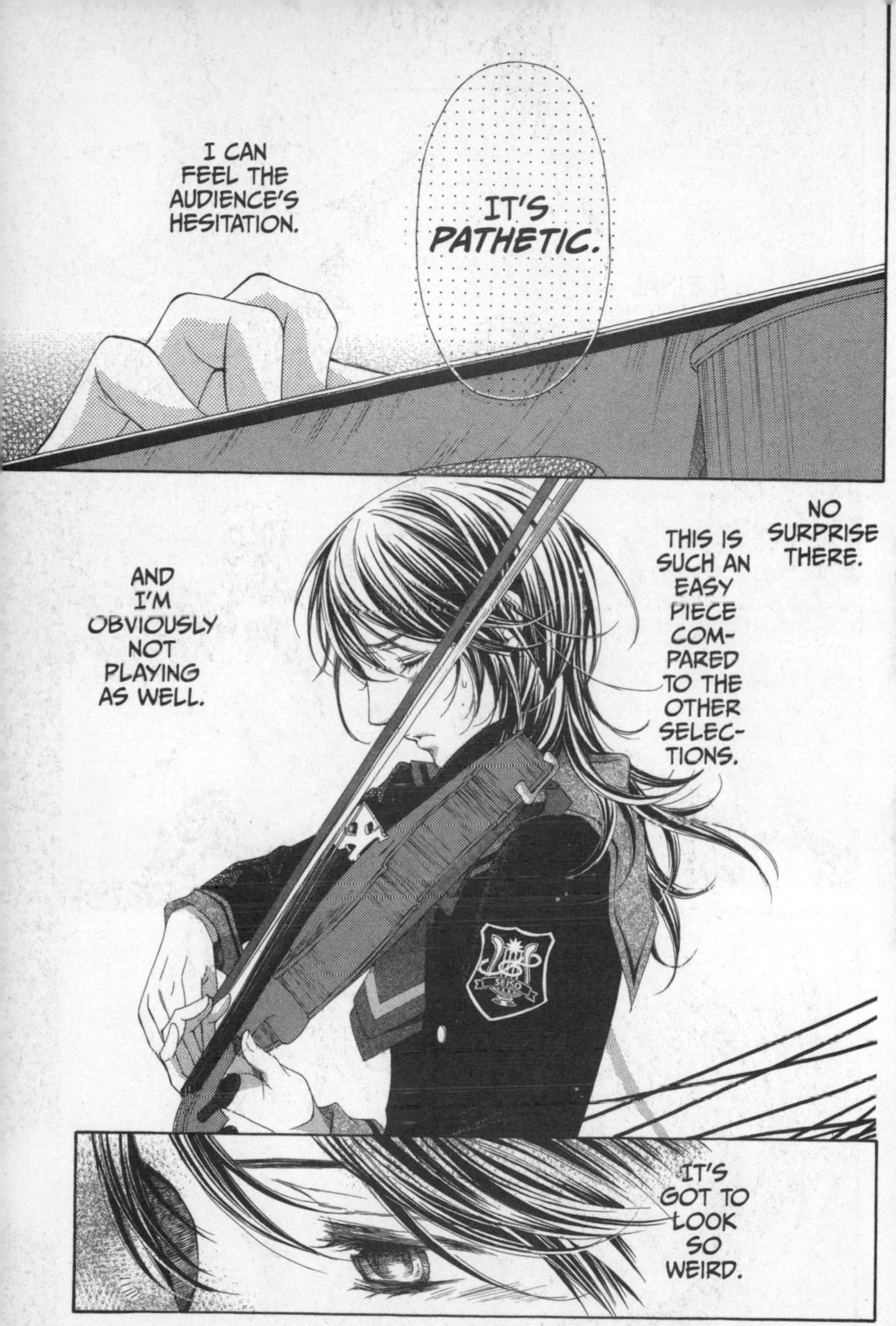
IT'S PATHETIC.
I CAN FEEL THE AUDIENCE'S HESITATION.
NO SURPRISE THERE.
THIS IS SUCH AN EASY PIECE COMPARED TO THE OTHER SELECTIONS.
AND I'M OBVIOUSLY NOT PLAYING AS WELL.
IT'S GOT TO LOOK SO WEIRD.

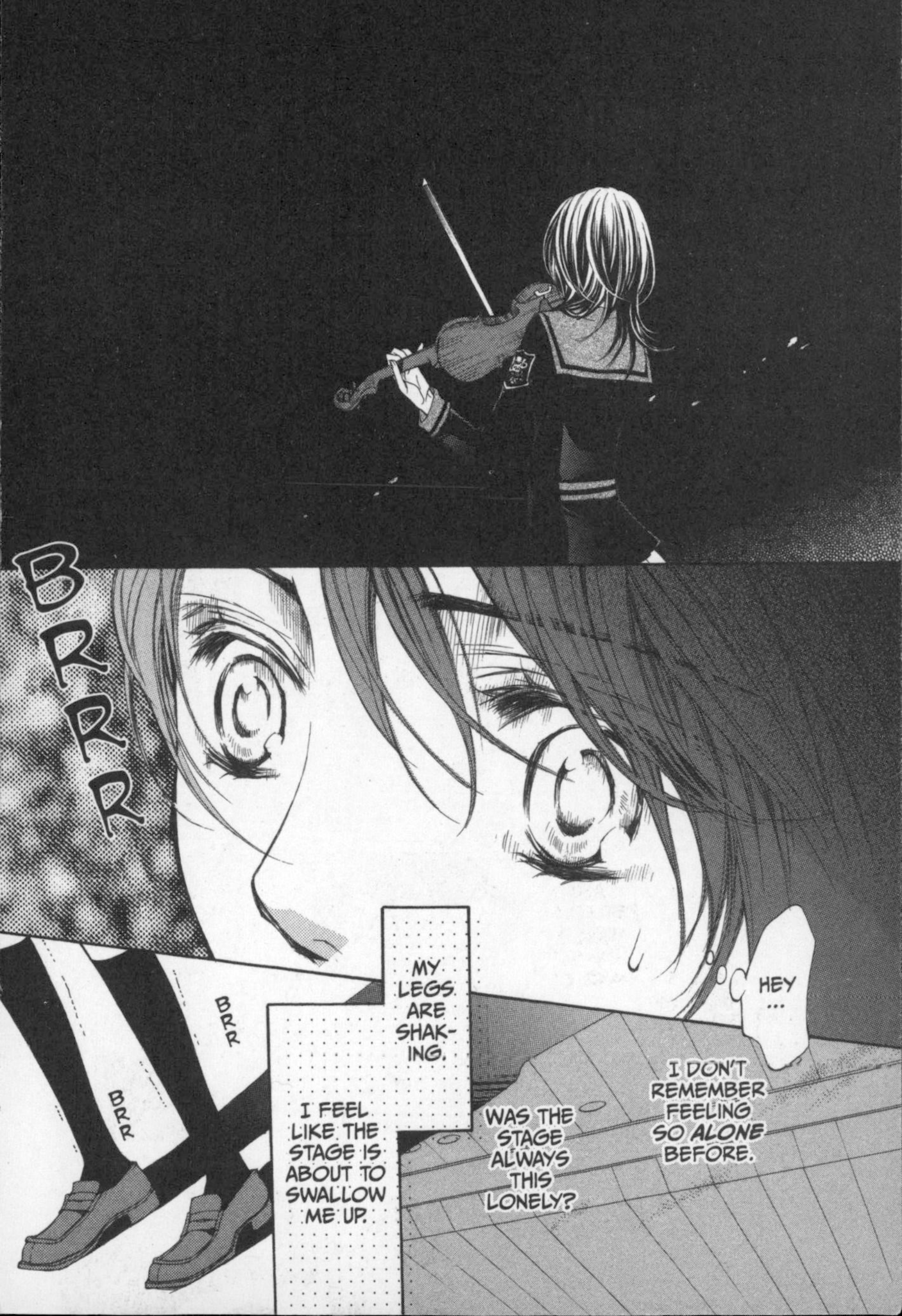
BRRRR
HEY ...
I DON'T REMEMBER FEELING SO *ALONE* BEFORE.
WAS THE STAGE ALWAYS THIS LONELY?
MY LEGS ARE SHAK-ING.
I FEEL LIKE THE STAGE IS ABOUT TO SWALLOW ME UP.
BRR
BRR

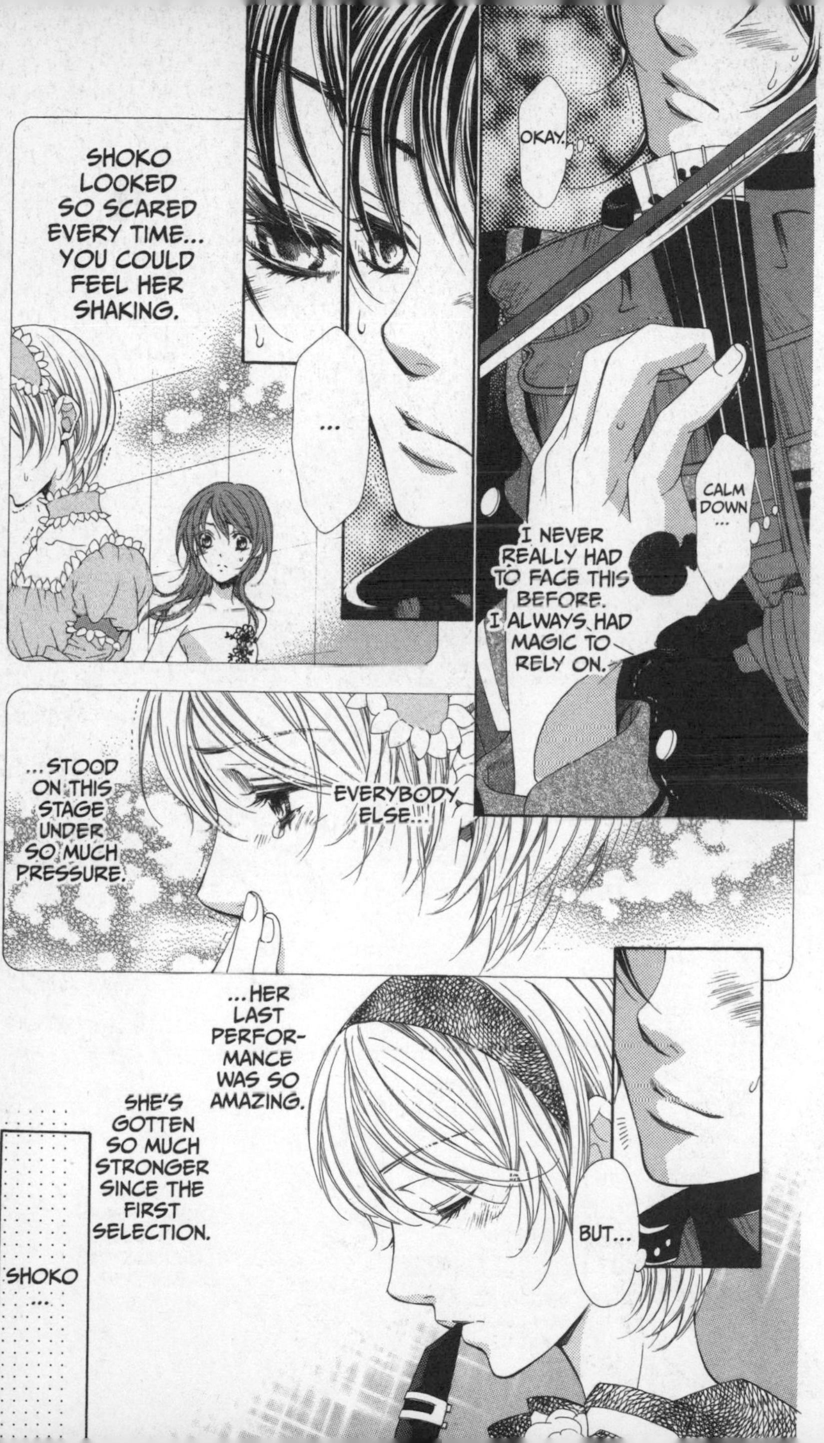
OKAY.
CALM DOWN...
I NEVER REALLY HAD TO FACE THIS BEFORE. I ALWAYS HAD MAGIC TO RELY ON.
...
SHOKO LOOKED SO SCARED EVERY TIME... YOU COULD FEEL HER SHAKING.
EVERYBODY ELSE...
...STOOD ON THIS STAGE UNDER SO MUCH PRESSURE.
BUT...
...HER LAST PERFORMANCE WAS SO AMAZING.
SHE'S GOTTEN SO MUCH STRONGER SINCE THE FIRST SELECTION.
SHOKO...

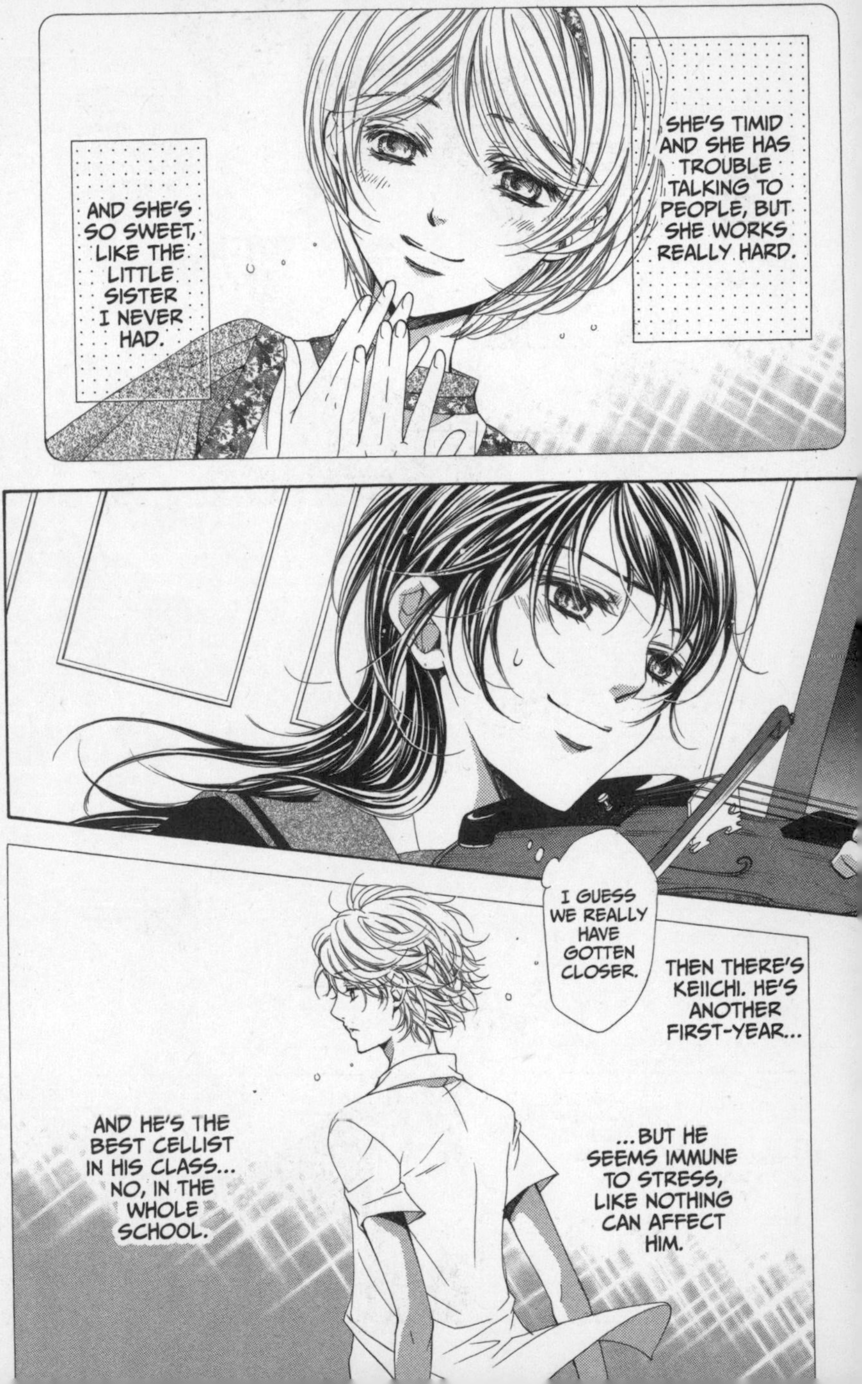
SHE'S TIMID AND SHE HAS TROUBLE TALKING TO PEOPLE, BUT SHE WORKS REALLY HARD.
AND SHE'S SO SWEET, LIKE THE LITTLE SISTER I NEVER HAD.
I GUESS WE REALLY HAVE GOTTEN CLOSER.
THEN THERE'S KEIICHI. HE'S ANOTHER FIRST-YEAR...
AND HE'S THE BEST CELLIST IN HIS CLASS... NO, IN THE WHOLE SCHOOL.
...BUT HE SEEMS IMMUNE TO STRESS, LIKE NOTHING CAN AFFECT HIM.

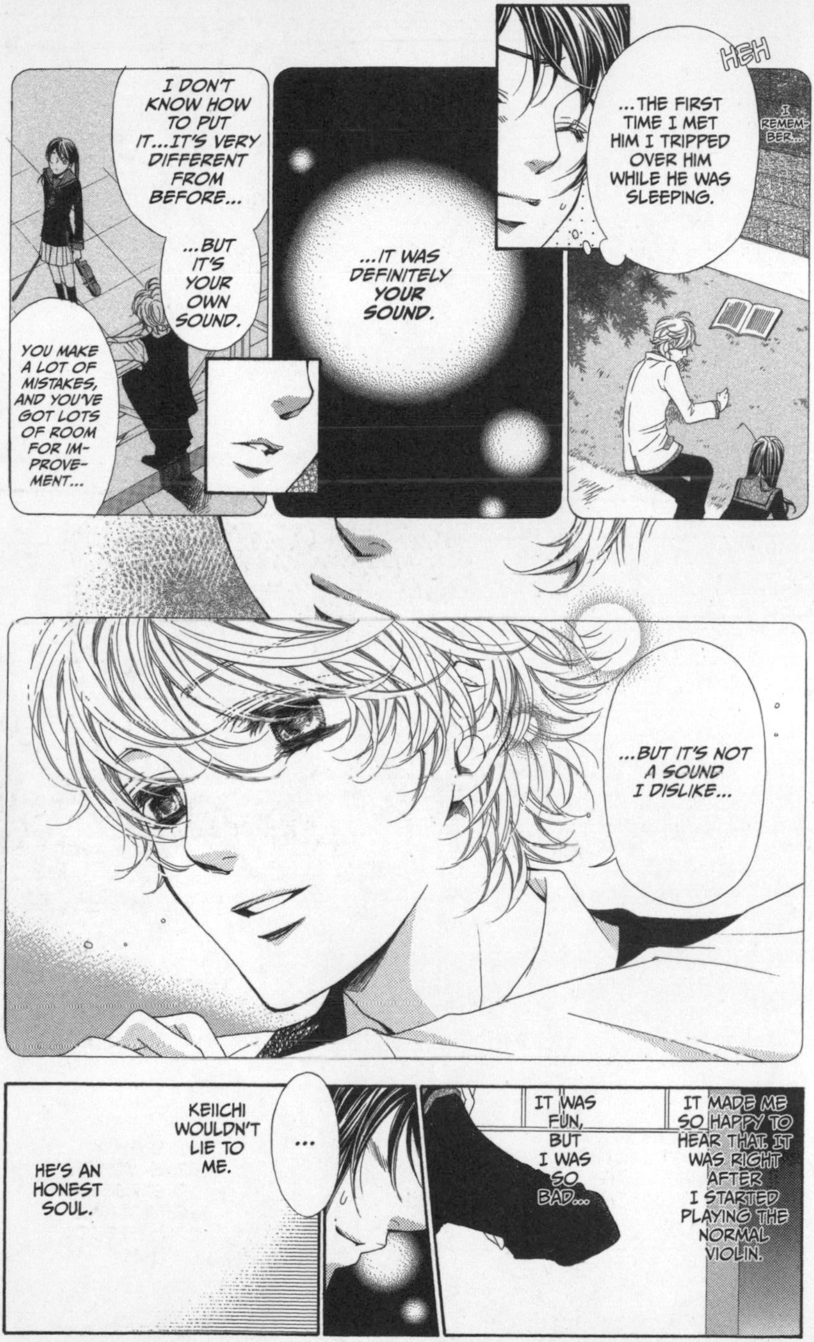
HEH
I REMEMBER...
...THE FIRST TIME I MET HIM I TRIPPED OVER HIM WHILE HE WAS SLEEPING.
...IT WAS DEFINITELY YOUR SOUND.
I DON'T KNOW HOW TO PUT IT...IT'S VERY DIFFERENT FROM BEFORE...
...BUT IT'S YOUR OWN SOUND.
YOU MAKE A LOT OF MISTAKES, AND YOU'VE GOT LOTS OF ROOM FOR IMPROVEMENT...
...BUT IT'S NOT A SOUND I DISLIKE...
IT MADE ME SO HAPPY TO HEAR THAT. IT WAS RIGHT AFTER I STARTED PLAYING THE NORMAL VIOLIN.
IT WAS FUN, BUT I WAS SO BAD...
...
KEIICHI WOULDN'T LIE TO ME.
HE'S AN HONEST SOUL.

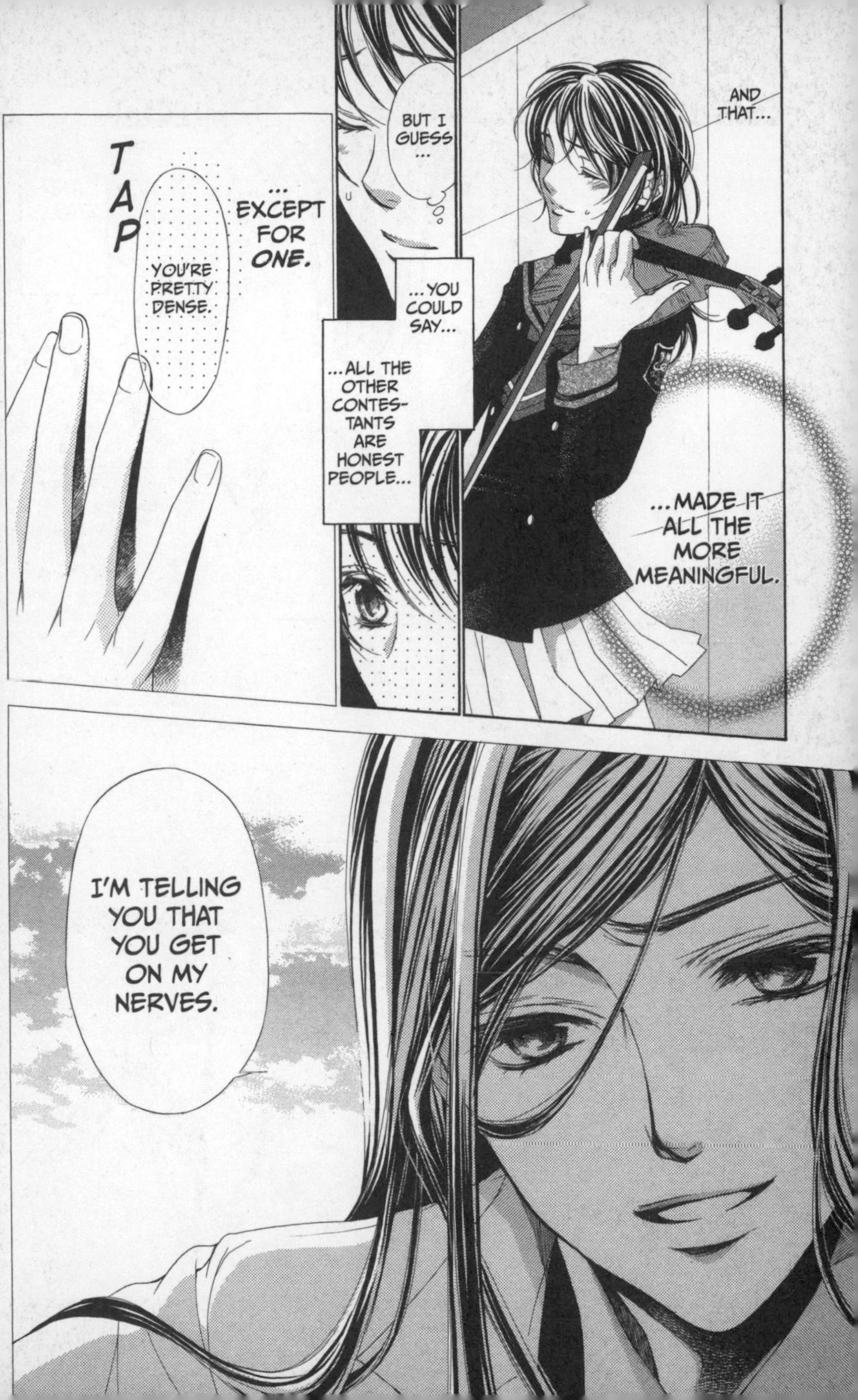
AND THAT...
...MADE IT ALL THE MORE MEANINGFUL.
BUT I GUESS...
...YOU COULD SAY...
...ALL THE OTHER CONTESTANTS ARE HONEST PEOPLE...
...EXCEPT FOR ONE.
TAP
YOU'RE PRETTY DENSE.
I'M TELLING YOU THAT YOU GET ON MY NERVES.

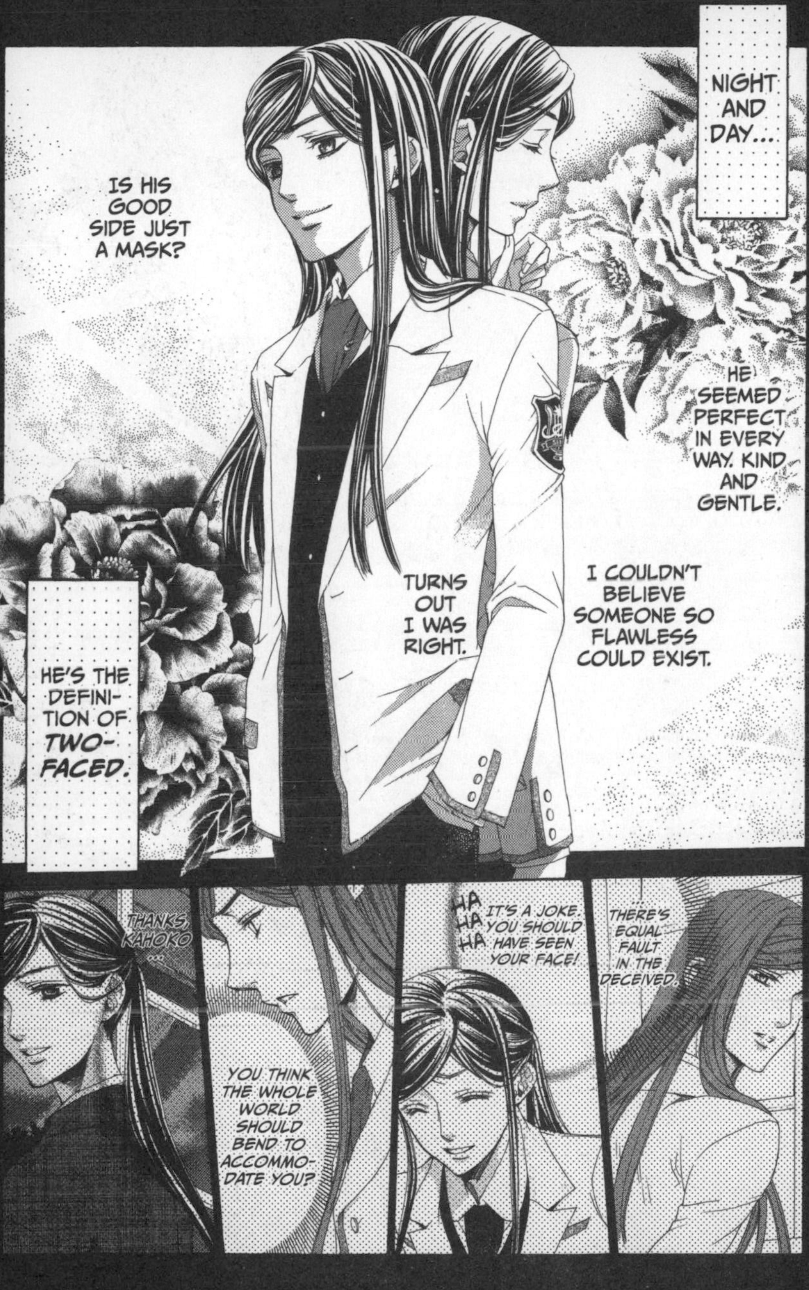
NIGHT AND DAY...
HE SEEMED PERFECT IN EVERY WAY. KIND AND GENTLE.
I COULDN'T BELIEVE SOMEONE SO FLAWLESS COULD EXIST.
IS HIS GOOD SIDE JUST A MASK?
TURNS OUT I WAS RIGHT.
HE'S THE DEFINITION OF *TWO-FACED.*
...THERE'S EQUAL FAULT IN THE DECEIVED.
HA HA HA
IT'S A JOKE. YOU SHOULD HAVE SEEN YOUR FACE!
YOU THINK THE WHOLE WORLD SHOULD BEND TO ACCOMMODATE YOU?
THANKS, KAHOKO...

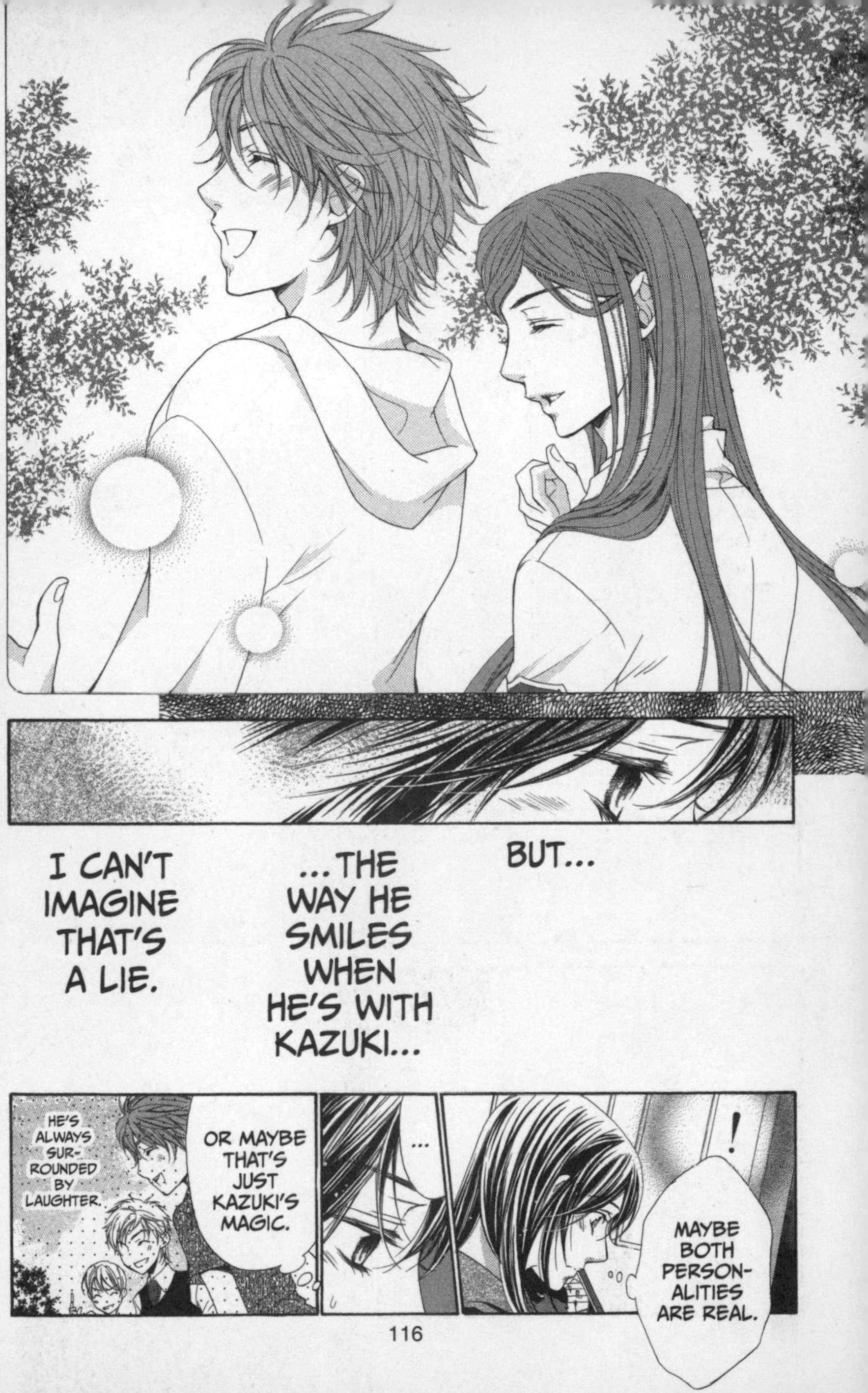
BUT...
...THE WAY HE SMILES WHEN HE'S WITH KAZUKI...
I CAN'T IMAGINE THAT'S A LIE.
!
MAYBE BOTH PERSON-ALITIES ARE REAL.
...
HE'S ALWAYS SUR-ROUNDED BY LAUGHTER.
OR MAYBE THAT'S JUST KAZUKI'S MAGIC.

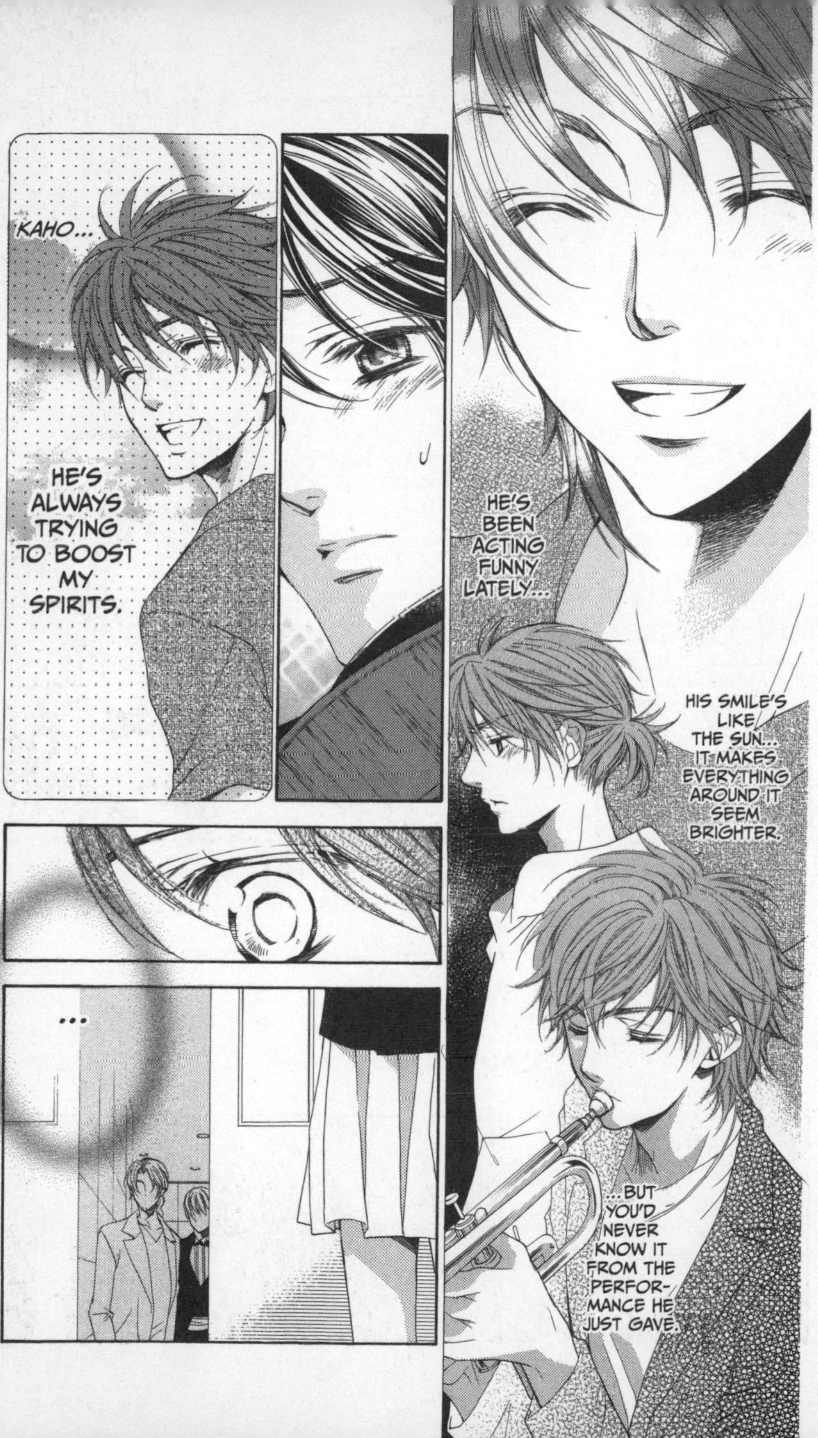
HE'S BEEN ACTING FUNNY LATELY...
HIS SMILE'S LIKE THE SUN... IT MAKES EVERYTHING AROUND IT SEEM BRIGHTER.
...BUT YOU'D NEVER KNOW IT FROM THE PERFORMANCE HE JUST GAVE.
KAHO...
HE'S ALWAYS TRYING TO BOOST MY SPIRITS.
...

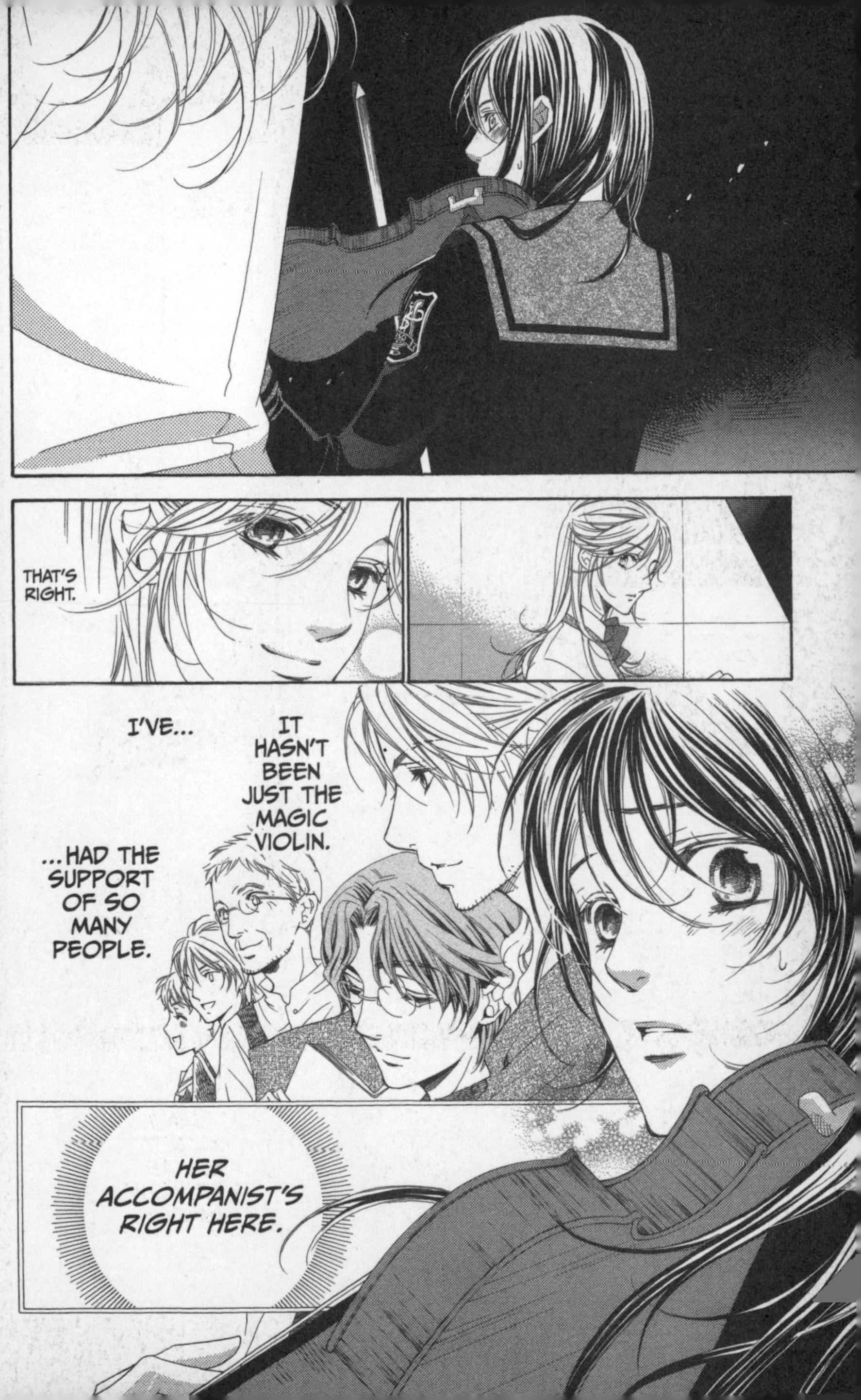
THAT'S RIGHT.
IT HASN'T BEEN JUST THE MAGIC VIOLIN.
I'VE...
...HAD THE SUPPORT OF SO MANY PEOPLE.
HER ACCOMPANIST'S RIGHT HERE.

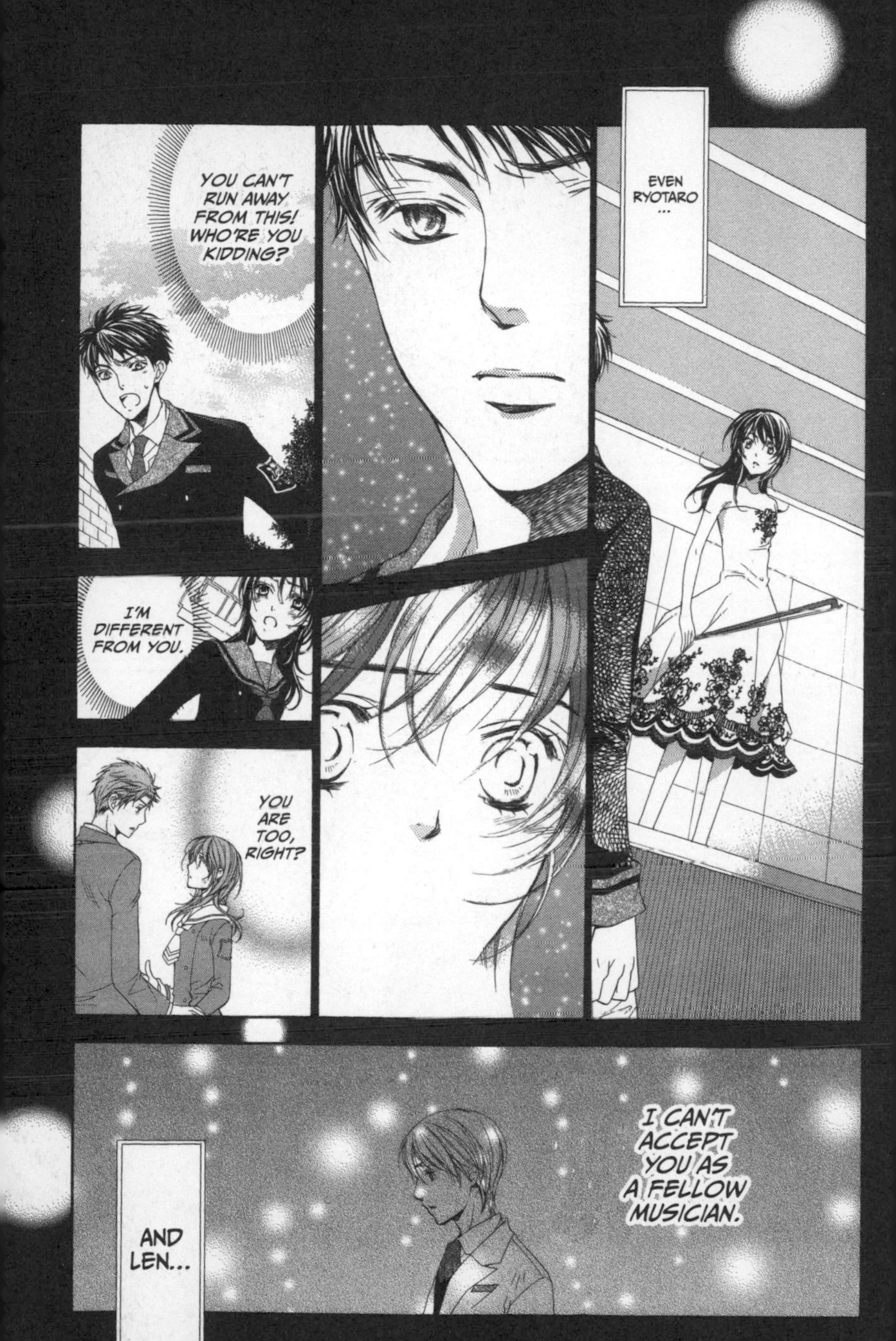

EVEN RYOTARO ...
YOU CAN'T RUN AWAY FROM THIS! WHO'RE YOU KIDDING?
I'M DIFFERENT FROM YOU.
YOU ARE TOO, RIGHT?
I CAN'T ACCEPT YOU AS A FELLOW MUSICIAN.
AND LEN...

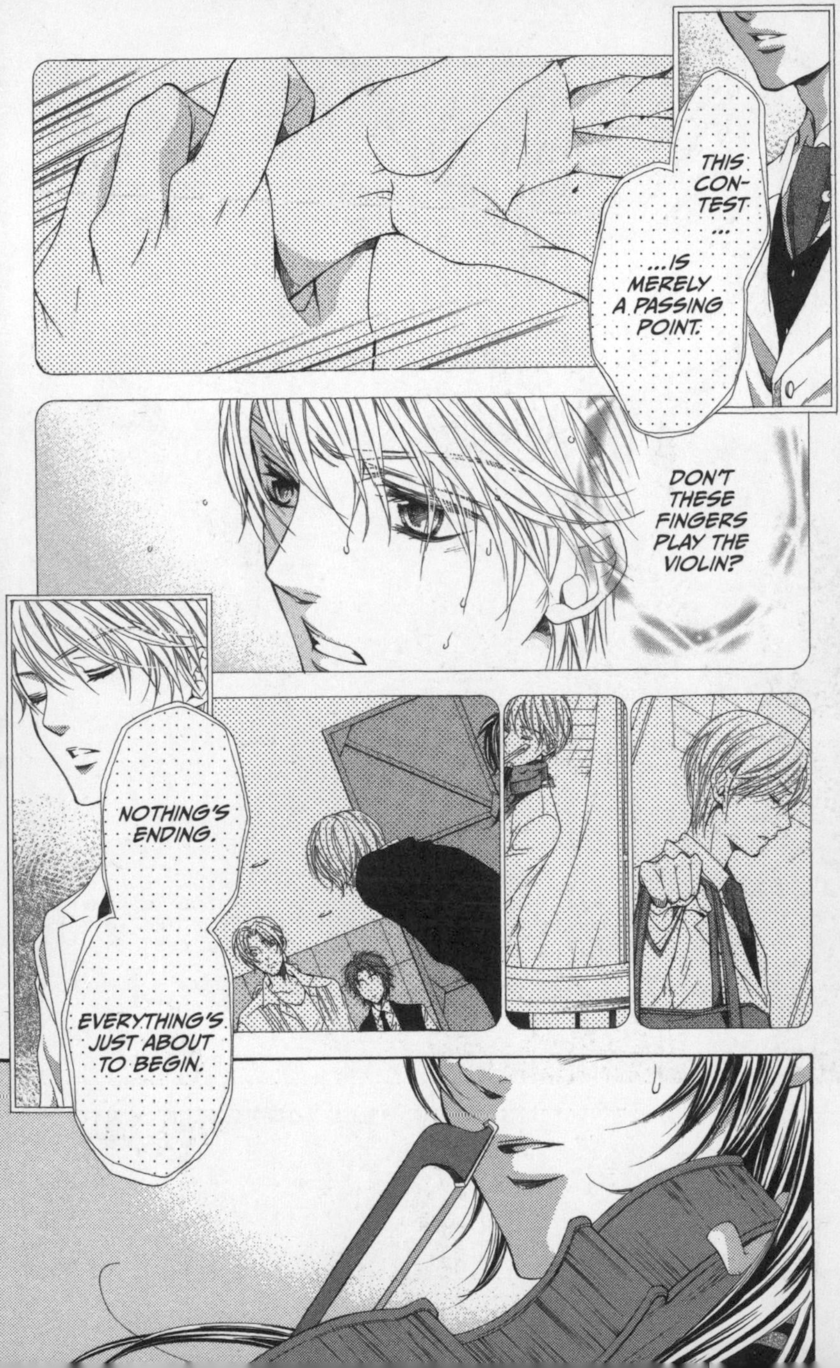
THIS CONTEST ...
...IS MERELY A PASSING POINT.
DON'T THESE FINGERS PLAY THE VIOLIN?
NOTHING'S ENDING.
EVERYTHING'S JUST ABOUT TO BEGIN.

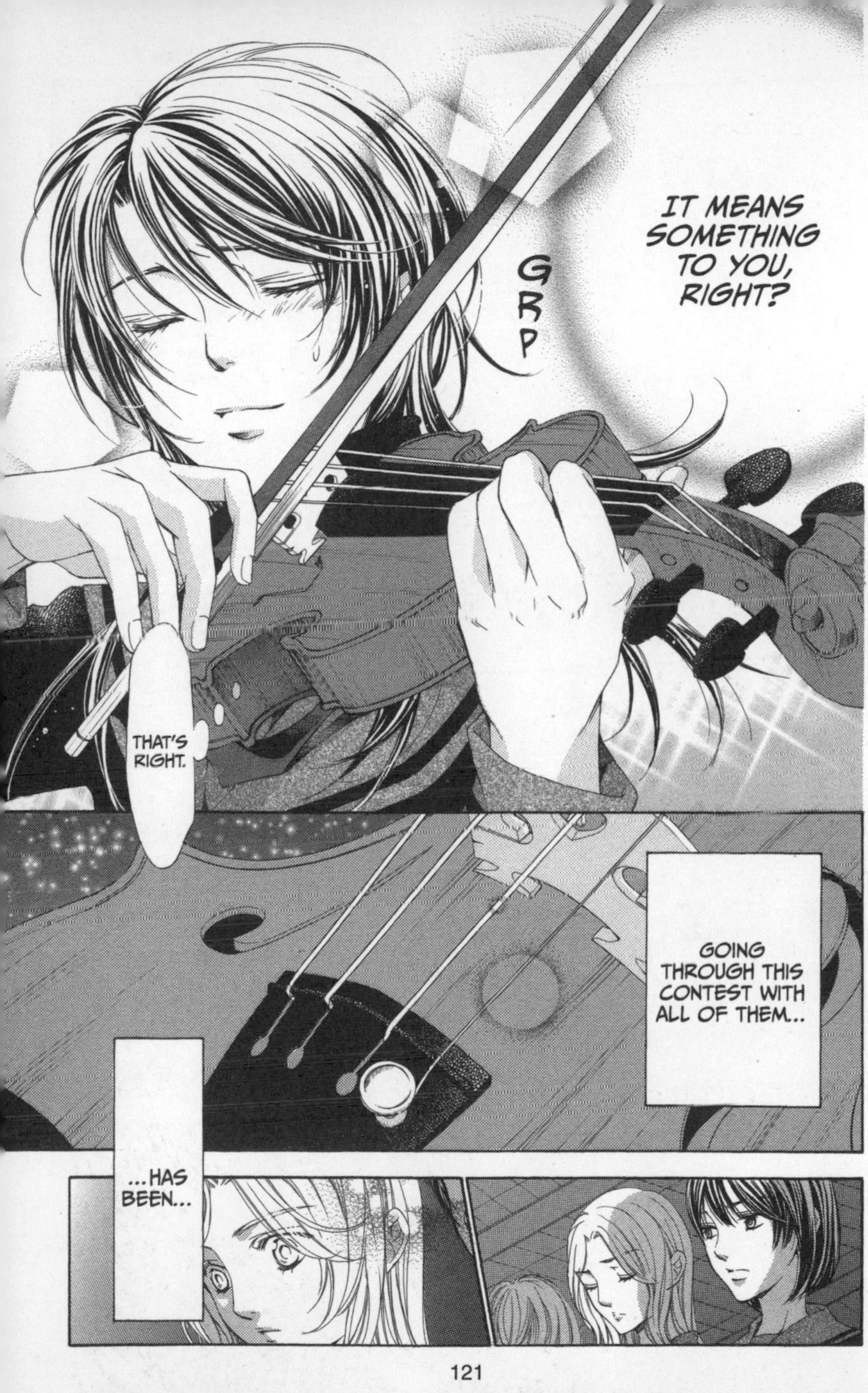
IT MEANS SOMETHING TO YOU, RIGHT?
GRP
THAT'S RIGHT.
GOING THROUGH THIS CONTEST WITH ALL OF THEM...
...HAS BEEN...

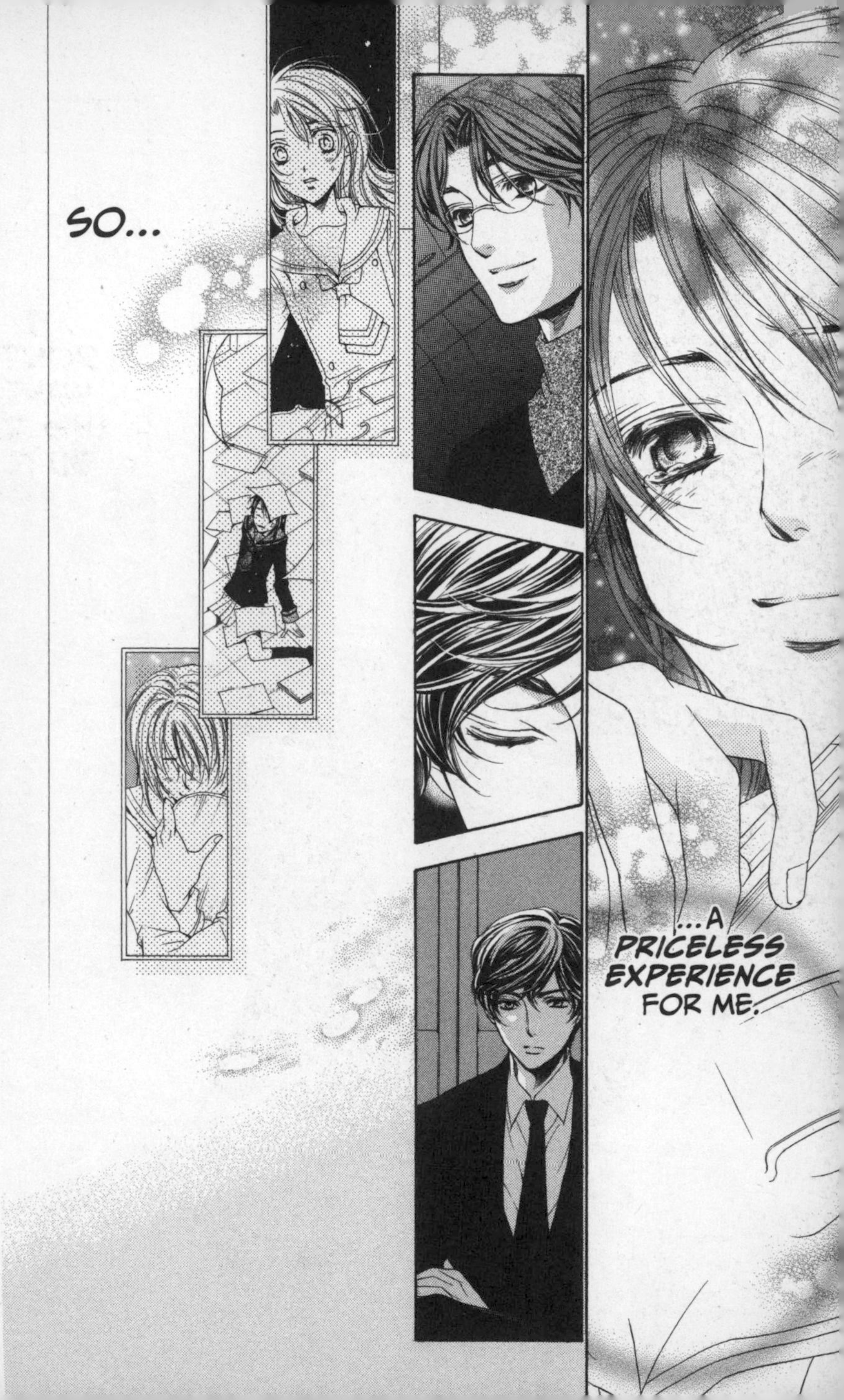
SO...
...A PRICELESS EXPERIENCE FOR ME.

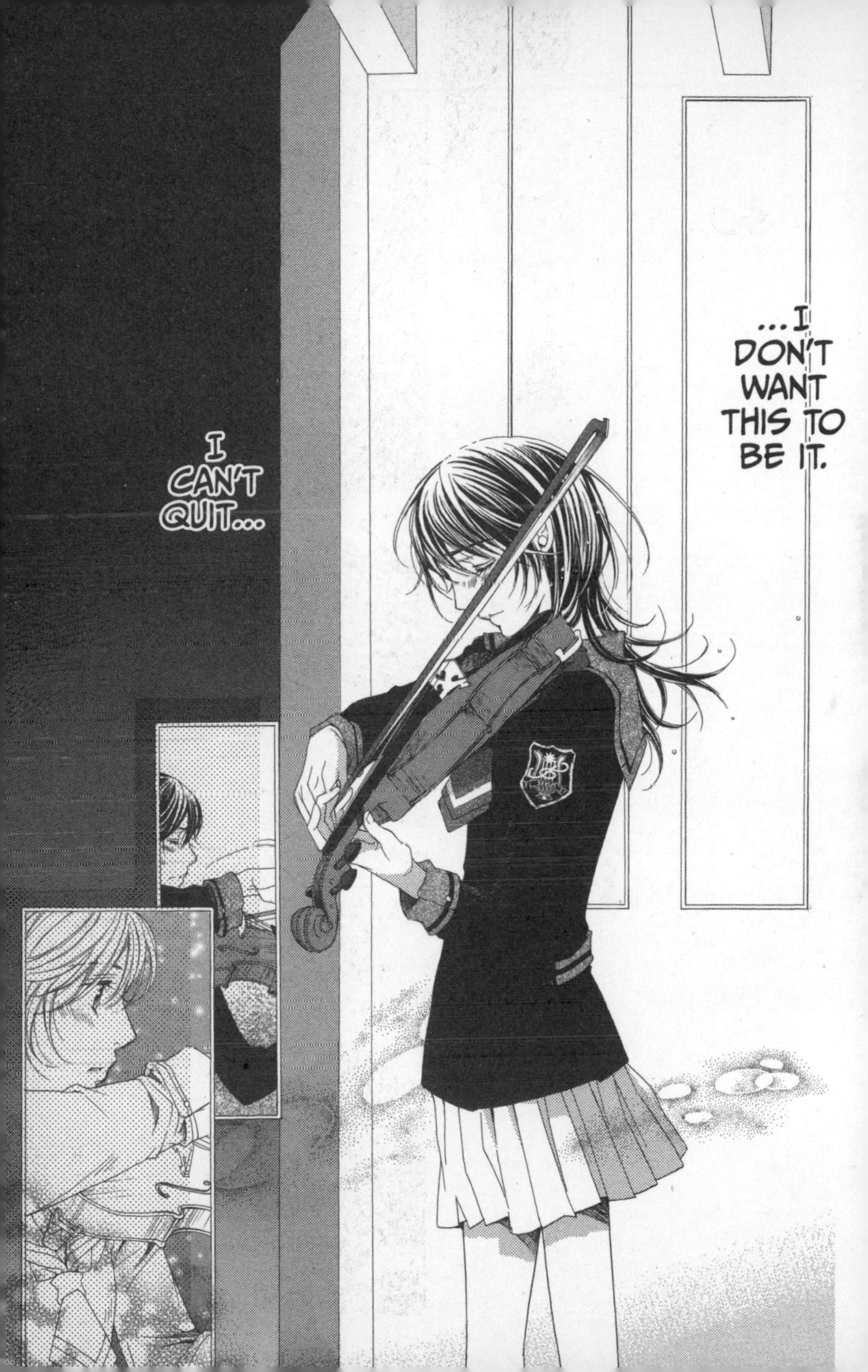
...I DON'T WANT THIS TO BE IT.
I CAN'T QUIT...

...FOR LOVE
OF THE VIOLIN.

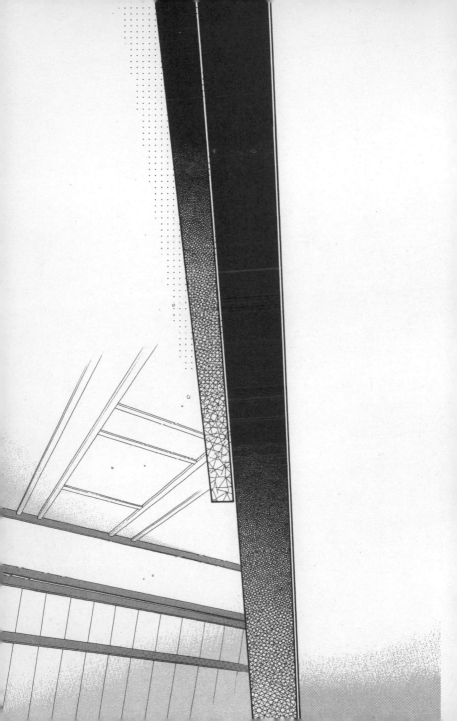

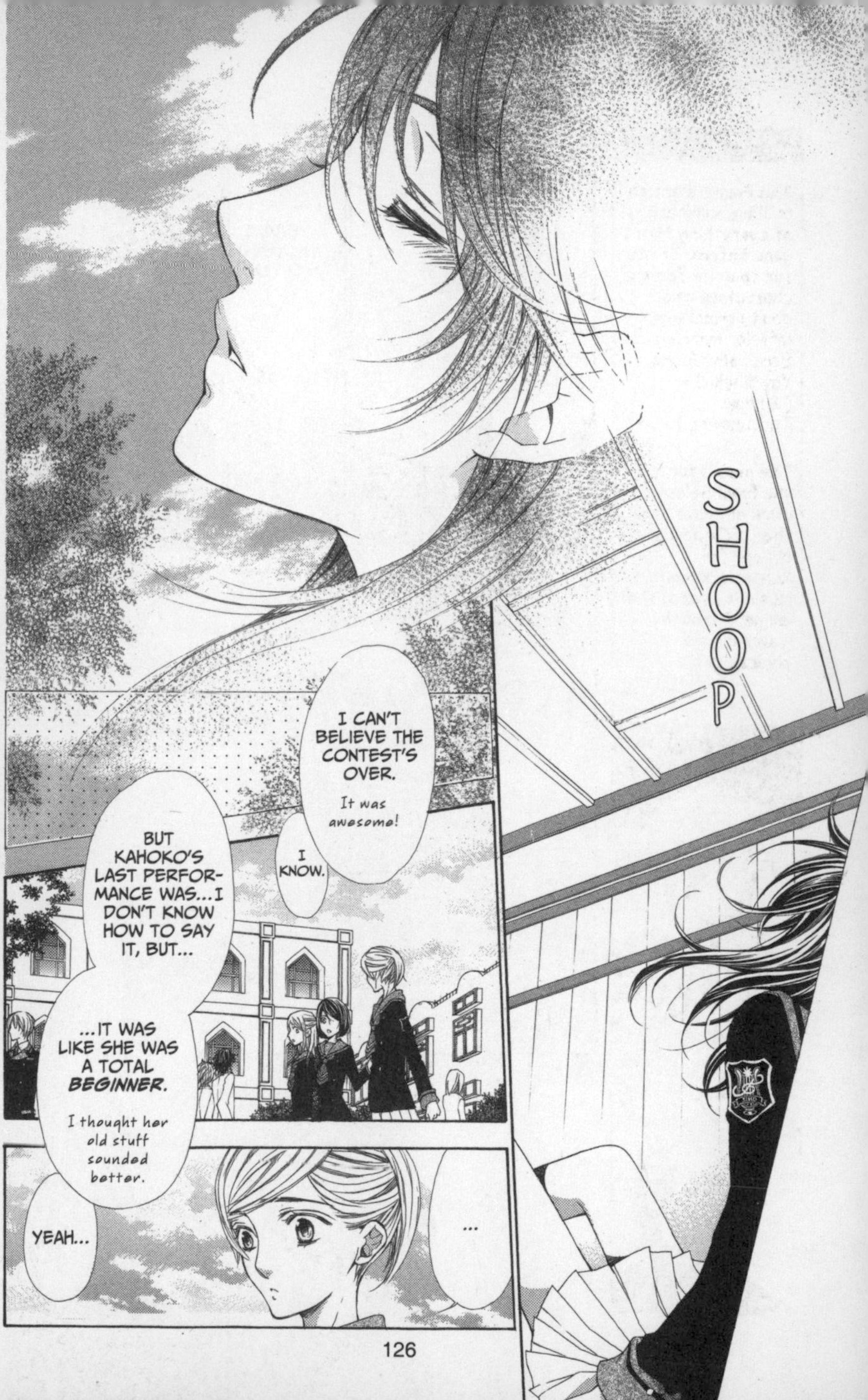
SHOOP
I CAN'T BELIEVE THE CONTEST'S OVER.
It was awesome!
I KNOW.
BUT KAHOKO'S LAST PERFORMANCE WAS...I DON'T KNOW HOW TO SAY IT, BUT...
...IT WAS LIKE SHE WAS A TOTAL *BEGINNER*.
I thought her old stuff sounded better.
...
YEAH...

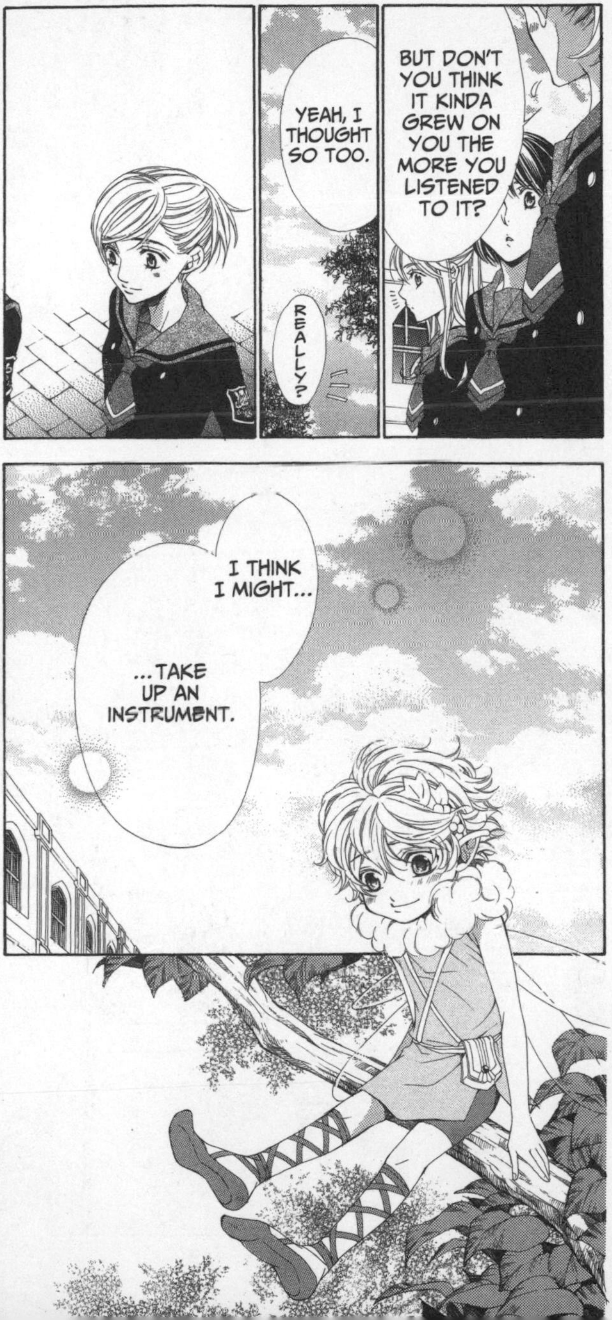
BUT DON'T YOU THINK IT KINDA GREW ON YOU THE MORE YOU LISTENED TO IT?
YEAH, I THOUGHT SO TOO.
REALLY?
I THINK I MIGHT...
...TAKE UP AN INSTRUMENT.

The Final Selection is like a summary of everything that's gone before. It was fun to write for the characters who don't normally get interior monologues. Especially Shoko. Yay Shoko!! ←
(I know.
I'm annoying.)

The pieces for the Final Selection were all taken from the *La Corda* game except for Kahoko's. Kahoko's music is used in the anime. I thought it was a good choice.

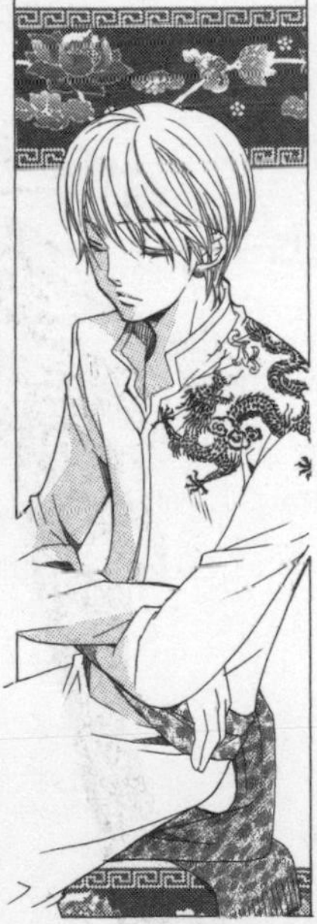

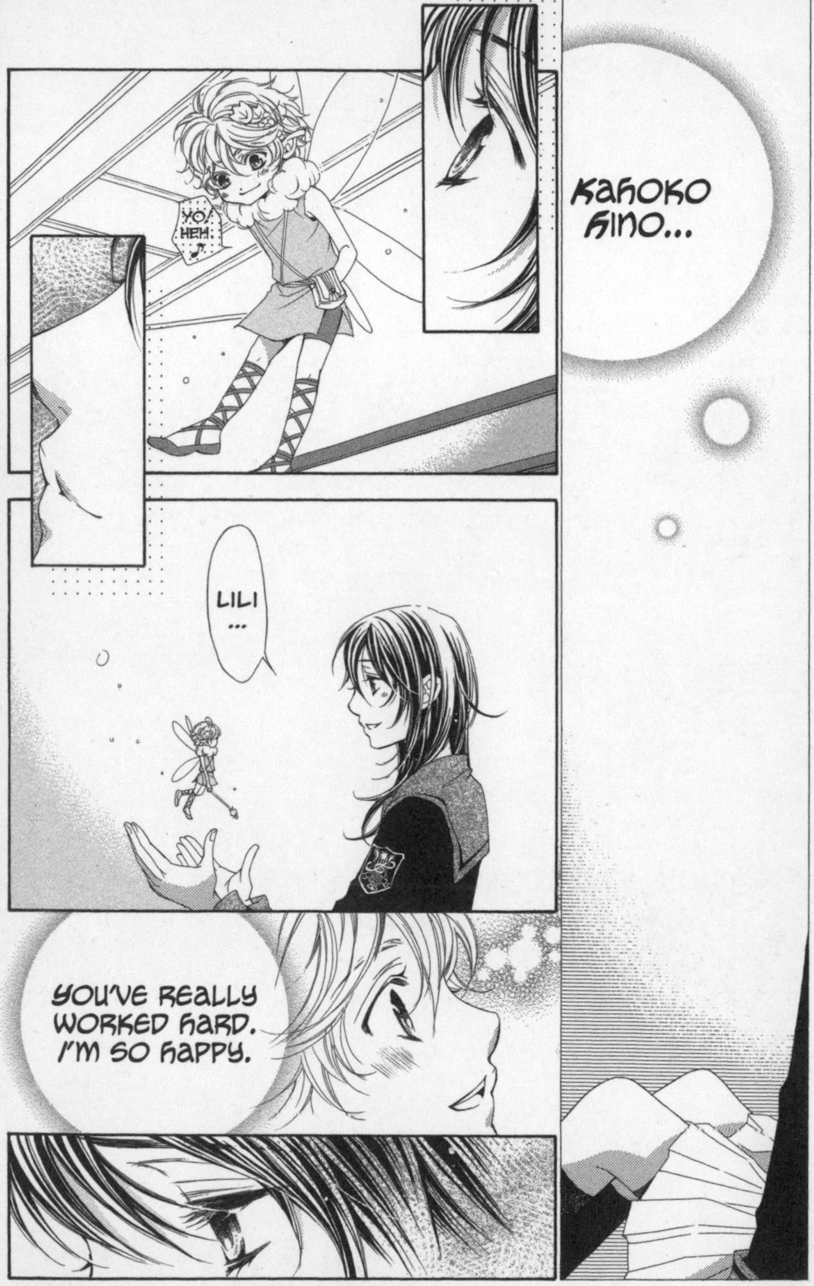
KAHOKO HINO...
YO! HEH ♪
LILI ...
YOU'VE REALLY WORKED HARD. I'M SO HAPPY.

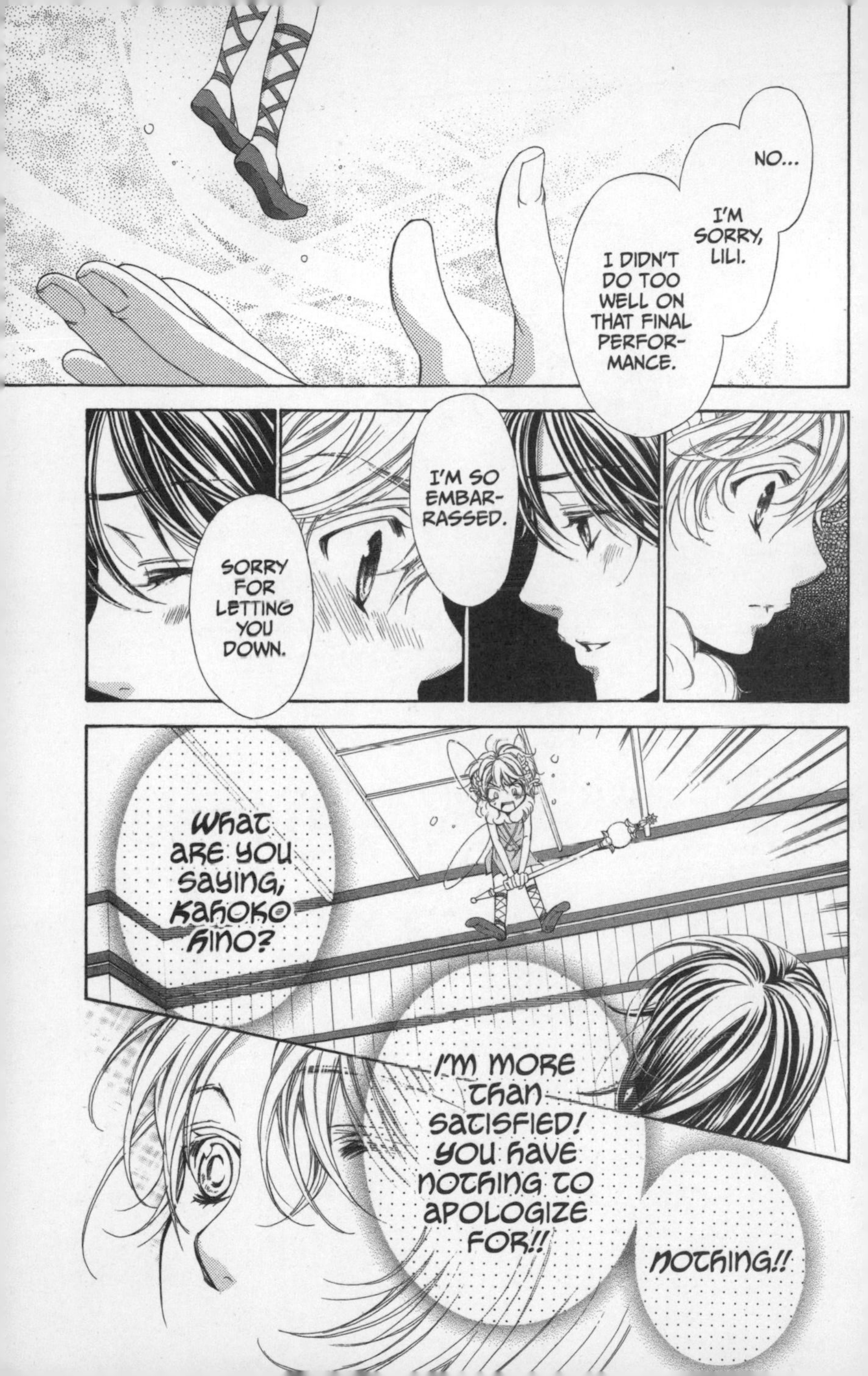
NO...
I'M SORRY, LILI.
I DIDN'T DO TOO WELL ON THAT FINAL PERFORMANCE.
I'M SO EMBARRASSED.
SORRY FOR LETTING YOU DOWN.
What are you saying, Kahoko Hino?
I'm more than satisfied! You have nothing to apologize for!!
Nothing!!

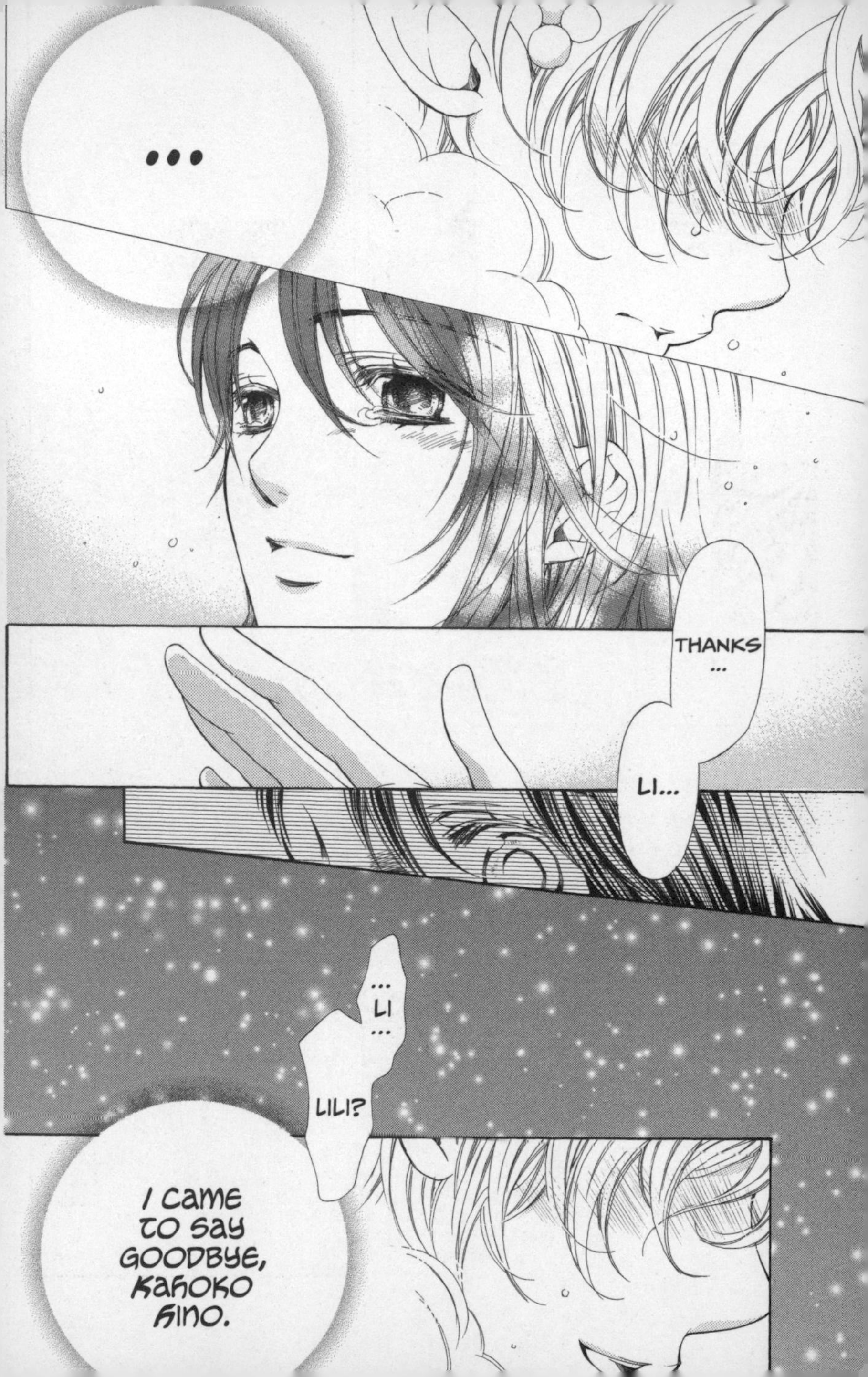
...
THANKS ...
LI...
... LI ...
LILI?
I CAME TO SAY GOODBYE, KAHOKO HINO.

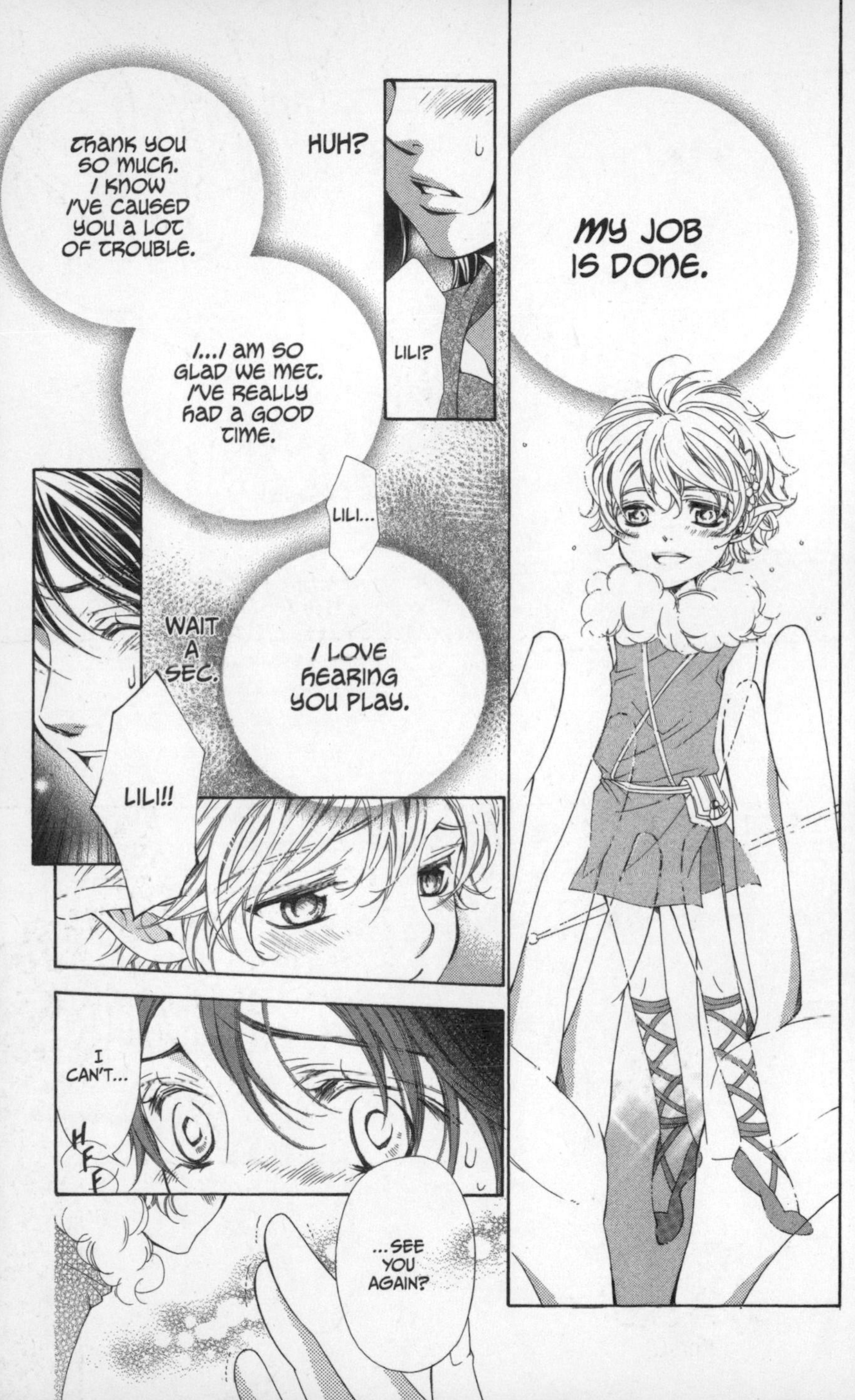
MY JOB IS DONE.
HUH?
THANK YOU SO MUCH. I KNOW I'VE CAUSED YOU A LOT OF TROUBLE.
LILI?
I...I AM SO GLAD WE MET. I'VE REALLY HAD A GOOD TIME.
LILI...
I LOVE HEARING YOU PLAY.
WAIT A SEC.
LILI!!
I CAN'T...
HFF
...SEE YOU AGAIN?

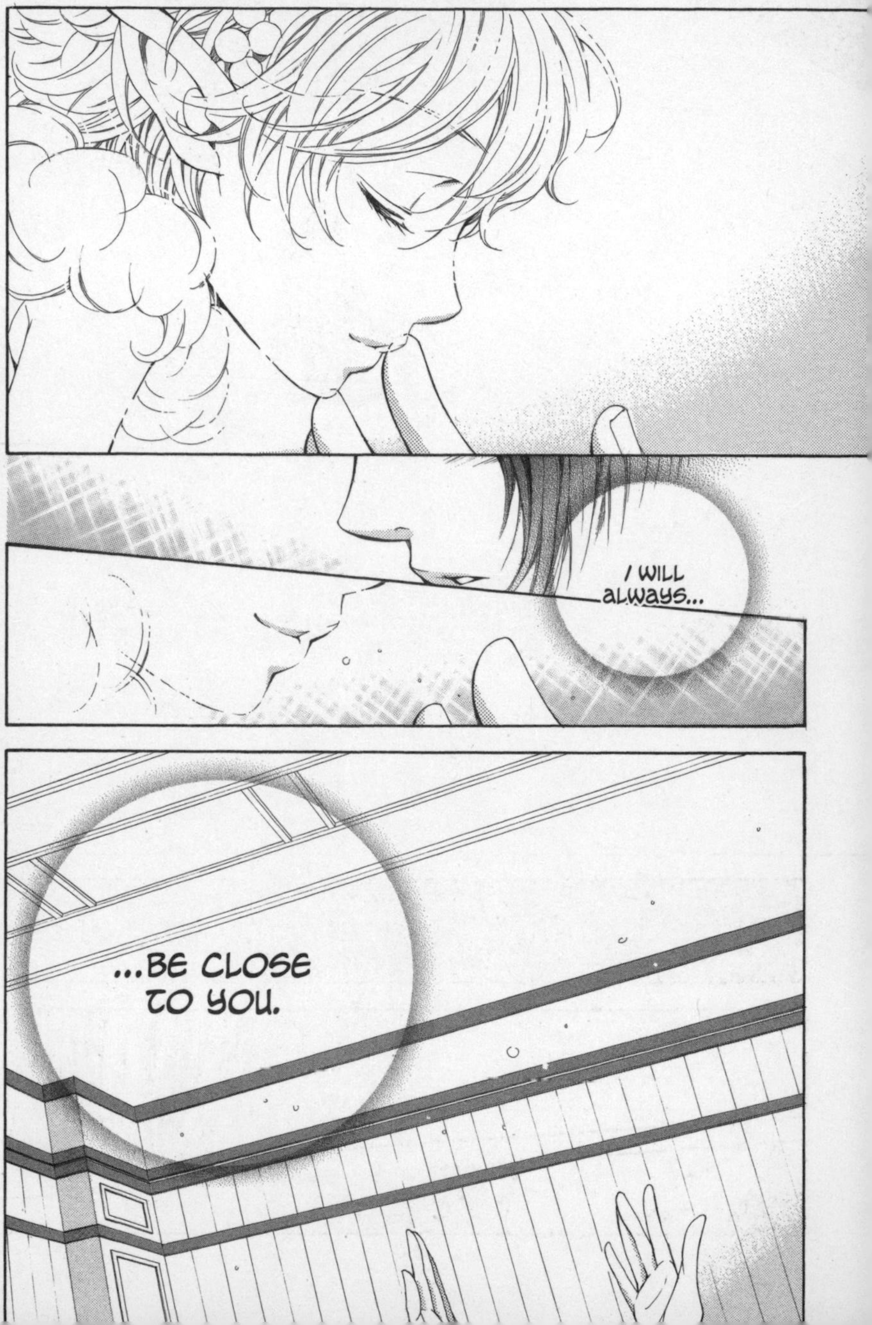
I WILL always...
...BE CLOSE TO YOU.

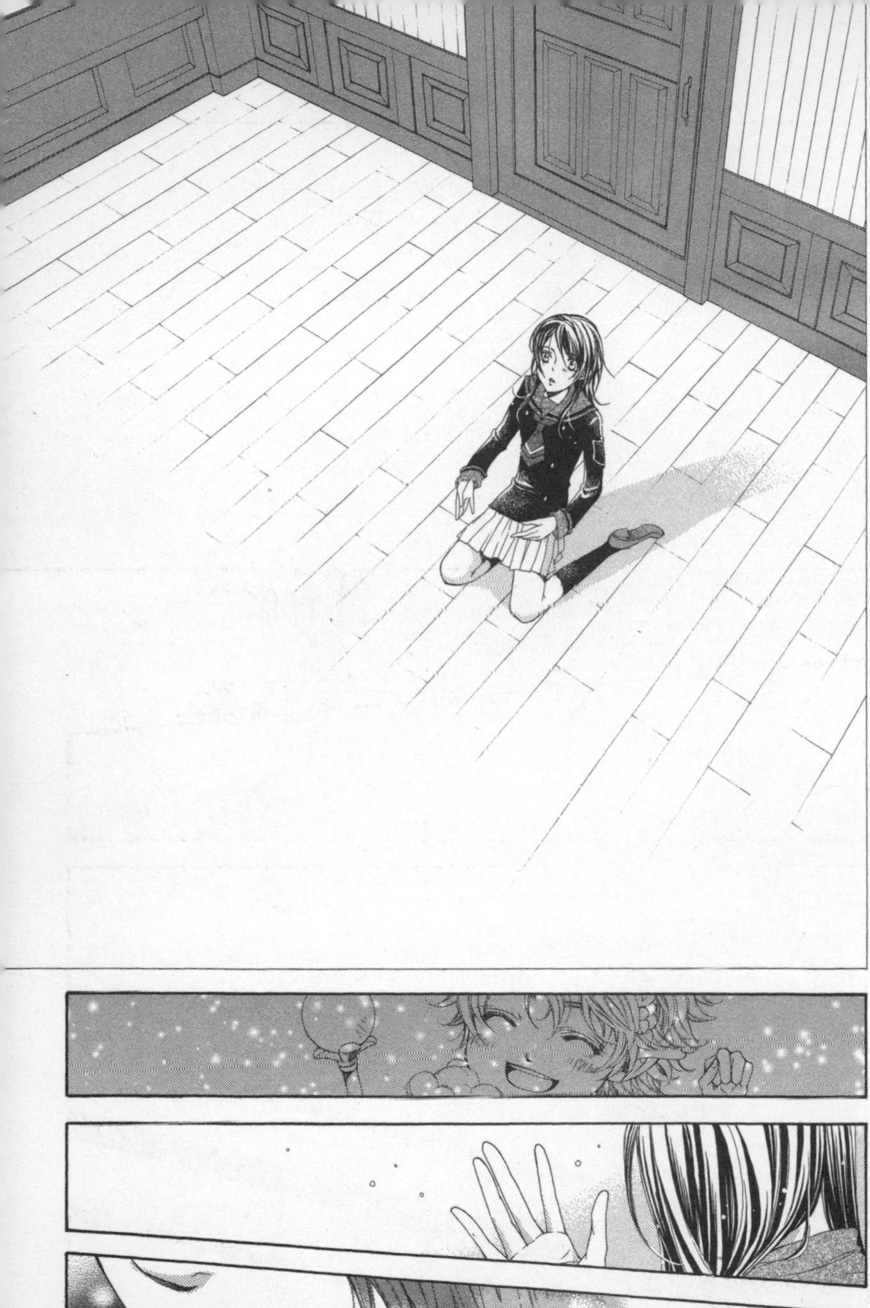

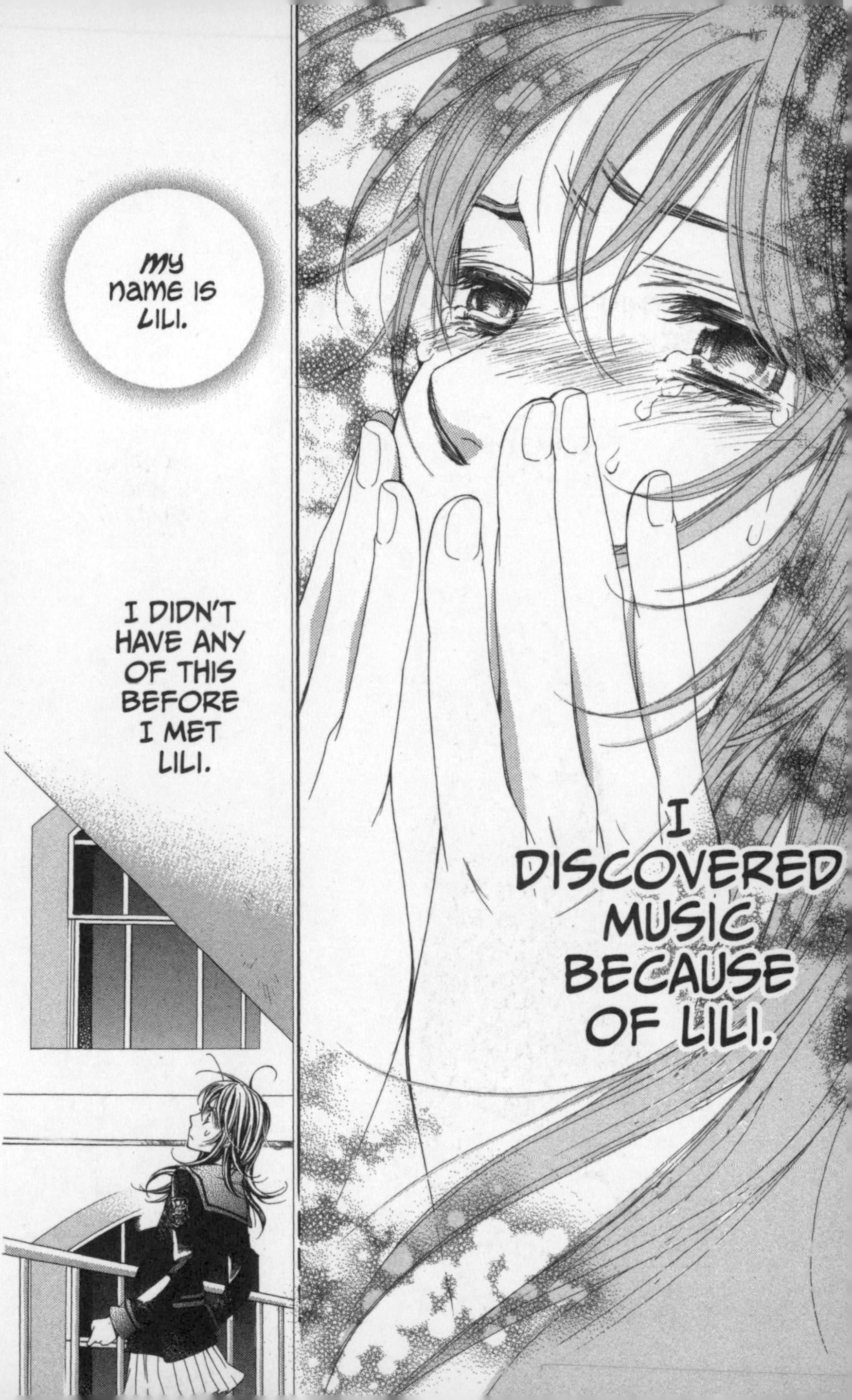
I DISCOVERED MUSIC BECAUSE OF LILI.
my name is LILI.
I DIDN'T HAVE ANY OF THIS BEFORE I MET LILI.

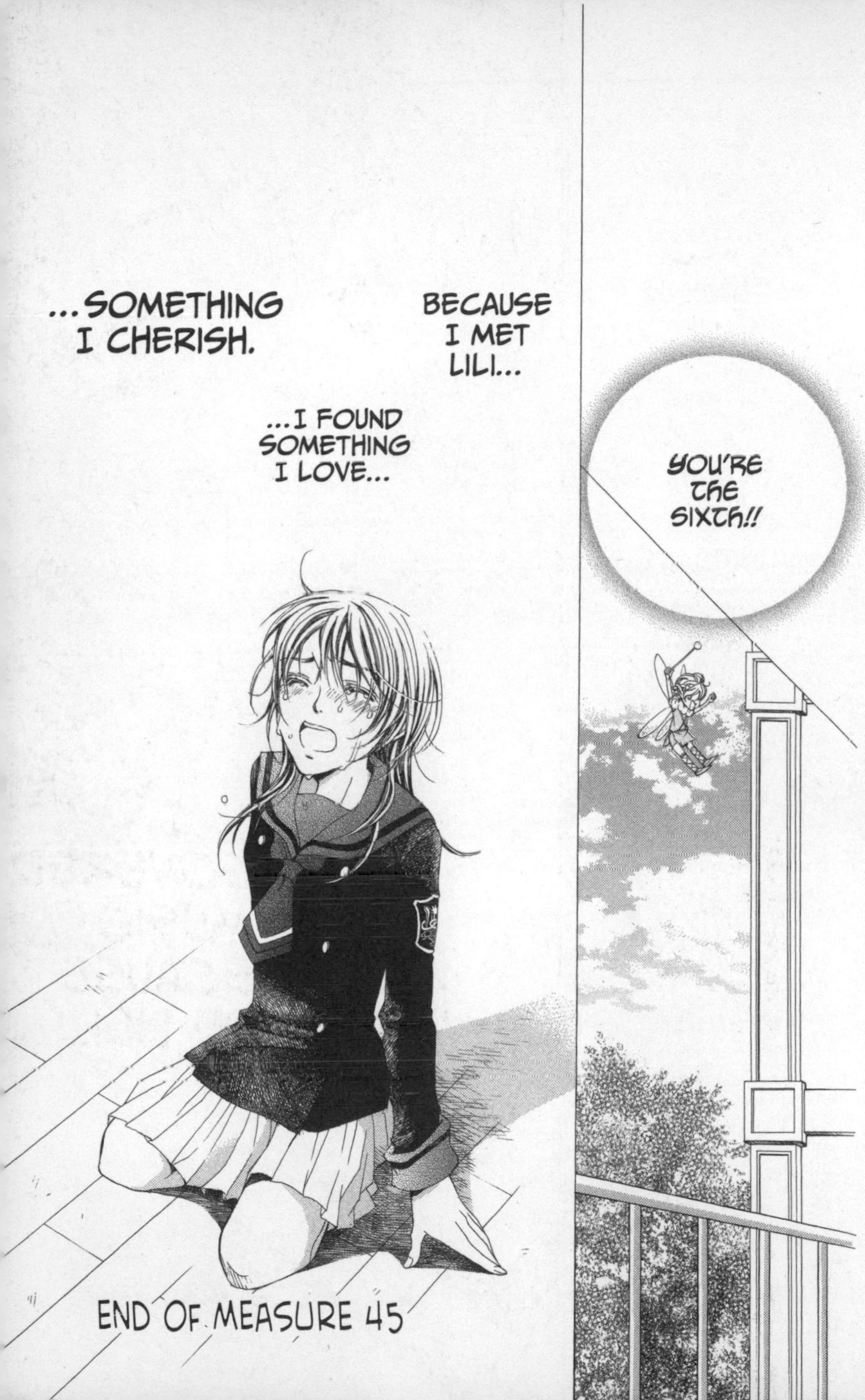
YOU'RE THE SIXTH!!
BECAUSE I MET LILI...
...I FOUND SOMETHING I LOVE...
...SOMETHING I CHERISH.

END OF MEASURE 45

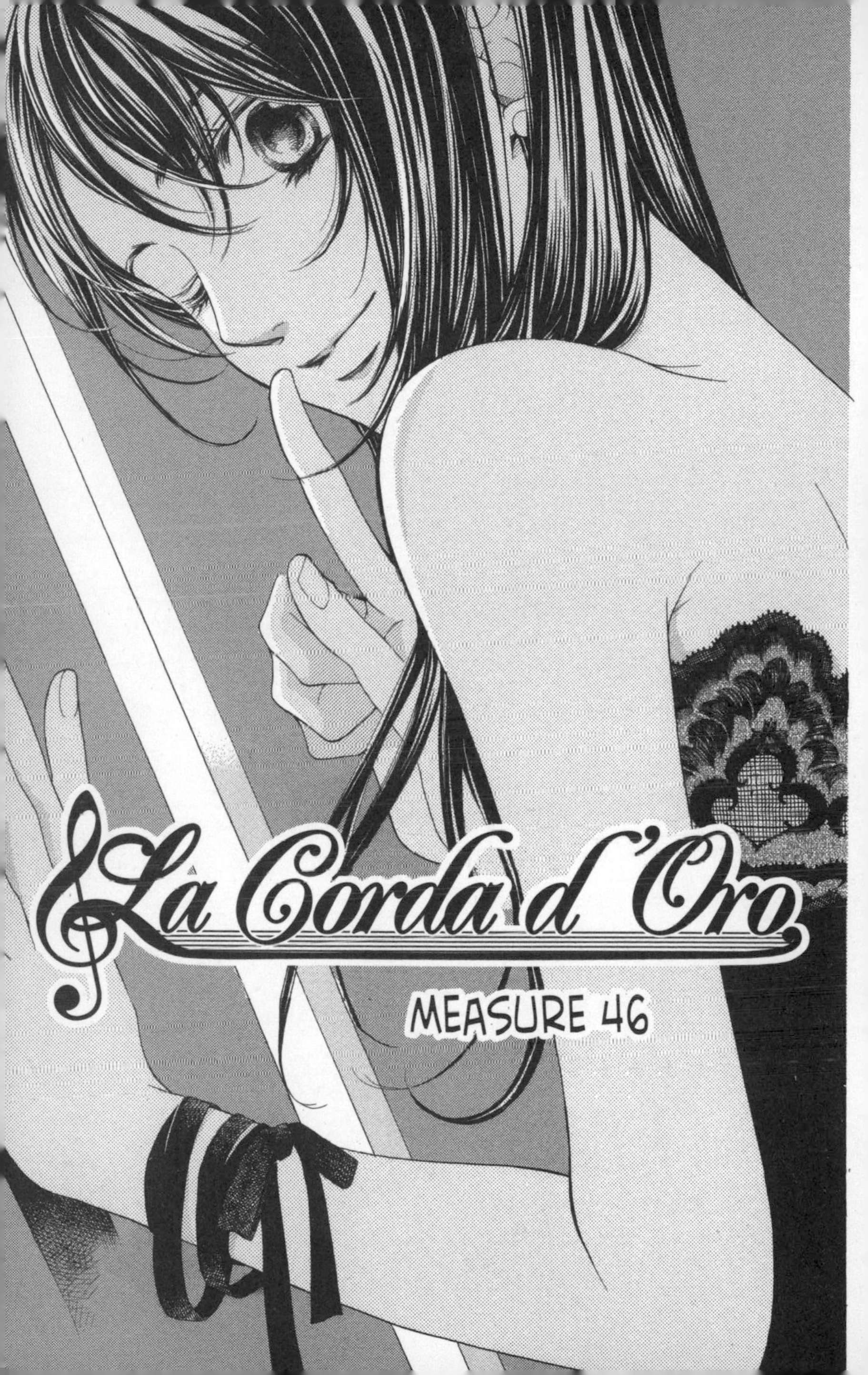
La Corda d'Oro
MEASURE 46

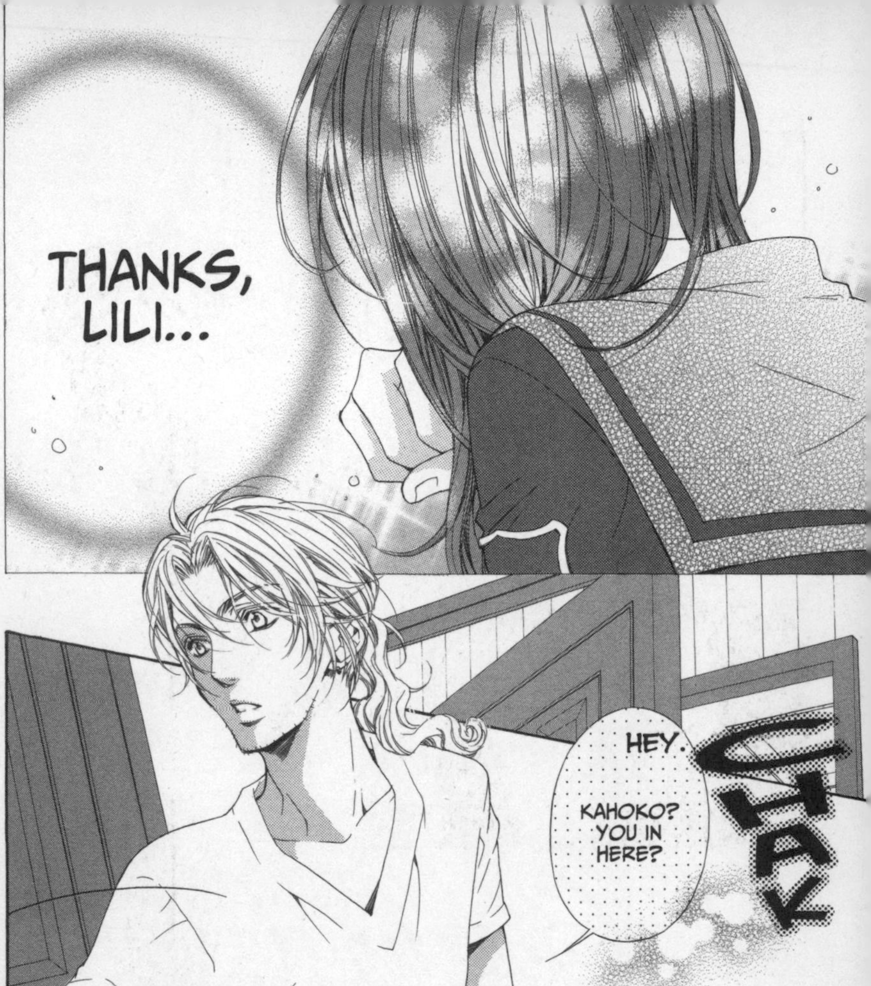
THANKS, LILI...
HEY.
KAHOKO? YOU IN HERE?
CHAK

Daily Happenings 38
Ito-san on stage...

The other day I was invited to see Ito-san, who does the voice of Ryotaro, perform. But I got lost on the way from the train station, and as I was walking around aimlessly I saw a pair of florists carrying big bouquets in front of me. On closer inspection I learned that the flowers were for Morita-san, who does Kazuki's voice.

I tailed them and arrived safely at my destination. ♡ Thank you so much! (← Who am I thanking?)
The performance was wonderful and I had a great time.
Live performances are so cool.♡

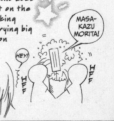

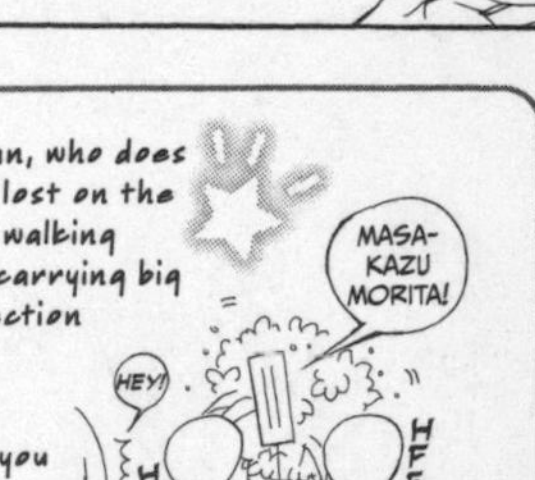
MASA-KAZU MORITA!
HEY!
HFF
HFF

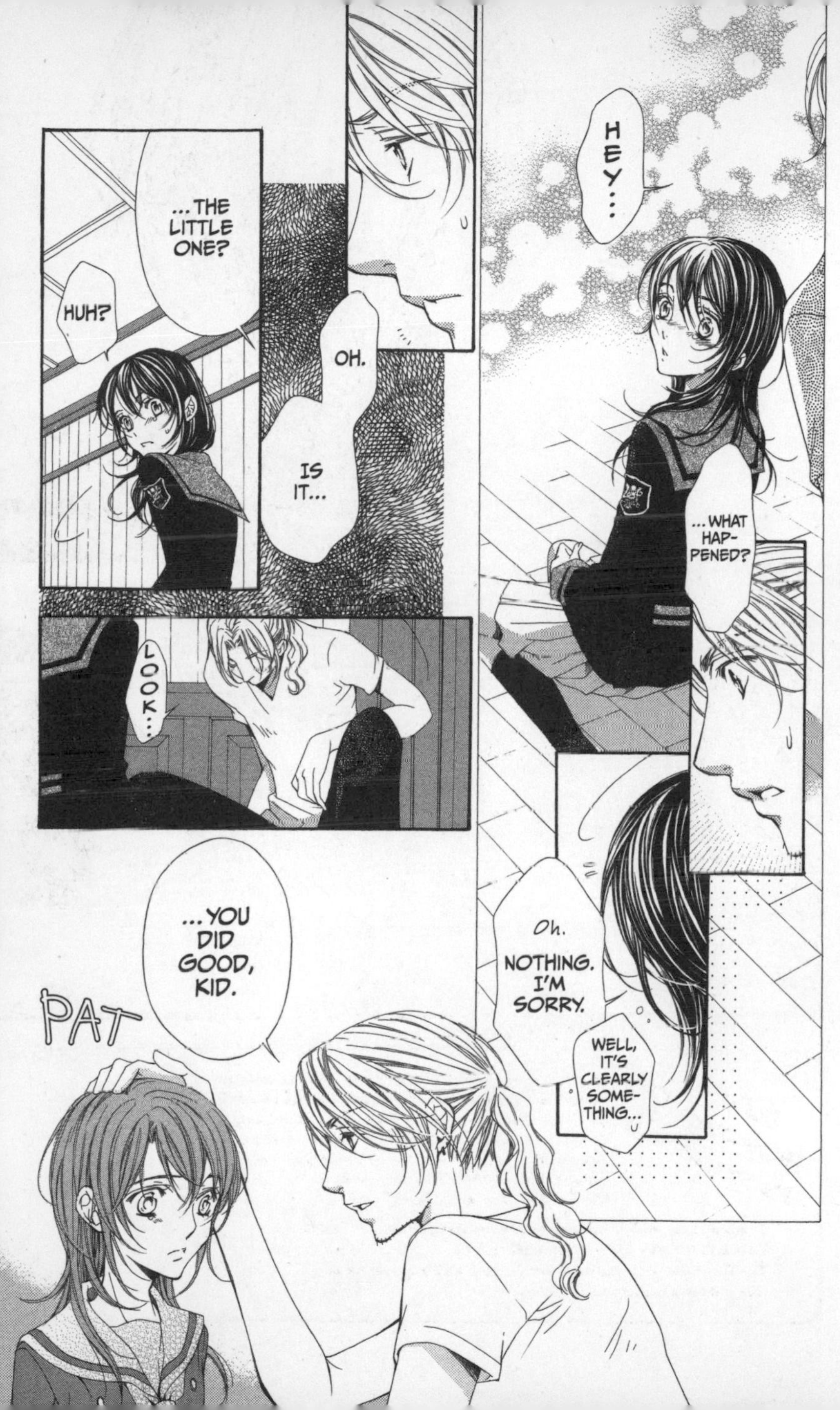
HEY...
...WHAT HAP-PENED?
Oh.
NOTHING. I'M SORRY.
WELL, IT'S CLEARLY SOME-THING...
OH.
IS IT...
...THE LITTLE ONE?
HUH?
LOOK...
...YOU DID GOOD, KID.
PAT

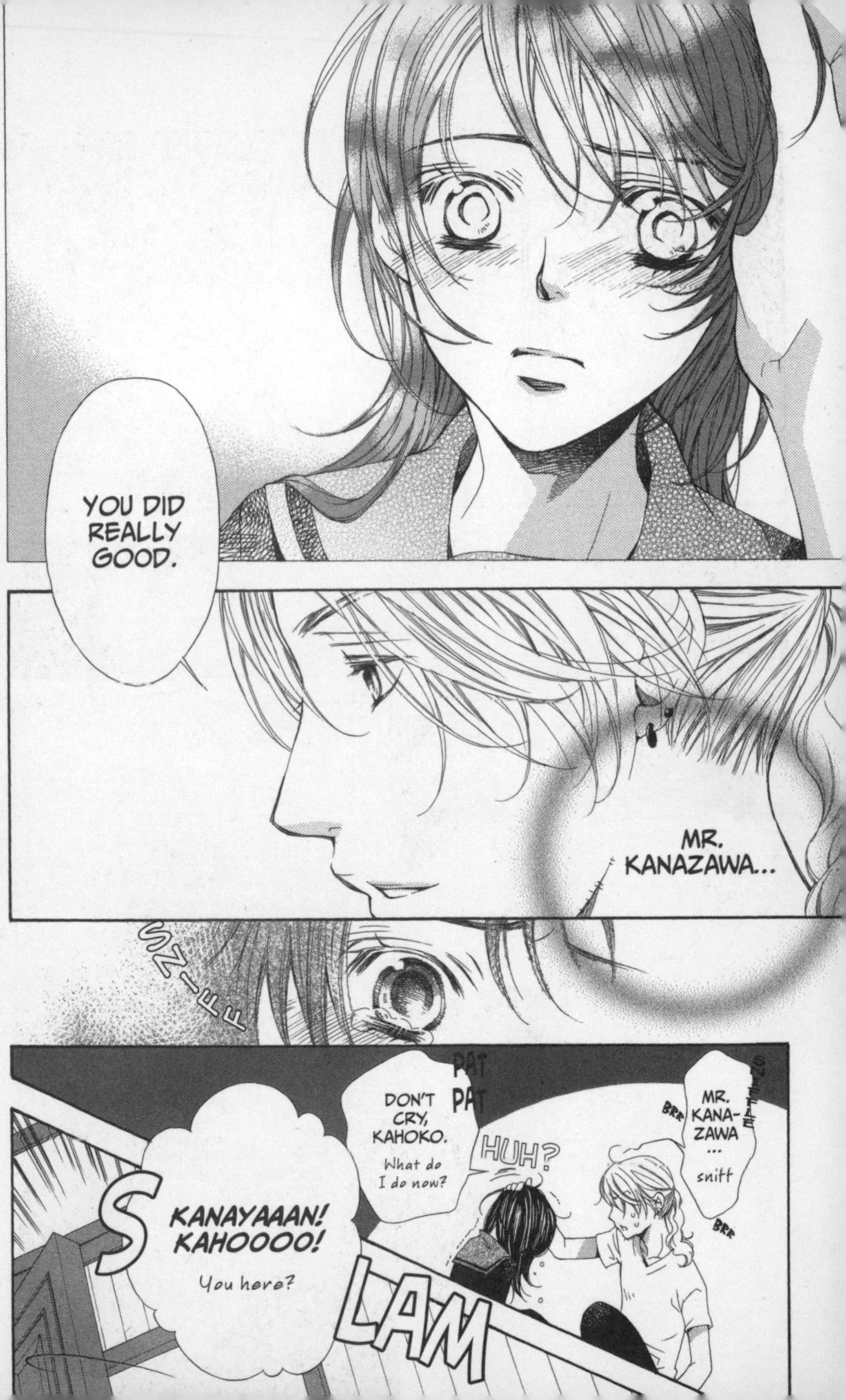
YOU DID REALLY GOOD.
MR. KANAZAWA...
FF-ZZS
SNIFFLE
MR. KANA-ZAWA ...
sniff
BRR
BRR
PAT PAT
DON'T CRY, KAHOKO.
What do I do now?
HUH?
SLAM
KANAYAAAN! KAHOOOO!
You here?

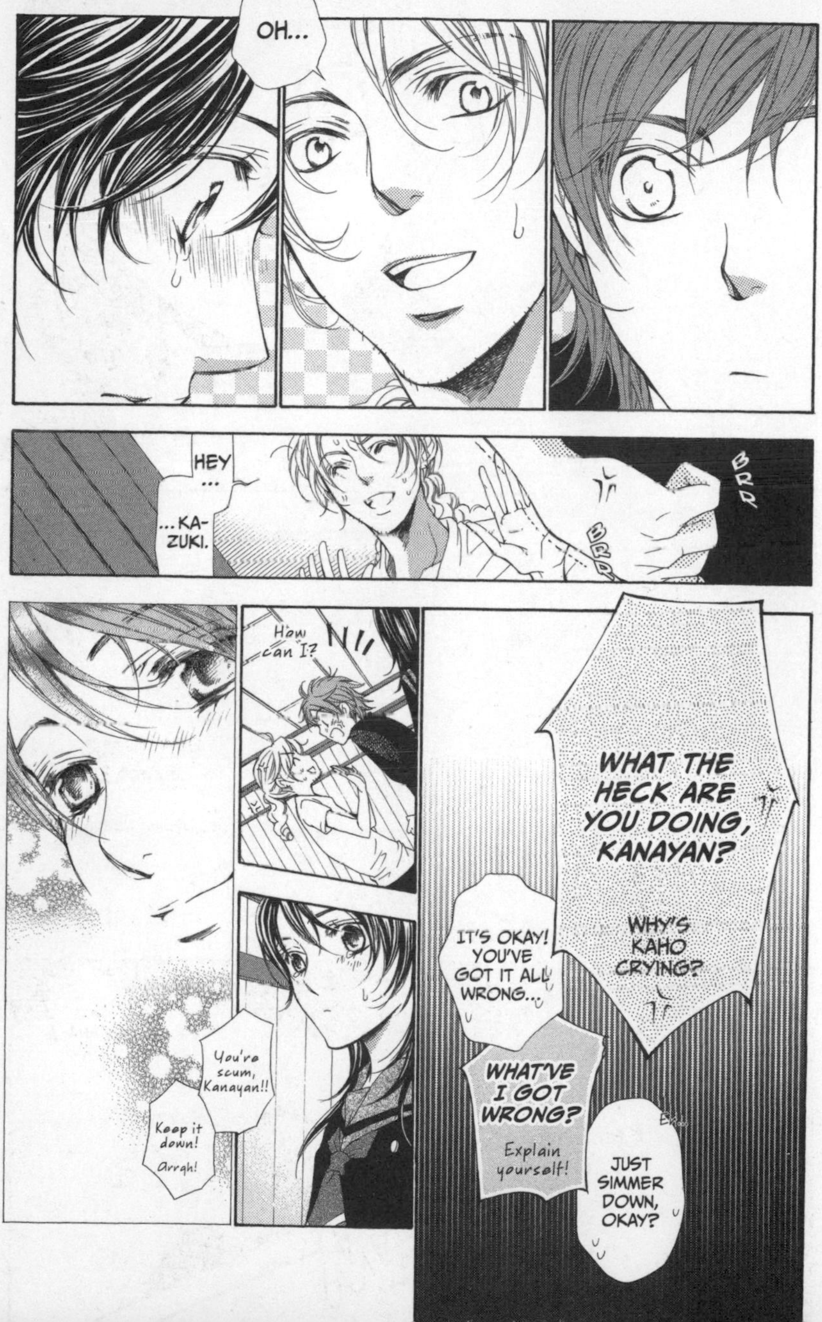
OH...
BRR
HEY ...
...KA-ZUKI.
BRR
WHAT THE HECK ARE YOU DOING, KANAYAN?
WHY'S KAHO CRYING?
IT'S OKAY! YOU'VE GOT IT ALL WRONG...
WHAT'VE I GOT WRONG?
Explain yourself!
JUST SIMMER DOWN, OKAY?
How can I?
You're scum, Kanayan!!
Keep it down!
Arrgh!

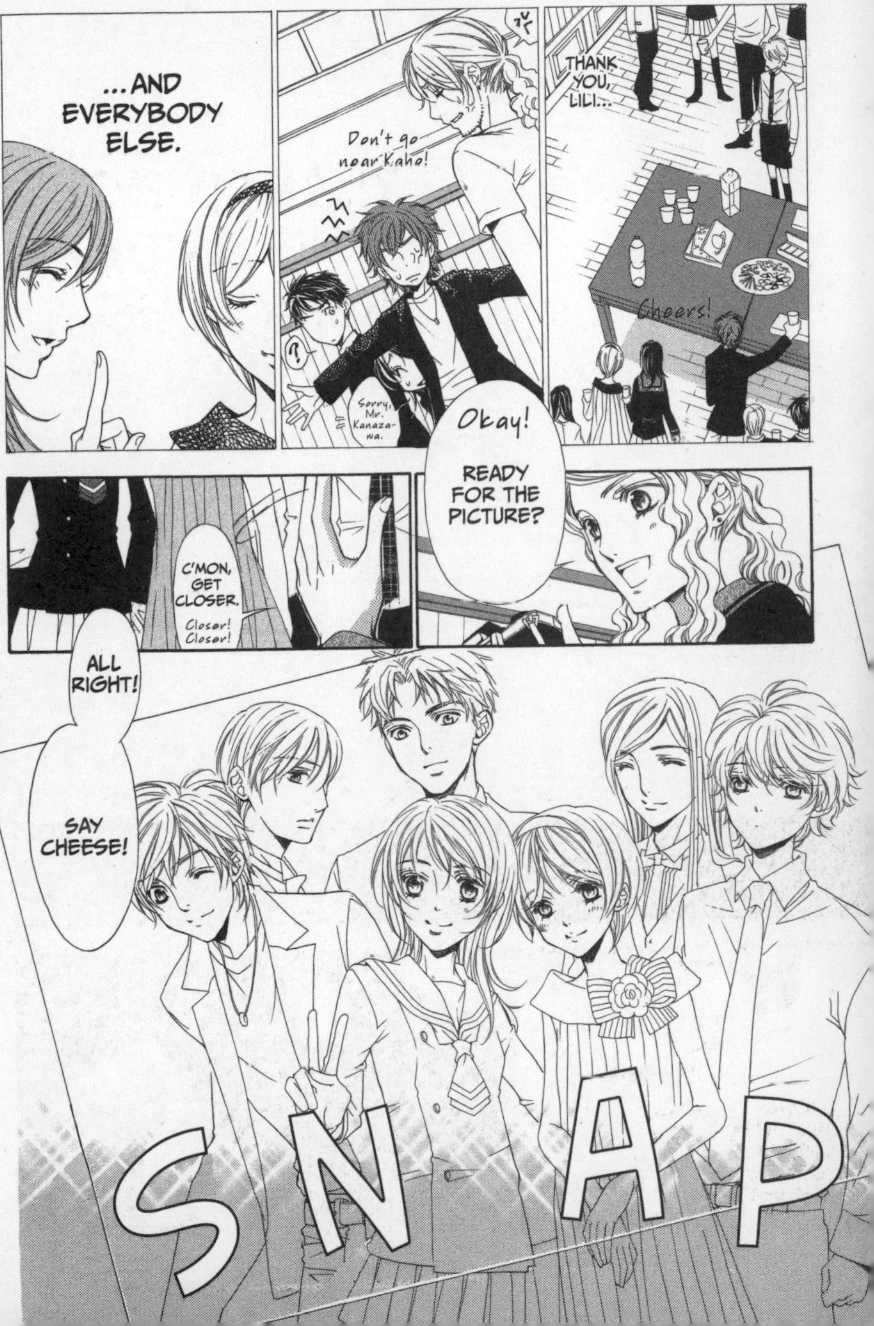
THANK YOU, LILI...
Cheers!
Don't go near Kaho!
Sorry, Mr. Kanazawa.
...AND EVERYBODY ELSE.
Okay! READY FOR THE PICTURE?
C'MON, GET CLOSER.
Closer! Closer!
ALL RIGHT! SAY CHEESE!
SNAP

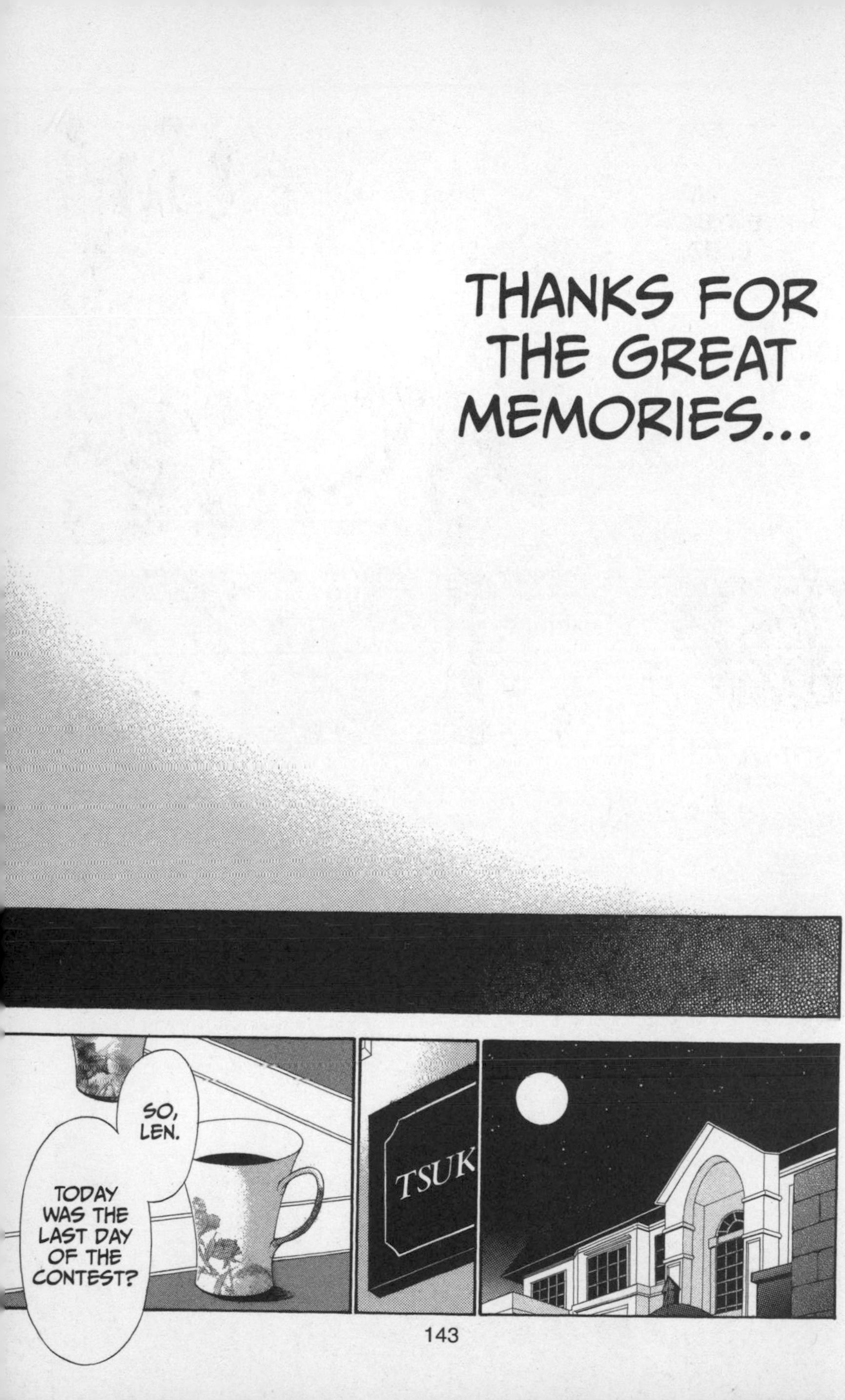
THANKS FOR THE GREAT MEMORIES...
TSUK
SO, LEN.
TODAY WAS THE LAST DAY OF THE CONTEST?

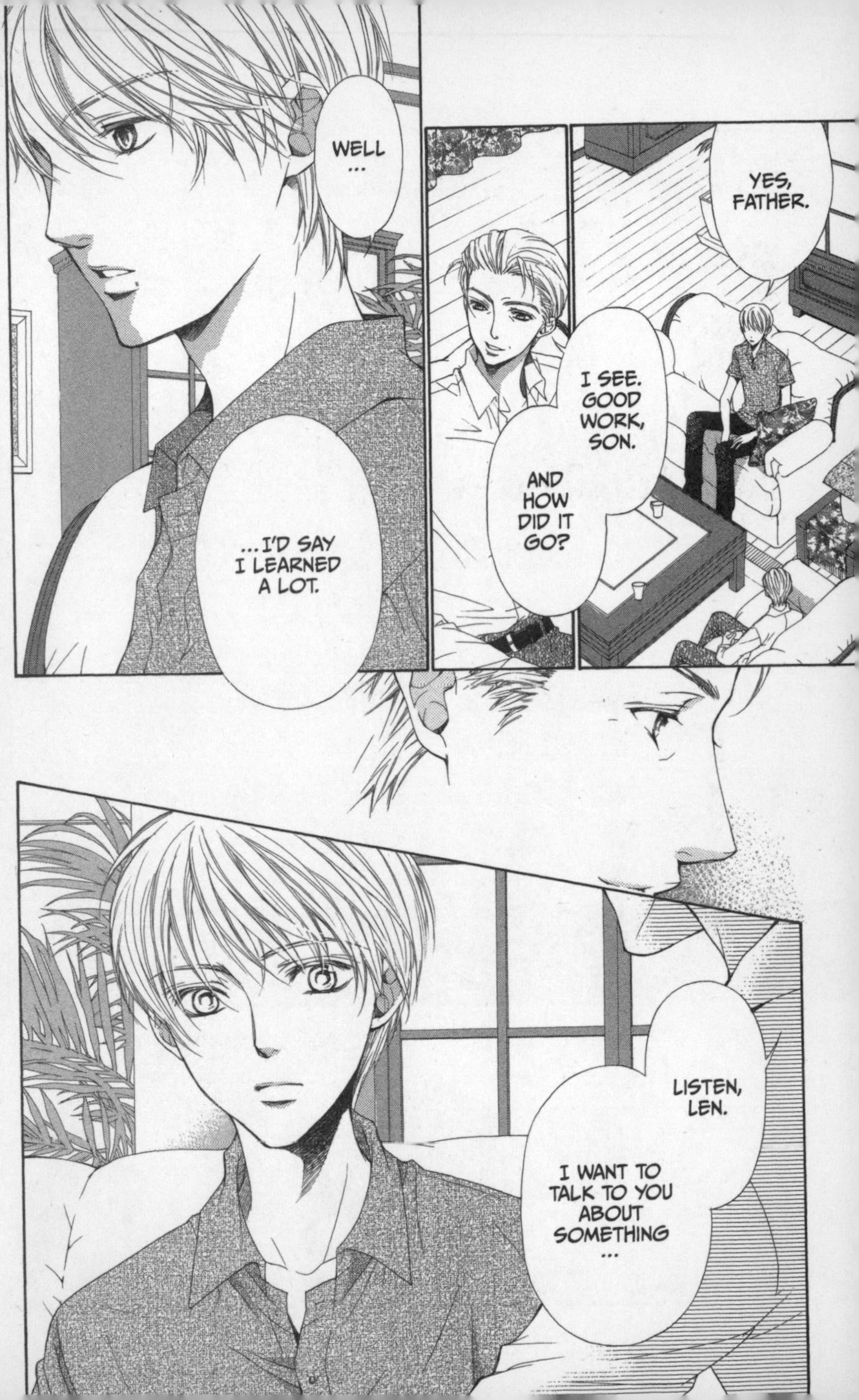
YES, FATHER.
I SEE. GOOD WORK, SON.
AND HOW DID IT GO?
WELL ...
...I'D SAY I LEARNED A LOT.
LISTEN, LEN.
I WANT TO TALK TO YOU ABOUT SOMETHING ...

LEN MUST'VE COME FIRST IN THE FINAL SELECTION.

Hey, Keiichi's third.

I TOTALLY THOUGHT IT'D BE AZUMA.

WOW, LEN'S AWESOME.

First place!

AHH
AHH
AHH
AHH
AHH

YEAH. I BET KEIICHI WAS SECOND, RYOTARO WAS THIRD...

...AND KAZUKI WAS FOURTH...

Seiso Academy School Music C[o]
Final Placement

First	Music School	Class 2-A	Len Tsuki
Second	Music School	Class 3-B	Azuma Yu
Third	Music School	Class 1-A	Keiichi Shi
Fourth	General Education	Class 2-5	Ryotaro Tsuchiura
Fifth	Music School	Class 3-B	Kazuki Hihara
Sixth	Music School	Class 1-B	Shoko Fuyuumi
Seventh	General Education	Class 2-2	Kahoko Hino

...FOLLOWED BY SHOKO, AZUMA AND KAHOKO.

SMACK

OWW!

145

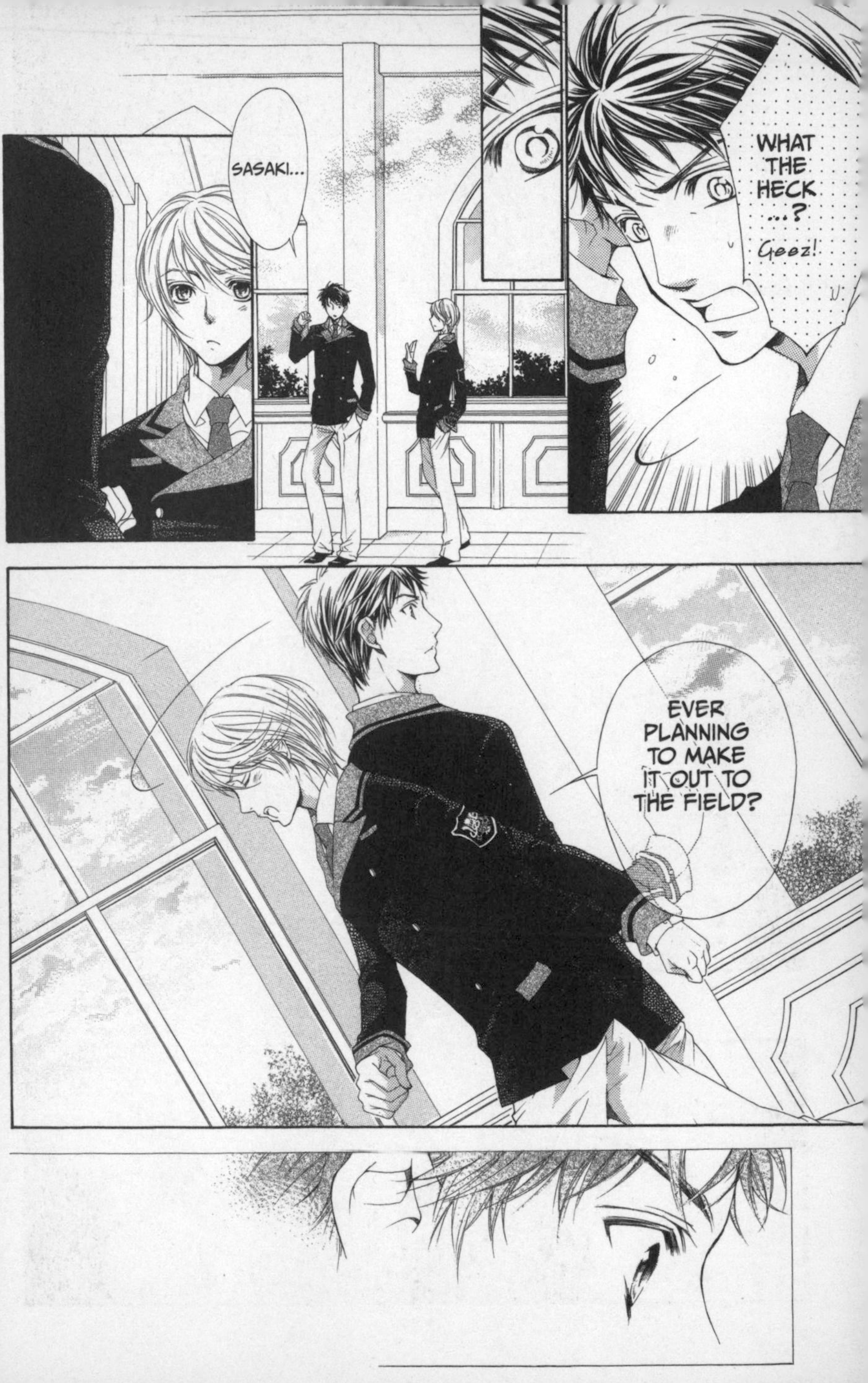
WHAT THE HECK ...?
Geez!
SASAKI...
EVER PLANNING TO MAKE IT OUT TO THE FIELD?

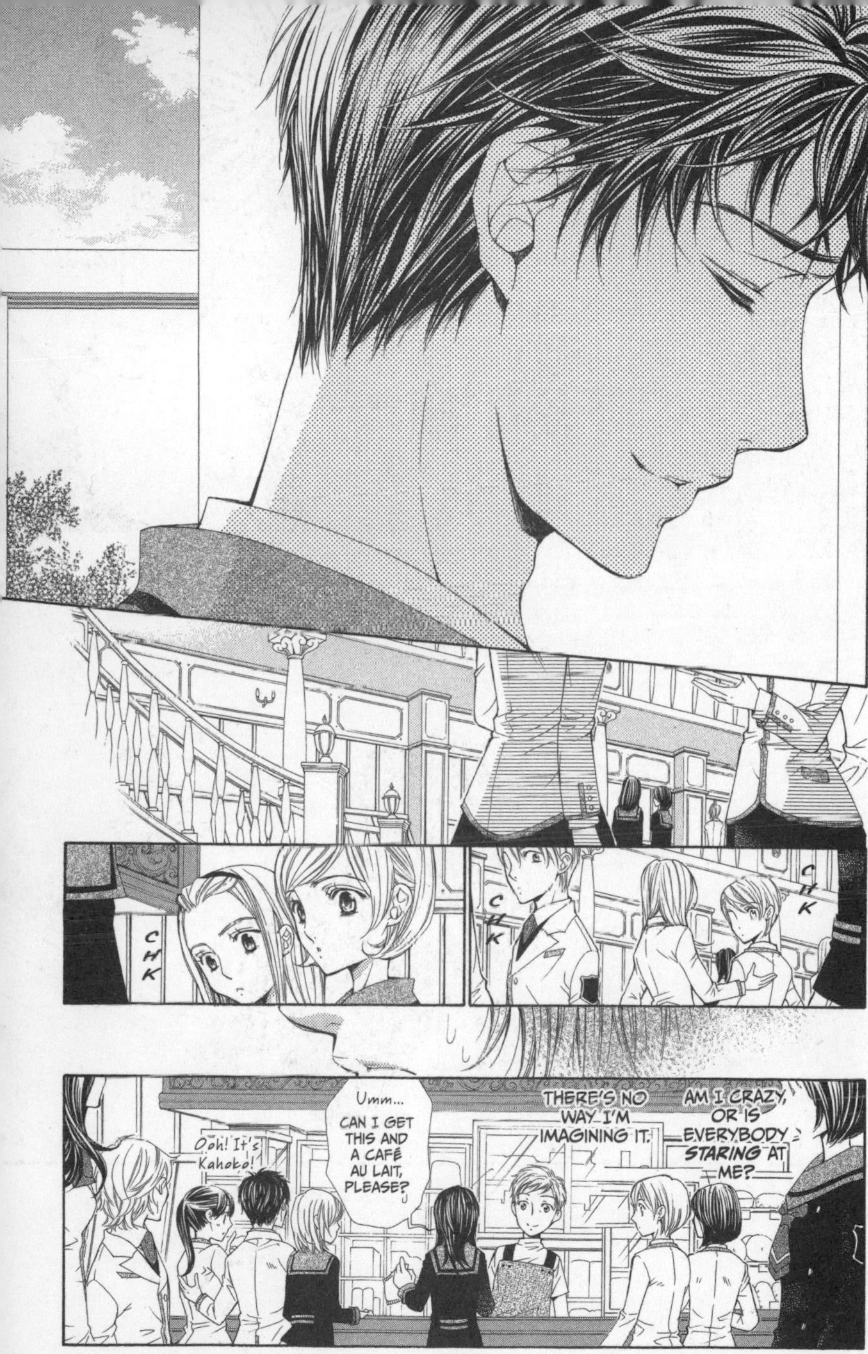
CHK
CHK
CHK
AM I CRAZY, OR IS EVERYBODY STARING AT ME?
THERE'S NO WAY I'M IMAGINING IT.
Umm... CAN I GET THIS AND A CAFÉ AU LAIT, PLEASE?
Ooh! It's Kahoko!

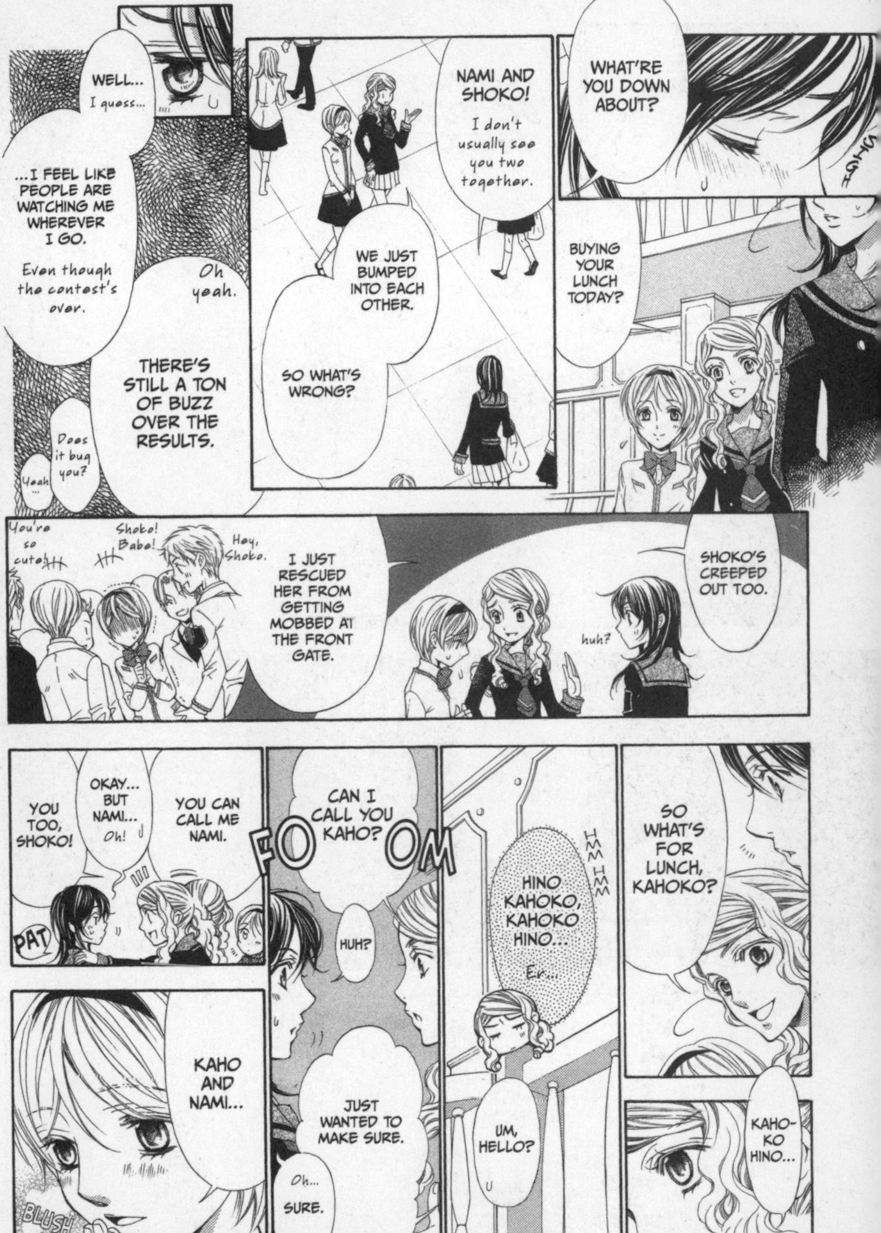
WHAT'RE YOU DOWN ABOUT?
BUYING YOUR LUNCH TODAY?
NAMI AND SHOKO!
I don't usually see you two together.
WE JUST BUMPED INTO EACH OTHER.
SO WHAT'S WRONG?
WELL...
I guess...
...I FEEL LIKE PEOPLE ARE WATCHING ME WHEREVER I GO.
Even though the contest's over.
Oh yeah.
THERE'S STILL A TON OF BUZZ OVER THE RESULTS.
Does it bug you?
Yeah...
SHOKO'S CREEPED OUT TOO.
huh?
I JUST RESCUED HER FROM GETTING MOBBED AT THE FRONT GATE.
Hey, Shoko.
Shoko! Babe!
You're so cute!
SO WHAT'S FOR LUNCH, KAHOKO?
KAHO-KO HINO...
HMM HMM
HINO KAHOKO, KAHOKO HINO...
Er...
UM, HELLO?
CAN I CALL YOU KAHO?
FOOM
HUH?
JUST WANTED TO MAKE SURE.
Oh...
SURE.
YOU CAN CALL ME NAMI.
OKAY... BUT NAMI...
Oh!
YOU TOO, SHOKO!
PAT
KAHO AND NAMI...
BLUSH

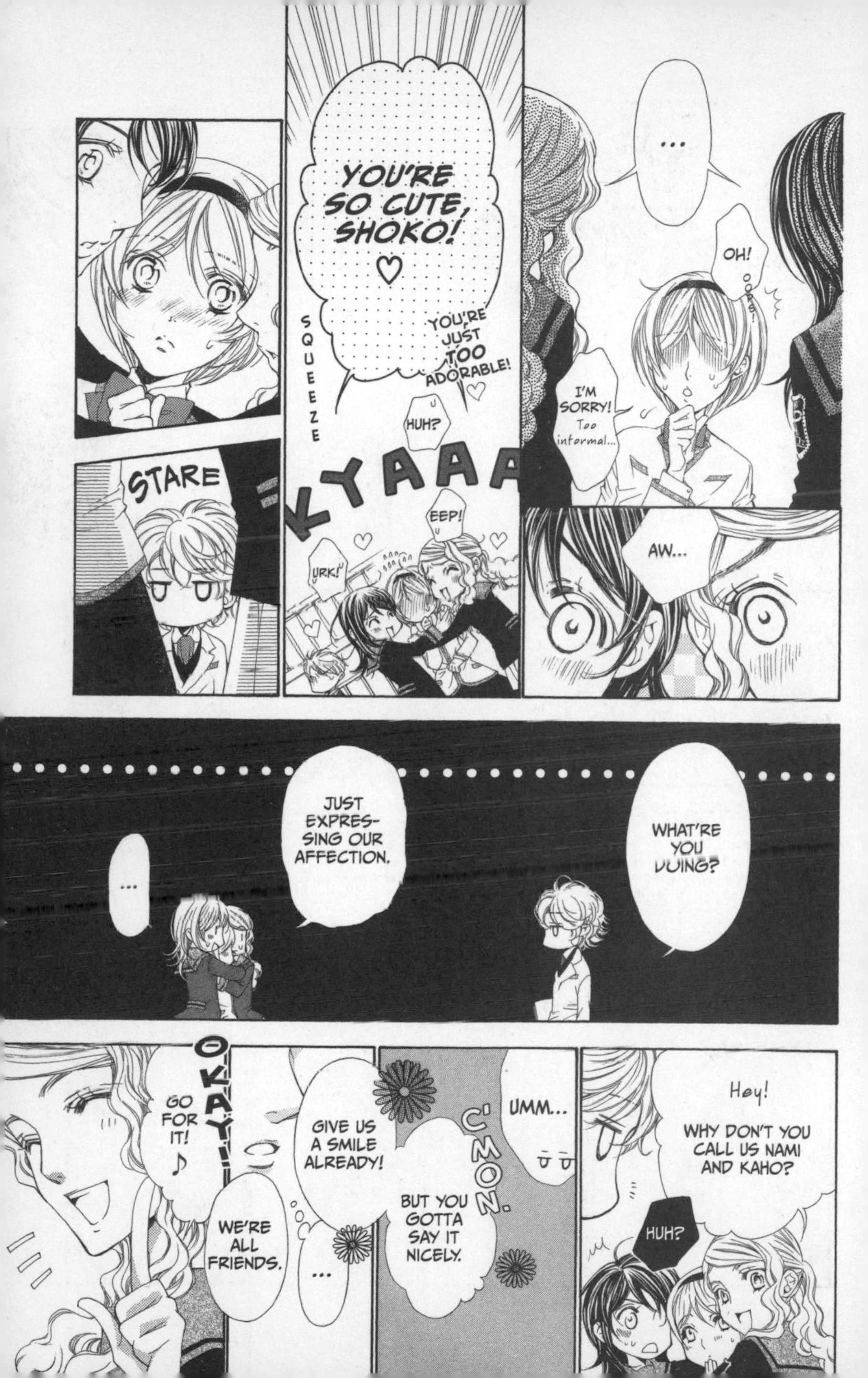
...
OH!
OOPS!
I'M SORRY! Too informal...
AW...
YOU'RE SO CUTE, SHOKO! ♡
YOU'RE JUST TOO ADORABLE! ♡
SQUEEZE
HUH?
KYAAA
EEP!
URK!
STARE
WHAT'RE YOU DOING?
JUST EXPRES-SING OUR AFFECTION.
...
Hey!
WHY DON'T YOU CALL US NAMI AND KAHO?
HUH?
UMM...
C'MON.
BUT YOU GOTTA SAY IT NICELY.
GIVE US A SMILE ALREADY!
WE'RE ALL FRIENDS.
...
OKAY!
GO FOR IT! ♪

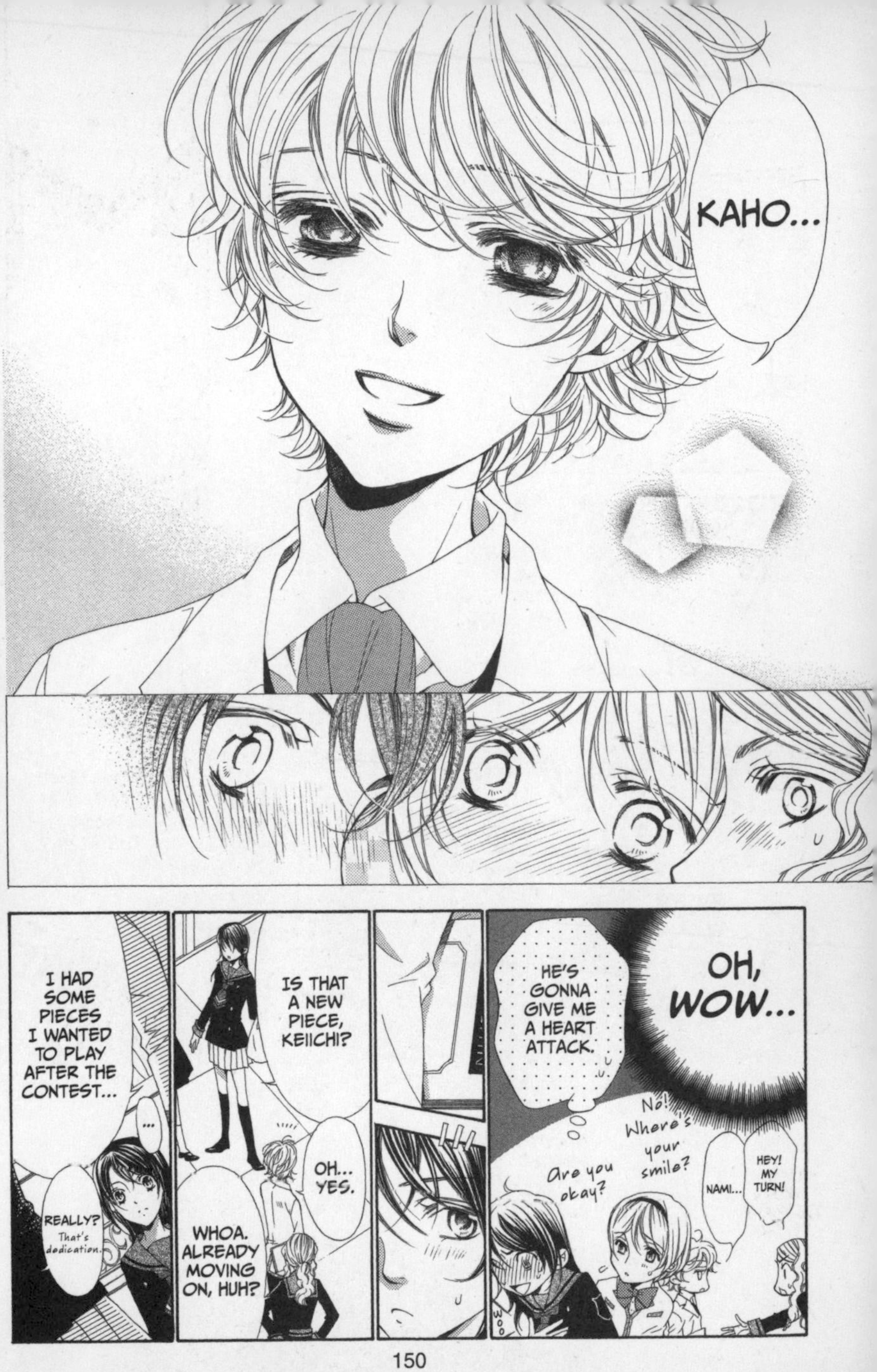
KAHO...
OH, WOW...
HE'S GONNA GIVE ME A HEART ATTACK.
No! Where's your smile?
HEY! MY TURN!
NAMI...
Are you okay?
IS THAT A NEW PIECE, KEIICHI?
OH... YES.
WHOA. ALREADY MOVING ON, HUH?
I HAD SOME PIECES I WANTED TO PLAY AFTER THE CONTEST...
...
REALLY? That's dedication.

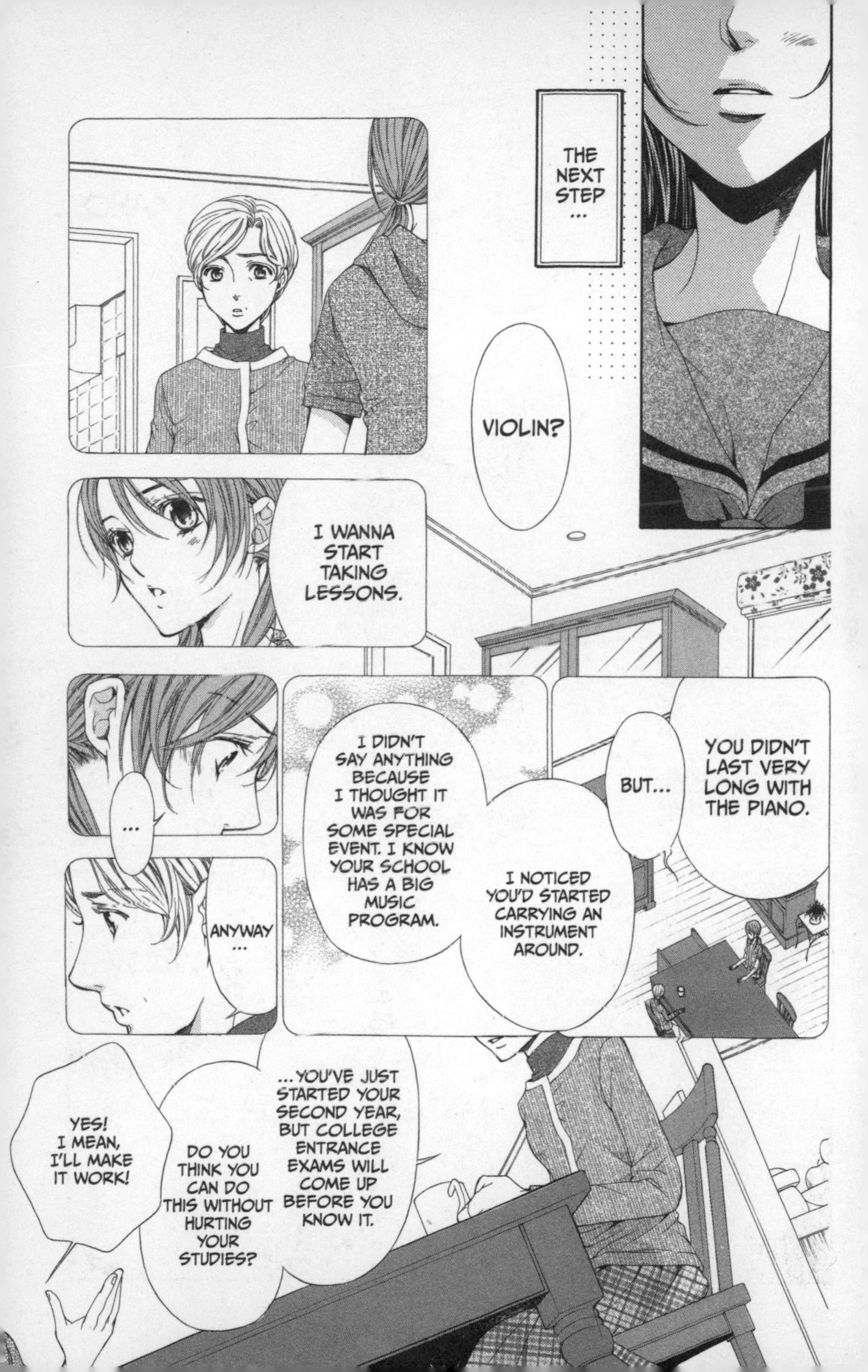
THE NEXT STEP ...
VIOLIN?
I WANNA START TAKING LESSONS.
YOU DIDN'T LAST VERY LONG WITH THE PIANO.
BUT...
I NOTICED YOU'D STARTED CARRYING AN INSTRUMENT AROUND.
I DIDN'T SAY ANYTHING BECAUSE I THOUGHT IT WAS FOR SOME SPECIAL EVENT. I KNOW YOUR SCHOOL HAS A BIG MUSIC PROGRAM.
...
ANYWAY ...
...YOU'VE JUST STARTED YOUR SECOND YEAR, BUT COLLEGE ENTRANCE EXAMS WILL COME UP BEFORE YOU KNOW IT.
DO YOU THINK YOU CAN DO THIS WITHOUT HURTING YOUR STUDIES?
YES! I MEAN, I'LL MAKE IT WORK!

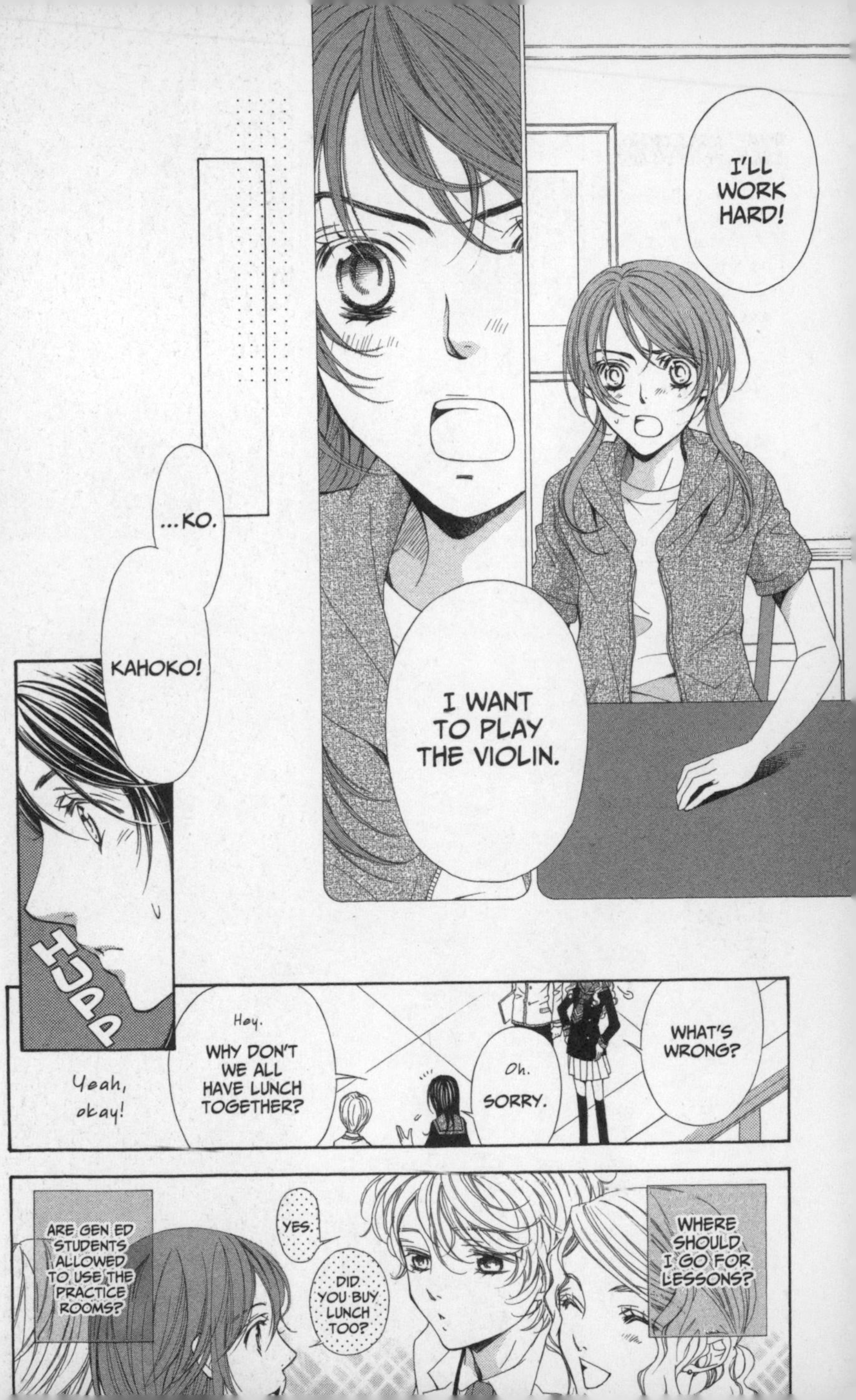
I'LL WORK HARD!
I WANT TO PLAY THE VIOLIN.
...KO.
KAHOKO!
WHAT'S WRONG?
Oh.
SORRY.
Hey.
WHY DON'T WE ALL HAVE LUNCH TOGETHER?
Yeah, okay!
WHERE SHOULD I GO FOR LESSONS?
YES.
DID YOU BUY LUNCH TOO?
ARE GEN ED STUDENTS ALLOWED TO USE THE PRACTICE ROOMS?

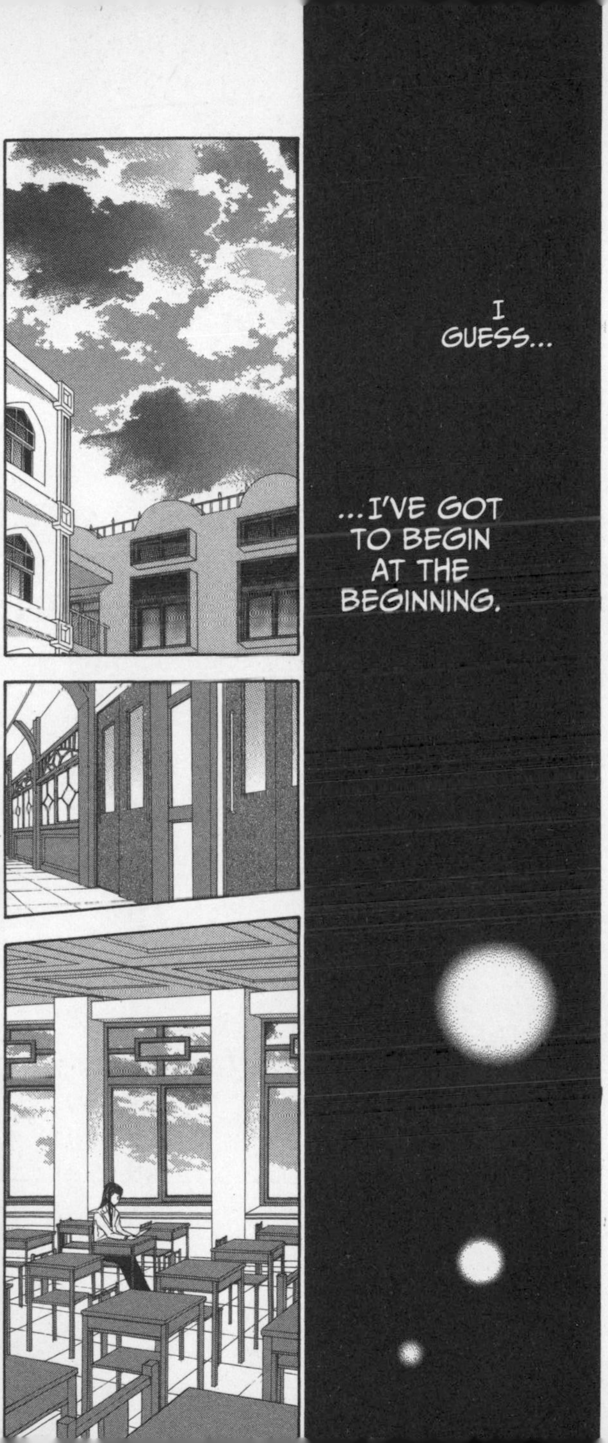
I GUESS...
...I'VE GOT TO BEGIN AT THE BEGINNING.

Thank you again for reading. We're already up to volume 10... I'm indebted to everyone. To my editor, who puts up with all my problems, to everybody who assists me on the art, to my family, my friends, Koei and of course all my readers... I have the support of so many people. Thank you very much.

2008 Yuki Kure

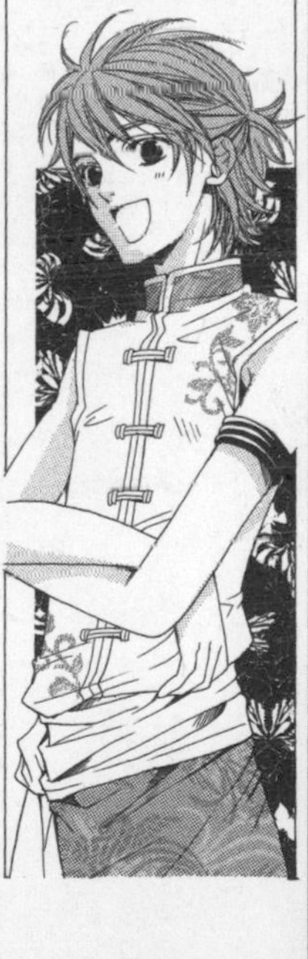

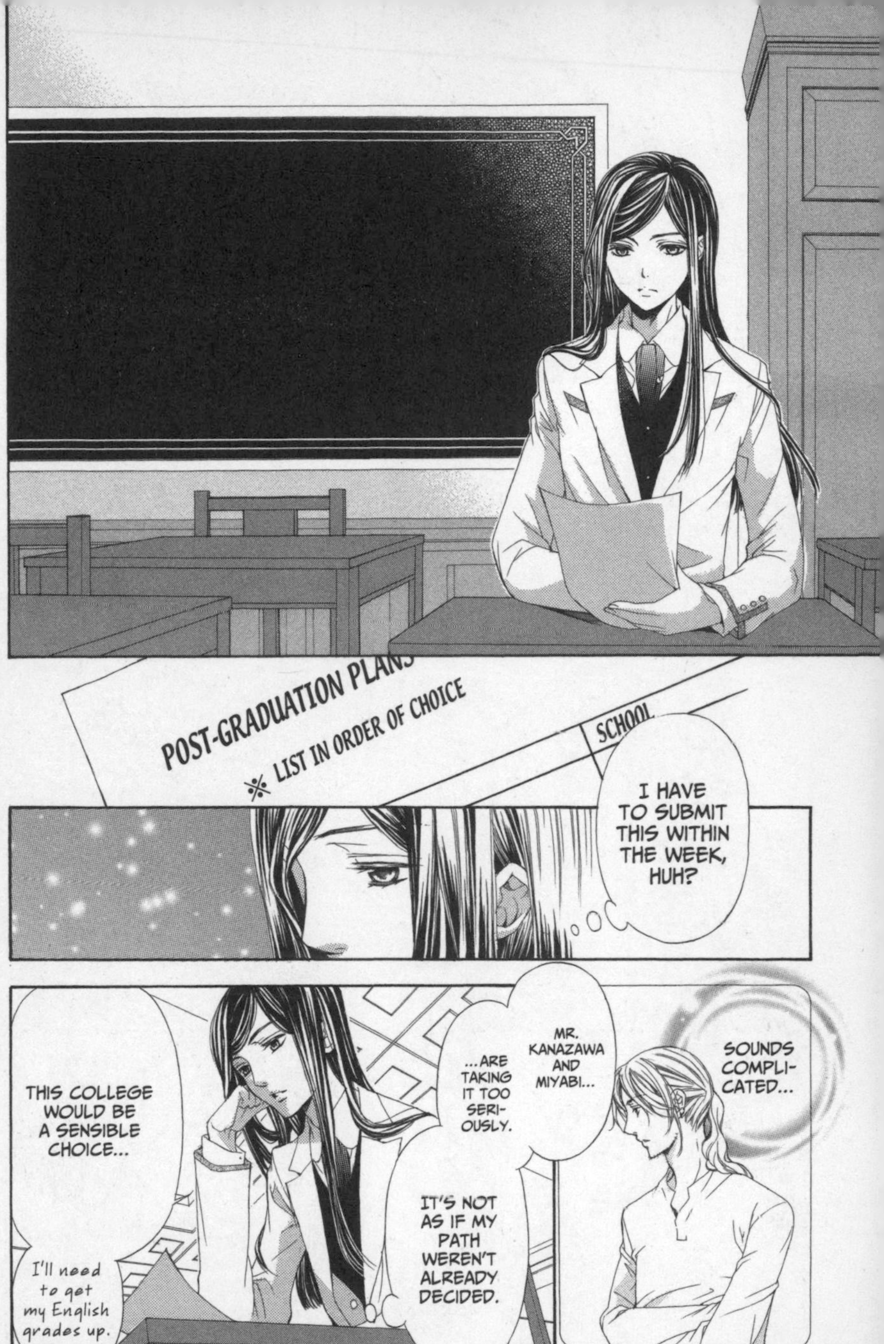
POST-GRADUATION PLANS
※ LIST IN ORDER OF CHOICE
SCHOOL
I HAVE TO SUBMIT THIS WITHIN THE WEEK, HUH?
SOUNDS COMPLICATED...
MR. KANAZAWA AND MIYABI...
...ARE TAKING IT TOO SERIOUSLY.
IT'S NOT AS IF MY PATH WEREN'T ALREADY DECIDED.
THIS COLLEGE WOULD BE A SENSIBLE CHOICE...
I'll need to get my English grades up.

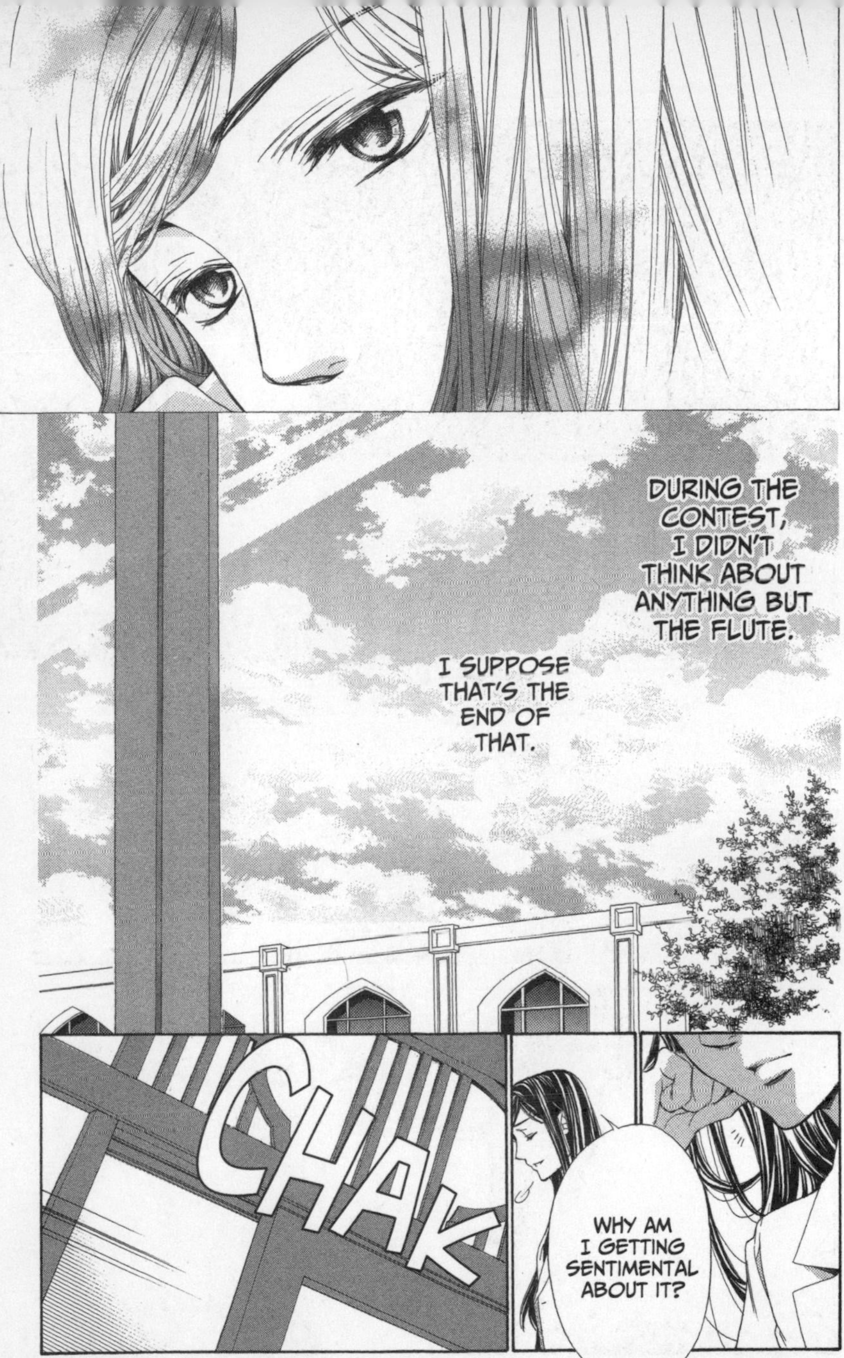
DURING THE CONTEST, I DIDN'T THINK ABOUT ANYTHING BUT THE FLUTE.
I SUPPOSE THAT'S THE END OF THAT.
WHY AM I GETTING SENTIMENTAL ABOUT IT?
CHAK

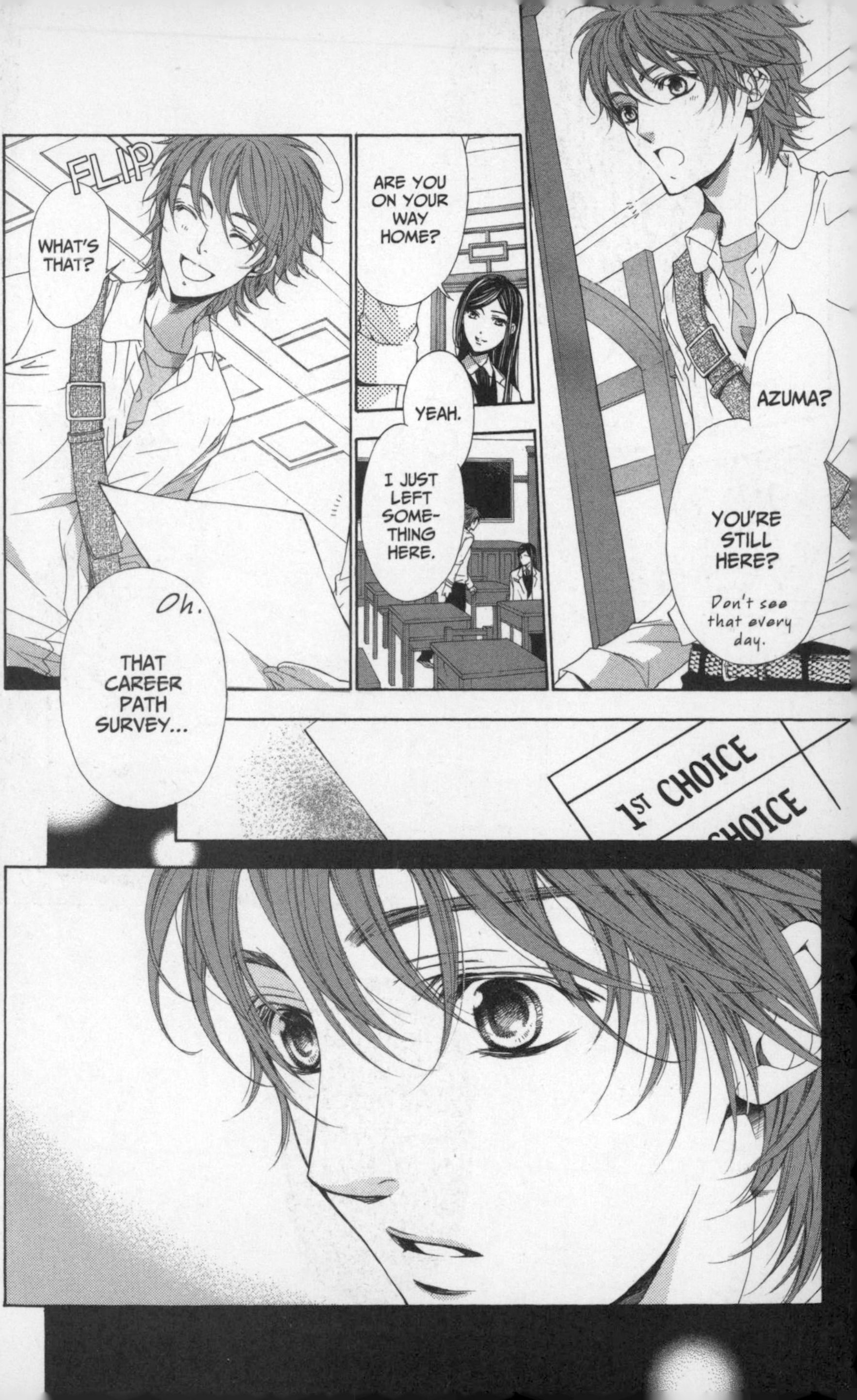
AZUMA?
YOU'RE STILL HERE?
Don't see that every day.
ARE YOU ON YOUR WAY HOME?
YEAH.
I JUST LEFT SOMETHING HERE.
FLIP
WHAT'S THAT?
Oh.
THAT CAREER PATH SURVEY...
1ST CHOICE
CHOICE

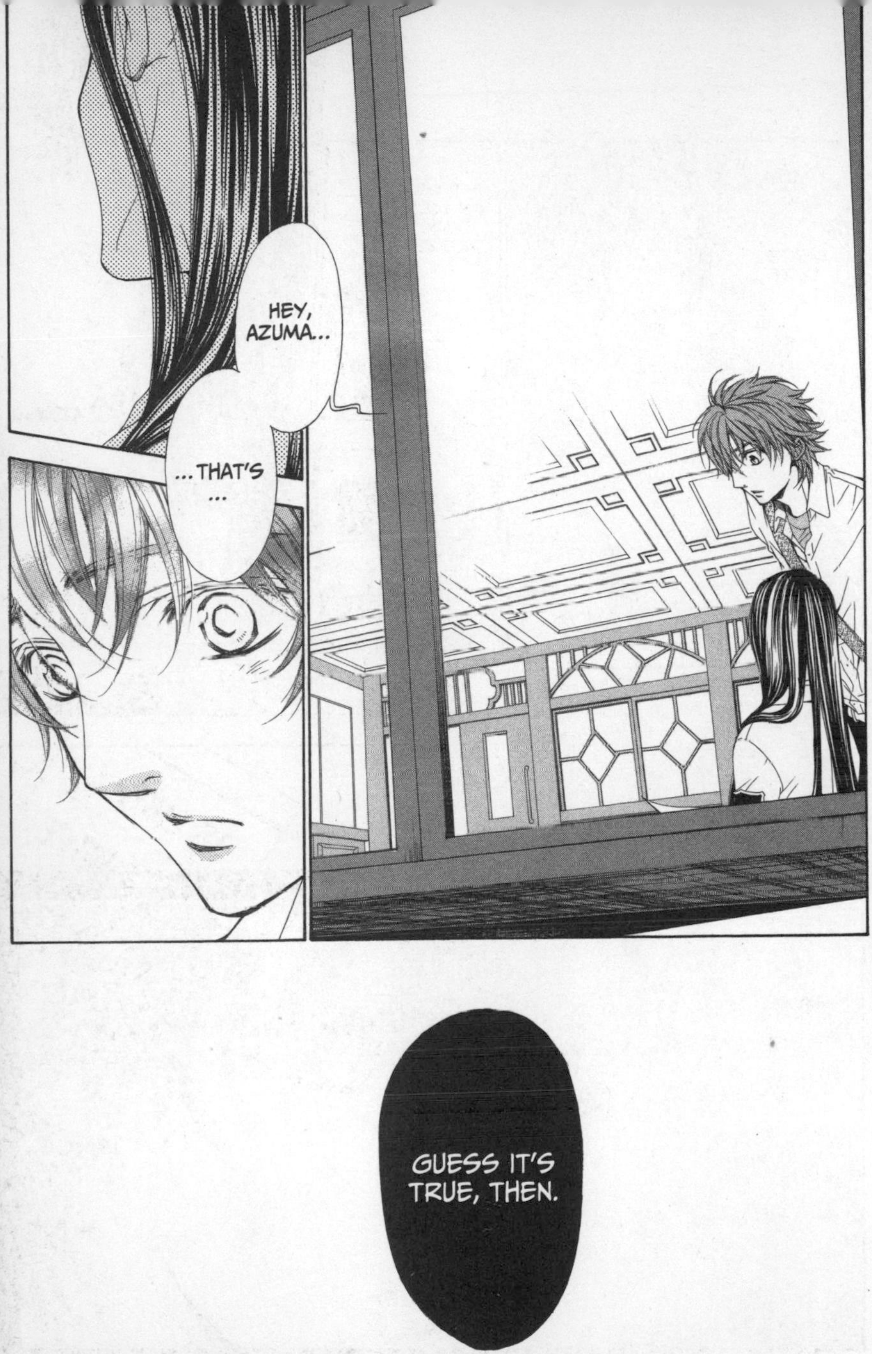
HEY, AZUMA...
...THAT'S ...
GUESS IT'S TRUE, THEN.

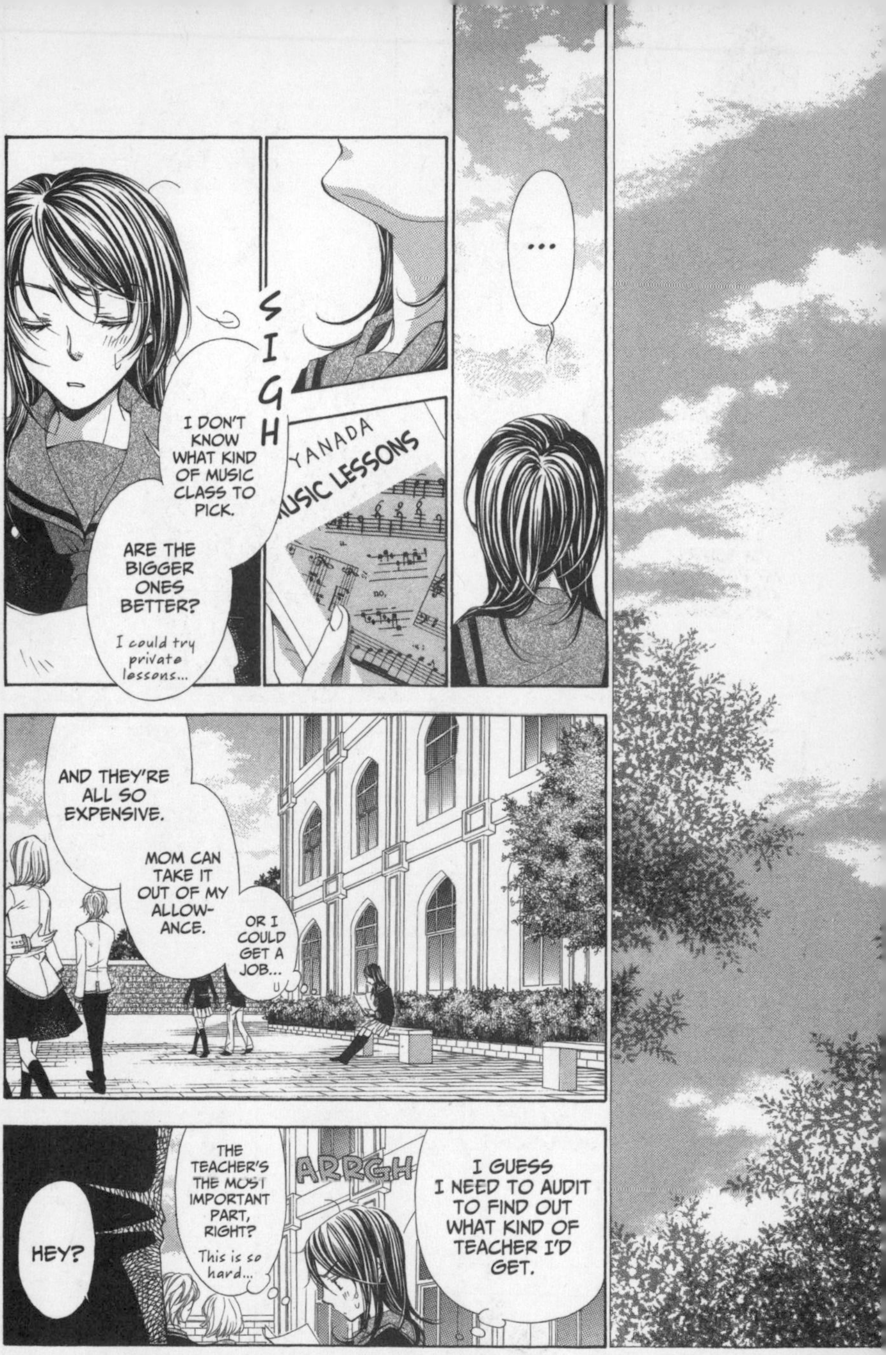
...
SIGH
YANADA
USIC LESSONS
I DON'T KNOW WHAT KIND OF MUSIC CLASS TO PICK.
ARE THE BIGGER ONES BETTER?
I could try private lessons...
AND THEY'RE ALL SO EXPENSIVE.
MOM CAN TAKE IT OUT OF MY ALLOW-ANCE.
OR I COULD GET A JOB...
I GUESS I NEED TO AUDIT TO FIND OUT WHAT KIND OF TEACHER I'D GET.
ARRGH
THE TEACHER'S THE MOST IMPORTANT PART, RIGHT?
This is so hard...
HEY?

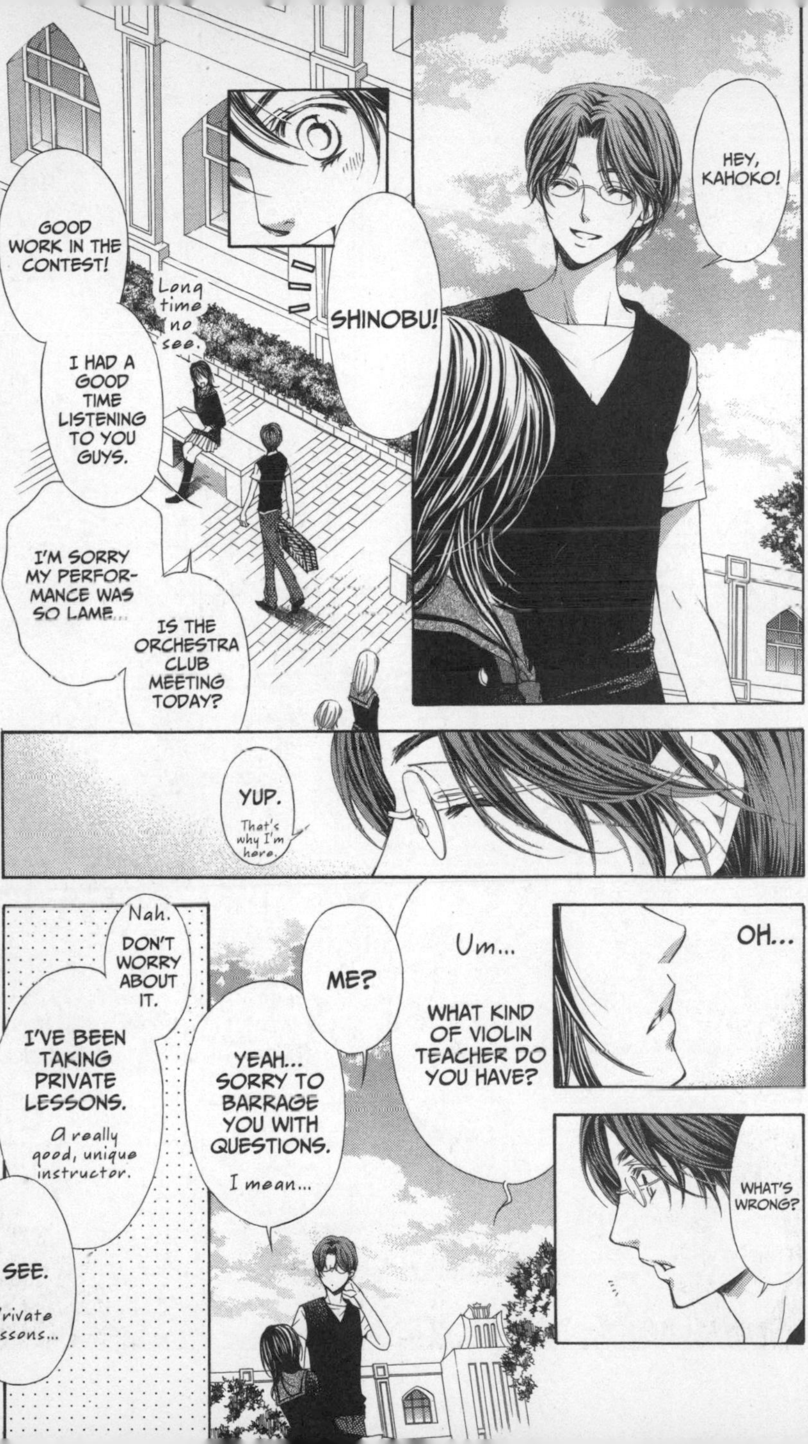
HEY, KAHOKO!
SHINOBU!
GOOD WORK IN THE CONTEST!
Long time no see.
I HAD A GOOD TIME LISTENING TO YOU GUYS.
I'M SORRY MY PERFORMANCE WAS SO LAME...
IS THE ORCHESTRA CLUB MEETING TODAY?
YUP.
That's why I'm here.
OH...
WHAT'S WRONG?
Um...
WHAT KIND OF VIOLIN TEACHER DO YOU HAVE?
ME?
YEAH... SORRY TO BARRAGE YOU WITH QUESTIONS.
I mean...
Nah.
DON'T WORRY ABOUT IT.
I'VE BEEN TAKING PRIVATE LESSONS.
A really good, unique instructor.
I SEE.
Private lessons...

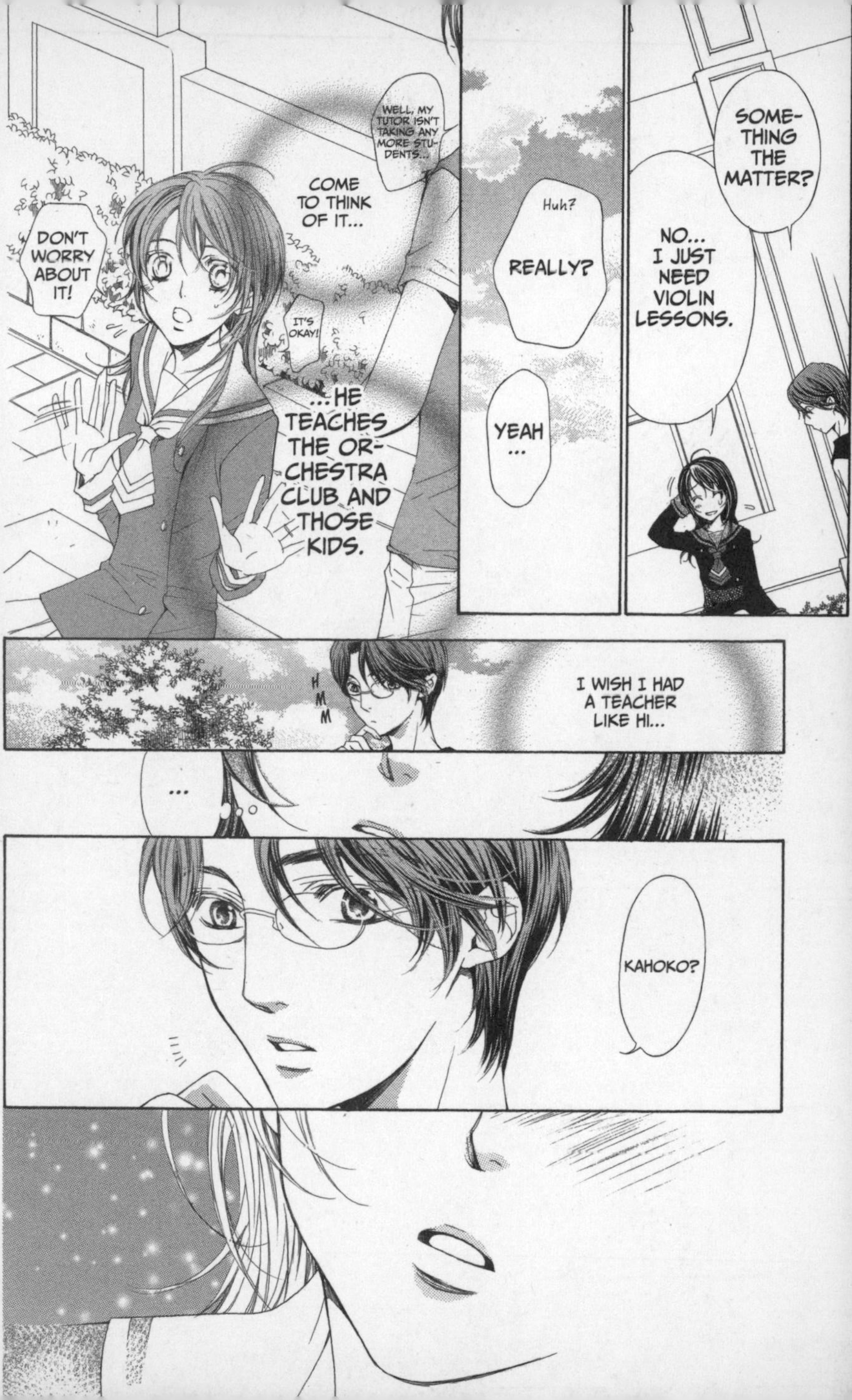
SOME-THING THE MATTER?
NO... I JUST NEED VIOLIN LESSONS.
Huh?
REALLY?
YEAH ...
WELL, MY TUTOR ISN'T TAKING ANY MORE STU-DENTS...
COME TO THINK OF IT...
...HE TEACHES THE OR-CHESTRA CLUB AND THOSE KIDS.
IT'S OKAY!
DON'T WORRY ABOUT IT!
I WISH I HAD A TEACHER LIKE HI...
HMM
...
KAHOKO?

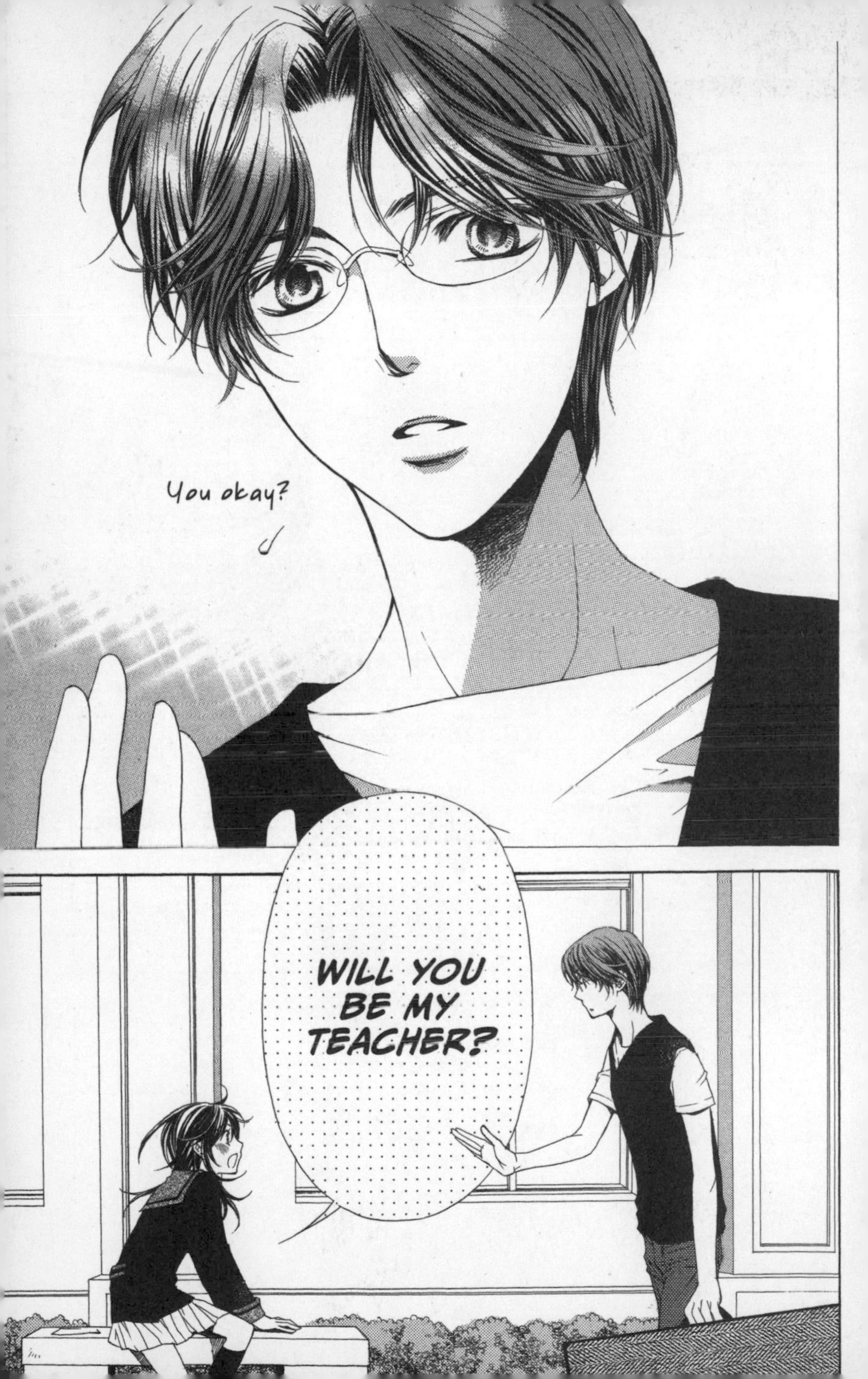
You okay?
WILL YOU BE MY TEACHER?

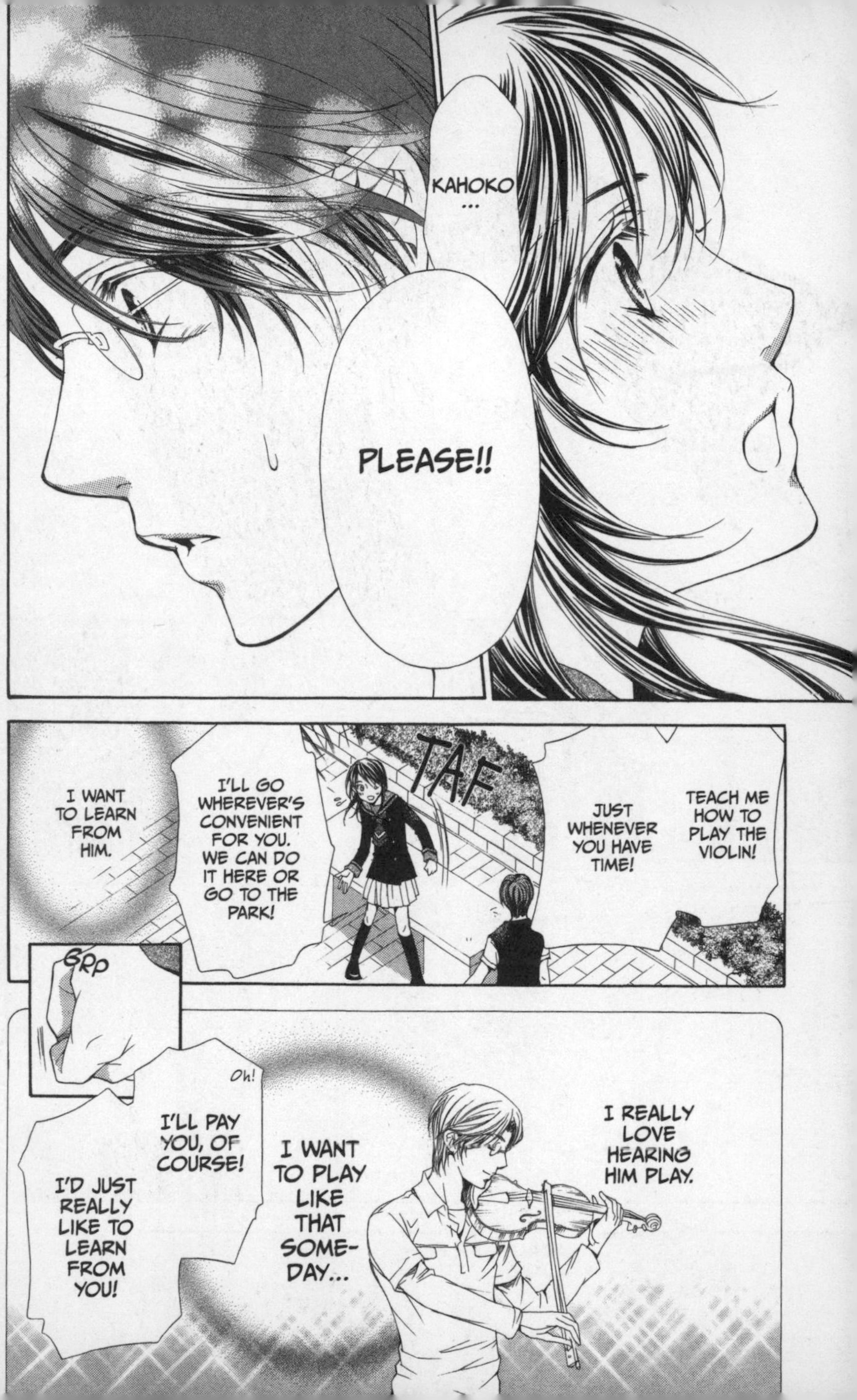
KAHOKO ...
PLEASE!!
TEACH ME HOW TO PLAY THE VIOLIN!
JUST WHENEVER YOU HAVE TIME!
TAF
I'LL GO WHEREVER'S CONVENIENT FOR YOU. WE CAN DO IT HERE OR GO TO THE PARK!
I WANT TO LEARN FROM HIM.
GRP
I REALLY LOVE HEARING HIM PLAY.
I WANT TO PLAY LIKE THAT SOME-DAY...
Oh!
I'LL PAY YOU, OF COURSE!
I'D JUST REALLY LIKE TO LEARN FROM YOU!

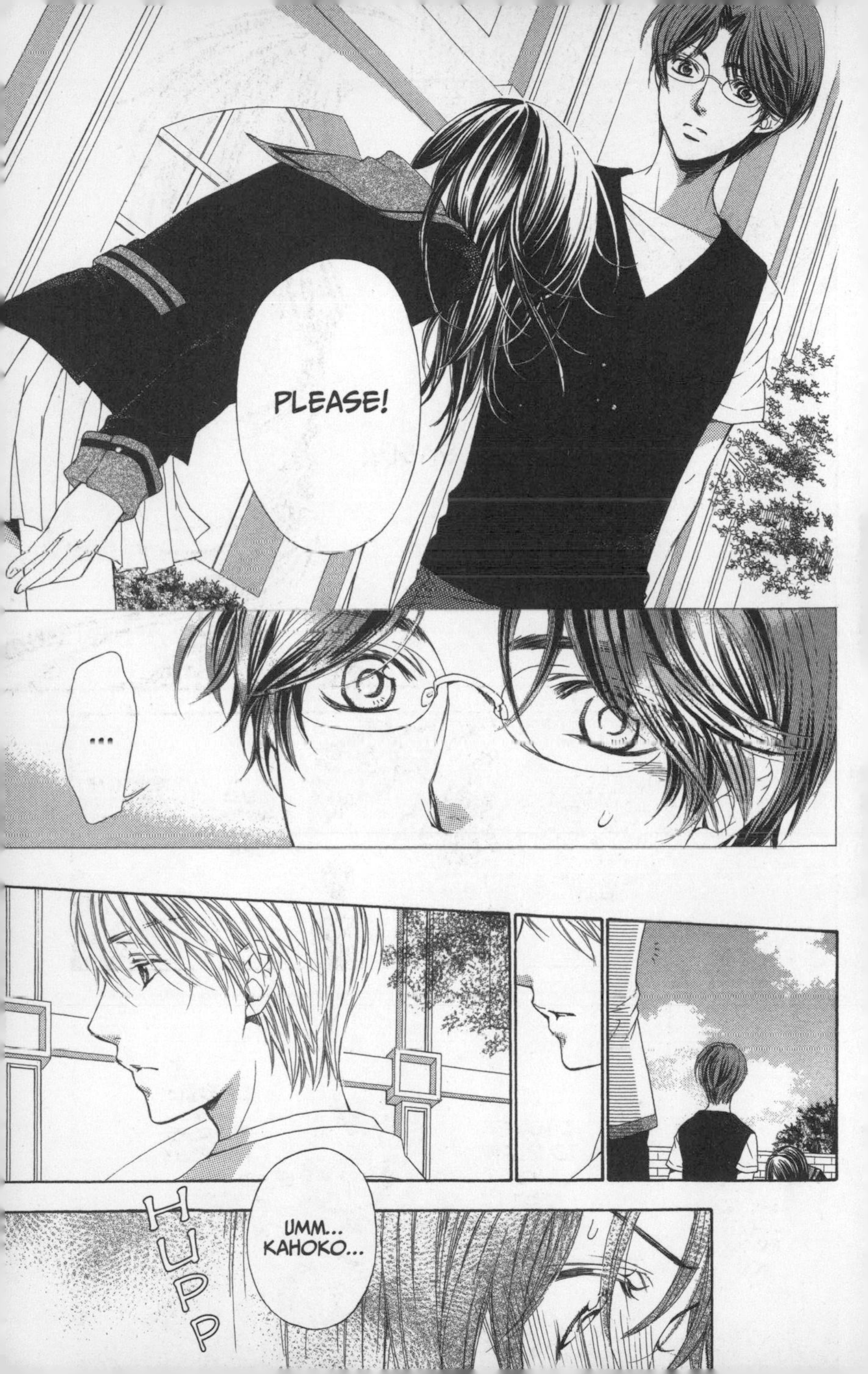
PLEASE!
...
HUPP
UMM... KAHOKO...

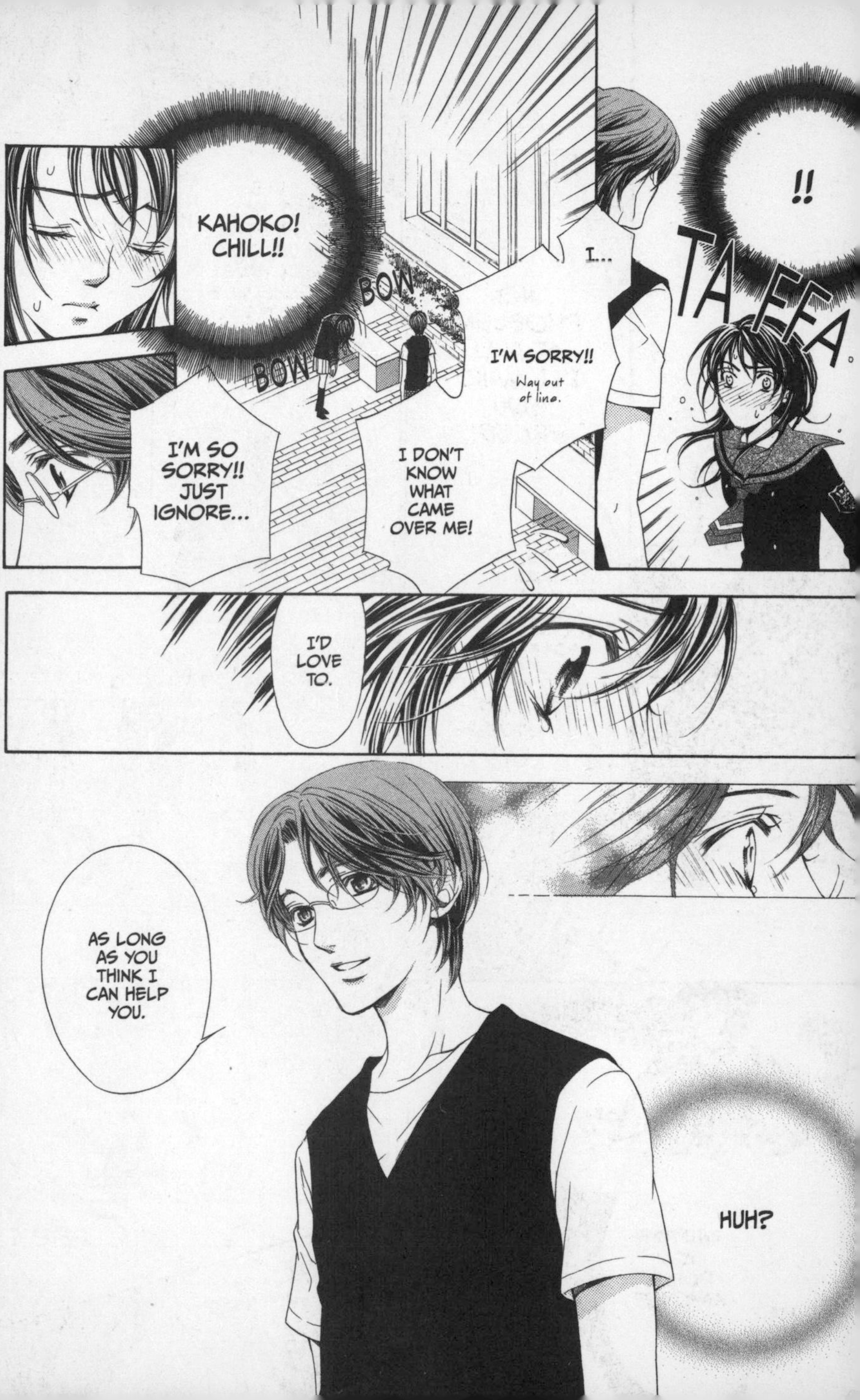
!!
TAFFA
I...
I'M SORRY!!
Way out of line.
I DON'T KNOW WHAT CAME OVER ME!
BOW
BOW
KAHOKO! CHILL!!
I'M SO SORRY!! JUST IGNORE...
I'D LOVE TO.
AS LONG AS YOU THINK I CAN HELP YOU.
HUH?

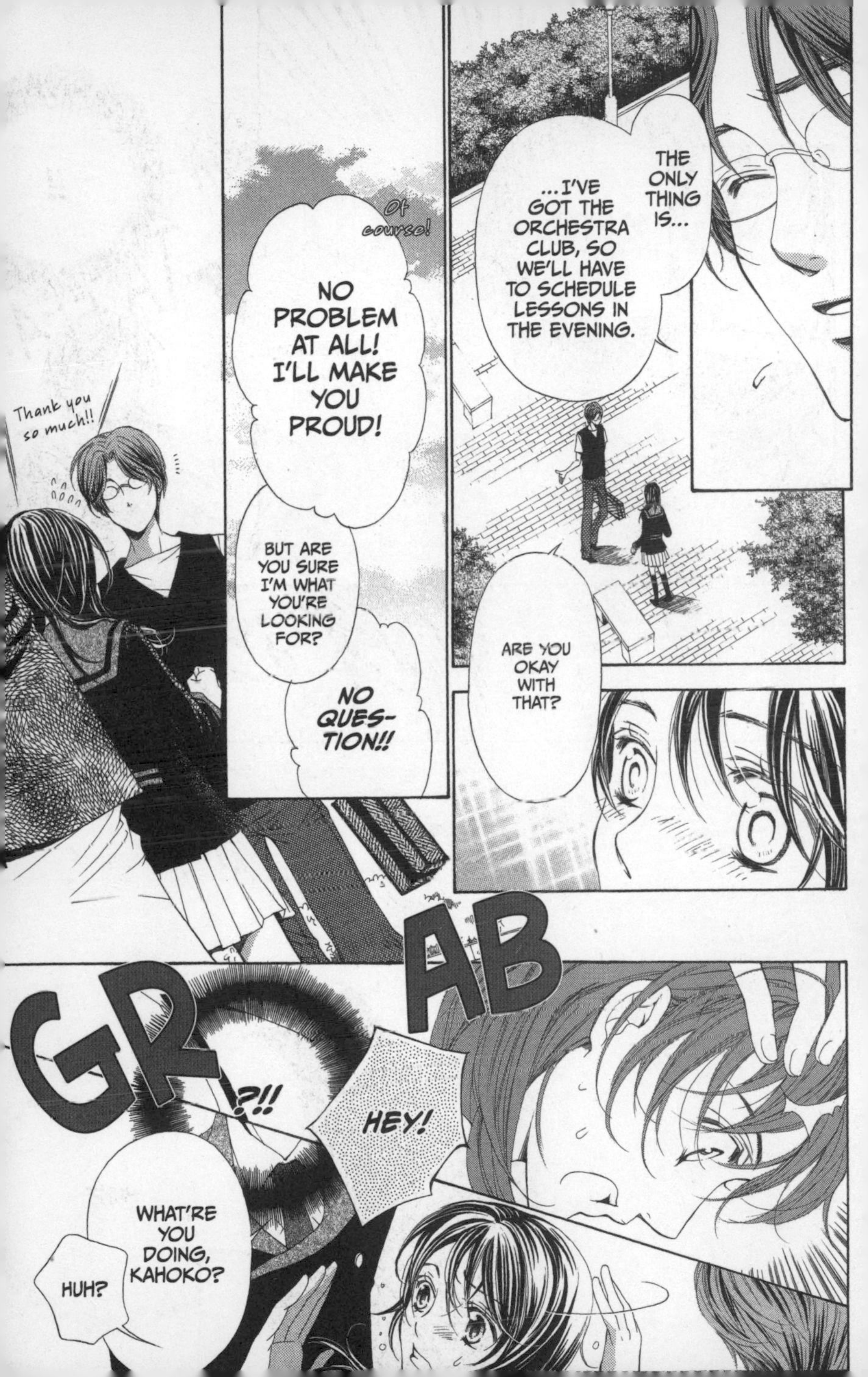
THE ONLY THING IS...
...I'VE GOT THE ORCHESTRA CLUB, SO WE'LL HAVE TO SCHEDULE LESSONS IN THE EVENING.
ARE YOU OKAY WITH THAT?
Of course!
NO PROBLEM AT ALL! I'LL MAKE YOU PROUD!
BUT ARE YOU SURE I'M WHAT YOU'RE LOOKING FOR?
NO QUES-TION!!
Thank you so much!!
GRAB
HEY!
?!!
WHAT'RE YOU DOING, KAHOKO?
HUH?

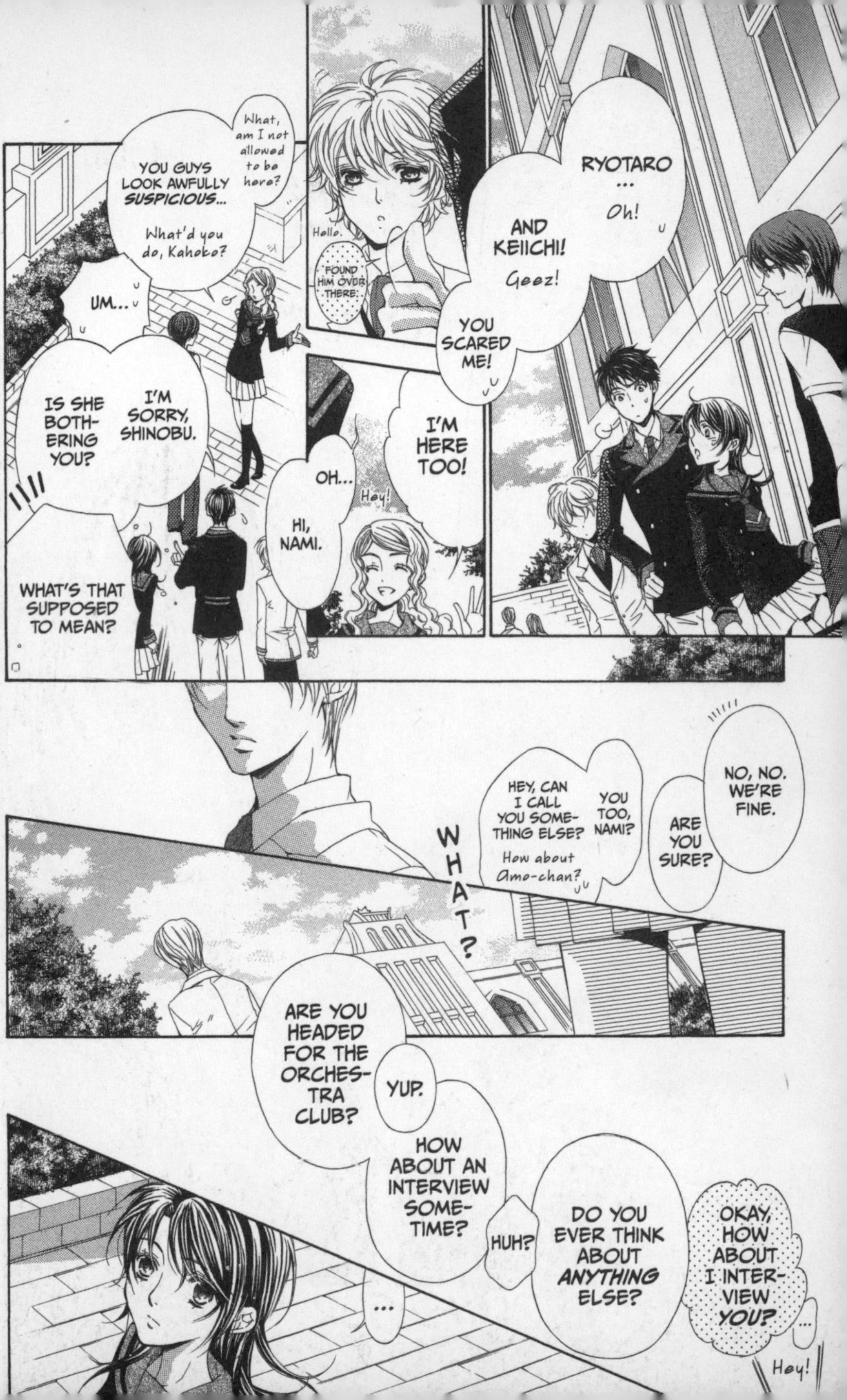
RYOTARO ...
Oh!
AND KEIICHI!
Geez!
YOU SCARED ME!
Hello.
FOUND HIM OVER THERE.
I'M HERE TOO!
Hey!
OH...
HI, NAMI.
What, am I not allowed to be here?
YOU GUYS LOOK AWFULLY *SUSPICIOUS*...
What'd you do, Kahoko?
UM...
I'M SORRY, SHINOBU.
IS SHE BOTHERING YOU?
WHAT'S THAT SUPPOSED TO MEAN?
NO, NO. WE'RE FINE.
ARE YOU SURE?
YOU TOO, NAMI?
HEY, CAN I CALL YOU SOMETHING ELSE?
How about Amo-chan?
WHAT?
ARE YOU HEADED FOR THE ORCHESTRA CLUB?
YUP.
HOW ABOUT AN INTERVIEW SOMETIME?
HUH?
DO YOU EVER THINK ABOUT *ANYTHING* ELSE?
OKAY, HOW ABOUT I INTERVIEW *YOU*?
...
Hey!
...

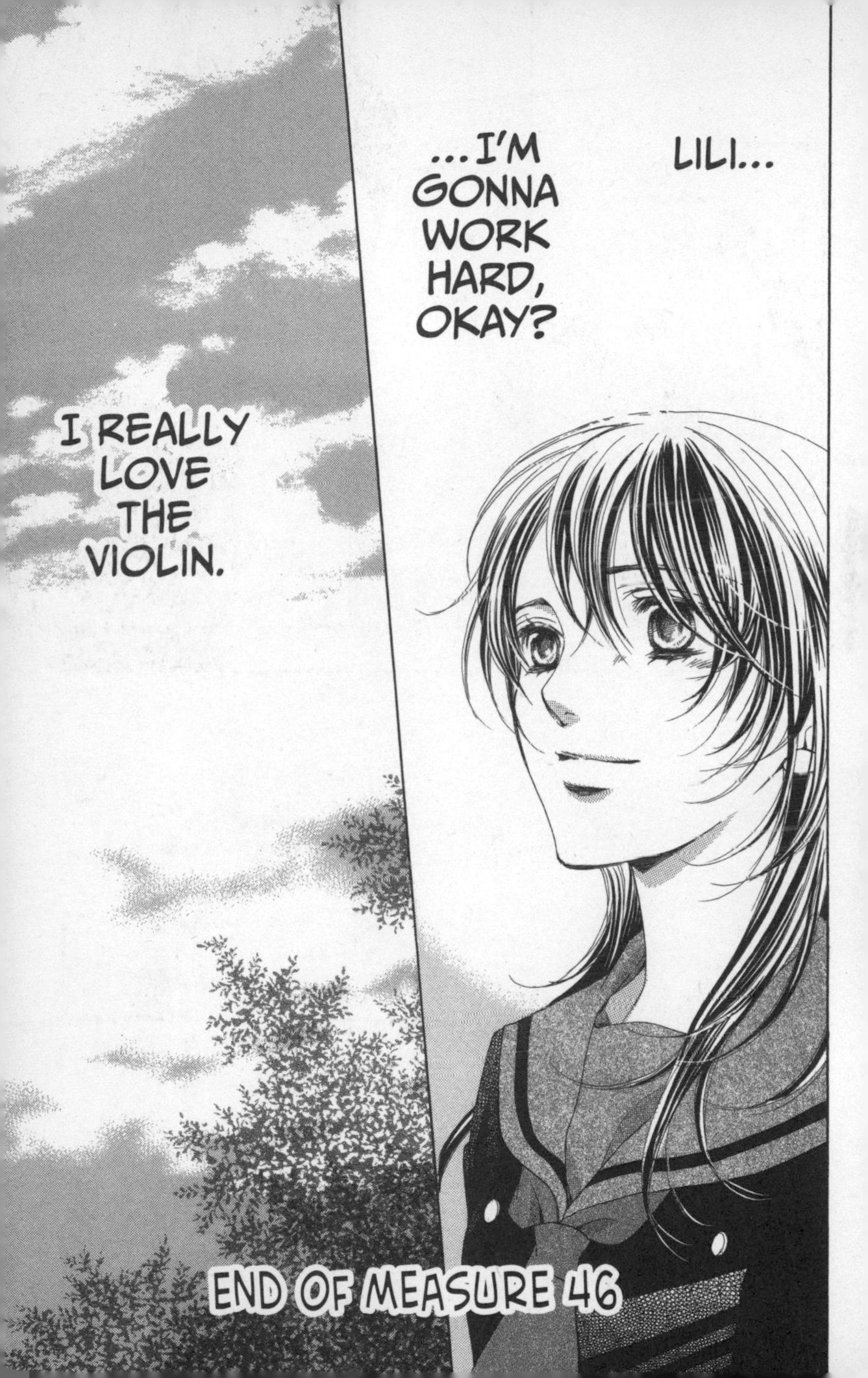
LILI...
...I'M GONNA WORK HARD, OKAY?
I REALLY LOVE THE VIOLIN.
END OF MEASURE 46

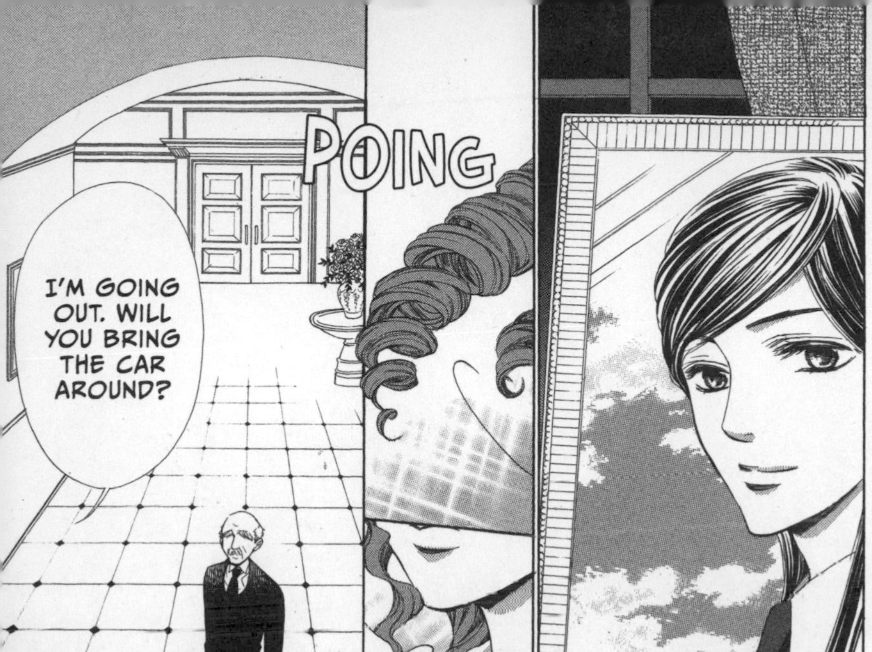
POING
I'M GOING OUT. WILL YOU BRING THE CAR AROUND?
La Corda d'Oro

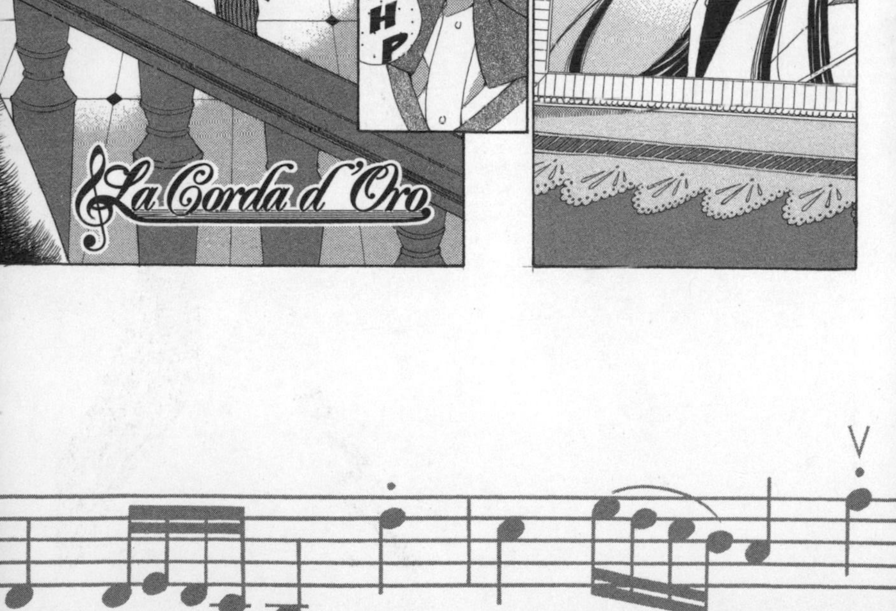

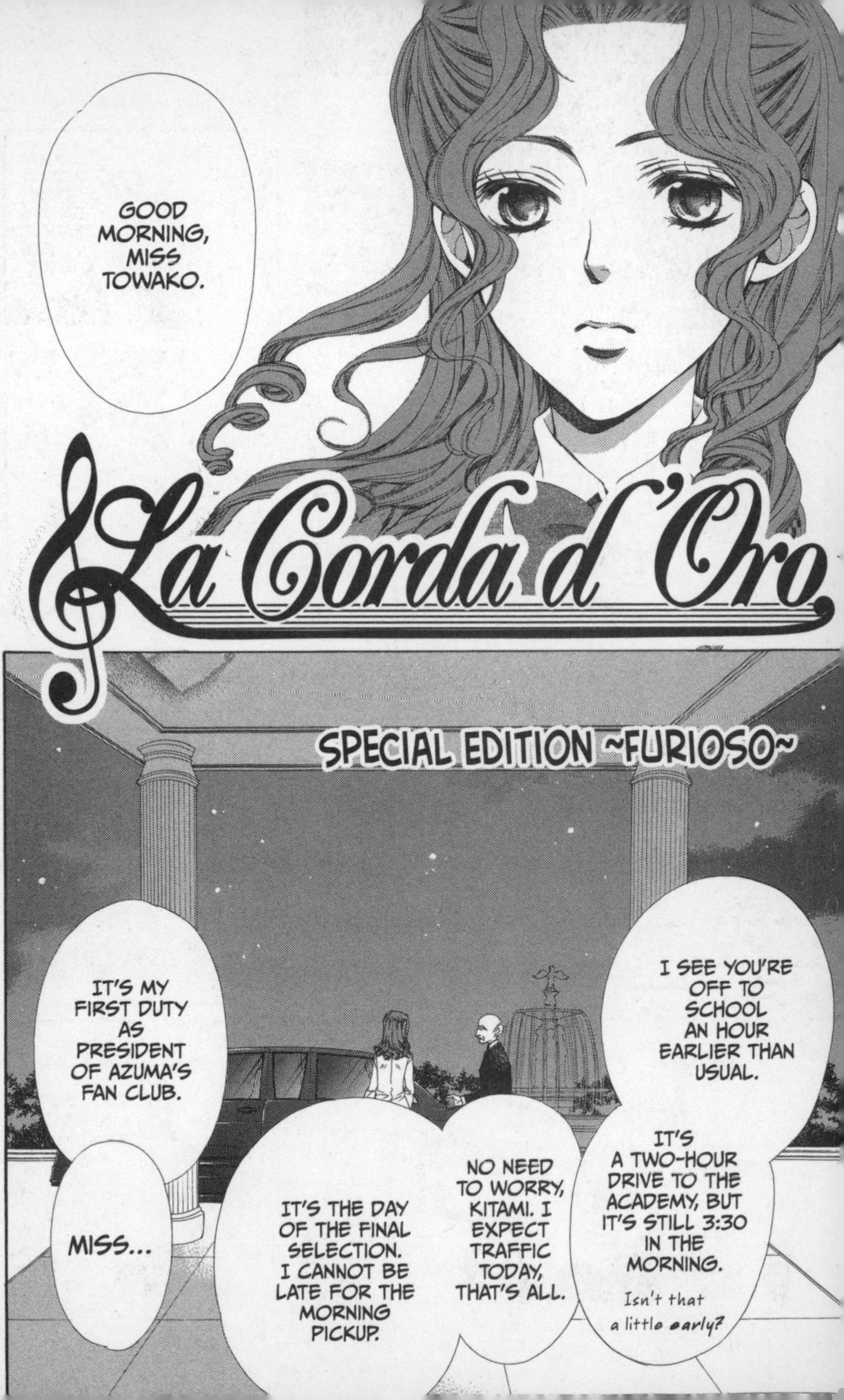

GOOD MORNING, MISS TOWAKO.
La Corda d'Oro
SPECIAL EDITION ~FURIOSO~
I SEE YOU'RE OFF TO SCHOOL AN HOUR EARLIER THAN USUAL.
IT'S MY FIRST DUTY AS PRESIDENT OF AZUMA'S FAN CLUB.
IT'S A TWO-HOUR DRIVE TO THE ACADEMY, BUT IT'S STILL 3:30 IN THE MORNING.
Isn't that a little early?
NO NEED TO WORRY, KITAMI. I EXPECT TRAFFIC TODAY, THAT'S ALL.
IT'S THE DAY OF THE FINAL SELECTION. I CANNOT BE LATE FOR THE MORNING PICKUP.
MISS...

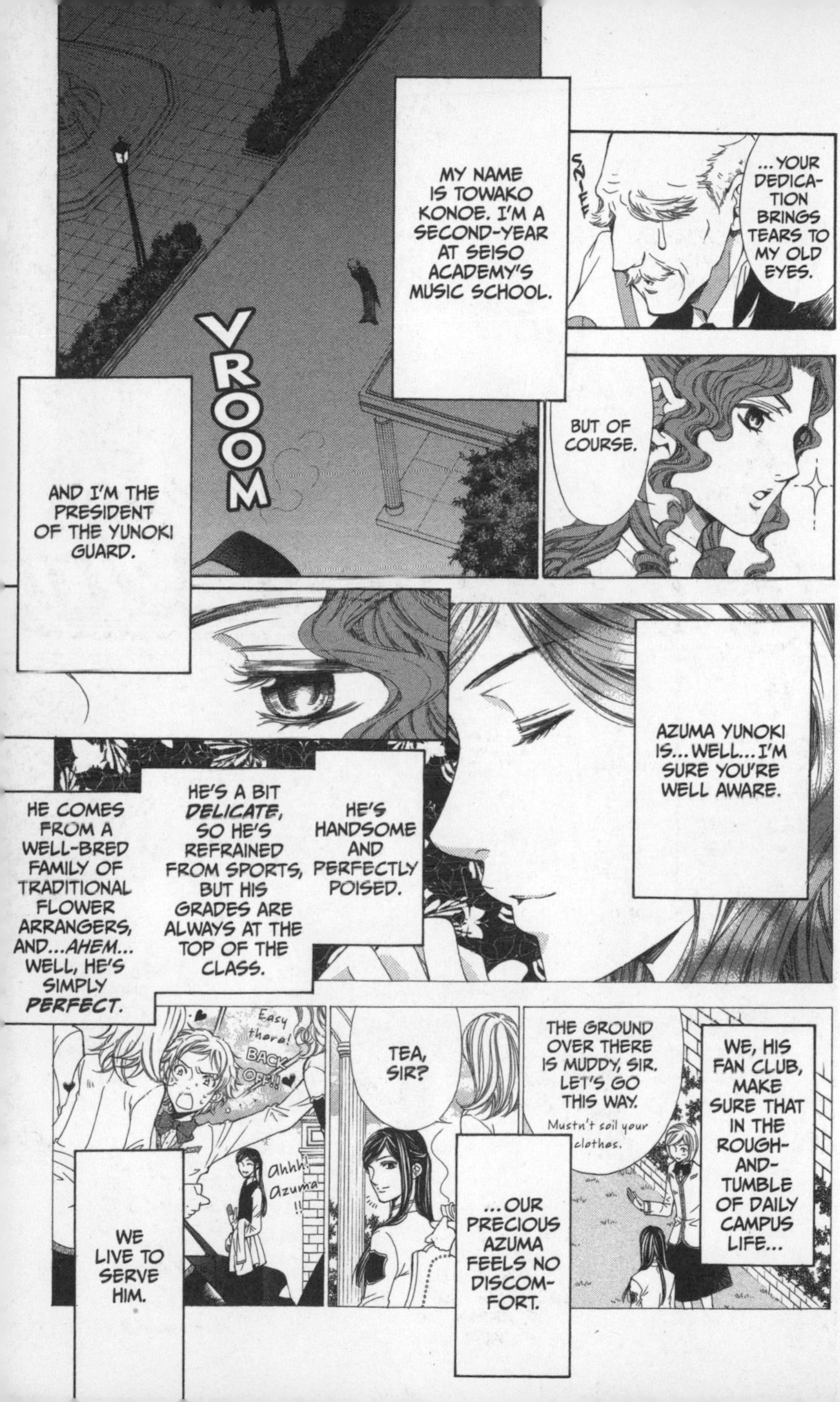
SNIFF
...YOUR DEDICATION BRINGS TEARS TO MY OLD EYES.
MY NAME IS TOWAKO KONOE. I'M A SECOND-YEAR AT SEISO ACADEMY'S MUSIC SCHOOL.
BUT OF COURSE.
VROOM
AND I'M THE PRESIDENT OF THE YUNOKI GUARD.
AZUMA YUNOKI IS...WELL...I'M SURE YOU'RE WELL AWARE.
HE'S HANDSOME AND PERFECTLY POISED.
HE'S A BIT *DELICATE*, SO HE'S REFRAINED FROM SPORTS, BUT HIS GRADES ARE ALWAYS AT THE TOP OF THE CLASS.
HE COMES FROM A WELL-BRED FAMILY OF TRADITIONAL FLOWER ARRANGERS, AND...*AHEM*... WELL, HE'S SIMPLY *PERFECT*.
WE, HIS FAN CLUB, MAKE SURE THAT IN THE ROUGH-AND-TUMBLE OF DAILY CAMPUS LIFE...
THE GROUND OVER THERE IS MUDDY, SIR. LET'S GO THIS WAY.
Mustn't soil your clothes.
...OUR PRECIOUS AZUMA FEELS NO DISCOMFORT.
TEA, SIR?
Easy there!
BACK OFF!!
Ahhh! Azuma!!
WE LIVE TO SERVE HIM.

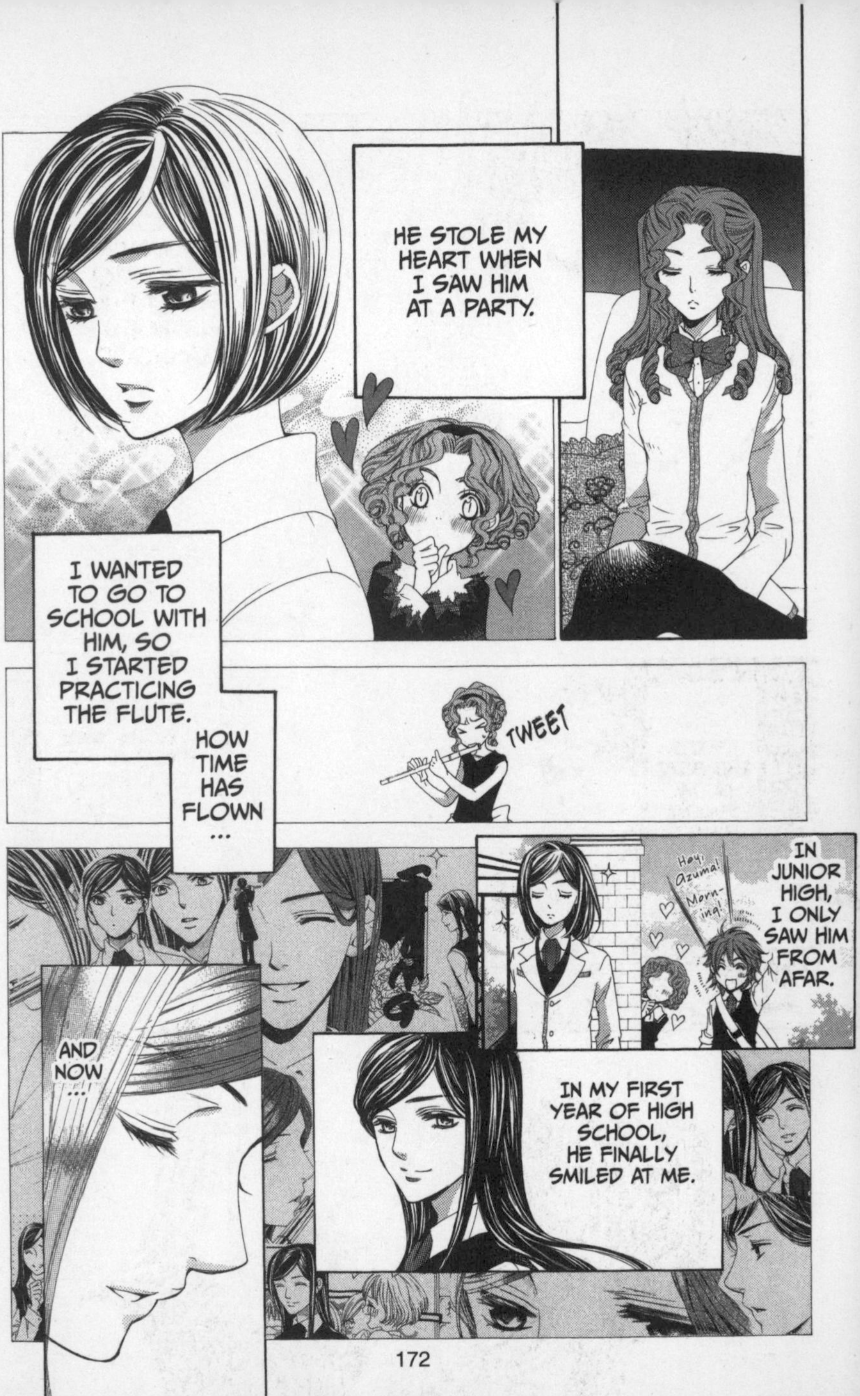
HE STOLE MY HEART WHEN I SAW HIM AT A PARTY.
I WANTED TO GO TO SCHOOL WITH HIM, SO I STARTED PRACTICING THE FLUTE.
TWEET
HOW TIME HAS FLOWN ...
Hey, Azuma!
Morning!
IN JUNIOR HIGH, I ONLY SAW HIM FROM AFAR.
IN MY FIRST YEAR OF HIGH SCHOOL, HE FINALLY SMILED AT ME.
AND NOW ...

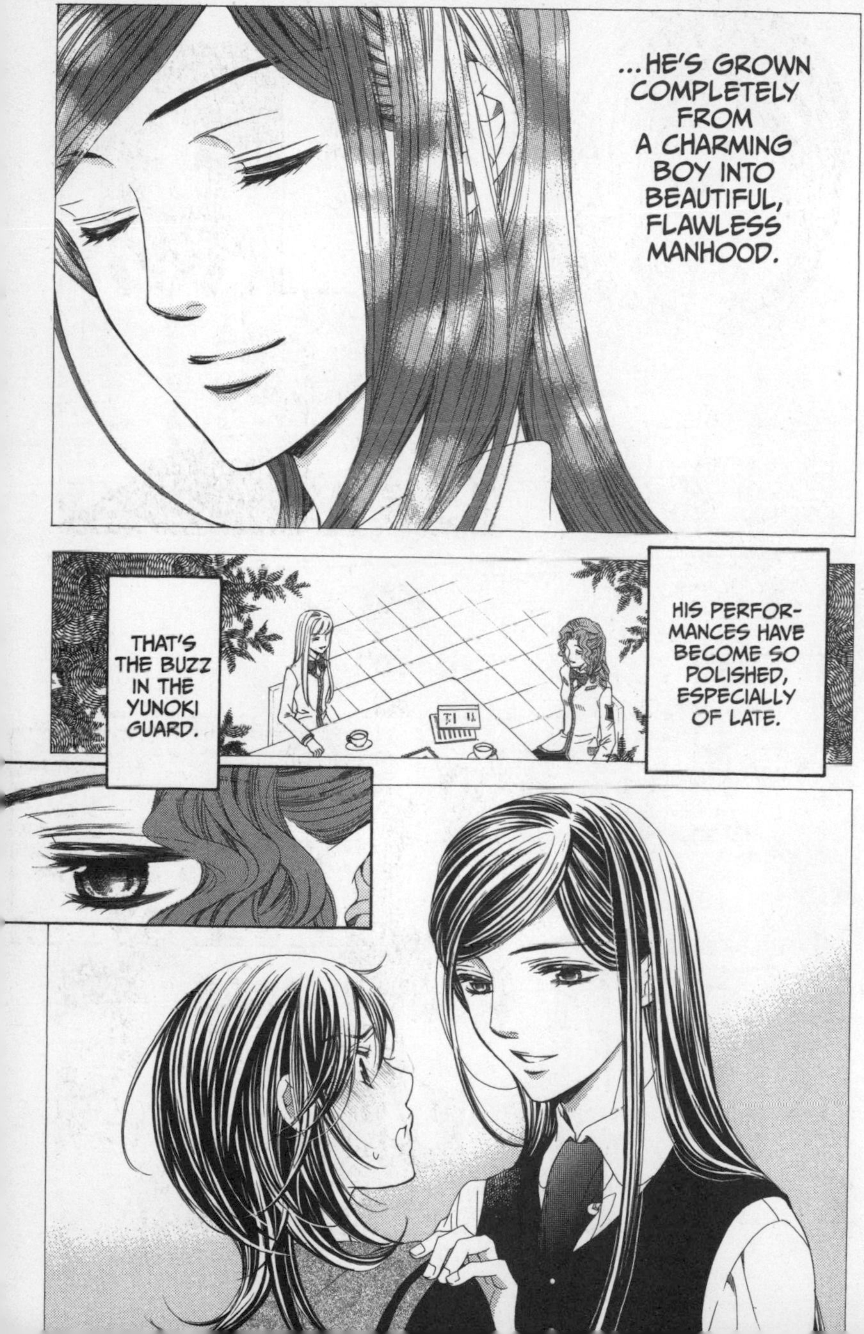
...HE'S GROWN COMPLETELY FROM A CHARMING BOY INTO BEAUTIFUL, FLAWLESS MANHOOD.
HIS PERFORMANCES HAVE BECOME SO POLISHED, ESPECIALLY OF LATE.
THAT'S THE BUZZ IN THE YUNOKI GUARD.

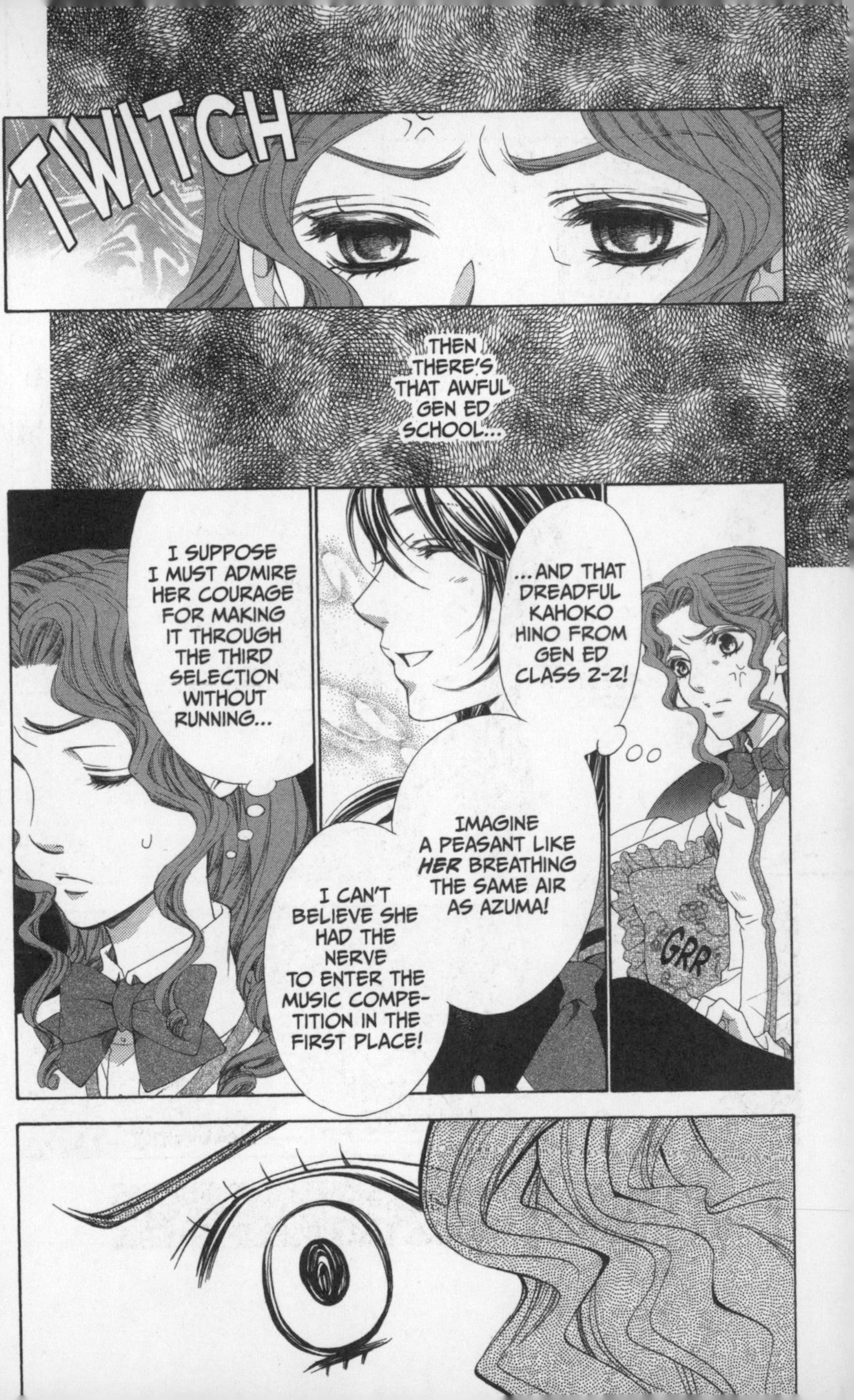
TWITCH
THEN THERE'S THAT AWFUL GEN ED SCHOOL...
GRR
...AND THAT DREADFUL KAHOKO HINO FROM GEN ED CLASS 2-2!
IMAGINE A PEASANT LIKE HER BREATHING THE SAME AIR AS AZUMA!
I CAN'T BELIEVE SHE HAD THE NERVE TO ENTER THE MUSIC COMPETITION IN THE FIRST PLACE!
I SUPPOSE I MUST ADMIRE HER COURAGE FOR MAKING IT THROUGH THE THIRD SELECTION WITHOUT RUNNING...

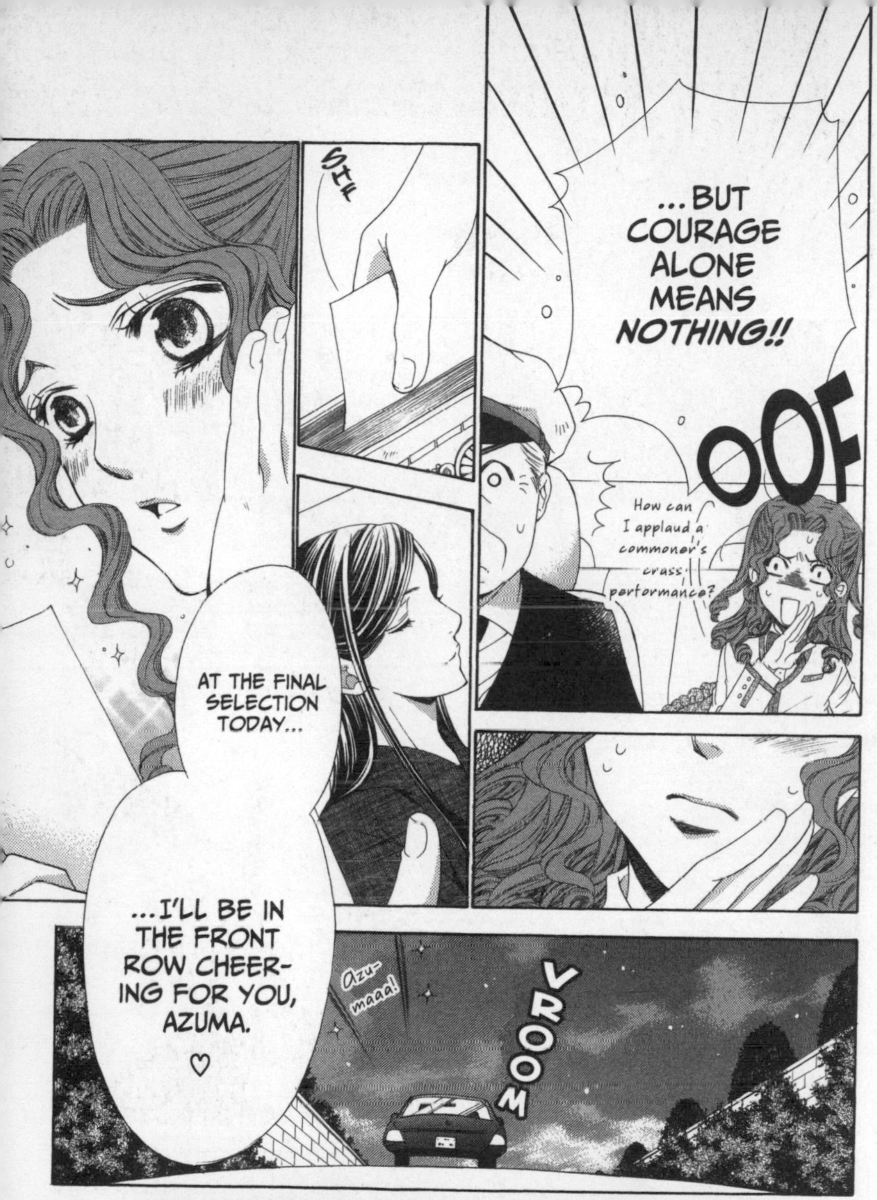
...BUT COURAGE ALONE MEANS NOTHING!!
OOF
How can I applaud a commoner's crass performance?
SHF
AT THE FINAL SELECTION TODAY...
...I'LL BE IN THE FRONT ROW CHEERING FOR YOU, AZUMA. ♡
Azu-maaa!
VROOM

[redacted]

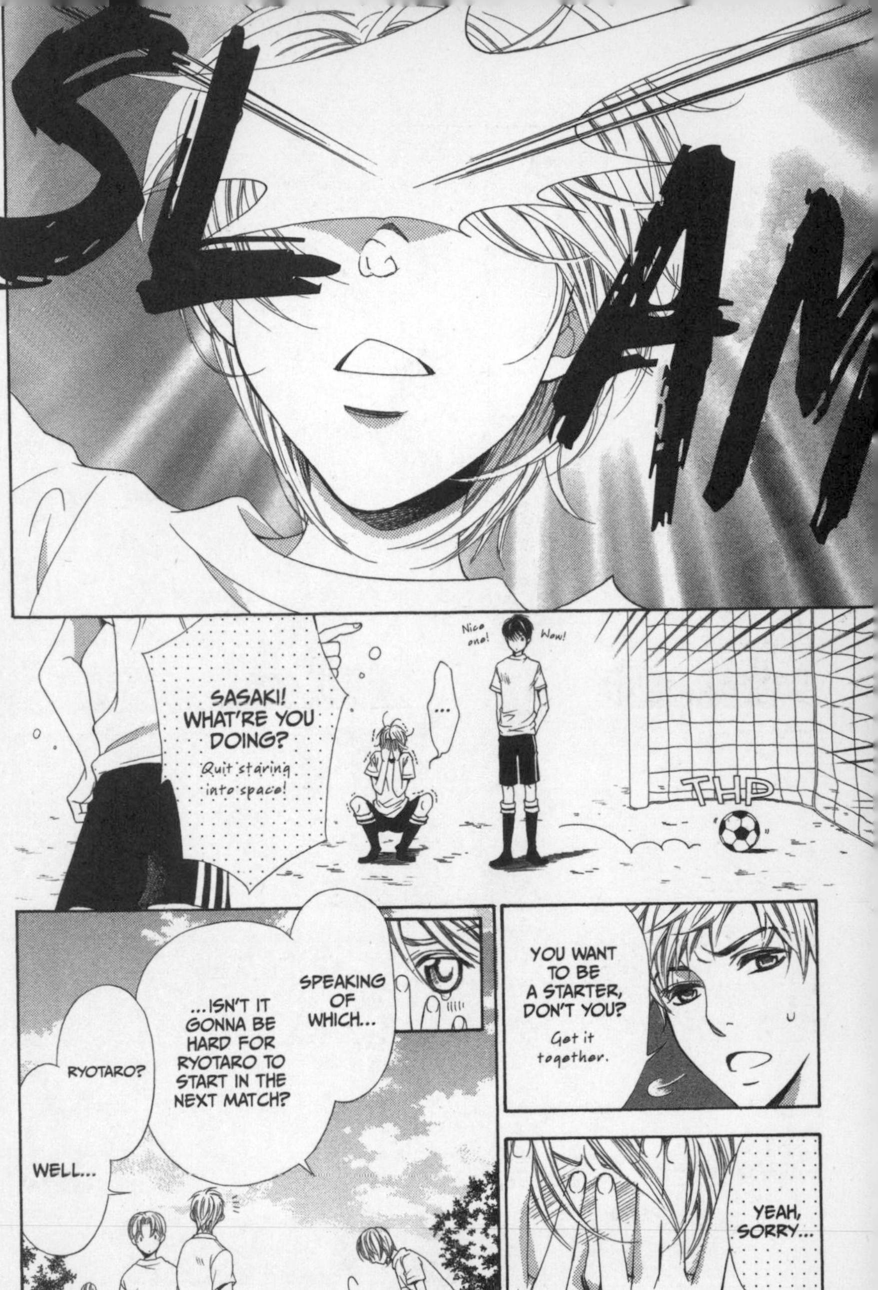
SLAM
Wow!
Nice one!
...
SASAKI! WHAT'RE YOU DOING?
Quit staring into space!
THP
YOU WANT TO BE A STARTER, DON'T YOU?
Get it together.
YEAH, SORRY...
SPEAKING OF WHICH...
...ISN'T IT GONNA BE HARD FOR RYOTARO TO START IN THE NEXT MATCH?
RYOTARO?
WELL...

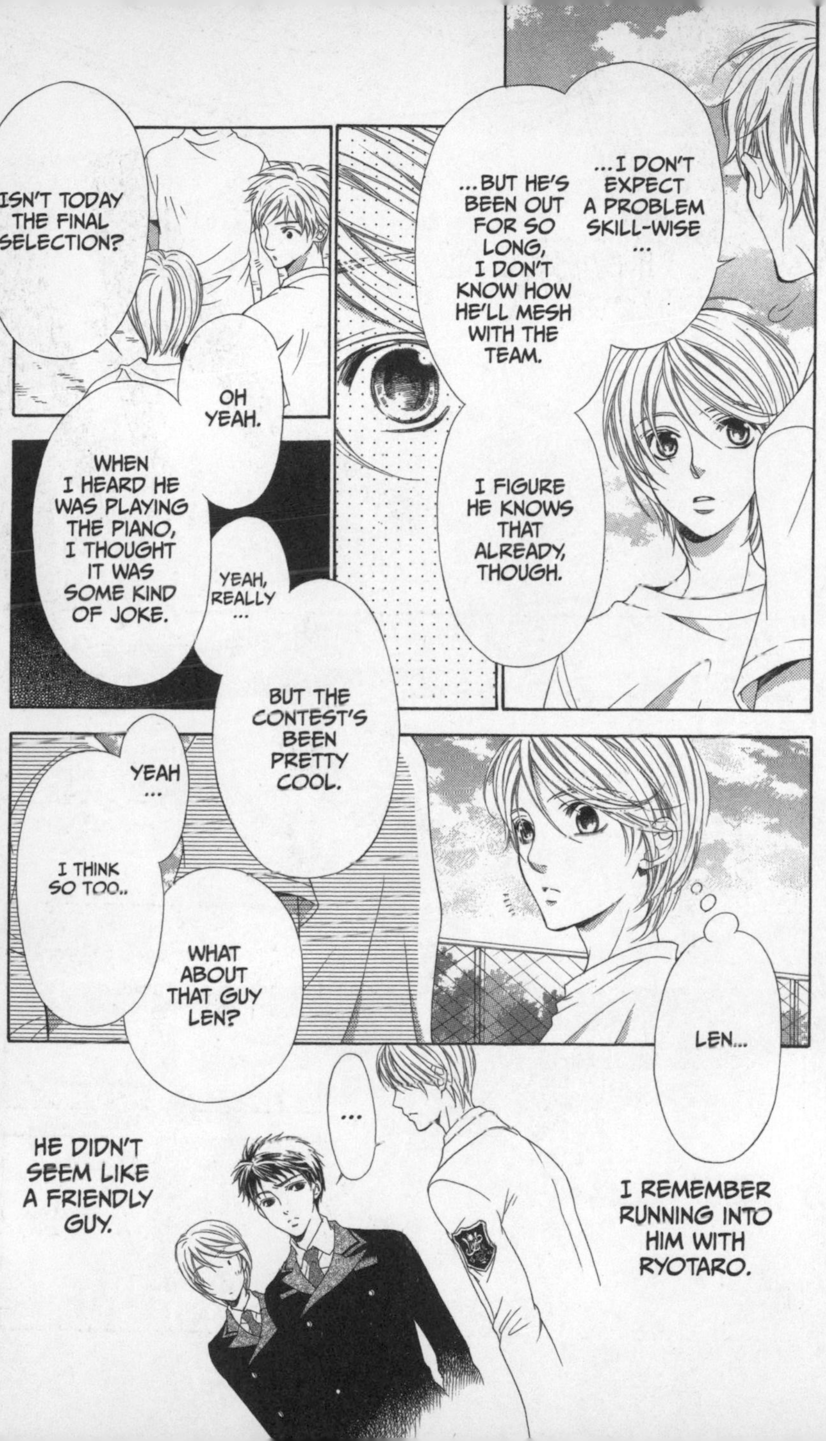
...I DON'T EXPECT A PROBLEM SKILL-WISE ...
...BUT HE'S BEEN OUT FOR SO LONG, I DON'T KNOW HOW HE'LL MESH WITH THE TEAM.
I FIGURE HE KNOWS THAT ALREADY, THOUGH.
ISN'T TODAY THE FINAL SELECTION?
OH YEAH.
WHEN I HEARD HE WAS PLAYING THE PIANO, I THOUGHT IT WAS SOME KIND OF JOKE.
YEAH, REALLY ...
BUT THE CONTEST'S BEEN PRETTY COOL.
YEAH ...
I THINK SO TOO..
WHAT ABOUT THAT GUY LEN?
LEN...
I REMEMBER RUNNING INTO HIM WITH RYOTARO.
...
HE DIDN'T SEEM LIKE A FRIENDLY GUY.

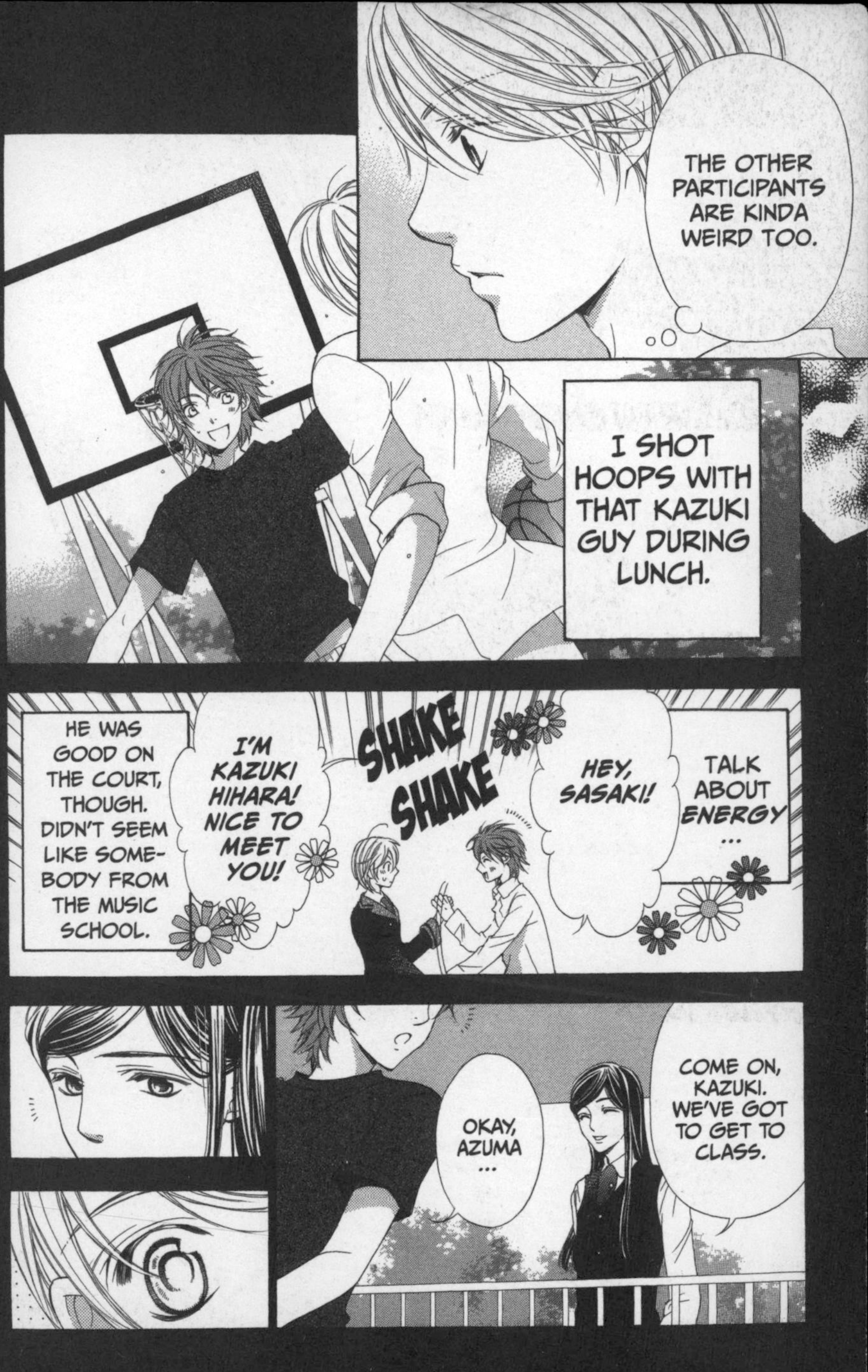
THE OTHER PARTICIPANTS ARE KINDA WEIRD TOO.
I SHOT HOOPS WITH THAT KAZUKI GUY DURING LUNCH.
TALK ABOUT ENERGY ...
HEY, SASAKI!
SHAKE SHAKE
I'M KAZUKI HIHARA! NICE TO MEET YOU!
HE WAS GOOD ON THE COURT, THOUGH. DIDN'T SEEM LIKE SOME-BODY FROM THE MUSIC SCHOOL.
COME ON, KAZUKI. WE'VE GOT TO GET TO CLASS.
OKAY, AZUMA ...

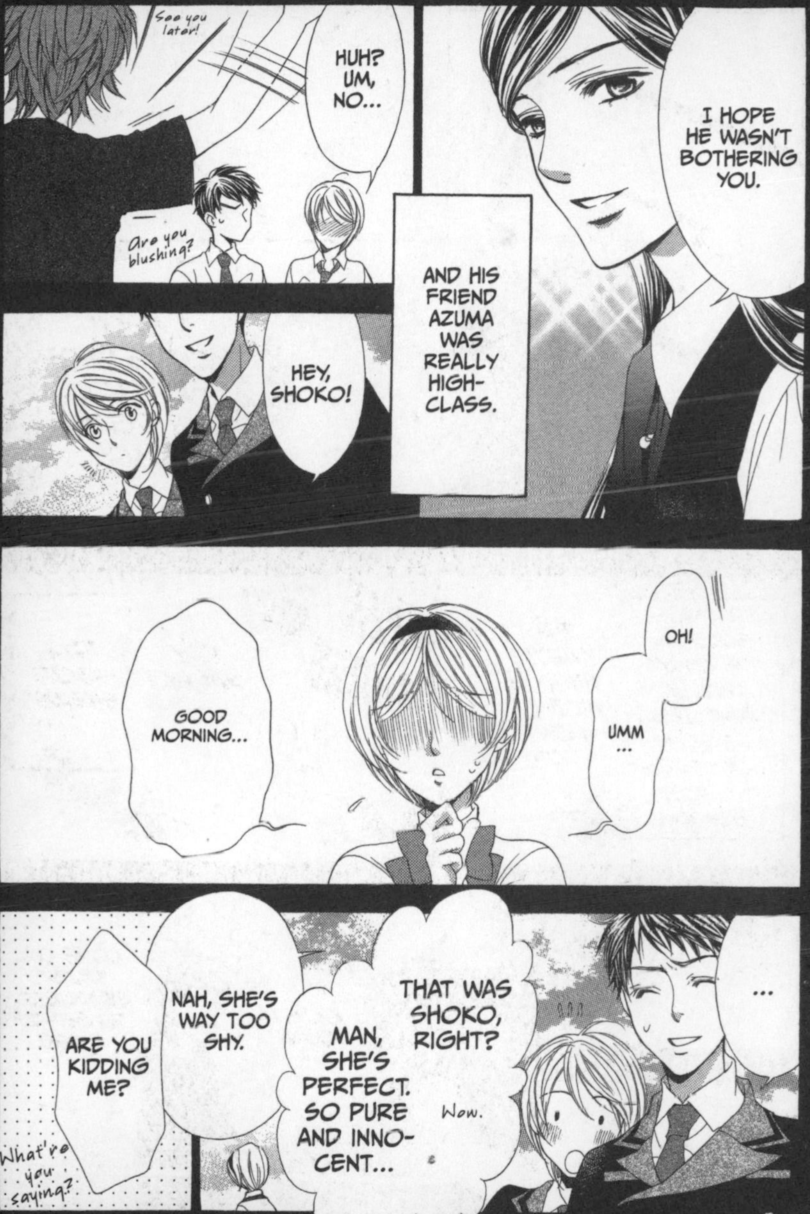
I HOPE HE WASN'T BOTHERING YOU.
AND HIS FRIEND AZUMA WAS REALLY HIGH-CLASS.
See you later!
HUH? UM, NO...
Are you blushing?
HEY, SHOKO!
OH!
UMM ...
GOOD MORNING...
...
THAT WAS SHOKO, RIGHT?
MAN, SHE'S PERFECT. SO PURE AND INNO-CENT...
Wow.
NAH, SHE'S WAY TOO SHY.
ARE YOU KIDDING ME?
What're you saying?

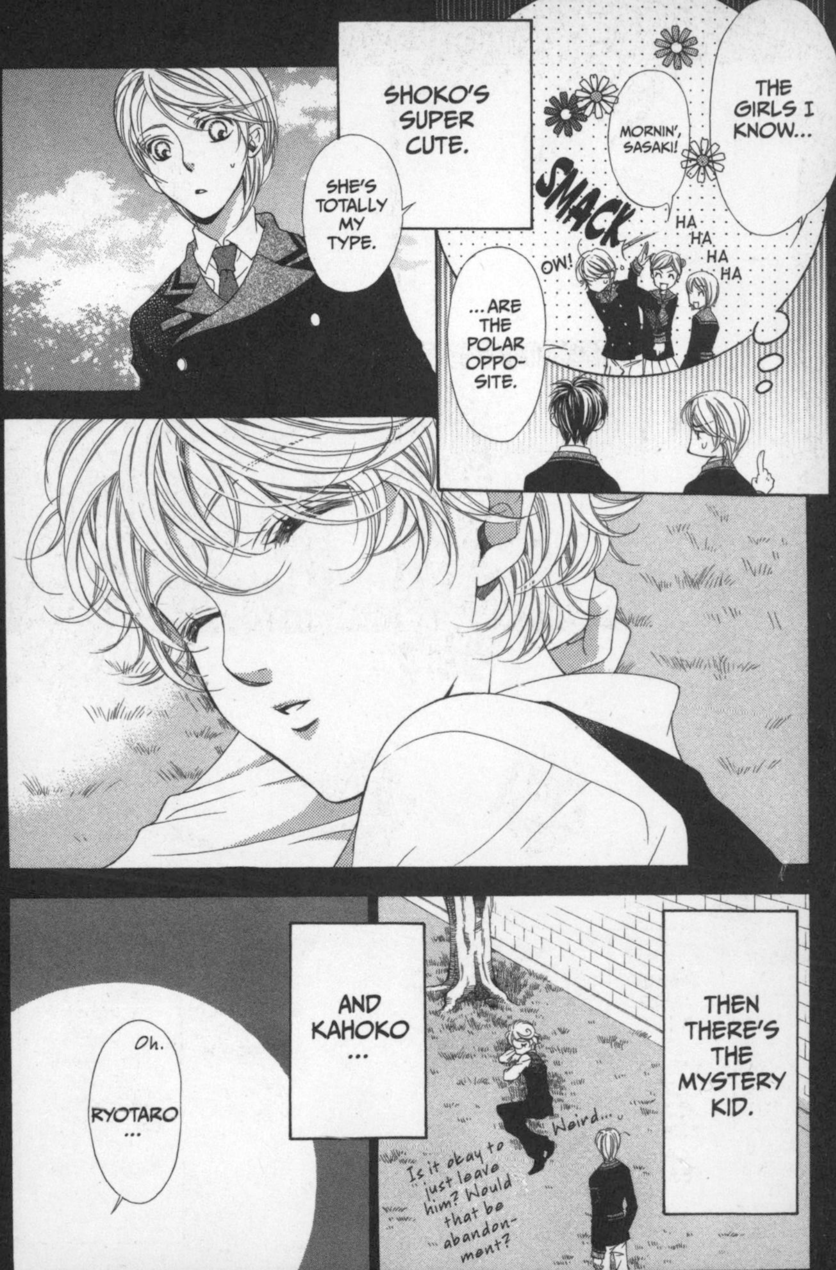
THE GIRLS I KNOW...
MORNIN', SASAKI!
SMACK
OW!
HA HA HA HA
...ARE THE POLAR OPPOSITE.
SHOKO'S SUPER CUTE.
SHE'S TOTALLY MY TYPE.
THEN THERE'S THE MYSTERY KID.
Weird...
Is it okay to just leave him? Would that be abandonment?
AND KAHOKO...
Oh.
RYOTARO...

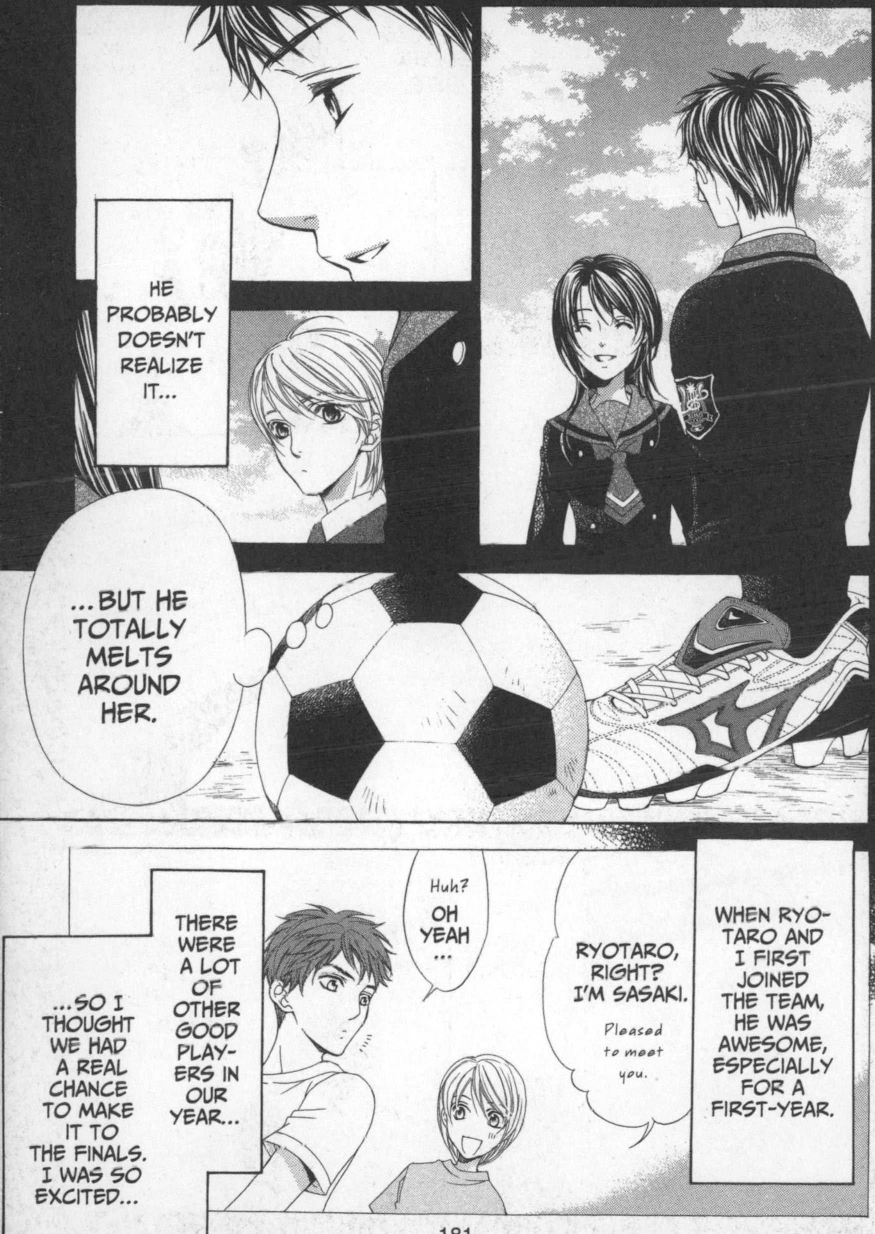
HE PROBABLY DOESN'T REALIZE IT...
...BUT HE TOTALLY MELTS AROUND HER.
WHEN RYOTARO AND I FIRST JOINED THE TEAM, HE WAS AWESOME, ESPECIALLY FOR A FIRST-YEAR.
RYOTARO, RIGHT? I'M SASAKI.
Pleased to meet you.
Huh?
OH YEAH...
THERE WERE A LOT OF OTHER GOOD PLAYERS IN OUR YEAR...
...SO I THOUGHT WE HAD A REAL CHANCE TO MAKE IT TO THE FINALS. I WAS SO EXCITED...

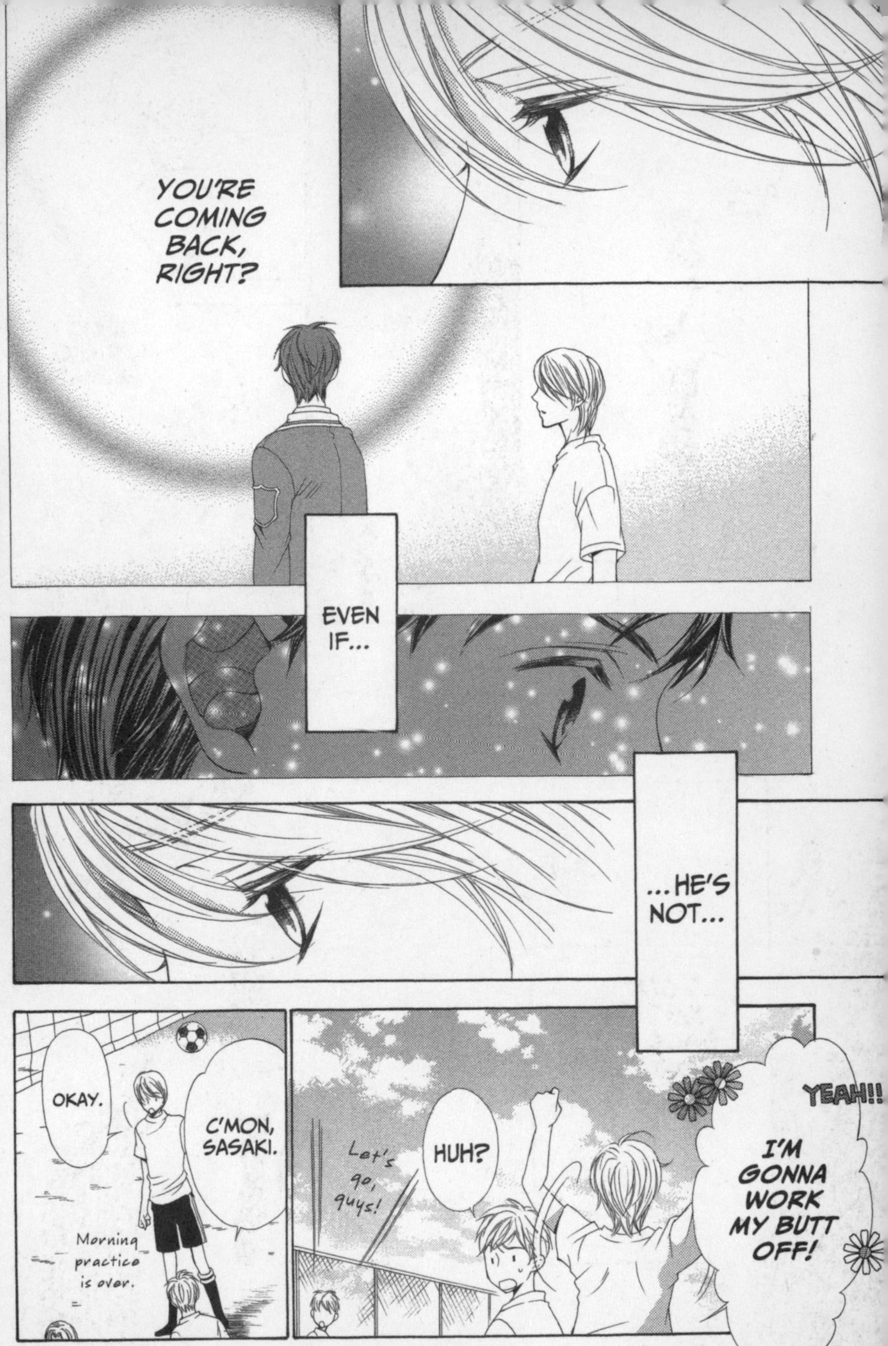
YOU'RE COMING BACK, RIGHT?
EVEN IF...
...HE'S NOT...
YEAH!!
I'M GONNA WORK MY BUTT OFF!
HUH?
Let's go, guys!
C'MON, SASAKI.
OKAY.
Morning practice is over.

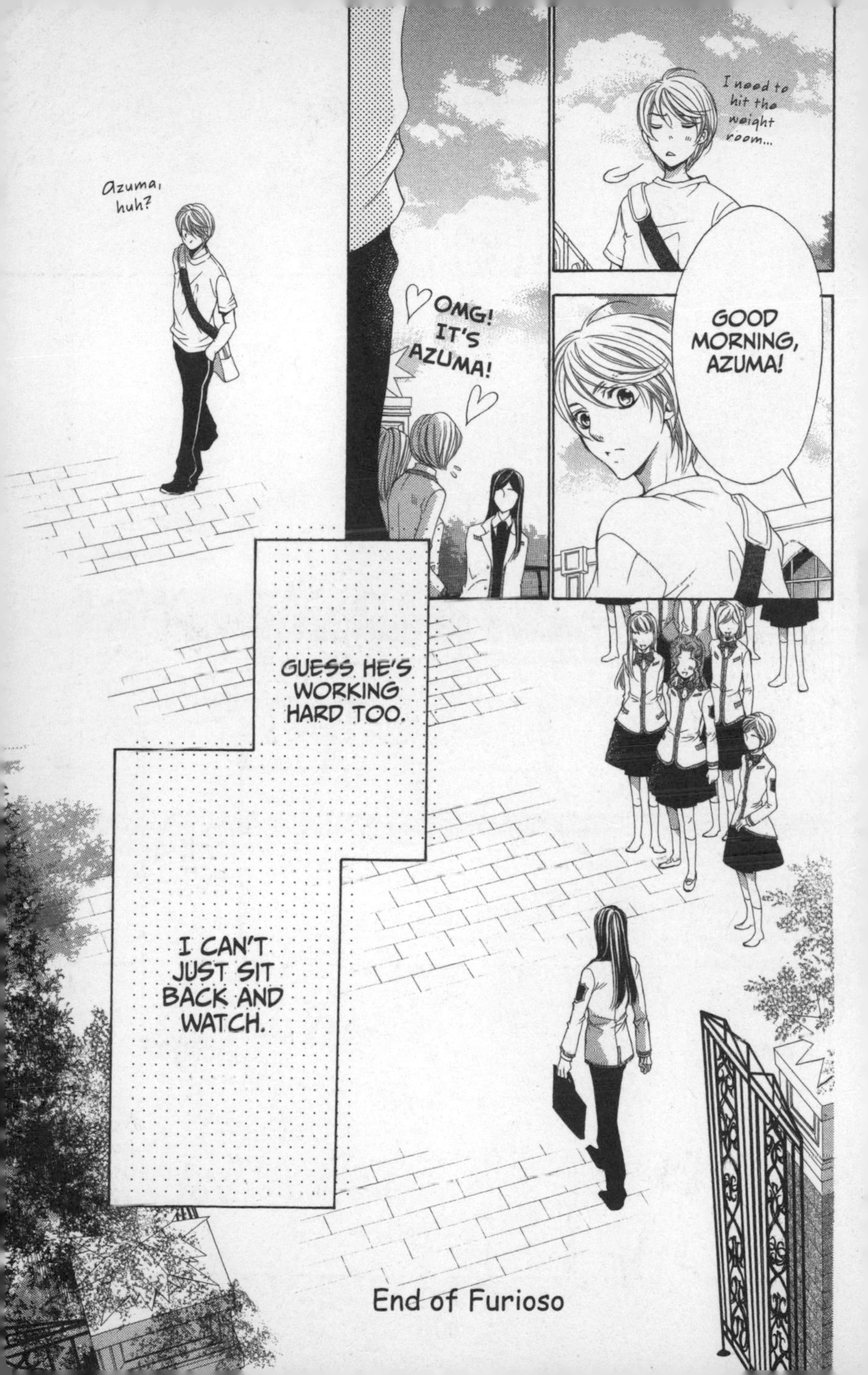
I need to hit the weight room...
GOOD MORNING, AZUMA!
OMG! IT'S AZUMA!
Azuma, huh?
GUESS HE'S WORKING HARD TOO.
I CAN'T JUST SIT BACK AND WATCH.

End of Furioso

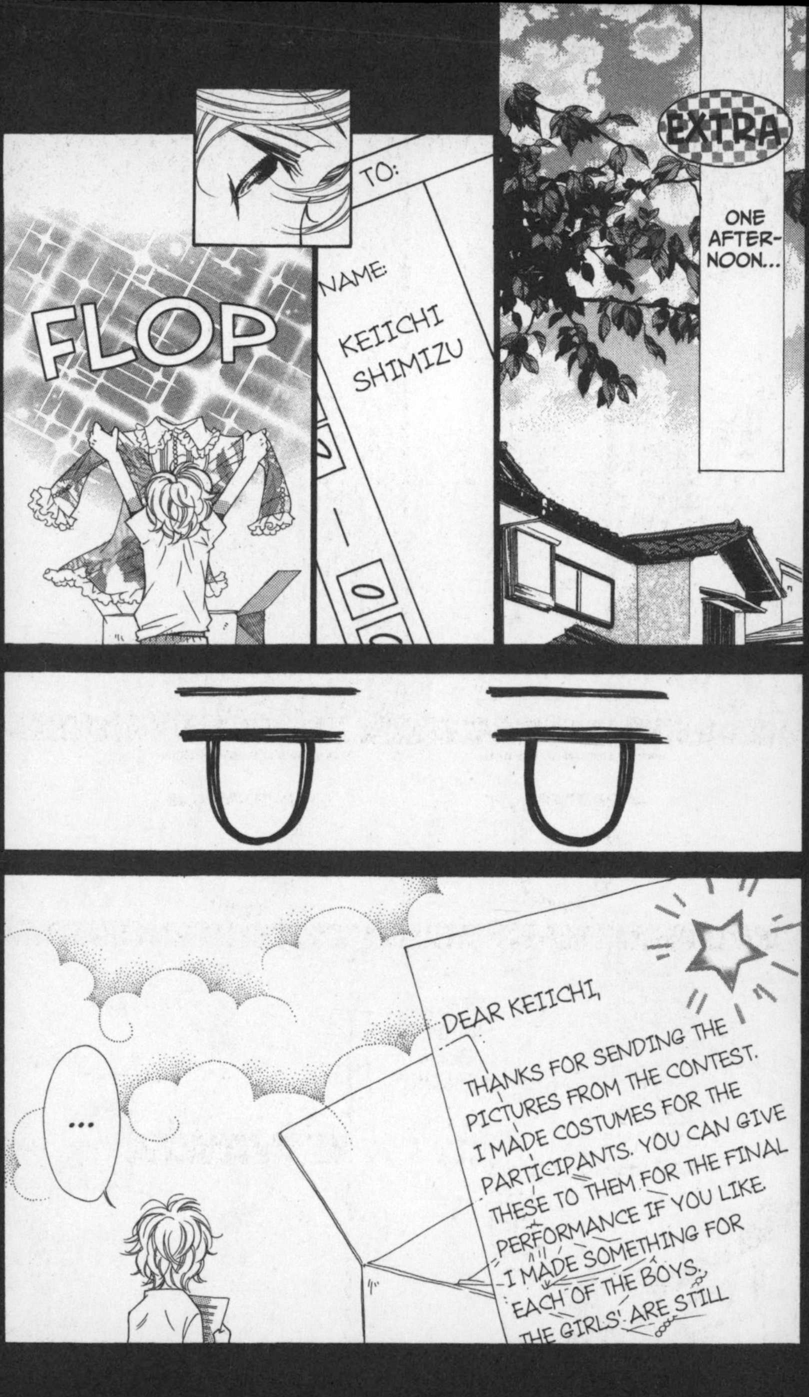

EXTRA
ONE AFTER-NOON...
TO:
NAME:
KEIICHI SHIMIZU
FLOP
DEAR KEIICHI,
THANKS FOR SENDING THE PICTURES FROM THE CONTEST. I MADE COSTUMES FOR THE PARTICIPANTS. YOU CAN GIVE THESE TO THEM FOR THE FINAL PERFORMANCE IF YOU LIKE. I MADE SOMETHING FOR EACH OF THE BOYS. THE GIRLS' ARE STILL
...

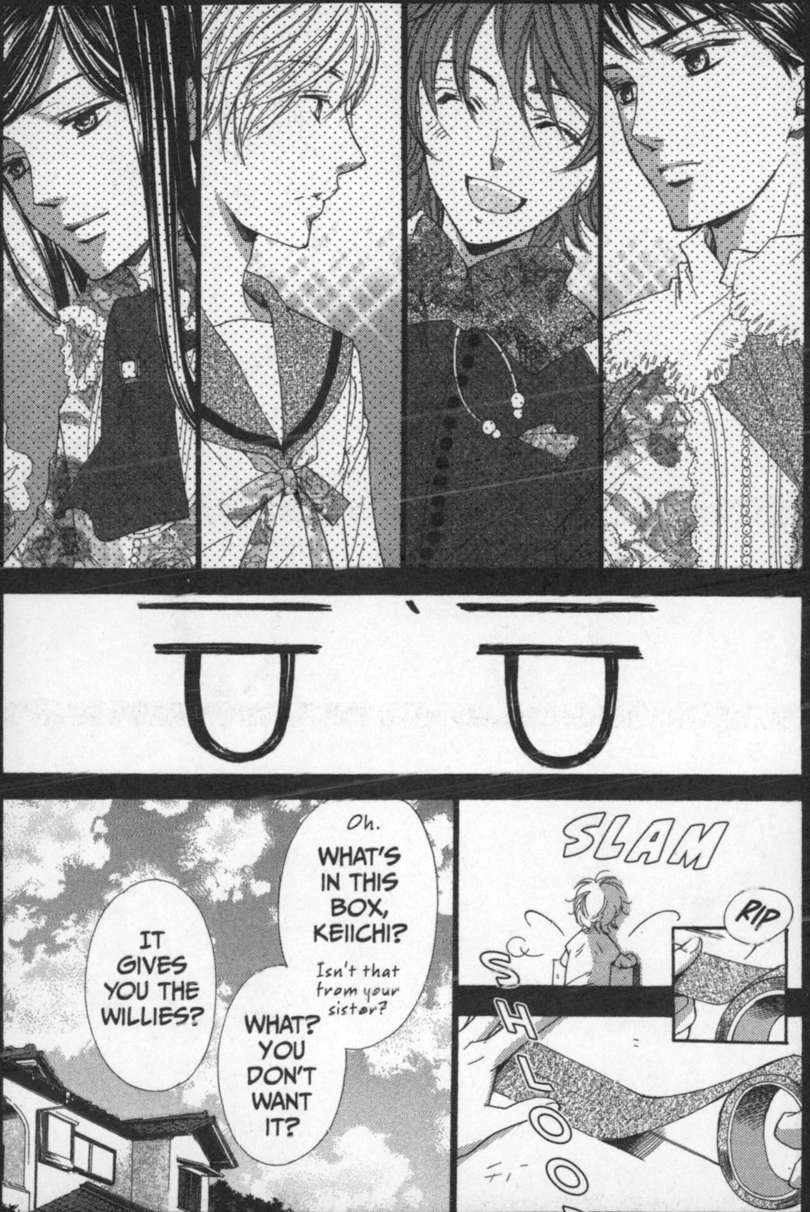
SLAM
RIP
SHLOOOP
Oh.
WHAT'S IN THIS BOX, KEIICHI?
Isn't that from your sister?
WHAT? YOU DON'T WANT IT?
IT GIVES YOU THE WILLIES?

The End

SPECIAL THANKS

A.Kashima
C.Karasawa
M.Shiino
M.Hiyama
N.Sato
S.Asahina
S.Takagi
W.Hibiki

La Corda d'Oro End Notes

You can appreciate music just by listening to it, but knowing the story behind a piece can help enhance your enjoyment. In that spirit, here is background information about some of the topics mentioned in *La Corda d'Oro*. Enjoy!

Page 34, panel 1: *Fantasie* by Fauré
Gabriel Fauré (1845-1924), known as the "French Brahms," was the foremost French composer of his time. His many works include the opera *Penelope*, two famous piano quartets and his *mélodies*, or French art songs. He was also a music teacher whose style strongly influenced the musicians of the day. The *Fantasie* Azuma plays is probably his Opus 79, composed for flute and piano.

Page 45, panel 1: Beethoven's *Romance* no. 2
One of the great composer's most eternally popular pieces, this was one of two romances for violin and orchestra that Beethoven composed between 1798 and 1802.

Page 49, panel 2-4: Tzigane, Wieniawski, Paganini
Three demanding composers. Niccolò Paganini (1782-1840) was both a great composer and a violin virtuoso who helped establish modern violin technique. He emphasized agility with the fingers and bow rather than intonation and traditional bowing; Len's mastery of fast, complex pieces suggests that Paganini fits his style.

Page 57, panel 1: *Hungarian Rhapsody* by Popper
David Popper (1843-1913) was a great cellist from Prague who composed many pieces for his own instrument. His *Hungarian Rhapsody* is a short piece designed to highlight the unique sound of the cello. Popper was a fast and prolific composer; he would often run up a bill at a local restaurant, run home, compose a piece on the spot, sell it to his publisher and return to pay the bill.

Page 66, panel 1: *Variations on a Theme by Paganini* by Brahms
Brahms wrote this series of variations for solo piano based on the piece Caprice no. 24 in A minor by Niccolò Paganini. Each of the two sections ends in a challenging virtuoso finale.

Page 75, Author's Note: New Year's
The week of New Year's Day is one of the biggest holidays on the Japanese calendar. Schools and businesses close, and there are festivals, parties and religious ceremonies everywhere. It sounds like Kure's celebration was pretty low-key.

Page 81, panel 1: *Farandole* by Bizet
Bizet wrote this music for Alphonse Daudet's play *L'Arlésienne* (The Woman from Arles), about a tragic romance between a cosmopolitan woman from the city of Arles and a peasant in southern France. The music contrasts two lively themes: a march adapted from a French folk song and a theme based on the *farandole*, a traditional southern French dance. Because the title character never appears in the play, the French often use *Arlésienne* to refer to someone or something that's unexpectedly absent.

Page 86, panel 6: Debussy's *Rêverie*
Claude Debussy (1862-1918) was one of the most important composers of the nineteenth century and a pioneer of French Impressionist music, a term he personally disliked. His *Rêverie* was originally composed for solo piano.

Page 170: Furioso
In musical notation, *furioso* means "play furiously."

Yuki Kure made her debut in 2000 with the story *Chijo yori Eien ni* (Forever from the Earth), published in monthly *LaLa* magazine. *La Corda d' Oro* is her first manga series published. Her hobbies are watching soccer games and collecting small goodies.

LA CORDA D'ORO
Vol. 10
The Shojo Beat Manga Edition

STORY AND ART BY
YUKI KURE
ORIGINAL CONCEPT BY
RUBY PARTY

English Translation & Adaptation/Mai Ihara
Touch-up Art & Lettering/HudsonYards
Design/Izumi Evers
Editor/Shaenon K. Garrity

Editor in Chief, Books/Alvin Lu
Editor in Chief, Magazines/Marc Weidenbaum
VP, Publishing Licensing/Rika Inouye
VP, Sales & Product Marketing/Gonzalo Ferreyra
VP, Creative/Linda Espinosa
Publisher/Hyoe Narita

Printed in Canada

Published by VIZ Media, LLC
P.O. Box 77010
San Francisco, CA 94107

Shojo Beat Manga Edition
10 9 8 7 6 5 4 3 2 1
First printing, April 2009

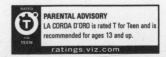

store.viz.com

Tell us what you think about Shojo Beat Manga!

Our survey is now available online. Go to:

shojobeat.com/mangasurvey

Help us make our product offerings better!